THE EARLY HISTORY OF ROME

THE EARLY HISTORY OF ROME
Books I–V of the Ab Urbe Condita

LIVY

TRANSLATED BY B. O. FOSTER

INTRODUCTION TO THE NEW EDITION
BY MATTHEW PEACOCK

BARNES & NOBLE

NEW YORK

THE BARNES & NOBLE
LIBRARY OF ESSENTIAL READING

Introduction to the New Edition and Suggested Reading
© 2005 by Barnes & Noble, Inc.

Originally published circa 25 BCE

This 2005 edition published by Barnes & Noble, Inc.

Barnes & Noble, Inc.
122 Fifth Avenue
New York, NY 10011

ISBN: 978-0-7607-7023-8

Printed and bound in the United States of America

5 7 9 10 8 6 4

CONTENTS

INTRODUCTION TO THE NEW EDITION   VII

INTRODUCTION   XV

BOOK I   3

SUMMARY OF BOOK I   77

BOOK II   80

SUMMARY OF BOOK II   158

BOOK III   161

SUMMARY OF BOOK III   247

BOOK IV   249

SUMMARY OF BOOK IV   321

BOOK V   323

SUMMARY OF BOOK V   389

ENDNOTES   391

SUGGESTED READING   413

INTRODUCTION TO THE
NEW EDITION

THE EARLY HISTORY OF ROME DESCRIBES THE FOUNDING OF A SMALL monarchical state in central Italy and its struggle to survive. It tells the story of the overthrow of the kings and of the development of the Roman Republic. It depicts the qualities and organization which allowed the early Romans to overcome internal disputes and foreign enemies and to recover after the nearly total destruction of their city in 390 BC. Livy is the most important source of information we have for the history of early Rome. He writes with fairness, humanity, and an irresistible enthusiasm for the courage, honesty, and self-sacrifice that to him exemplified what it was to be Roman.

Titus Livius was born in Patavium (modern Padua) in northern Italy in 59 BC or slightly earlier. Thanks to the wool trade in particular, in peacetime the town was one of the most prosperous in Italy. Given that he was able to devote so much of his life to writing history, it is reasonable to suppose that Livy's family must have been fairly wealthy. We cannot be sure exactly when he started writing, though references to contemporary events in book 1, section 19, seem to show that books one through five were published between about 27 and 25 BC. At this time, Rome was emerging from two decades of bitter civil war and one of Livy's aims in writing was to remind the Romans of the virtues that had made them great because he believed they were in danger of forgetting them altogether. This work, which he called the *Ab Urbe Condita*— "From the Founding of the City"—eventually comprised 142 books, covered Roman history down to 9 BC and took Livy forty years to write.

In his preface, Livy writes that Rome had reached the point "when we can endure neither our vices nor their cure." However, by book 9, he is found saying that Rome ". . . has defeated a thousand armies and will defeat a thousand more, provided that our love of the peace which we are now enjoying and our concern for civil concord endure forever." At the same time as Livy was recreating and preserving the past of Rome in words, Caesar's adopted son Augustus, victor of the civil wars and emperor in all but name, was rebuilding and ensuring the survival of Rome in reality. Although Livy remained a republican at heart, he may well have gradually or grudgingly come to accept that Rome was recovering under the new monarchical government. He was never an Augustan propagandist—we are told that one of the later books of his history, now lost, praised Brutus and Cassius, Caesar's murderers—but Livy managed to stay on good terms with Augustus because he shared many of the new regime's values and objectives. Augustus too wanted to see a rebuilt Rome based on high moral standards, peace at home and success abroad, following in the footsteps of the great Romans of old. After Augustus' death, however, the transmission of power to the Emperor Tiberius showed once and for all that the monarchy was to be no short-term response to a national emergency. Livy published his final volumes at the beginning of Tiberius' reign and, it seems, he died soon afterwards.

Livy is often described as a moral (or moralizing) historian. As well as history, he was said by Seneca to have written philosophical dialogues, and if this is true, they might have been in the form of fictional discussions between historical characters. Livy genuinely believed that Rome's troubles were the result of moral decline from its early high standards. In this volume, particular episodes, such as the Battle of the Allia in book 5, or even whole books, such as book 3, are structured around expressions of particular virtues (loyalty at the Allia, moderation in book 3). Livy offers many lessons about human nature, yet the circumstances of composition, that is the civil wars and the end of political freedom, indicate that the element of escapism in Livy's history should not be underestimated, especially in the early books. Much of Livy's narrative does not contain any obvious moral "message." His narrative is based on the rhythms of the Roman year. Within the regular business of each year, he often builds up one or more specific episodes. The episodes which do have a particular moral theme are very often those which Livy wants to give the maximum emotional or intellectual appeal. To engage the reader with the story, the full measure of credit or blame is given, but usually through the warmth or coldness of the descriptive language rather than by a direct comment from the author. The duty of a Roman historian was to entertain as well as to instruct and neither of these aims was more important than the other or independent of the other.

Livy was a great admirer of the republican statesman and orator Cicero (106–43 BC), for his prose style in particular. Although Cicero never wrote history himself, beyond the sketch of early Rome in his philosophical work *On the Republic,* he still argued that history should be written by orators, both for the good of orators, who needed historical examples for their speeches, and for the good of history, which deserved to be written well. Stylistically, Cicero was advocating, no doubt, his own favored brand of Latin, flowing, reassuring, encouraging, architectural, far removed from the unsettling ferocity of other writers of the period, such as Sallust and, it seems, Pollio, and from the terse, unemotional, logical Latin of men like Brutus. On the other hand, Livy's Latin is not as formal as Cicero's. He prefers gentle irony to Cicero's barbed wit. He is not afraid to use vocabulary that Cicero would have avoided and adopts different registers for different occasions, from the very plain Latin he uses for election results and other public notices, to the highly ornate and impassioned language found in the key episodes and many of his speeches.

Not long before Livy, it may have been the usual practice for historians writing in Latin (unlike Greek) to report people's words *indirectly.* Cato said that Minucius Thermus was a liar and a cheat—that is indirect speech. Cato said, "Minucius Thermus, you are a liar and a cheat"—that is direct speech (though Classical Latin did not use quotation marks). Pompeius Trogus, another Augustan historian, therefore criticized Livy and Sallust for including direct speech in their histories at all. Although Livy quite often writes lengthy passages of indirect speech featuring a good deal of rhetorical sophistication, nevertheless direct speech is naturally better at conveying the character of the speaker and he uses its possibilities to the fullest. His speeches were, in fact, later published separately in compendium editions. They often occur in pairs, giving both sides of a debate; the first one will look unanswerable, but Livy, switching sides, will find a way to answer it. Speeches were a way for all historians to clarify issues, feelings, and characters at a particular moment, to add variety to a narrative and to demonstrate their erudition. Thus most of the speeches in Livy have little claim to historical accuracy.

With regard to the sources of information used by Livy, there are two questions to consider. First, by identifying where Livy got his information, we gain some insight to determine how reliable Livy can be expected to be. Second, there is the question of how far other ancient evidence and modern archaeology can be used to gauge how reliable Livy actually is.

Within a year or two of Livy's finishing his first books, Virgil published the *Aeneid,* describing the adventures of the refugees from the Trojan War who became the mythical ancestors of the Roman race. The period covered in Livy's books 1 through 5, as well as being irretrievably bound up with myth, was in any event of considerable antiquity and obscurity by Livy's own day. He deals with the mythical origins of Rome (the Trojans settle in the Patavium area first) and the time of the kings in book 1. Thus, approximately one third of the total timeframe of the *Ab Urbe Condita* is dealt with in just 0.7% of the work's total length. By comparison, Livy's contemporary Dionysius of Halicarnassus, who wrote in Greek, and who probably used much the same sources as Livy, took four books to reach the overthrow of the kings. Thus Livy can at least be said to have cut down the mythological elements of early Roman history to a minimum.

Livy tells us which sources he is using more often than many ancient Greek or Roman historians. He occasionally gives us a clue as to how he judges between one literary source and another, on the basis of the reputation of the writer, for instance, or the agreement of a majority of his sources, or even of probability. Although documents, visible building remains, and other tangible evidence going back to at least the sixth century BC were all available in Livy's Rome, and although Livy certainly makes frequent references to Roman landmarks and buildings, most of Livy's sources must have been literary. Examples of these include Fabius Pictor, a senator of the late third century BC, who wrote a history in Greek; Quintus Ennius (239–169 BC), who wrote an epic poem on Roman history; Polybius (210–131 BC), who included some useful material on early Rome in his Greek history of his own times; and Cato the Censor (234–148 BC), who wrote a seven-book history of Rome called the *Origines*. Cato was the first Roman to write history in Latin prose: Pictor was the first Roman to write history of any sort. Greek literature was many centuries older than Roman, but the Greek historians did not really become interested in Roman history until Rome was powerful enough to be noticed by them, that is, not until the fourth or third centuries BC, though sometimes histories of other cities which Livy also mentions can be used to provide parallel dating evidence. Also important to Livy's narrative are the so-called "annalists," a term which is now used mainly to refer to writers of the late second and early first centuries BC who arranged their material in a year-by-year format. The term is also often used negatively nowadays; the annalists' accuracy and methods do not always compare well with Greek historians and Cicero associated them with a plain and unappealing prose style. However, the annalistic tradition for early Rome must go back at least in part to original documents.

Republican Romans also had access to information about the distant past of Rome in the writings of the "antiquarians." These were Roman scholars who often carried out original research into individual aspects of Roman culture. The most influential of these was M. Terentius Varro (116–27 BC), who wrote many hundreds of volumes and who standardized the dating of early Roman history. Although Livy can rarely be proven to be using antiquarian information (one rare example is 5.33 on the Gauls) and there are occasions when he can be proven to have ignored it, the results of antiquarian research must have filtered into the historical tradition and thence into Livy's work in ways we cannot now isolate.

All of these writers must have drawn on oral tradition to some extent, that is, on a combination of folk tale, traditional songs, and plays and the stories of aristocratic families about their ancestors. The Romans also maintained many truly ancient religious, legal, and cultural practices, which could shed much light on the past. Genuinely ancient documents were available; one famous example being the treaty between Rome and the city of Carthage which Polybius saw and dated to the beginning of the Republic. On the other hand, it is not very reassuring that, when in book 4, Livy tells us that his literary sources disagreed as to a certain entry in one of the official lists of early magistrates (the "Linen Books"), he also says that he did not (or could not) go back to the original document to check. This may not be Livy's fault: It may have been more difficult, either physically or politically, to check original documents under the Augustan regime, than it had been in the Late Republic.

As well as the basic lists of elected officials of the Republic (the *Fasti*), various priestly colleges kept records of the year's main events, the most important being the *Annales Maximi*, kept by the chief priest (*Pontifex Maximus*). These records listed, for each year, the names of the magistrates, plus military and religious business, plagues and famines and laws. This material clearly forms the backbone of Livy's history and although he probably obtained it secondhand, the information itself has a good claim to be reliable. Cicero tells us that the *Annales Maximi* went back to the beginning Rome. This can be doubted, but when he also tells us that these records referred to an eclipse on the June 5, "around 350 years after the founding of the city," we are on firm ground. Modern astronomy tells us that there was a solar eclipse visible from Rome on 21 June 400 BC, which for our purposes is certainly close enough to confirm the authenticity of the *Annales Maximi* at least from 400 BC onwards. Livy's history gets progressively more detailed from this point on, and it is not unreasonable to suppose that records for the fourth century were more detailed than those for the fifth.

As far as we can tell, Livy is usually several steps removed from what we would call a primary source of information. Yet it is also clear that reliable evidence underlies his narrative. His picture of a powerful and prosperous sixth-century Rome under the kings is also supported by the sophistication of the temples of that period. Livy seems to indicate that temple building declined in the fifth century; that picture is again supported by archaeology. There are traces of quite widespread destruction in the city of Rome which can be dated to around 500 BC: This evidence certainly fits well enough with Varro's date of 509 for the expulsion of the kings (Livy's own lists of consuls indicate a date in around 502). On its own, the precise synchronism between the beginning of the Roman democracy and the beginning of the Athenian, even with the conscientious Polybius backing up Dionysius, looks suspiciously like a Roman attempt to prove that they were just as good as the Greeks. The archaeology backs up Livy, and Livy allows us to make sense of the archaeology. Because the process is circular, we cannot call this proof. The closest we can get to proof is by bringing in alternative literary evidence — a passage in Dionysius, book 7, which appears to originate from a respectable and ancient Greek source and gives a date for the Battle of Aricia of 504 BC. This fits well with Livy's narrative: He does not give a precise date for the battle, but puts in the context of events following the creation of the Republic. Conversely, archaeology seems to indicate that the destruction of Rome by the Gauls was not nearly as serious as Livy claims, but then his picture of a still-strong Rome in book 6 seems to contradict the emotional book 5 picture anyway. Archaeology is most useful for illuminating the material culture and everyday life that Livy and the other literary sources rarely describe. When brought to bear directly on Livy, we are still trying to do the same thing that Livy was trying to do, to write a consistent, meaningful story.

Matthew Peacock wrote his doctoral thesis on Livy while studying at St. Hugh's College, Oxford; having also taught in Oxford, he is now Lecturer in Roman History at the National University of Ireland, Galway.

INTRODUCTION

I

FROM ENTRIES IN JEROME'S RE-WORKING OF THE *CHRONICLE* OF Eusebius we learn that Titus Livius the Patavian was born in 59 BC, the year of Caesar's first consulship, and died in his native town (the modern Padua) in AD 17. Of his parents nothing is known. They were presumably well-to-do, for their son received the training in Greek and Latin literature and in rhetoric which constituted the standard curriculum of that time, and was afterwards able to devote a long life to the unremunerative work of writing. That he was by birth an aristocrat is no more than an inference from his outstanding sympathy with the senatorial party. Livy's childhood witnessed the conquest of Gaul and Caesar's rapid rise to lordship over the Roman world. These early years he doubtless passed in his northern home. Patavium laid claim to great antiquity. Livy tells us himself in his opening chapter the legend of its founding by the Trojan Antenor, and elsewhere describes with unmistakable satisfaction the vain attempt of the Spartan Cleonymus (in 302 BC) to subdue the Patavians.[1] They defended themselves with equal vigor and success against the aggressions of the Etruscans and the inroads of the Gauls, and in the war with Hannibal cast in their lot with Rome. In 49 BC, when Livy was ten years old, the town became a Roman municipality and its citizens were enrolled in the Fabian tribe. The place was a great center of trade, especially in wool,[2] and under Augustus was perhaps the wealthiest city in Italy, next to Rome,[3] to which in some respects it presented a striking contrast, since the Patavians maintained the simple manners and strict morality which had long gone out of fashion in the cosmopolitan capital.[4] We cannot say how old Livy was when he left Patavium, but it is probable that his tastes and character had been permanently influenced by the old-world traditions of his native town. Did he go to Rome with the intention of pursuing there the career of a rhetorician and subsequently become interested in historical studies? It may have been so. Perhaps he had already resolved to write history and wished to make use of the libraries and other sources of information which were lacking in a provincial town. Certain passages in his earlier books[5] indicate that he was already familiar with the City when he began his great work, about 27 BC,[6] and a reference to a conversation with Augustus in Book IV seems to argue that it was not long till he was on a friendly footing with the Emperor.[7] He doubtless continued to reside in Rome, with occasional visits to Patavium and other places in Italy, till near the end of his long life.

Livy seems never to have held any public office, but to have given himself up entirely to literature. Seneca says that he wrote dialogues which one might classify under history as well as under philosophy, besides books which were professedly philosophical.[8] And Quintilian quotes a letter from Livy to his son which was very likely an essay on the training of the orator, for in the passage cited he advises the young man to read Demosthenes and Cicero, and then such as most nearly resembled them.[9] So, in another place, Quintiliar tells us that he finds in Livy that there was a certain teacher who bade his pupils *obscure* what they said.[10] It may have been in this same essay that he made the criticism on Sallust which seemed to the elder Seneca to be unjust, that he had not only appropriated a sentence from Thucydides but had spoilt it in the process.[11] And there is another passage in Seneca where Livy is credited with having quoted approvingly a *mot* of the rhetorician Miltiades against orators who affected archaic and sordid words, which may also be an echo of the letter.[12] If Livy was about thirty-two years old when he began to write history it is probable that this essay was composed some years later, for it is unlikely to have been written before the son was about sixteen.[13] We may therefore think of the historian as putting aside his magnum opus for a season, to be of use in the education of the boy, who, whether or no he profited by his father's instructions in rhetoric, at all events became a writer, and is twice named by the elder Pliny as one of his authorities, in Books V and VI of the *Natural History,* which deal with geography. In a sepulchral inscription found in Padua, which may be that of our Livy, two sons are named—Titus Livius Priscus and Titus Livius Longus, and their mother's name is given as Cassia.[14] The only other item of information we possess about the family is supplied by the elder Seneca, who mentions a son-in-law, named Lucius Magius, as a declaimer who had some following for a time, though men rather endured him for the sake of his father-in-law than praised him for his own.[15]

Of Livy's social life in Rome we know nothing more than that he enjoyed the friendship of Augustus, and probably, as we have seen, from an early date in his stay in Rome.[16] The intimacy was apparently maintained till the end of the Emperor's life, for it cannot have been much before AD 14 that Livy, as related by Suetonius,[17] advised his patron's grand-nephew Claudius (born 9 BC) to take up the writing of history. The good relations subsisting between the Emperor and the historian do honor to the sense and candor of both. Livy gloried in the history of the republic, yet he could but acquiesce in the new order of things. And the moral and religious reforms of Augustus, his wish to revive the traditions of an elder day, his respect for the forms inherited from a time when Rome was really governed by a senate, must have commanded Livy's hearty approval. On the other side, when Livy's great history was appealing to men's patriotism and displaying the ideal Rome as no other literary work (with the possible exception of the contemporaneous *Aeneid*) had ever done, it was easy for the Emperor to smile at the scholar's exaggerated admiration of Pompey,[18] and even to overlook the frankness of his query whether more of good or of harm had come to the state from the birth of Julius Caesar.[19] Livy died three years after Augustus, in 17 AD, at the ripe age of seventy-six. If he continued working at his history up to the last he had devoted more than forty years to the gigantic enterprise. Jerome says that he died in Patavium. We can only conjecture whether he was overtaken by death while making a visit to his old home, or had retired thither, with the coming in of the new régime, to spend his declining years. The latter is perhaps the more likely assumption. The character of Tiberius can have possessed little claim to the sympathy of Livy, and life in Rome may well have lost its charm for him, now that his old patron was no more.

II

Livy seems to have called his history simply *Ab Urbe Condita*, "From the Founding of the City,"[20] just as Tacitus was later to call his Annals *Ab Excessu Divi Augusti*, "From the death of the Divine Augustus." He began with the legend of Aeneas, and brought his narrative down to the death of Drusus (and the defeat of Quintilius Varus?[21]) in 9 BC. There is no reason to think that Livy intended, as some have supposed, to go on to the death of Augustus. In the preface to one of the lost books he remarked that he had already earned enough of reputation and might have ceased to write, were it not that his restless spirit was sustained by work.[22] He probably toiled on till his strength failed him, with no fixed goal in view, giving his history to the public in parts, as these were severally completed. The following table, taken from Schanz,[23] is an attempt to reconstruct these instalments:

Books I–V. From the founding of the City to its conquest by the Gauls (387–386 BC).

VI–XV. To the subjugation of Italy (265 BC).

XVI–XX. The Punic wars to the beginning of the war with Hannibal (219 BC).

XXI–XXX. The war with Hannibal (to 201 BC).

XXXI–XL. To the death of King Philip of Macedon (179 BC).

XLI–LXX. To the outbreak of the Social War (91 BC).

LXXI–LXXX. The Social War to the death of Marius (86 BC).

LXXXI–XC. To the death of Sulla (78 BC).

XCI–CVIII. From the war with Sertorius to the Gallic War (58 BC).

CIX–CXVI. From the beginning of the Civil Wars to the death of Caesar (44 BC).

CXVII–CXXXIII. To the death of Antony and Cleopatra (30 BC).

CXXXIV–CXLII. The principate of Augustus to the death of Drusus (9 BC).

It will be noticed that certain portions fall naturally into decades (notably XXI–XXX), or pentads (e.g., I–V). Elsewhere, and particularly in that part of the work which deals with the writer's own times, no such symmetry is discernible. Later however it became the uniform practice of the copyists to divide the history into decades. This is clearly seen in the wholly distinct and independent MS tradition of the several surviving sections.

Only about a quarter of the whole work has been preserved. We have the Preface and Books I–X, covering the period from Aeneas to the year 293 BC; Books XXI–XXX describing the Second Punic War; and Books XXXI–XLV, which continue the story of Rome's conquests down to the year 167 BC and the victories of Lucius Aemilius Paulus.[24]

For the loss of the other books the existence from the first century of our era of a handy abridgment is no doubt largely responsible. It is to this Martial alludes in the following distich (XIV cxc.):

> *Pellibus exiguis artatur Livius ingens,*
> *Quem mea non totum bibliotheca capit.*[25]

If we had this *Epitome*[26] it would be some slight compensation for the disappearance of the original books, but we have only a compend of it, the so-called *Periochae,* and certain excerpts thought to have been made from another summary of it, no longer extant, which scholars refer to as the *Chronicon,* to wit, the fragments of the *Oxyrhynchus Papyrus,* the *Prodigiorum Liber* of Obsequens, and the consular lists of Cassiodorius.

The *Periochae,* or summaries of the several Books (only CXXXVI and CXXXVII are wanting), are the most valuable of these sources for supplying the gaps in our text of Livy. Their author narrates briefly what seem to him the leading events in each book, adding a reference to other matters treated in the original.[27] The *Periochae* are thus a kind of compromise between a book of excerpts for the use of readers who for any reason could not or would not go to the unabridged Livy, and a table of contents for the convenience of those who did.[28] They are usually printed with editions of Livy, and are included in this one. It may be noted here that *Per. I.* exists in a double recension, of which B appears from its style to be of a piece with those of all the other books, while A is thought to have come from the *Chronicon*.

In 1903 a papyrus was discovered at Oxyrhynchus which contained fragments of a compend of Roman history which was based on Livy, though it seems not to have been taken from Livy directly but from the *Chronicon*, which was also, as we have said, the source of Obsequens and Cassiodorius. The MS is assigned to the third century, and the book must therefore have been composed in that or a still earlier period. It contains eight columns of uncial writing. Of these 1–3 preserve a selection of the events recorded in Livy, Books XXXVII–XL, (which we have), while 4–8 deal with the subject-matter of Books XLVIII–LV. But there is a column gone between column six and column seven, which treated of the years 143 and 142 BC.

Magnus Aurelius Cassiodorus Senator lived about 480 to 575, and was Consul in 514, under Theodoric. Among his writings was a chronicle, from Adam to AD 519. For the earlier periods he used Eusebius and Jerome, but from the expulsion of Tarquinius to AD 31 he names as his authorities Titus Livius and Aufidius Bassus. His list of consuls for this period shows kinship with the *Oxyrhynchus Papyrus* and Obsequens.

In his *Prodigiorum Liber* Julius Obsequens enumerates in chronological order the portents which occurred from the year 190 to the year 12 BC. In its original form the catalogue probably began, as the title in the MS indicates,[29] with the year 249. The little book is of unknown date: Schanz thinks it is a product of the fourth century of our era, when paganism made its last struggle against Christianity.[30] Rossbach inclines to a somewhat earlier date.[31] In any case Rossbach has shown that the author was a believer in prodigies, and therefore a pagan.

III

In his preface to the whole work Livy gives a satisfactory account of his conception of history and the ends he himself had in view. He begins with an apology for adding to the already large number of Roman histories. Those who attempt this theme hope, he says, to surpass their predecessors either in accuracy or style, and it is doing Livy no injustice to infer that in his own case it was the belief that he could make the story of Rome more vivid and readable than anyone had yet done which gave him the courage to undertake the task. But whether he succeeds or not, he will be glad, he tells us, to have done what he could for the memory of the foremost people of the world. He recognizes the immense labor which confronts him, in consequence of the more than seven hundred years which he must deal with, and admits that it will be labor thrown away on most of his readers, who will have little patience with the earlier history in their eagerness to be reading of the civil wars and the events of their own generation. "I myself, on the contrary," he continues—and the sentiment reveals at once the man's romantic spirit—"shall seek in this an additional reward for my toil, that I may turn my back upon the evils which our age has witnessed for so many years, so long at least as I am absorbed in the recollection of the brave days of old."[32] He refers to the marvellous tales which were associated with the founding of the City as to matters of no great consequence. He declines to vouch for their authenticity, though he means to set them down as he finds them; and he apparently regards them as possessing a certain symbolic truth, at least. But the really important thing in Rome's history is the way her power was founded on morality and discipline, waxed mighty with the maintenance of these, and was now fallen upon evil days through their decay. For the use of historical study lies in its application to life. The story of a great people is fraught with examples and warnings, both for the individual and for the state. And no nation is better worth studying than Rome, for in none did righteousness and primitive simplicity so long resist the encroachments of wealth and luxury.

It was the ethical aspect of history then that chiefly appealed to Livy, and he chose Rome for his subject because the rise of the Roman empire seemed to him the best example of the fruition of those qualities which he wished to inculcate. To do this he must first of all win the interest of his readers, and if morality is his goal style is certainly the road by which he hopes to lead men towards it. We must therefore fix our attention on these two things if we would approach Livy's work in the spirit of his ancient readers, and understand their almost unqualified approval of it.

For Livy's success was both immediate and lasting. I have already referred to the frank way in which he himself recognized his fame, in the preface to one of the books of his History, and the younger Pliny tells a delightful story of an enthusiastic Spanish admirer who travelled from Cadiz to Rome solely to behold the great writer, and having gratified his curiosity returned forthwith to his home.[33] Livy's magnanimity was warmly praised by the elder Seneca, who said that he was by nature a most candid judge of all great talents,[34] and it is a striking testimony to the justice of this observation that the modern reader's admiration for Hannibal is largely a reflection of Livy's, which all his prejudice against Rome's most formidable enemy could not altogether stifle. Tacitus too admired Livy, whom he considered the most eloquent of the older historians, as Fabius Rusticus was of the more recent.[35] Quintilian compared him with Herodotus, and spoke of the wonderful fascination of his narrative, his great fairness, and the inexpressible eloquence of the speeches, in which everything was suited not only to the circumstances but to the speaker.[36] Quintilian also praised his representation of the emotions, particularly the gentler ones, in which field he said he had no superior. Livy shared with Virgil the honor of being the most widely read of Latin writers, and in consequence incurred the resentment of the mad Caligula, who lacked but little of casting out their works and their portraits from all the libraries, alleging of Livy that he was verbose and careless.[37] Even Quintilian could tax him with prolixity,[38] though he seems to have owned that it was but the defect of a quality, for he elsewhere speaks of his "milky richness."[39] The only other jarring note in the general chorus of admiration is sounded by the critic Asinius

Pollio, who reproached Livy's style with "Patavinity," by which he perhaps meant that it was tainted with an occasional word or idiom peculiar to the historian's native dialect.[40] Owing chiefly to its intrinsic excellence, but partly no doubt to the accidental circumstance that it covered the whole field of Roman History, Livy's work became the standard source-book from which later writers were to draw their materials. We have already seen how it was epitomized and excerpted. Other writers who took their historical data from Livy were Lucan and Silius Italicus, Asconius, Valerius Maximus, Frontinus, Florus, and the Greeks Cassius Dio and Plutarch. Avienus, in the fourth century, turned Livy into *iambic senarii,* a *tour de force* which has not come down to us.[41] In the fifth he is cited by Pope Gelasius,[42] and the grammarian Priscian used him in the sixth. Comparatively little read in the Middle Ages, Livy found a warm admirer in Dante, who used him in the second book of his *De Monarchia,* and in the *Divina Commedia* refers to him naively as "*Livio . . . che non erra.*"[43] The Italians of the Renaissance seized upon Livy's History with avidity. The poet Beccadelli sold a country-place to enable him to purchase a copy by the hand of Poggio. Petrarch was among those who hoped for the recovery of the lost decades, and Pope Nicholas V. exerted himself without avail to discover them. With the emendations in Books XXI–XXVI by Laurentius Valla[44] the critical study of the text was inaugurated. The year 1469 saw the first printed edition of the History, which was produced in Rome. Early in the sixteenth century Machiavelli wrote his famous *Discorsi sul Primo Libro delle Deche di Tito Livio.* It is not too much to say that from the Revival of Learning to the present time Livy has been generally recognized as one of the world's great writers. The English scholar Munro pronounced him owner of what is "perhaps the greatest prose style that has ever been written in any age or language,"[45] and his history seemed to Niebuhr a "a colossal masterpiece."[46]

The qualities which gave Livy his lofty place in literature are easily discovered. He was a high-minded patriot, inspired with a genuine desire to promote the welfare of his country. An idealist of the most pronounced type, he was endowed—as not all idealists are—with a breadth of sympathy which enabled him to judge men with charity, and to discern in the most diverse characters whatever admirable traits they might possess. In him a passionate love of noble deeds and a rare insight into the workings of the mind and heart were united with a strength of imagination which enabled him to clothe the shadowy names of Rome's old worthies with the flesh and blood of living men. Finally, his mastery of all the resources of language is only equalled by his never-failing tact and sense of fitness in the use of them.[47] It is difficult to describe in a few words so complex an instrument as Livy's style. Perhaps it might fairly be said that it is distinguished by the attributes of warmth and amplitude. The Livian period, less formal and regular than that of Cicero, whom Livy so greatly admired,[48] is fully as intricate, and reveals an amazing sensitiveness to the rhetorical possibilities inherent in word-order.[49] To the first decade, and especially Book I, Livy has, consciously no doubt, given a slightly archaic and poetical color, in keeping with the subject-matter[50]; and his extraordinary faculty for visualizing and dramatizing the men and events of Roman story reminds us even more insistently of Quintilian's dictum that history is a kind of prose poetry.[51]

Yet despite his many remarkable gifts it is only too clear that Livy was deficient in some of the most essential qualifications for producing such a history of Rome as would satisfy the standards of our own day. Neither well informed nor specially interested in politics or the art of war, and lacking even such practical knowledge of constitutional matters as scores of his contemporaries must have gained from participating in the actual business of the state, he undertook to trace the development of the greatest military power (save one) that the world has ever seen, and the growth of an empire which has taught the principles of organization and government to all succeeding ages. Nor was this lack of technical knowledge the only or indeed the heaviest handicap that Livy was compelled to carry. His mind was fundamentally uncritical, and he was unable to subject his authorities to such a judicial examination as might have made it possible for him to choose the safer guides and reject the less trustworthy. Towards original documents he manifests an almost incredible indifference.[52] As regards the earlier period, he himself remarks that the

Gauls in burning Rome had swept away the "pontifical commentaries" and pretty much all the other public and private records,[53] but there is nothing to indicate that he made much use of even such shreds of evidence as survived the fire, or that he referred, in writing of a later period, to so important a source as the *Annales Maximi,* though they had been published in 123 BC, in eighty books, by P. Mucius Scaevola. He excuses himself from transcribing the expiatory hymn composed by Livius Andronicus, and publicly sung, in the year 207 BC, by a chorus of girls, as a thing too uncouth for modern taste.[54] He seems never to have bothered to examine the terrain of so important a battle as Cannae, and his account of the operations there shows that he had no very clear notion of the topography of the field. It would be easy to multiply instances. There is an example at II. xli. 10, where he refers to an inscription, but without having himself consulted it, as his contemporary, Dionysius of Halicarnassus, did.[55]

Livy's history supplanted the works of the annalists, which have consequently perished, so that it is impossible to ascertain with exactness his relation to his sources. His own references to them are rather casual. He makes no attempt to indicate his authorities systematically, but cites them in certain cases where they conflict with one another, or where he is sceptical of their statements and does not choose to assume the responsibility for them.[56] Often he does not give names, but contents himself with a phrase like, "men say," or "I find in certain writers." For the first decade he derived his materials from a number of annalists. The oldest of these were Q. Fabius Pictor and L. Cincius Alimentus, both of whom wrote in Greek and lived in the time of Hannibal, in which both men fought. Another was L. Calpurnius Piso Frugi, who opposed the Gracchi and was consul in 133.[57] Cato's valuable history, the *Origines,*[58] he seems not to have used until he came to treat of the events in which Cato himself played a part. It was to writers who lived nearer his own day, whose style caused Livy to rank them above their less sophisticated but no doubt far more trustworthy predecessors that he mainly resorted. Such were Valerius Antias, whose seventy-five books were certainly the most abundant source available, and are thought to have covered the history of Rome to the death of Sulla; C. Licinius Macer, tribune of the plebs in seventy-three, who wrote from the democratic standpoint; and Q. Aelius Tubero, who took part in the Civil War on the side of Pompey, and brought down his annals to his own times.

For the third decade Livy used Polybius,[59] though whether directly or through a Roman intermediary, and whether for the whole or only a part of the ten books, are questions still *sub iudice*. For this decade he also drew upon L. Coelius Antipater, a writer whose treatise on the Second Punic War in seven books[60] had introduced into Roman literature the genre of the historical monograph.

In the fourth and fifth decades Livy's main reliance seems to have been Polybius, in describing eastern affairs, and the annalists Q. Claudius Quadrigarius[61] and Valerius Antias, in treating of Italy and Spain. A recent critic[62] has found reason for thinking that Livy used Valerius as his chief authority for western matters (controlling his statements however by those of Claudius) until, coming to the prosecution of Scipio (see Book XXXVIII), he found so much in Valerius that was incredible that his mistrust, which had hitherto been confined to that annalist's reports of numbers (see e.g., XXXIII. x. 8.) caused him to take Claudius thenceforth for his principal guide.

This unscientific attitude towards the sources was the product partly of Livy's own characteristics, partly of the conception of history as a means of edification and entertainment prevalent in ancient times.[63] Another shortcoming, which would have to be insisted on if we were criticising him as though he were a contemporary, is his inability to clear his mind of ideas belonging to his own day in considering the men and institutions of the past, though this again is a limitation which he shares with his age.

It is evident that the student of history must use Livy with caution, especially in those portions of his work where his statements cannot be tested by comparison with those of Polybius. Yet, quite apart from his claims upon our attention as a supreme literary artist, it would be hard to overrate his importance as an historian, which is chiefly of two sorts. In the first place, uncritical though he is, we have no one to put in his place, and his pages are our best authority for long stretches of Roman history. In the second place he possesses a very positive excellence to add to this accidental one, in the fidelity and spirit with which he depicts for us the Roman's own idea of Rome. Anyone of half a dozen annalists would have served as well as Livy to tell us what the Romans *did,* but it required genius to make us realize as Livy does what the Romans *were.* No mere critical use of documents could ever make the Roman character live again as it lives for us in his "pictured page." The People and the State are idealized no doubt by the patriotic imagination of this extraordinary writer, but a people's ideals are surely not the least significant part of their history.[64]

IV

We have seen that each of the extant decades was handed down in a separate tradition. The manuscripts of the later portions will be briefly described in introductory notes to the volumes in which they are contained. Books I–X are preserved in a twofold MS tradition. One family is represented by a single MS, the Verona palimpsest (*V*). The portion of this codex which contains the Livy consists of sixty leaves, on which are preserved fragments of Books III–VI, written in uncial characters of the fourth century. These fragments were deciphered and published by Mommsen in 1868. The other family is the so-called Nichomachean. This edition, as it may be called, of the first decade was produced under the auspices of Q. Aurelius Symmachus, who was consul in 391 AD. He appears to have commissioned Tascius Victorianus to prepare an amended copy of Books I–X, and the latter's subscription *(Victorianus emendabam dominis Symmachis)* is found after every book as far as the ninth. In Books VI–VIII the subscription of Victorianus is preceded by one of Nichomachus Flavianus, son-in-law of Symmachus *(Nichomachus Flavianus v. c. III. praefect. urbis emendavi apud Hennam),* and in Books III–V by one of Nichomachus Dexter, a son of Flavianus *(Tili Livi Nichomachus Dexter v.c. emendavi ab urbe condita),* who adds the information, in subscribing Book V., that he had used the copy of his kinsman Clementianus. To this origin all the MSS now extant are referred, with the exception of the *Veronensis.* The most famous member of the family is the *Mediceus,* a minuscule codex of the tenth or eleventh century containing the ten books and written with great fidelity—even in absurdities—to its exemplar. It has been shown to be the work of at least three scribes. The MS abounds with dittographies and other errors, but is possibly the most valuable of its class, because of its honesty. For a full description of this and the other Nichomachean MSS the reader should consult the Oxford edition of Livy, Books I–V, by Conway and Walters. A list of all the MSS used in that edition is given at the end of this introduction.

The *editio princeps,* edited by Andreas, afterwards Bishop of Aleria, was issued in Rome in 1469. In 1518 came the Aldine edition. The first complete edition of all the books now extant was also brought out at Rome, in 1616, by Lusignanus. Of modern editions may be mentioned those of Gronovius, Leyden, 1645 and 1679; Drakenborch (with notes of Duker and others, and the supplements of Freinsheimius), Leyden, 1738–1746; Alschefski, Berlin, 1841–1846 (critical edition of Books I–X and XXI–XXIII), and Berlin, 1843–44 (text of Books I–X and XXI–XXX); Madvig and Ussing, Copenhagen[4], 1886 ff. (Madvig's *Emendationes Livianae*—a classic of criticism—had appeared at Copenhagen in 1860); Hertz, Leipsic, 1857–1863; Weissenborn (Teubner text, revised by M. Müller and W. Heraeus) Leipsic, 1881 ff.; Luchs, Books XXI–XXV and XXVI–XXX, Berlin, 1888–1889 (best critical apparatus for third decade); Zingerle, Leipsic, 1888–1908; Weissenborn and H. J. Müller, Berlin, 1880–1909 (best explanatory edition of the whole of Livy, with German notes; the several volumes are more or less frequently republished in revised editions); M. Müller, F. Luterbacher, E. Wölfflin, H. J. Müller, and F. Friedersdorff (Books I–X and XXI–XXX, separate volumes, with German notes) Leipsic, various dates; Books I. and II. are in their second edition (II. by W. Heraeus).

Of the numerous editions of parts of the first decade which are provided with English notes may be cited: Book I. by Sir J. Seeley, Oxford, 1874; by H. J. Edwards, Cambridge, 1912; Books I. and II. by J. B. Greenough, Boston, 1891; Book II. by R. S. Conway, Cambridge, 1901; Books II. and III. by H. M. Stephenson, London, 1882; Book III. by P. Thoresby Jones, Oxford, 1914; Book IV. by H. M. Stephenson,

Cambridge, 1890; Books V–VII by A. R. Cluer and P. E. Matheson, Oxford, 1904²; Book IX by W. B. Anderson, Cambridge, 1909. For the first decade the critical edition by Conway and Walters, of which the first half was published by the Oxford University Press in 1914, is the standard. There are translations of the whole of Livy by Philemon Holland, London, 1600; by George Baker, London, 1797; and by Rev. Canon Roberts, now in course of publication in Everyman's Library, London, 1912 ff. Books XXI–XXV have been done by A. J. Church and W. J. Brodribb, London, 1890. Of books concerned wholly or in part with Livy the following may be mentioned: H. Taine, *Essai sur Tite Live*, Paris, 1856; J. Wight Duff, *A Literary History of Rome*, London and New York, 1909; O. Riemann, *Etudes sur la Langue el la Grammaire de Tite-Live*, Paris, 1885; C, Wachsmuth, *Einleitung in das Studium der alten Geschichte*, Leipsic, 1895; H. Darnley Naylor, *Latin and English Idiom, an Object Lesson from Livy's Preface,* and *More Latin and English Idiom*, Cambridge, 1909 and 1915. For further information about the bibliography of Livy, including the great mass of pamphlets and periodical articles, the student may consult Schanz, *Geschichte der römischen Litteratur* ii. 1³, Munich, 1911 (in Iwan von Müller's *Handbuch der Klassischen Altertumswissenschaft)* and the various *Jahresberichte,* by H. J. Müller and others, which Schanz lists on p. 418.

LIVY

FROM THE FOUNDING OF THE CITY

BOOK I

PREFACE

WHETHER I AM LIKELY TO ACCOMPLISH ANYTHING WORTHY OF THE labor, if I record the achievements of the Roman people from the foundation of the city, I do not really know, nor if I knew would I dare to avouch it; perceiving as I do that the theme[1] is not only old but hackneyed, through the constant succession of new historians, who believe either that in their facts they can produce more authentic information, or that in their style they will prove better than the rude attempts of the ancients. Yet, however this shall be, it will be a satisfaction to have done myself as much as lies in me to commemorate the deeds of the foremost people of the world; and if in so vast a company of writers my own reputation should be obscure, my consolation would be the fame and greatness of those whose renown will throw mine into the shade. Moreover, my subject involves infinite labor, seeing that it must be traced back above seven hundred years, and that proceeding from slender beginnings it has so increased as now to be burdened by its own magnitude; and at the same time I doubt not that to most readers the earliest origins and the period immediately succeeding them will give little pleasure, for they will be in haste to reach these modern times, in which the might of a people which has long been very powerful is working its own undoing. I myself, on the contrary, shall seek in this an additional reward for my toil, that I may avert my gaze from the troubles which our age has been witnessing for so many years, so long at least as I am absorbed in the recollection of the brave days of old, free from every care which, even if it could not divert the historian's mind from the truth, might nevertheless cause it anxiety.[2]

Such traditions as belong to the time before the city was founded, or rather was presently to be founded, and are rather adorned with poetic legends than based upon trustworthy historical proofs, I purpose neither to affirm nor to refute. It is the privilege of antiquity to mingle divine things with human, and so to add dignity to the beginnings of cities; and if any people ought to be allowed to conse-crate their origins and refer them to a divine source, so great is the military glory of the Roman People that when they profess that their Father and the Father of their Founder was none other than Mars, the nations of the earth may well submit to this also with as good a grace as they submit to Rome's dominion. But to such legends as these, however they shall be regarded and judged, I shall, for my own part, attach no great importance. Here are the questions to which I would have every reader give his close attention—what life and morals were like; through what men and by what policies, in peace and in war, empire was established and enlarged: then let him note how, with the gradual relaxation of discipline, morals first gave way, as it were, then sank lower and lower, and finally began the downward plunge[3] which has brought us to the present time, when we can endure neither our vices nor their cure.

What chiefly makes the study of history wholesome and profitable is this, that you behold the lessons of every kind of experience set forth as on a conspicuous monument;[4] from these you may choose for yourself and for your own state what to imitate, from these mark for avoidance what is shameful in the conception and shame-ful in the result. For the rest, either love of the task I have set myself deceives me, or no state was ever greater, none more righteous or richer in good examples, none ever was where avarice and luxury came into the social order so late, or where humble means and thrift were so highly esteemed and so long held in honor. For true it is that the less men's wealth was, the less was their greed. Of late, riches have brought in avarice, and excessive pleasures the longing to carry wantonness and license to the point of ruin for oneself and of universal destruction.

But complaints are sure to be disagreeable, even when they shall perhaps be necessary; let the beginning, at all events, of so great an enterprise have none. With good omens rather would we begin, and, if historians had the same custom which poets have, with prayers and entreaties to the gods and goddesses, that they might grant us to bring to a successful issue the great task we have undertaken.

I. First of all, then, it is generally agreed that when Troy was taken vengeance was wreaked upon the other Trojans, but that two, Aeneas and Antenor, were spared all the penalties of war by the Achivi, owing to long-standing claims of hospitality, and because they had always advocated peace and the giving back of Helen. They then experienced various vicissitudes. Antenor, with a company of Eneti who had been expelled from Paphlagonia in a revolution and were looking for a home and a leader—for they had lost their king, Pylaemenes, at Troy[5]—came to the inmost bay of the Adriatic. There, driving out the Euganei, who dwelt between the sea and the Alps, the Eneti and Trojans took possession of those lands. And in fact the place where they first landed is called Troy, and the district is therefore known as Trojan, while the people as a whole are called the Veneti. Aeneas, driven from home by a similar misfortune, but guided by fate to undertakings of greater consequence, came first to Macedonia; thence was carried, in his quest of a place of settlement, to Sicily; and from Sicily laid his course towards the land of Laurentum. This place too is called Troy. Landing there, the Trojans, as men who, after their all but immeasurable wanderings, had nothing left but their swords and ships, were driving booty from the fields, when King Latinus and the Aborigines, who then occupied that country, rushed down from their city and their fields to repel with arms the violence of the invaders. From this point the tradition follows two lines. Some say that Latinus, having been defeated in the battle, made a peace with Aeneas, and later an alliance of marriage.[6] Others maintain that when the opposing lines had been drawn up, Latinus did not wait for the charge to sound, but advanced amidst his chieftains and summoned the captain of the strangers to a parley. He then inquired what men they were, whence they had come, what mishap had caused them to leave their home, and what they sought in landing on the coast of Laurentum. He was told that the people were Trojans and their leader Aeneas, son of Anchises and Venus; that their city had been burnt, and that, driven from home, they were looking for a dwelling-place and a site where they might build a city. Filled with wonder at the renown of the race and the hero, and at his spirit, prepared alike for war or peace, he gave him his right hand in solemn pledge of lasting friendship. The commanders then made a treaty, and the armies saluted each other. Aeneas became a guest in the house of Latinus; there the latter, in the presence of his household gods, added a domestic treaty to the public one, by giving his daughter in marriage to Aeneas. This event removed any doubt in the minds of the Trojans that they had brought their wanderings to an end at last in a permanent and settled habitation. They founded a town, which Aeneas named Lavinium, after his wife. In a short time, moreover, there was a male scion of the new marriage, to whom his parents gave the name of Ascanius.

II. War was then made upon Trojans and Aborigines alike. Turnus was king of the Rutulians, and to him Lavinia had been betrothed before the coming of Aeneas. Indignant that a stranger should be preferred before him, he attacked, at the same time, both Aeneas and Latinus. Neither army came off rejoicing from that battle. The Rutulians were beaten: the victorious Aborigines and Trojans lost their leader Latinus. Then Turnus and the Rutulians, discouraged at their situation, fled for succor to the opulent and powerful Etruscans and their king Mezentius, who held sway in Caere, at that time an important town. Mezentius had been, from the very beginning, far from pleased at the birth of the new city; he now felt that the Trojan state was growing much more rapidly than was altogether safe for its neighbors, and readily united his forces with those of the Rutulians. Aeneas, that he might win the goodwill of the Aborigines to confront so formidable an array, and that all might possess not only the same rights but also the same name, called both nations Latins;[7] and from that time on the Aborigines were no less ready and faithful than the Trojans in the service of King Aeneas. Accordingly, trusting to this friendly spirit of the two peoples, which were growing each day more united, and, despite the power of Etruria, which had filled with the glory of her name not only the lands but the sea as well, along the whole extent of Italy from the Alps to the Sicilian Strait, Aeneas declined to defend himself behind his walls, as he might have done, but led out his troops to battle. The fight which ensued was a victory for the Latins: for Aeneas it was, besides, the last of his mortal labors. He lies buried, whether it is fitting and right to term him god or man, on the banks of the river Numicus; men, however, call him Jupiter Indiges.[8]

III. Ascanius, Aeneas' son, was not yet ripe for authority; yet the authority was kept for him, unimpaired, until he arrived at manhood. Meanwhile, under a woman's regency, the Latin State and the kingdom of his father and his grandfather stood unshaken—so strong was Lavinia's character—until the boy could claim it. I shall not discuss the question—for who could affirm for certain so ancient a matter? whether this boy was Ascanius, or an elder brother, born by Creusa while Ilium yet stood, who accompanied his father when he fled from the city, being the same whom the Julian family call Iulus and claim as the author of their name. This Ascanius, no matter where born, or of what mother—it is agreed in any case that he was Aeneas' son—left Lavinium, when its population came to be too large, for it was already a flourishing and wealthy city for those days, to his mother, or stepmother, and founded a new city himself below the Alban Mount. This was known from its position, as it lay stretched out along the ridge, by the name of Alba Longa. From the settlement of Lavinium to the planting of the colony at Alba Longa was an interval of some thirty years. Yet the nation had grown so powerful, in consequence especially of the defeat of the Etruscans, that even when Aeneas died, and even when a woman became its regent and a boy began his apprenticeship as king, neither Mezentius and his Etruscans nor any other neighbors dared to attack them. Peace had been agreed to on these terms, that the River Albula, which men now call the Tiber, should be the boundary between the Etruscans and the Latins. Next Silvius reigned, son of Ascanius, born, as it chanced, in the forest. He begat Aeneas Silvius, and he Latinus Silvius. By him several colonies were planted, and called the Ancient Latins. Thereafter the cognomen Silvius was retained by all who ruled at Alba. From Latinus came Alba, from Alba Atys, from Atys Capys, from Capys Capetus, from Capetus Tiberinus. This last king was drowned in crossing the River Albula, and gave the stream the name which has been current with later generations. Then Agrippa, son of Tiberinus, reigned, and after Agrippa Romulus Silvius was king, having received the power from his father. Upon the death of Romulus by lightning, the kingship passed from him to Aventinus. This king was buried on that hill, which is now a part of the city of Rome, and gave his name to the hill. Proca ruled next. He begat Numitor and Amulius; to Numitor, the elder, he bequeathed the ancient realm of the Silvian family. Yet violence proved more potent than a father's wishes or respect for seniority. Amulius drove out his brother and ruled in his stead. Adding crime to crime, he destroyed Numitor's male issue; and Rhea Silvia, his brother's daughter, he appointed a Vestal under pretense of honoring her, and by consigning her to perpetual virginity, deprived her of the hope of children.

IV. But the Fates were resolved, as I suppose, upon the founding of this great City, and the beginning of the mightiest of empires, next after that of Heaven. The Vestal was ravished, and having given birth to twin sons, named Mars as the father of her doubtful offspring, whether actually so believing, or because it seemed less wrong if a god were the author of her fault. But neither gods nor men protected the mother herself or her babes from the king's cruelty; the priestess he ordered to be manacled and cast into prison, the children to be committed to the river. It happened by singular good fortune that the Tiber having spread beyond its banks into stagnant pools afforded nowhere any access to the regular channel of the river, and the men who brought the twins were led to hope that being infants they might be drowned, no matter how sluggish the stream. So they made shift to discharge the king's command, by exposing the babes at the nearest point of the overflow, where the fig tree Ruminalis—formerly, they say, called Romularis—now stands. In those days this was a wild and uninhabited region. The story persists that when the floating basket in which the children had been exposed was left high and dry by the receding water, a she-wolf, coming down out of the surrounding hills to slake her thirst, turned her steps towards the cry of the infants, and with her teats gave them suck so gently, that the keeper of the royal flock found her licking them with her tongue. Tradition assigns to this man the name of Faustulus, and adds that he carried the twins to his hut and gave them to his wife Larentia to rear. Some think that Larentia, having been free with her favors, had got the name of "she-wolf" among the shepherds, and that this gave rise to this marvellous story.[9] The boys, thus born and reared, had no sooner attained to youth than they began—yet without neglecting the farmstead or the flocks—to range the glades of the mountains for game. Having in this way gained both strength and resolution, they would now not only face wild beasts, but would attack robbers laden with their spoils, and divide up what they took from them among the shepherds, with whom they shared their toils and pranks, while their band of young men grew larger everyday.

V. They say that the Palatine was even then the scene of the merry festival of the Lupercalia which we have today, and that the hill was named Pallantium, from Pallanteum, an Arcadian city, and then Palatium.[10] There Evander, an Arcadian of that stock, who had held the place many ages before the time of which I am writing, is said to have established the yearly rite, derived from Arcadia, that youths should run naked about in playful sport, doing honor to Lycaean Pan, whom the Romans afterwards called Inuus. When the young men were occupied in this celebration, the rite being generally known, some robbers who had been angered by the loss of their plunder laid an ambush for them, and although Romulus successfully defended himself, captured Remus and delivered up their prisoner to King Amulius, even lodging a complaint against him. The main charge was that the brothers made raids on the lands of Numitor, and pillaged them, with a band of young fellows which they had got together, like an invading enemy. So Remus was given up to Numitor to be punished. From the very beginning Faustulus had entertained the suspicion that they were children of the royal blood that he was bringing up in his house; for he was aware both that infants had been exposed by order of the king, and that the time when he had himself taken up the children exactly coincided with that event. But he had been unwilling that the matter should be disclosed prematurely, until opportunity offered or necessity compelled. Necessity came first; accordingly, driven by fear, he revealed the facts to Romulus. It chanced that Numitor too, having Remus in custody, and hearing that the brothers were twins, had been reminded, upon considering their age and their far from servile nature, of his grandsons. The inquiries he made led him to the same conclusion, so that he was almost ready to acknowledge Remus. Thus on every hand the toils were woven about the king. Romulus did not assemble his company of youths—for he was not equal to open violence—but commanded his shepherds to come to the palace at an appointed time, some by one way, some by another, and so made his attack upon the king; while from the house of Numitor came Remus, with another party which he had got together, to help his brother. So Romulus slew the king.

VI. At the beginning of the fray Numitor exclaimed that an enemy had invaded the city and attacked the palace, and drew off the active men of the place to serve as an armed garrison for the defense of the citadel; and when he saw the young men approaching, after they had dispatched the king, to congratulate him, he at once summoned a council, and laid before it his brother's crimes against himself, the parentage of his grandsons, and how they had been born, reared, and recognized. He then announced the tyrant's death, and declared himself to be responsible for it. The brothers advanced with their band through the midst of the crowd, and hailed their grandfather king, whereupon such a shout of assent arose from the entire throng as confirmed the new monarch's title and authority.

The Alban state being thus made over to Numitor, Romulus and Remus were seized with the desire to found a city in the region where they had been exposed and brought up. And in fact the population of Albans and Latins was too large; besides, there were the shepherds. All together, their numbers might easily lead men to hope that Alba would be small, and Lavinium small, compared with the city which they should build. These considerations were interrupted by the curse of their grandsires, the greed of kingly power, and by a shameful quarrel which grew out of it, upon an occasion innocent enough. Since the brothers were twins, and respect for their age could not determine between them, it was agreed that the gods who had those places in their protection should choose by augury who should give the new city its name, who should govern it when built. Romulus took the Palatine for his augural quarter, Remus the Aventine.

VII. Remus is said to have been the first to receive an augury, from the flight of six vultures. The omen had been already reported when twice that number appeared to Romulus. Thereupon each was saluted king by his own followers, the one party laying claim to the honor from priority, the other from the number of the birds. They then engaged in a battle of words and, angry taunts leading to bloodshed, Remus was struck down in the affray. The commoner story is that Remus leaped over the new walls in mockery of his brother, whereupon Romulus in great anger slew him, and in menacing wise added these words withal, "So perish whoever else shall leap over my walls!"[11] Thus Romulus acquired sole power, and the city, thus founded, was called by its founder's name.

His first act was to fortify the Palatine, on which he had himself been reared. To other gods he sacrificed after the Alban custom, but employed the Greek for Hercules, according to the institution of Evander. The story is as follows: Hercules, after slaying Geryones, was driving off his wondrously beautiful cattle, when, close to the river Tiber, where he had swum across it with the herd before him, he found a green spot, where he could let the cattle rest and refresh themselves with the abundant grass; and being tired from his journey he lay down himself. When he had there fallen into a deep sleep, for he was heavy with food and wine, a shepherd by the name of Cacus, who dwelt hard by and was insolent by reason of his strength, was struck with the beauty of the animals, and wished to drive them off as plunder. But if he had driven the herd into his cave, their tracks would have been enough to guide their owner to the place in his search; he therefore chose out those of the cattle that were most remarkable for their beauty, and turning them the other way, dragged them into the cave by their tails. At daybreak Hercules awoke. Glancing over the herd, and perceiving that a part of their number was lacking, he proceeded to the nearest cave, in case there might be footprints leading into it. When he saw that they were all turned outward and yet did not lead to any other place, he was confused and bewildered, and made ready to drive his herd away from that uncanny spot. As the cattle were being driven off, some of them lowed, as usually happens, missing those which had been left behind. They were answered with a law by the cattle shut up in the cave, and this made Hercules turn back. When he came towards the cave, Cacus would have prevented his approach with force, but received a blow from the hero's club, and calling in vain upon the shepherds to protect him, gave up the ghost. Evander, an exile from the Peloponnese, controlled that region in those days, more through personal influence than sovereign power. He was a man revered for his wonderful invention of letters,[12] a new thing to men unacquainted with the arts, and even more revered because of the divinity which men attributed to his mother Carmenta, whom those tribes had admired as a prophetess before the Sibyl's coming into Italy. Now this Evander was then attracted by the concourse of shepherds, who, crowding excitedly about the stranger, were accusing him as a murderer caught red-handed. When he had been told about the deed and the reason for it, and had marked the bearing of the man and his figure, which was somewhat ampler and more august than a mortal's, he inquired who he was. Upon learning his name, his father, and his birthplace, he exclaimed, "Hail, Hercules, son of Jupiter! You are he, of whom my mother, truthful interpreter of Heaven, foretold to me that you should be added to the number of the gods, and that an altar should be dedicated to you here which the nation one day to be the most powerful on earth should call the Greatest Altar, and should serve according to your rite." Hercules gave him his hand, and declared that he accepted the omen, and would fulfill the prophecy by establishing and dedicating an altar. Then and there men took a choice victim from the herd, and for the first time made sacrifice to Hercules. For the ministry and the banquet they employed the Potitii and the Pinarii, being the families of most distinction then living in that region. It so fell out that the Potitii were there at the appointed time, and to them were served the inwards; the Pinarii came after the inwards had been eaten, in season for the remainder of the feast. Thence came the custom, which persisted as long as the Pinarian family endured, that they should not partake of the inwards at that sacrifice. The Potitii, instructed by Evander, were priests of this cult for many generations, until, having delegated to public slaves the solemn function of their family, the entire stock of the Potitii died out. This was the only sacred observance, of all those of foreign origin, which Romulus then adopted, honoring even then the immortality won by worth to which his own destiny was leading him.[13]

VIII. When Romulus had duly attended to the worship of the gods, he called the people together and gave them the rules of law, since nothing else but law could unite them into a single body politic. But these, he was persuaded, would only appear binding in the eyes of a rustic people in case he should invest his own person with majesty, by adopting emblems of authority. He therefore put on a more august state in every way, and especially by the assumption of twelve lictors.[14] Some think the twelve birds which had given him an augury of kingship led him to choose this number. For my part, I am content to share the opinion of those who derive from the neighboring Etruscans (whence were borrowed the curule chair and purple-bordered toga) not only the type of attendants but their number as well—a number which the Etruscans themselves are thought to have chosen because each of the twelve cities which united to elect the king contributed one lictor.

Meanwhile the City was expanding and reaching out its walls to include one place after another, for they built their defenses with an eye rather to the population which they hoped one day to have than to the numbers they had then. Next, lest his big City should be empty, Romulus resorted to a plan for increasing the inhabitants which had long been employed by the founders of cities, who gather about them an obscure and lowly multitude and pretend that the earth has raised up sons to them. In the place which is now enclosed, between the two groves as you go up the hill,[15] he opened a sanctuary. Thither fled, from the surrounding peoples, a miscellaneous rabble, without distinction of bond or free, eager for new conditions; and these constituted the first advance in power towards that greatness at which Romulus aimed. He had now no reason to be dissatisfied with his strength, and proceeded to add policy to strength. He appointed a hundred senators, whether because this number seemed to him sufficient, or because there were no more than a hundred who could be designated Fathers.[16] At all events, they received the designation of Fathers from their rank, and their descendants were called patricians.

IX. Rome was now strong enough to hold her own in war with any of the adjacent states; but owing to the want of women a single generation was likely to see the end of her greatness, since she had neither prospect of posterity at home nor the right of intermarriage with her neighbors. So, on the advice of the senate, Romulus sent envoys round among all the neighboring nations to solicit for the new people an alliance and the privilege of intermarrying. Cities, they argued, as well as all other things, take their rise from the lowliest beginnings. As time goes on, those which are aided by their own worth and by the favor of Heaven achieve great power and renown. They said they were well assured that Rome's origin had been blessed with the favor of Heaven, and that worth would not be lacking; their neighbors should not be reluctant to mingle their stock and their blood with the Romans, who were as truly men as they were. Nowhere did the embassy obtain a friendly hearing. In fact men spurned, at the same time that they feared, both for themselves and their descendants, that great power which was then growing up in their midst; and the envoys were frequently asked, on being dismissed, if they had opened a sanctuary for women as well as for men, for in that way only would they obtain suitable wives. This was a bitter insult to the young Romans, and the matter seemed certain to end in violence. Expressly to afford a fitting time and place for this, Romulus, concealing his resentment, made ready solemn games in honor of the equestrian Neptune, which he called Consualia.[17] He then bade proclaim the spectacle to the surrounding peoples, and his subjects prepared to celebrate it with all the resources within their knowledge and power, that they might cause the occasion to be noised abroad and eagerly expected. Many people—for they were also eager to see the new city—gathered for the festival, especially those who lived nearest, the inhabitants of Caenina, Crustumium, and Antemnae. The Sabines, too, came with all their people, including their children and wives. They were hospitably entertained in every house, and when they had looked at the site of the city, its walls, and its numerous buildings, they marvelled that Rome had so rapidly grown great. When the time came for the show, and people's thoughts and eyes were busy with it, the preconcerted attack began. At a given signal the young Romans darted this way and that, to seize and carry off the maidens. In most cases these were taken by the men in whose path they chanced to be. Some, of exceptional beauty, had been marked out for the chief senators, and were carried off to their houses by plebeians to whom the office had been entrusted. One, who far excelled the rest in mien and loveliness, was seized, the story relates, by the gang of a certain Thalassius. Being repeatedly asked for whom they were bearing her off, they kept shouting that no one should touch her, for they were taking her to Thalassius, and this was the origin of the wedding-cry.[18] The sports broke up in a panic, and the parents of the maidens fled sorrowing. They charged the Romans with the crime of violating hospitality, and invoked the gods to whose solemn games they had come, deceived in violation of religion and honor. The stolen maidens were no more hopeful of their plight, nor less indignant. But Romulus himself went amongst them and explained that the pride of their parents had caused this deed, when they had refused their neighbors the right to intermarry; nevertheless the daughters should be wedded and become co-partners in all the possessions of the Romans, in their citizenship and, dearest privilege of all to the human race, in their children; only let them moderate their anger, and give their hearts to those to whom fortune had given their persons. A sense of injury had often given place to affection, and they would find their husbands the kinder for this reason, that every man would earnestly endeavor not only to be a good husband, but also to console his wife for the home and parents she had lost. His arguments were seconded by the wooing of the men, who excused their act on the score of passion and love, the most moving of all pleas to a woman's heart.

X. The resentment of the brides was already much diminished at the very moment when their parents, in mourning garb and with tears and lamentations, were attempting to arouse their states to action. Nor did they confine their complaints to their home towns, but thronged from every side to the house of Titus Tatius, king of the Sabines; and thither, too, came official embassies, for the name of Tatius was the greatest in all that country. The men of Caenina, Crustumium, and Antemnae, were those who had had a share in the wrong. It seemed to them that Tatius and the Sabines were procrastinating, and without waiting for them these three tribes arranged for a joint campaign. But even the Crustuminians and Antemnates moved too slowly to satisfy the burning anger of the Caeninenses, and accordingly that nation invaded alone the Roman territory. But while they were dispersed and engaged in pillage, Romulus appeared with his troops and taught them, by an easy victory, how ineffectual is anger without strength. Their army he broke and routed, and pursued it as it fled; their king he killed in battle and despoiled; their city, once their leader was slain, he captured at the first assault. He then led his victorious army back, and being not more splendid in his deeds than willing to display them, he arranged the spoils of the enemy's dead commander upon a frame, suitably fashioned for the purpose, and, carrying it himself, mounted the Capitol. Having there deposited his burden, by an oak which the shepherds held sacred, at the same time as he made his offering he marked out the limits of a temple to Jupiter, and bestowed a title upon him. "Jupiter Feretrius," he said, "to thee I, victorious Romulus, myself a king, bring the panoply of a king, and dedicate a sacred precinct within the bounds which I have even now marked off in my mind, to be a seat for the spoils of honor which men shall bear hither in time to come, following my example, when they have slain kings and commanders of the enemy." This was the origin of the first temple that was consecrated in Rome.[19] It pleased Heaven, in the sequel, that while the founder's words should not be in vain, when he declared that men should bring spoils thither in the after time, yet the glory of that gift should not be staled by a multitude of partakers. Twice only since then, in all these years with their many wars, have the spoils of honor been won; so rarely have men had the good fortune to attain to that distinction.[20]

XI. While the Romans were thus occupied in the City, the army of the Antemnates seized the opportunity afforded by their absence, and made an inroad upon their territory; but so swiftly was the Roman levy led against them that they, too, were taken off their guard while scattered about in the fields. They were therefore routed at the first charge and shout, and their town was taken. As Romulus was exulting in his double victory, his wife Hersilia, beset with entreaties by the captive women, begged him to forgive their parents and receive them into the state; which would, in that case, gain in strength by harmony. He readily granted her request. He then set out to meet the Crustuminians, who were marching to attack him. They offered even less resistance than their allies had done, for their ardor had been quenched by the defeats of the others. Colonies were sent out to both places, though most of the colonists preferred to enroll for Crustumium on account of the fertility of its soil. On the other hand, many persons left Crustumium and came to live in Rome, chiefly parents and kinsmen of the captured women.

The last to attack Rome were the Sabines, and this war was by far the gravest of all, for passion and greed were not their motives, nor did they parade war before they made it. To their prudence they even added deception. Spurius Tarpeius commanded the Roman citadel. This man's maiden daughter was bribed with gold by Tatius to admit armed men into the fortress: she happened at that time to have gone outside the walls to fetch water for a sacrifice.[21] Once within, they threw their shields upon her and killed her so, whether to make it appear that the citadel had been taken by assault, or to set an example, that no one might anywhere keep faith with a traitor. There is also a legend that because most of the Sabines wore heavy golden bracelets on their left arms and magnificent jewelled rings, she had stipulated for what they had on their left arms, and that they had therefore heaped their shields upon her, instead of gifts of gold. Some say that, in virtue of the compact that they should give her what they wore on their arms, she flatly demanded their shields and, her treachery being perceived, forfeited her life to the bargain she herself had struck.[22]

XII. Be that as it may, the Sabines held the citadel. Next day the Roman army was drawn up, and covered the ground between the Palatine Hill and the Capitoline, but the Sabines would not come down till rage and eagerness to regain the citadel had goaded their enemy into marching up the slope against them. Two champions led the fighting, the Sabine Mettius Curtius on the one side, and the Roman Hostius Hostilius on the other. Hostius held the Romans firm, despite their disadvantage of position, by the reckless courage he displayed in the thick of the fray. But when he fell, the Roman line gave way at once and fled towards the old gate of the Palatine. Romulus himself was swept along in the crowd of the fugitives, till lifting his sword and shield to heaven, he cried, "O Jupiter, it was thy omen that directed me when I laid here on the Palatine the first foundations of my City. The fortress is already bought by a crime and in the possession of the Sabines, whence they are come, sword in hand, across the valley to seek us here. But do thou, father of gods and men, keep them back from this spot at least; deliver the Romans from their terror, and stay their shameful flight! I here vow to thee, Jupiter the Stayer, a temple, to be a memorial to our descendants how the City was saved by thy present help." Having uttered this prayer he exclaimed, as if he had perceived that it was heard, "Here, Romans, Jupiter Optimus Maximus commands us to stand and renew the fight!" The Romans did stand, as though directed by a voice from Heaven, Romulus himself rushing into the forefront of the battle. Mettius Curtius, on the Sabine side, had led the charge down from the citadel, and driven the Romans in disorder over all that ground which the Forum occupies. He was not now far from the gate of the Palatine, shouting, "We have beaten our faithless hosts, our cowardly enemies! They know now how great is the difference between carrying off maidens and fighting with men!" While he pronounced this boast a band of gallant youths, led on by Romulus, assailed him. It chanced that Mettius was fighting on horseback at the time, and was therefore the more easily put to flight. As he fled, the Romans followed; and the rest of their army, too, fired by the reckless daring of their king, drove the Sabines before them. Mettius plunged into a swamp, his horse becoming unmanageable in the din of the pursuit, and even the Sabines were drawn off from the general engagement by the danger to so great a man. As for Mettius, heartened by the gestures and shouts of his followers and the encouragement of the throng, he made his escape; and the Romans and the Sabines renewed their battle in the valley that lies between the two hills. But the advantage rested with the Romans.

XIII. Then the Sabine women, whose wrong had given rise to the war, with loosened hair and torn garments, their woman's timidity lost in a sense of their misfortune, dared to go amongst the flying missiles, and rushing in from the side, to part the hostile forces and disarm them of their anger, beseeching their fathers on this side, on that their husbands, that fathers-in-law and sons-in-law should not stain themselves with impious bloodshed, nor pollute with parricide the suppliants' children, grandsons to one party and sons to the other. "If you regret," they continued, "the relationship that unites you, if you regret the marriage-tie, turn your anger against us; we are the cause of war, the cause of wounds, and even death to both our husbands and our parents. It will be better for us to perish than to live, lacking either of you, as widows or as orphans." It was a touching plea, not only to the rank and file, but to their leaders as well. A stillness fell on them, and a sudden hush. Then the leaders came forward to make a truce, and not only did they agree on peace, but they made one people out of the two. They shared the sovereignty, but all authority was transferred to Rome. In this way the population was doubled, and that some concession might after all be granted the Sabines, the citizens were named Quirites, from the town of Cures.[23] As a reminder of this battle they gave the name of Curtian Lake to the pool where the horse of Curtius first emerged from the deep swamp and brought his rider to safety.[24]

The sudden exchange of so unhappy a war for a joyful peace endeared the Sabine women even more to their husbands and parents, and above all to Romulus himself. And so, when he divided the people into thirty *curiae*, he named these wards after the women.[25] Undoubtedly the number of the women was somewhat greater than this, but tradition does not tell whether it was their age, their own or their husbands' rank, or the casting of lots, that determined which of them should give their names to the wards. At the same time there were formed three centuries of knights: the Ramnenses were named after Romulus; the Titienses after Titus Tatius; the name and origin of the Luceres are alike obscure.[26] From this time forth the two kings ruled not only jointly but in harmony.

XIV. Some years later the kinsmen of King Tatius maltreated the envoys of the Laurentians, and when their fellow-citizens sought redress under the law of nations, Titus yielded to his partiality for his relations and to their entreaties. In consequence of this he drew down their punishment upon himself, for at Lavinium, whither he had gone to the annual sacrifice, a mob came together and killed him. This act is said to have awakened less resentment than was proper in Romulus, whether owing to the disloyalty that attends a divided rule, or because he thought Tatius had been not unjustly slain. He there-fore declined to go to war; but yet, in order that he might atone for the insults to the envoys and the murder of the king, he caused the covenant between Rome and Lavinium to be renewed.

Thus with the Laurentians peace was preserved against all expec-tation; but another war broke out, much nearer, and indeed almost at the city gates. The men of Fidenae, perceiving the growth of a power which they thought too near themselves for safety, did not wait till its promised strength should be realized, but began war themselves. Arming the young men, they sent them to ravage the land between the City and Fidenae. Thence they turned to the left—for the Tiber stopped them on the right—and by their devastations struck terror into the farmers, whose sudden stampede from the fields into the City brought the first tidings of war. Romulus led forth his army on the instant, for delay was impossible with the enemy so near, and pitched his camp a mile from Fidenae. Leaving there a small guard, he marched out with all his forces. A part of his men he ordered to lie in ambush, on this side and on that, where thick underbrush afforded cover; advancing with the greater part of the infantry and all the cavalry, and delivering a disorderly and provoking attack, in which the horsemen galloped almost up to the gates, he accomplished his purpose of drawing out the enemy. For the flight, too, which had next to be feigned, the cavalry engagement afforded a favorable pretext. And when not only the cavalry began to waver, as if undecided whether to fight or run, but the infantry also fell back, the city gates were quickly thronged by the enemy, who poured out and hurled themselves against the Roman line, and in the ardor of attack and pursuit were drawn on to the place of ambuscade. There the Romans suddenly sprang out and assailed the enemy's flanks, while, to add to their terror, the standards of the detachment which had been left on guard were seen advancing from the camp; thus threatened by so many dangers the men of Fidenae scarcely afforded time for Romulus and those whom they had seen riding off with him to wheel about, before they broke and ran, and in far greater disorder than that of the pretended fugitives whom they had just been chasing—for the flight was a real one this time—sought to regain the town. But the Fidenates did not escape their foes; the Romans followed close upon their heels, and before the gates could be shut burst into the city, as though they both formed but a single army.

XV. From Fidenae the war-spirit, by a kind of contagion, spread to the Veientes, whose hostility was aroused by their kinship with the Fidenates, Etruscans like themselves, and was intensified by the danger which lay in their very proximity to Rome, if her arms should be directed against all her neighbors. They made an incursion into Roman territory which more resembled a marauding expedition than a regular campaign; and so, without having entrenched a camp or waited for the enemy's army, they carried off their booty from the fields and brought it back to Veii. The Romans, on the contrary, not finding their enemy in the fields, crossed the Tiber, ready and eager for a decisive struggle. When the Veientes heard that they were making a camp, and would be advancing against their city, they went out to meet them, preferring to settle the quarrel in the field of battle rather than to be shut up and compelled to fight for their homes and their town. Without employing strategy to aid his forces, the Roman king won the battle by the sheer strength of his seasoned army, and routing his enemies, pursued them to their walls. But the city was strongly fortified, besides the protection afforded by its site, and he refrained from attacking it. Their fields, indeed, he laid waste as he returned, more in revenge than from a desire for booty, and this disaster, following upon their defeat, induced the Veientes to send envoys to Rome and sue for peace. They were deprived of a part of their land, and a truce was granted them for a hundred years.

Such were the principal achievements of the reign of Romulus, at home and in the field, nor is any of them incompatible with the belief in his divine origin and the divinity which was ascribed to the king after his death, whether one considers his spirit in recovering the kingdom of his ancestors, or his wisdom in founding the City and in strengthening it by warlike and peaceful measures. For it was to him, assuredly, that Rome owed the vigor which enabled her to enjoy an untroubled peace for the next forty years. Nevertheless, he was more liked by the commons than by the senate, and was preeminently dear to the hearts of his soldiers. Of these he had three hundred for a bodyguard, to whom he gave the name of Celeres,[27] and kept them by him, not only in war, but also in time of peace.

XVI. When these deathless deeds had been done, as the king was holding a muster in the Campus Martius, near the swamp of Capra, for the purpose of reviewing the army, suddenly a storm came up, with loud claps of thunder, and enveloped him in a cloud so thick as to hide him from the sight of the assembly; and from that moment Romulus was no more on earth.[28] The Roman soldiers at length recovered from their panic, when this hour of wild confusion had been succeeded by a sunny calm; but when they saw that the royal seat was empty, although they readily believed the assertion of the senators, who had been standing next to Romulus, that he had been caught up on high in the blast, they nevertheless remained for sometime sorrowful and silent, as if filled with the fear of orphanhood. Then, when a few men had taken the initiative, they all with one accord hailed Romulus as a god and a god's son, the King and Father of the Roman City, and with prayers besought his favor that he would graciously be pleased forever to protect his children. There were some, I believe, even then who secretly asserted that the king had been rent in pieces by the hands of the senators, for this rumor, too, got abroad, but in very obscure terms; the other version obtained currency, owing to men's admiration for the hero and the intensity of their panic. And the shrewd device of one man is also said to have gained new credit for the story. This was Proculus Julius, who, when the people were distracted with the loss of their king and in no friendly mood towards the senate, being, as tradition tells, weighty in council, were the matter never so important, addressed the assembly as follows: "Quirites, the Father of this City, Romulus, descended suddenly from the sky at dawn this morning and appeared to me. Covered with confusion, I stood reverently before him, praying that it might be vouchsafed me to look upon his face without sin.[29] 'Go,' said he, 'and declare to the Romans the will of Heaven that my Rome shall be the capital of the world; so let them cherish the art of war, and let them know and teach their children that no human strength can resist Roman arms.' So saying," he concluded, "Romulus departed on high." It is wonderful what credence the people placed in that man's tale, and how the grief for the loss of Romulus, which the plebeians and the army felt, was quieted by the assurance of his immortality.

XVII. The senators meanwhile were engaged in a struggle for the coveted kingship. So far it had not come to a question of anyone person, for nobody stood out with special prominence in the new nation; instead, a strife of factions was waging between the two stocks. Those of Sabine origin, having had no king on their side since the death of Tatius, feared that despite their equal rights they might lose their hold upon the sovereign power, and hence desired that the king should be chosen from their own body. The original Romans spurned the idea of an alien king. Various, however, as were men's inclinations, to be ruled by a king was their universal wish, for they had not yet tasted the sweetness of liberty. Then the senators became alarmed, lest the state wanting a ruler and the army a leader, and many neighboring states being disaffected, some violence might be offered from without. All therefore were agreed that there should be some head, but nobody could make up his mind to yield to his fellow. And so the hundred senators shared the power among themselves, establishing ten decuries and appointing one man for each decury to preside over the administration. Ten men exercised authority; only one had its insignia and lictors. Five days was the period of his power, which passed in rotation to all; and for a year the monarchy lapsed. This interval was called, as it was, an interregnum, a name which even yet obtains. Murmurs then arose among the plebs that their servitude had been multiplied; that a hundred masters had been given them instead of one. No longer, it seemed, would they endure anything short of a king, and a king, too, of their own choosing. Perceiving that such ideas were in the wind, the senators thought it would be well to proffer spontaneously a thing which they were on the verge of losing, and obtained the favor of the people by granting them supreme power on such terms as to part with no greater prerogative than they retained. For they decreed that when the people should have named a king, their act should only be valid in case the senators ratified it. Even now, in voting for laws and magistrates, the same right is exercised, but is robbed of its significance; before the people can begin to vote, and when the result of the election is undetermined, the Fathers ratify it. On the present occasion the interrex summoned the assembly and spoke as follows: "May prosperity, favor, and fortune attend our action! Quirites, choose your king. Such is the pleasure of the Fathers, who, in their turn, if your choice fall upon one worthy to be called Romulus' successor, will confirm your election." This so pleased the plebs, that, unwilling to appear outdone in generosity, they merely resolved and ordered that the senate should decree who should be king in Rome.

XVIII. A great reputation for justice and piety was enjoyed in those days by Numa Pompilius. Cures, a town of the Sabines, was his home, and he was deeply versed, so far as anyone could be in that age, in all law, divine and human. The teacher to whom he owed his learning was not, as men say, in default of another name, the Samian Pythagoras; for it is well established that Servius Tullius was king at Rome, more than a hundred years after this time, when Pythagoras gathered about him, on the farthest coasts of Italy, in the neighborhood of Metapontum, Heraclea, and Croton, young men eager to share his studies.[30] And from that country, even if he had been contemporary, how could his fame have reached the Sabines? Again, in what common language could he have induced anyone to seek instruction of him? Or under whose protection could a solitary man have made his way through so many nations differing in speech and customs? It was Numa's native disposition, then, as I incline to believe, that tempered his soul with noble qualities, and his training was not in foreign studies, but in the stern and austere discipline of the ancient Sabines, a race incorruptible as any race of the olden time. When Numa's name had been proposed, the Roman senators perceived that the Sabines would gain the ascendancy if a king were to be chosen from that nation; yet nobody ventured to urge his own claims in preference to those of such a man, nor the claim of any other of his faction, nor those, in short, of any of the senators or citizens. And so they unanimously voted to offer the sovereignty to Numa Pompilius. Being summoned to Rome he commanded that, just as Romulus had obeyed the augural omens in building his city and assuming regal power, so too in his own case the gods should be consulted. Accordingly an augur (who thereafter, as a mark of honor, was made a priest of the state in permanent charge of that function) conducted him to the citadel and caused him to sit down on a stone, facing the south. The augur seated himself on Numa's left, having his head covered, and holding in his right hand the crooked staff without a knot which they call a *lituus*. Then, looking out over the City and the country beyond, he prayed to the gods, and marked off the heavens by a line from east to west, designating as "right" the regions to the south, as "left" those to the north, and fixing in his mind a landmark opposite to him and as far away as the eye could reach; next shifting the crook to his left hand and, laying his right hand on Numa's head, he uttered the following prayer: "Father Jupiter, if it is Heaven's will that this man Numa Pompilius, whose head I am touching, be king in Rome, do thou exhibit to us unmistakable signs within those limits which I have set." He then specified the auspices which he desired should be sent, and upon their appearance Numa was declared king, and so descended from the augural station.

XIX. When he had thus obtained the kingship, he prepared to give the new City, founded by force of arms, a new foundation in law, statutes, and observances. And perceiving that men could not grow used to these things in the midst of wars, since their natures grew wild and savage through warfare, he thought it needful that his warlike people should be softened by the disuse of arms, and built the temple of Janus at the bottom of the Argiletum, as an index of peace and war, that when open it might signify that the nation was in arms, when closed that all the peoples round about were pacified. Twice since Numa's reign has it been closed: once in the consulship of Titus Manlius, after the conclusion of the First Punic War; the second time, which the gods permitted our own generation to witness, was after the battle of Actium, when the emperor Caesar Augustus had brought about peace on land and sea.[31] Numa closed the temple after first securing the goodwill of all the neighboring tribes by alliances and treaties. And fearing lest relief from anxiety on the score of foreign perils might lead men who had hitherto been held back by fear of their enemies and by military discipline into extravagance and idleness, he thought the very first thing to do, as being the most efficacious with a populace which was ignorant and, in those early days, uncivilized, was to imbue them with the fear of Heaven. As he could not instil this into their hearts without inventing some marvellous story, he pretended to have nocturnal meetings with the goddess Egeria, and that hers was the advice which guided him in the establishment of rites most approved by the gods, and in the appointment of special priests for the service of each.

And first of all he divided the year into twelve months, according to the revolutions of the moon. But since the moon does not give months of quite thirty days each, and eleven days are wanting to the full complement of a year as marked by the sun's revolution, he inserted intercalary months in such a way that in the twentieth year the days should fall in with the same position of the sun from which they had started, and the period of twenty years be rounded out. He also appointed days when public business might not be carried on, and others when it might, since it would sometimes be desirable that nothing should be brought before the people.

XX. He then turned his attention to the appointment of priests, although he performed very many priestly duties himself, especially those which now belong to the Flamen Dialis. But inasmuch as he thought that in a warlike nation there would be more kings like Romulus than like Numa, and that they would take the field in person, he did not wish the sacrificial duties of the kingly office to be neglected, and so appointed a flamen for Jupiter, as his perpetual priest, and provided him with a conspicuous dress and the royal curule chair. To him he added two other flamens, one for Mars, the other for Quirinus. In like manner he designated virgins for Vesta's service—a priesthood, this, that derived from Alba and so was not unsuited to the founder's stock. That they might be perpetual priestesses of the temple, he assigned them a stipend from the public treasury, and by the rule of virginity and other observances invested them with awe and sanctity. He likewise chose twelve Salii for Mars Gradivus, and granted them the distinction of wearing the embroidered tunic and over it a bronze breastplate, and of bearing the divine shields which men call *ancilia*,[32] while they proceeded through the City, chanting their hymns to the triple beat of their solemn dance. He next chose as pontifex Numa Marcius, son of Marcus, one of the senators, and to him he intrusted written directions, full and accurate, for performing the rites of worship; with what victims, on what days, in what temple, sacrifices should be offered, and from what sources money was to be disbursed to pay their costs. All other public and private sacrifices he likewise made subject to the decrees of the pontifex, that there might be someone to whom the commons could come for advice, lest any confusion should arise in the religious law through the neglect of ancestral rites and the adoption of strange ones. And not merely ceremonies relating to the gods above, but also proper funeral observances and the propitiation of the spirits of the dead were to be taught by the pontifex as well, and also what prodigies manifested by lightning or other visible sign were to be taken in hand and averted. With the purpose of eliciting this knowledge from the minds of the gods, Numa dedicated an altar on the Aventine to Jupiter Elicius, and consulted the god by augury, that he might learn what portents were to be regarded.

XXI. The consideration and disposal of these matters diverted the thoughts of the whole people from violence and arms. Not only had they something to occupy their minds, but their constant preoccupation with the gods, now that it seemed to them that concern for human affairs was felt by the heavenly powers, had so tinged the hearts of all with piety, that the nation was governed by its regard for promises and oaths, rather than by the dread of laws and penalties. And while Numa's subjects were spontaneously imitating the character of their king, as their unique exemplar, the neighboring peoples also, who had hitherto considered that it was no city but a camp that had been set up in their midst, as a menace to the general peace, came to feel such reverence for them, that they thought it sacrilege to injure a nation so wholly bent upon the worship of the gods. There was a grove watered by a perennial spring which flowed through the midst of it, out of a dark cave. Thither Numa would often withdraw, without witnesses, as if to meet the goddess; so he dedicated the grove to the Camenae, alleging that they held counsel there with his wife Egeria. He also established an annual worship of Faith, to whose chapel he ordered that the flamens should proceed in a two-horse hooded carriage, and should wrap up their arms as far as the fingers before sacrificing, as a sign that faith must be kept, and that even in men's clasped hands her seat is sacred. He established many other rites, as well as places of sacrifice, which the pontiffs called *Argei*.[33] But of all his services the greatest was this, that throughout his reign he guarded peace no less jealously than his kingdom. Thus two successive kings in different ways, one by war, the other by peace, promoted the nation's welfare. Romulus ruled thirty-seven years, Numa forty-three. The state was not only strong, but was also well organized in the arts both of war and of peace.

XXII. At Numa's death the state reverted to an interregnum. Then Tullus Hostilius, grandson of that Hostilius who had distinguished himself in the battle with the Sabines at the foot of the citadel, was declared king by the people, and the senate confirmed their choice. This monarch was not only unlike the last, but was actually more warlike than Romulus had been. Besides his youth and strength, the glory of his grandfather was also an incentive to him. So, thinking that the nation was growing decrepit from inaction, he everywhere sought excuses for stirring up war. It happened that the Roman rustics were driving off cattle from Alban territory, while the Albans were treating the Romans in the same way. The man who was then in power in Alba was Gaius Cluilius. Each side, at about the same time, sent envoys to demand restitution. Tullus had commanded his envoys to do nothing else till they had carried out his orders; he felt convinced that the Albans would refuse his demands, in which case he could declare war with a good conscience. The Alban representatives proceeded rather laxly. Received by Tullus with gracious and kindly hospitality, they attended in a friendly spirit the banquet which he gave in their honor. Meanwhile the Romans had been beforehand with them in seeking redress, and, being denied it by the Alban leader, had made a declaration of war, to take effect in thirty days. Returning, they reported these things to Tullus, who thereupon invited the Alban envoys to inform him of the object of their mission. They, knowing nothing of what had happened, at first spent sometime in apologies. They said they should be sorry to utter anything which might give offense to Tullus, but that they were compelled to do so by their orders; they had come to seek restitution; if it should be denied them they were commanded to declare war. To this Tullus replied: "Tell your king the Roman king calls the gods to witness which people first spurned the other's demand for redress and dismissed its envoys, that they may call down upon the guilty nation all the disasters of this war."

XXIII. With this answer the Albans returned to their city, and both sides prepared for war with the greatest energy—a civil war, to all intents and purposes, almost as if fathers were arrayed against sons; for both were of Trojan ancestry, since Lavinium had been planted from Troy, Alba from Lavinium, and from the line of the Alban kings had come the Romans. Still, the issue of the war made the struggle less deplorable, for no battle was fought, and when only the buildings of one of the cities had been destroyed, the two peoples were fused into one. The Albans were first in the field, and with a great army invaded the Roman territory. Their camp they pitched not more than five miles from the City, and surrounded it with a trench. (This was known for some centuries as the Cluilian Trench, from the name of the general, until in the course of time both trench and name disappeared.) In this camp Cluilius the Alban king died, and the Albans chose as dictator Mettius Fufetius. Meantime Tullus, emboldened principally by the death of the king, and asserting that Heaven's great powers would take vengeance upon all of the Alban name, beginning with their king himself, for their unscrupulous war, made a night march past the enemy's camp and led his army into the country of the Albans. This move drew Mettius out from his fortifications. Leading his troops the shortest way towards the enemy, he sent an envoy on ahead to say to Tullus that before they fought it was well that they should confer together; if Tullus would meet him he was confident he had that to say which would be of no less moment to the Roman state than to the Alban. Without rejecting this suggestion, Tullus nevertheless drew up his men in line of battle, in case the proposals should prove impracticable. On the other side the Albans also formed up. When both armies had been marshalled, the leaders, attended by a few of their nobles, advanced to the middle of the field. Then the Alban began as follows:

> Pillage and failure to make the amends demanded in accordance with our treaty I think I have myself heard named by our king, Cluilius, as the occasion of this war, and I doubt not, Tullus, but you make the same contention. But if truth is to be spoken, rather than sophistries, it is greed for dominion that is goading two kindred and neighboring peoples into war. Whether rightly or wrongly I do not attempt to determine; that is a question that may well have been considered by him who undertook the war; I am only the general appointed by the Albans to prosecute that war. But this is the point, Tullus, which I wish to suggest to you: Of the magnitude of the Etruscan power which encompasses us, and you especially, you are better aware than we, in proportion as you are nearer to that people. Great is their strength on land, exceedingly great on the sea. You must consider that the instant you give the signal for battle, the Tuscans will be watching our two armies, so that, when we have become tired and exhausted, they may attack at once the victor and the vanquished. In

Heaven's name, therefore, since we are not content with unquestioned liberty, but are proceeding to the doubtful hazard of dominion or enslavement, let us adopt some plan by which we may decide the question which nation shall rule the other, without a great disaster and much carnage on both sides.

Tullus made no objection, though inclined to war by nature no less than by his anticipation of victory. While both parties were considering what to do, a plan was hit upon for the execution of which Fortune herself supplied the means.

XXIV. It chanced that there were in each of these armies triplet brothers, not ill-matched either in age or in physical prowess. That they were Horatii and Curiatii is generally allowed, and scarcely any other ancient tradition is better known; yet, in spite of the celebrity of the affair, an uncertainty persists in regard to the names—to which people, that is, the Horatii belonged, and to which the Curiatii. The writers of history are divided. Still, the majority, I find, call the Roman brothers Horatii, and theirs is the opinion I incline to adopt. To these young men the kings proposed a combat in which each should fight for his own city, the dominion to belong with that side where the victory should rest. No objection was raised, and time and place were agreed on. Before proceeding with the battle, a treaty was made between the Romans and the Albans, providing that the nation whose citizens should triumph in this contest should hold undisputed sway over the other nation. One treaty differs from another in its terms, but the same procedure is always employed. On the present occasion we are told that they did as follows, nor has tradition preserved the memory of anymore ancient compact. The fetial[34] asked King Tullus, "Dost thou command me, King, to make a treaty with the *pater patratus* of the Alban People?" Being so commanded by the king, he said, "I demand of thee, King, the sacred herb." The king replied, "Thou shalt take it untainted." The fetial brought from the citadel an untainted plant. After this he asked the king, "Dost thou grant me, King, with my emblems and my companions, the royal sanction, to speak for the Roman People of the Quirites?"

The king made answer, "So far as may be without prejudice to myself and the Roman People of the Quirites, I grant it." The fetial was Marcus Valerius; he made Spurius Fusius *pater patratus,* touching his head and hair with the sacred sprig. The *pater patratus* is appointed to pronounce the oath, that is, to solemnize the pact; and this he accomplishes with many words, expressed in a long metrical formula which it is not worth while to quote. The conditions being then recited, he cries, "Hear, Jupiter; hear, *pater patratus* of the Alban People: hear ye, People of Alba: From these terms, as they have been publicly rehearsed from beginning to end, without fraud, from these tablets, or this wax, and as they have been this day clearly understood, the Roman People will not be the first to depart. If it shall first depart from them, by general consent, with malice aforethought, then on that day do thou, great Diespiter, so smite the Roman People as I shall here today smite this pig: and so much the harder smite them as thy power and thy strength are greater." When Spurius had said these words, he struck the pig with a flint. In like manner the Albans pronounced their own forms and their own oath, by the mouth of their own dictator and priests.

XXV. When the treaty had been established, the brothers armed themselves, in accordance with the agreement. On either side the soldiers urged on their champions. They reminded them that their fathers' gods, their native land, their parents, and all their countrymen, whether at home or with the army, had their eye only on their swords and their right hands. Eager for the combat, as well owing to their native spirit as to the shouts of encouragement which filled their ears, the brothers advanced into the space between the two lines of battle. The two armies were drawn up, each in front of its own camp, no longer in any immediate danger, but their concern as great as ever; and no wonder, since empire was staked on those few men's valor and good fortune! Alert, therefore, and in suspense, they concentrated their attention upon this unpleasing spectacle. The signal was given, and with drawn steel, like advancing battle-lines, the six young men rushed to the charge, breathing the courage of great armies. Neither side thought of its own danger, but of the nation's sovereignty or servitude, and how from that day forward their country must experience the fortune they should themselves create. The instant they encountered, there was a clash of shields and a flash of glittering blades, while a deep shudder ran through the onlookers, who, as long as neither side had the advantage, remained powerless to speak or breathe. Then, in the hand-to-hand fight which followed, wherein were soon exhibited to men's eyes not only struggling bodies and the play of the sword and shield, but also bloody wounds, two of the Romans fell, fatally wounded, one upon the other, while all three of the Albans were wounded. At the fall of the Romans a shout of joy burst from the Alban army, while the Roman levies now bade farewell to all their hopes; but not to their anxiety, for they were horrorstricken at the plight of the single warrior whom the three Curiatii had surrounded. He happened to have got no hurt, and though no match for his enemies together, was ready to fight them one at a time. So, to divide their attack, he fled, thinking that each of them would pursue him with what speed his wounds permitted. He had already run some little distance from the spot where they had fought, when, looking back, he saw that they were following at wide intervals and that one of them had nearly overtaken him. Facing about, he ran swiftly up to his man, and while the Alban host were calling out to the Curiatii to help their brother, Horatius had already slain him, and was hastening, flushed with victory, to meet his second antagonist. Then with a cheer, such as is often drawn from partisans by a sudden turn in a contest, the Romans encouraged their champion, and he pressed on to end the battle. And so, before the third Curiatius could come up—and he was not far off—Horatius dispatched the second. They were now on even terms, one soldier surviving on each side, but in hope and vigor they were far from equal. The one, unscathed and elated by his double victory, was eager for a third encounter. The other dragged himself along, faint from his wound and exhausted with running; he thought how his brothers had been slaughtered before him, and was a beaten man when he faced his triumphant foe. What followed was no combat. The Roman cried exultantly, "Two victims I have given to the shades of my brothers: the third I will offer up to the cause of this war, that Roman may rule Alban." His adversary could barely hold up his shield. With a downward thrust Horatius buried his sword in the Alban's throat, and despoiled him where he lay. The Romans welcomed their hero with jubilations and thanksgivings, and their joy was all the greater that they had come near despairing. The burial of their dead then claimed the attention of the two armies, with widely different feelings, since one nation was exalted with imperial power, the other made subject to a foreign sway. The graves may still be seen where each soldier fell: two Roman graves in one spot, nearer Alba; those of the three Albans towards Rome, but separated, just as they had fought.

XXVI. Before they left the field Mettius asked, in pursuance of the compact, what Tullus commanded him to do, and the Roman ordered him to hold his young men under arms, saying that he should employ their services, if war broke out with the Veientes. The armies then marched home. In the van of the Romans came Horatius, displaying his triple spoils. As he drew near the Porta Capena he was met by his unwedded sister, who had been promised in marriage to one of the Curiatii. When she recognized on her brother's shoulders the military cloak of her betrothed, which she herself had woven, she loosed her hair and, weeping, called on her dead lover's name. It enraged the fiery youth to hear his sister's lamentations in the hour of his own victory and the nation's great rejoicing. And so, drawing his sword and at the same time angrily upbraiding her, he ran her through the body. "Begone" he cried, "to your betrothed, with your ill-timed love, since you have forgot your brothers, both the dead and the living, and forgot your country! So perish every Roman woman who mourns a foe!"

Horrid as this deed seemed to the Fathers and the people, his recent service was an off-set to it; nevertheless he was seized and brought before the king for trial. The king, that he might not take upon himself the responsibility for so stern and unpopular a judgement, and for the punishment which must follow sentence, called together the council of the people and said: "In accordance with the law I appoint duumvirs to pass judgement upon Horatius for treason."[35] The dread formula of the law ran thus: "Let the duumvirs pronounce him guilty of treason; if he shall appeal from the duumvirs, let the appeal be tried; if the duumvirs win, let the lictor veil his head; let him bind him with a rope to a barren tree; let him scourge him either within or without the pomerium."[36] By the terms of this law duumvirs were appointed. They considered that they might not acquit, under that act, even one who was innocent, and having given a verdict of guilty, one of them pronounced the words, "Publius Horatius, I adjudge you a traitor; go, lictor, bind his hands." The lictor had approached and was about to fit the noose. Then Horatius, at the prompting of Tullus, who put a merciful construction upon the law, cried, "I appeal!" And so the appeal was tried before the people. What influenced men most of all in that trial was the assertion of Publius Horatius, the father, that his daughter had been justly slain; otherwise he should have used a father's authority and have punished his son, himself. He then implored them not to make him childless whom they had beheld a little while before surrounded by a goodly offspring. So saying, the old man embraced the youth, and pointing to the spoils of the Curiatii set up in the place which is now called "the Horatian Spears,"[37] he exclaimed, "This man you saw but lately advancing decked with spoils and triumphing in his victory; can you bear, Quirites, to see him bound beneath a fork and scourged and tortured? Hardly could Alban eyes endure so hideous a sight. Go, lictor, bind the hands which but now, with sword and shield, brought imperial power to the Roman People! Go, veil the head of the liberator of this city! Bind him to a barren tree! Scourge him within the pomerium, if you will—so it be amidst yonder spears and trophies of our enemies—or outside the pomerium—so it be amongst the graves of the Curiatii! For whither can you lead this youth where his own honors will not vindicate him from so foul a punishment?" The people could not withstand the father's tears, or the courage of Horatius himself, steadfast in every peril; and they acquitted him, more in admiration of his valor than from the justice of his cause. And so, that the flagrant murder might yet be cleansed away, by some kind of expiatory rite, the father was commanded to make atonement for his son at the public cost. He therefore offered certain piacular sacrifices, which were thenceforward handed down in the Horatian family, and, erecting a beam across the street, to typify a yoke, he made his son pass under it, with covered head. It remains to this day, being restored from time to time at the state's expense, and is known as "the Sister's Beam." Horatia's tomb, of hewn stone, was built on the place where she had been struck down.

XXVII. But the peace with Alba did not last long. The discontent of the people, who criticized the dictator for having confided the nation's welfare to three soldiers, broke down his weak character, and since honest measures had proved unsuccessful, he resorted to evil ones to regain the favor of his countrymen. Accordingly, just as in war he had sought peace, so now in time of peace he desired war. But seeing that his own state was richer in courage than in strength, he stirred up other tribes to make war openly after due declaration; while for his own people he reserved the part of the traitor under the disguise of friendship. The men of Fidenae, a Roman colony, and the Veientes, whom they admitted to a share in their designs, were induced to commence hostilities by a promise that the Albans would go over to their side. Fidenae having openly revolted, Tullus summoned Mettius and his army from Alba, and led his forces against the enemy. Crossing the Anio, he pitched his camp at the confluence of the rivers. The Veientine army had crossed the Tiber between that place and Fidenae. These troops, drawn up next the river, formed the right wing; on the left the Fidenates were posted, nearer the mountains. Tullus marshalled his own men against the Veientine enemy; the Albans he posted opposite the army of Fidenae. The Alban commander was as wanting in courage as in loyalty. Not daring, therefore, either to hold his ground or openly to desert, he drew off by imperceptible degrees in the direction of the mountains. Then, when he thought he had got near enough to them, he brought up his whole battle-line to an elevated position, and still irresolute, deployed his ranks with the object of consuming time. His purpose was to swing his forces to the side which fortune favored. At first the Romans posted next to the Albans were amazed when they perceived that their flank was being uncovered by the withdrawal of their allies; then a horseman galloped up to the king, and told him that the Albans were marching off. In this crisis Tullus vowed to establish twelve Salian priests,[38] and to build shrines to Pallor and Panic. The horseman he reprimanded in a loud voice, that the enemy might overhear him, and ordered him to go back and fight; there was no occasion for alarm; it was by his own command that the Alban army was marching round, that they might attack the unprotected rear of the Fidenates. He also ordered the cavalry to raise their spears. This manœuvre hid the retreat of the Alban army from a large part of the Roman foot-soldiers; those who had seen it, believing what the king had been heard to say, fought all the more impetuously. The enemy in their turn now became alarmed; they had heard Tullus' loud assertion, and many of the Fidenates, having had Romans among them as colonists, knew Latin. And so, lest the Albans should suddenly charge down from the hills and cut them off from their town, they beat a retreat. Tullus pressed them hard, and having routed the wing composed of the Fidenates, returned, bolder than ever, to the Veientes, who were demoralized by the panic of their neighbors. They, too, failed to withstand his attack, but their rout was stopped by the river in their rear. When they had fled thus far, some basely threw away their arms and rushed blindly into the water, others hesitated on the bank and were overtaken before they had made up their minds whether to flee or resist. Never before had the Romans fought a bloodier battle.

XXVIII. Then the Alban army, which had been a spectator of the battle, was led down into the plain. Mettius congratulated Tullus on the conquest of his enemies; Tullus replied kindly to Mettius, and commanded the Albans in a good hour to join their camp to that of the Romans. He then made preparations to perform, on the morrow, a sacrifice of purification. At dawn, when all things were in readiness, he issued to both armies the customary order, convoking them to an assembly. The heralds, beginning at the outskirts of the camp, called out the Albans first, who being moved by the very novelty of the occasion, took their stand close to the Roman king, that they might hear him harangue his army. The Roman troops, by previous arrangement, were armed and disposed around them, and the centurions were bidden to execute orders promptly. Then Tullus began as follows:

Romans, if ever anywhere in any war you have had reason to give thanks, first to the immortal gods and then to your own valor, it was in the battle of yesterday. For you fought not only against your enemies, but a harder and more dangerous fight—against the treachery and the perfidy of your allies. For, to undeceive you, I gave no orders that the Albans should draw off towards the mountains. What you heard was not my command, but a trick and a pretended command, devised in order that you might not know you were being deserted, and so be distracted from the fight; and that the enemy, thinking that they were being hemmed in on the rear, might be panic-stricken and flee. And yet this guilt which I am charging does not attach to all the Albans; they but followed their general, as you, too, would have done, had I desired to lead you off anywhere. It is Mettius yonder who led this march; Mettius, too, who contrived this war; Mettius who broke the treaty between Roman and Alban. Let another dare such a deed hereafter if I do not speedily visit such a punishment on him as shall be a conspicuous warning to all mankind.

Thereupon the centurions, sword in hand, surrounded Mettius, while the king proceeded: "May prosperity, favor, and fortune be with the Roman people and myself, and with you, men of Alba! I purpose to bring all the Alban people over to Rome, to grant citizenship to their commons, to enroll the nobles in the senate, to make one city and one state. As formerly from one people the Alban nation was divided into two, so now let it be reunited into one." Hearing these words the Alban soldiers, themselves unarmed and fenced in by armed men, were constrained, however their wishes might differ, by a common fear, and held their peace. Then Tullus said: "Mettius Fufetius, if you were capable of learning, yourself, to keep faith and abide by treaties, you should have lived that I might teach you this; as it is, since your disposition is incurable, you shall yet by your punishment teach the human race to hold sacred the obligations you have violated. Accordingly, just as a little while ago your heart was divided between the states of Fidenae and Rome, so now you shall give up your body to be torn two ways." He then brought up two four-horse chariots, and caused Mettius to be stretched out and made fast to them, after which the horses were whipped up in opposite directions, and bore off in each of the cars fragments of the mangled body, where the limbs held to their fastenings. All eyes were turned away from so dreadful a sight. Such was the first and last punishment among the Romans of a kind that disregards the laws of humanity. In other cases we may boast that with no nation have milder punishments found favor.

XXIX. While this was going on, horsemen had already been sent on to Alba to fetch the inhabitants to Rome, and afterwards the legions were marched over to demolish the city. When they entered the gates there was not, indeed, the tumult and panic which usually follow the capture of a city, when its gates have been forced or its walls breached with a ram or its stronghold stormed, when the shouts of the enemy and the rush of armed men through the streets throw the whole town into a wild confusion of blood and fire. But at Alba oppressive silence and grief that found no words quite overwhelmed the spirits of all the people; too dismayed to think what they should take with them and what leave behind, they would ask each other's advice again and again, now standing on their thresholds, and now roaming aimlessly through the houses they were to look upon for that last time. But when at length the horsemen began to be urgent, and clamorously commanded them to come out; when they could now hear the crash of the buildings which were being pulled down in the outskirts of the city; when the dust rising in different quarters had overcast the sky like a gathering cloud, then everybody made haste to carry out what he could, and forth they went, abandoning their lares and penates,[39] and the houses where they had been born and brought up. And now the streets were filled with an unbroken procession of emigrants, whose mutual pity, as they gazed at one another, caused their tears to start afresh; plaintive cries too began to be heard, proceeding chiefly from the women, when they passed the venerable temples beset by armed men, and left in captivity, as it seemed to them, their gods. When the Albans had quitted the city, the Romans everywhere levelled with the ground all buildings, both public and private, and a single hour gave over to destruction and desolation the work of the four hundred years during which Alba had stood. But the temples of the gods were spared, for so the king had decreed.

XXX. Rome, meanwhile, was increased by Alba's downfall. The number of citizens was doubled, the Caelian Hill was added to the City, and, that it might be more thickly settled, Tullus chose it for the site of the king's house and from that time onwards resided there. The chief men of the Albans he made senators, that this branch of the nation might grow too. Such were the Julii, the Servilii, the Quinctii, the Geganii, the Curiatii, and the Cloelii. He also built, as a consecrated place for the order he had enlarged, a senate-house, which continued to be called the Curia Hostilia as late as the time of our own fathers.[40] And that all the orders might gain some strength from the new people, he enrolled ten squadrons of knights[41] from among the Albans, and from the same source filled up the old legions and enlisted new ones.

Confiding in these forces, Tullus declared war on the Sabines, a nation second only at that time to the Etruscans in its wealth of men and arms. On either side there had been aggressions and refusals to grant satisfaction. Tullus complained that at the shrine of Feronia, in a crowded fair, Roman traders had been seized; the Sabines alleged that, before this, refugees from their country had fled to the grove of sanctuary, and had been detained in Rome. These were put forward as the causes of war. The Sabines, not forgetting that a portion of their own forces had been settled in Rome by Tatius and that the Roman state had recently been further strengthened by the addition of the Alban people, began themselves to look about for outside help. Etruria was close by, and the nearest of the Etruscans were the Veientes. There the resentment left over from the wars was the strongest incentive to revolt, and procured them some volunteers; while with certain vagrant and poverty-stricken plebeians even the prospect of pay was effectual. Official aid there was none, and the Veientes (for there is less to surprise us in the others) held firmly to the truce they had agreed upon with Romulus. While preparations for war were making on both sides with the greatest energy, and success appeared to hinge upon which should first take the field, Tullus anticipated his enemies and invaded the Sabine country. A desperate battle was fought near the Silva Malitiosa,[42] where, owing partly, it is true, to the strength of their infantry, but most of all to their newly augmented cavalry, the Roman army gained the mastery. The cavalry made a sudden charge; the ranks of the Sabines were thrown into disorder, and from that moment were unable, without heavy loss, either to hold their own in the fight or to extricate themselves by a retreat.

XXXI. After the defeat of the Sabines, when King Tullus and the entire Roman state were at a high pitch of glory and prosperity, it was reported to the king and senators that there had been a rain of stones on the Alban Mount. As this could scarce be credited, envoys were dispatched to examine the prodigy, and in their sight there fell from the sky, like hail-stones which the wind piles in drifts upon the ground, a shower of pebbles. They thought too that they heard a mighty voice issuing from the grove on the mountain-top, which commanded the Albans to celebrate, according to the fashion of their fathers, the sacrifices, which as though they had forsaken their gods along with their city, they had given over to oblivion, either adopting Roman rites, or in anger at their fortune, such as men sometimes feel, abandoning the worship of the gods. The Romans also, in consequence of the same portent, undertook an official nine days' celebration, whether so commanded by the divine utterance from the Alban Mount—for this too is handed down—or on the advice of soothsayers. At all events it remained a regular custom that whenever the same prodigy was reported there should be a nine days' observance.

Not very long after this Rome was afflicted with a pestilence. This caused a reluctance to bear arms, yet no respite from service was allowed by the warlike king (who believed, besides, that the young men were healthier in the field than at home) until he himself contracted a lingering illness. Then that haughty spirit was so broken, with the breaking of his health, that he who had hitherto thought nothing less worthy of a king than to devote his mind to sacred rites, suddenly became a prey to all sorts of superstitions great and small, and filled even the minds of the people with religious scruples. Men were now agreed in wishing to recall the conditions which had obtained under King Numa, believing that the only remedy left for their ailing bodies was to procure peace and forgiveness from the gods. The king himself, so tradition tells, in turning over the commentaries of Numa discovered there certain occult sacrifices performed in honor of Jupiter Elicius, and devoted himself in secret to those rites; but the ceremony was improperly undertaken or performed, and not only was no divine manifestation vouchsafed him, but in consequence of the wrath of Jupiter, who was provoked by his faulty observance, he was struck by a thunderbolt and consumed in the flames of his house. Tullus was greatly renowned in war and reigned thirty-two years.

XXXII. On the death of Tullus, the government reverted, in accordance with the custom established in the beginning, to the senators, who named an interrex. This official called together the comitia, and the people elected Ancus Marcius king, a choice which the Fathers ratified. Ancus Marcius was a grandson, on the mother's side, of King Numa Pompilius. When he began to rule he was mindful of his grandfather's glory, and considered that the last reign, excellent in all else, had failed to prosper in one respect, owing to neglect or misconduct of religious observances. Deeming it therefore a matter of the utmost consequence to perform the state sacrifices as Numa had established them, he bade the pontifex copy out all these from the commentaries of the king and display them in public on a whitened table. This act led the citizens, who were eager for peace, and also the neighboring nations, to hope that he would adopt the character and institutions of his grandfather. Hence the Latins, with whom a treaty had been made in the time of Tullus, plucked up courage, and raided Roman territory, and when called on by the Romans to make restitution, returned an arrogant answer, persuaded that the Roman king would spend his reign in inactivity amid shrines and altars. But the character of Ancus was well balanced, and he honored the memory of Romulus, as well as Numa. And besides having a conviction that peace had been more necessary to his grandfather's reign, when the nation had been both young and mettlesome, he also believed that the tranquillity, so free of attack, which had fallen to the lot of Numa would be no easy thing for himself to compass; his patience was being tried, and when proved would be regarded with contempt, and in short the times were better suited to the rule of a Tullus than a Numa. In order however that, as Numa had instituted religious practices in time of peace, he might himself give out a ceremonial of war, and that wars might not only be waged but also declared with some sort of formality, he copied from the ancient tribe of the Aequicoli the law, which the fetials now have,[43] by which redress is demanded.

When the envoy has arrived at the frontiers of the people from whom satisfaction is sought, he covers his head with a bonnet—the covering is of wool—and says: "Hear, Jupiter; hear, ye boundaries of"—naming whatever nation they belong to; "let righteousness hear! I am the public herald of the Roman People; I come duly and religiously commissioned; let my words be credited." Then he recites his demands, after which he takes Jupiter to witness: "If I demand unduly and against religion that these men and these things be surrendered to me, then let me never enjoy my native land." These words he rehearses when he crosses the boundary line, the same to what man soever first meets him, the same when he enters the city gates, the same when he has come into the market place, with only a few changes in the form and wording of the oath. If those whom he demands are not surrendered, at the end of three and thirty days—for such is the conventional number—he declares war thus: "Hear, Jupiter, and thou, Janus Quirinus, and hear all heavenly gods, and ye, gods of earth, and ye of the lower world; I call you to witness that this people"—naming whatever people it is—"is unjust, and does not make just reparation. But of these matters we will take counsel of the elders in our country, how we may obtain our right." Then the messenger returns to Rome for the consultation. Immediately the king would consult the Fathers, in some such words as these: "Touching the things, the suits, the causes, concerning which the *pater patratus* of the Roman People of the Quirites has made demands on the *pater patratus* of the Ancient Latins, and upon the men of the Ancient Latins, which things they have not delivered, nor fulfilled, nor satisfied, being things which ought to have been delivered, fulfilled, and satis-fied, speak,"—turning to the man whose opinion he was wont to ask first, "what think you?" Then the other would reply: "I hold that those things ought to be sought in warfare just and righteous; and so I consent and vote." The others were then asked the question, in their order, and when the majority of those present went over to the same opinion, war had been agreed upon. It was customary for the fetial to carry to the bounds of the other nation a cornet-wood spear, iron-pointed or hardened in the fire, and in the presence of not less than three grown men to say: "Whereas the tribes of the Ancient Latins and men of the Ancient Latins have been guilty of acts and offenses against the Roman People of the Quirites; and whereas the Roman People of the Quirites has commanded that war be made on the Ancient Latins, and the Senate of the Roman People has approved, agreed, and voted a war with the Ancient Latins; I therefore and the Roman People declare and make war on the tribes of the Ancient Latins and the men of the Ancient Latins." Having said this, he would hurl his spear into their territory. This is the manner in which at that time redress was sought from the Latins and war was declared, and the custom has been received by later generations.

XXXIII. Ancus delegated the care of the sacrifices to the flamens and other priests, and having enlisted a new army proceeded to Politorium, one of the Latin cities. He took this place by storm, and adopting the plan of former kings, who had enlarged the state by making her enemies citizens, transferred the whole population to Rome. The Palatine was the quarter of the original Romans; on the one hand were the Sabines, who had the Capitol and the Citadel; on the other lay the Caelian, occupied by the Albans. The Aventine was therefore assigned to the newcomers, and thither too were sent shortly afterwards the citizens recruited from the captured towns of Tellenae and Ficana. Politorium was then attacked a second time, for having been left empty it had been seized by the Ancient Latins, and this gave the Romans an excuse for razing the town, lest it should serve continually as a refuge for their enemies. In the end the Latin levies were all forced back upon Medullia, where for sometime the fighting was indecisive and victory shifted from one side to the other; for the city was protected by fortifications and was defended by a strong garrison, and from their camp in the open plain the Latin army several times came to close quarters with the Romans. At last, throwing all his troops into the struggle, Ancus succeeded first in defeating the enemy's army, and then in capturing the town, whence he returned to Rome enriched with immense spoils. On this occasion also many thousands of Latins were granted citizenship. These people, in order that the Aventine might be connected with the Palatine, were made to settle in the region of the Altar of Murcia. Janiculum was also annexed to the city, not from any lack of room, but lest it might someday become a stronghold of Rome's enemies. It was decided not only to fortify it, but also to connect it with the city, for greater ease in passing to and fro, by a bridge of piles, the first bridge ever built over the Tiber.[44] The Quirites' Ditch also, no small protection on the more level and accessible side of town, was the work of King Ancus.

When these enormous additions to the community had been effected, it was found that in so great a multitude the distinction between right and wrong had become obscured, and crimes were being secretly committed. Accordingly, to overawe men's growing lawlessness, a prison was built in the midst of the city, above the Forum.[45] And this reign was a period of growth, not only for the City, but also for her lands and boundaries. The Maesian Forest was taken from the Veientes, extending Rome's dominion clear to the sea; at the Tiber's mouth the city of Ostia was founded, and salt-works were established near-by; while in recognition of signal success in war the temple of Jupiter Feretrius was enlarged.

XXXIV. In the reign of Ancus one Lucumo, a man of energy and wealth, took up his residence in Rome, chiefly from ambition and the hope that he might there achieve a station such as he had found no opportunity of attaining in Tarquinii; for though he had been born there himself, his race was alien to that place also. He was the son of Demaratus of Corinth, who had been driven from home by a political upheaval. Happening to settle in Tarquinii, he had married there and had two sons, named Lucumo and Arruns. Lucumo survived his father and inherited all his property; Arruns died before his father, leaving his wife with child. Demaratus did not long survive Arruns, and, unaware that his son's wife was to become a mother, he died without making provision for his grandson in his will. When the babe was born his grandfather was dead, and having no share in the inheritance, he was given the name of Egerius,[46] in consequence of his penniless condition. Lucumo, on the other hand, was heir to the whole estate. The self-confidence implanted in his bosom by his wealth was heightened by his marriage with Tanaquil, who was a woman of the most exalted birth, and not of a character lightly to endure a humbler rank in her new environment than she had enjoyed in the condition to which she had been born. The Etruscans looked with disdain on Lucumo, the son of a banished man and a stranger. She could not endure this indignity, and forgetting the love she owed her native land, if she could only see her husband honored, she formed the project of emigrating from Tarquinii. Rome appeared to be the most suitable place for her purpose; amongst a new people, where all rank was of sudden growth and founded on worth, there would be room for a brave and strenuous man; the city had been ruled by Tatius the Sabine, it had summoned Numa to the sovereignty from Cures, even Ancus was the son of a Sabine mother, and could point to no noble ancestor but Numa. She had no trouble in persuading a man who was eager for distinction, to whom Tarquinii was only his mother's birthplace. They therefore gathered their possessions together and removed to Rome. They had come, as it happened, as far as Janiculum, when, as they were sitting in their covered waggon, an eagle poised on its wings gently descended upon them and plucked off Lucumo's cap, after which, rising noisily above the car and again stooping, as if sent from heaven for that service, it deftly replaced the cap upon his head, and departed on high. This augury was joyfully accepted, it is said, by Tanaquil, who was a woman skilled in celestial prodigies, as was the case with most Etruscans. Embracing her husband, she bade him expect transcendent greatness: such was the meaning of that bird, appearing from that quarter of the sky, and bringing tidings from that god; the highest part of the man had been concerned in the omen; the eagle had removed the adornment placed upon a mortal's head that it might restore it with the divine approbation. Such were their hopes and their reflections as they entered the city. Having obtained a house, they gave out the name of Lucius Tarquinius Priscus. The Romans regarded him with special interest, as a stranger and a man of wealth, and he steadily pushed his fortune by his own exertions, making friends wherever possible, by kind words, courteous hospitality, and benefactions, until his reputation extended even to the palace. He had not long been known in this way to the king before the liberality and adroitness of his services procured him the footing of an intimate friend. He was now consulted in matters both of public and private importance, in time of war and in time of peace, and having been tested in every way was eventually even named in the king's will as guardian of his children.

XXXV. Ancus reigned four and twenty years, a king inferior to none of his predecessors in the arts of peace and war and in the reputation they conferred. By this time his sons were nearly grown. Tarquinius was therefore all the more insistent in urging that the comitia should be held without delay to choose a king. When the meeting had been proclaimed, and the day drew near, he sent the boys away on a hunting expedition. Tarquinius was the first, they say, to canvass votes for the kingship and to deliver a speech designed to win the favor of the commons. He pointed out that it was no new thing he sought; he was not the first outsider to aim at the sovereignty in Rome—a thing which might have occasioned indignation and astonishment, but the third. Tatius indeed, had been not merely an alien but an enemy when he was made king; while Numa was a stranger to the City, and, far from seeking the kingship, had actually been invited to come and take it. As for himself, he had no sooner become his own master than he had removed to Rome with his wife and all his property. For the greater part of that period of life during which men serve the state he had lived in Rome, and not in the city of his birth. Both in civil life and in war he had had no mean instructor—King Ancus himself had taught him Roman laws and Roman rites. In subordination and deference to the king he had vied, he said, with all his hearers; in generosity to his fellow-subjects he had emulated the king himself. Hearing him advance these not unwarranted claims, the people, with striking unanimity, named him king. The result was that the man, so admirable in all other respects, continued even after he had obtained the sovereignty to manifest the same spirit of intrigue which had governed him in seeking it; and being no less concerned to strengthen his own power than to enlarge the state, he added a hundred members to the senate, who were known thenceforward as Fathers of the "lesser families," and formed a party of unwavering loyalty to the king, to whom they owed their admission to the Curia.[47]

His first war was with the Latins, whose town of Apiolae he took by storm. Returning thence with more booty than the rumors about the war had led people to expect, he exhibited games on a more splendid and elaborate scale than former kings had done. It was then that the ground was first marked out for the circus now called Maximus. Places were divided amongst the Fathers and the knights where they might each make seats for themselves; these were called "rows." They got their view from seats raised on props to a height of twelve feet from the ground. The entertainment was furnished by horses and boxers, imported for the most part from Etruria. From that time the Games continued to be a regular annual show, and were called indifferently the Roman and the Great Games. It was the same king, too, who apportioned building sites about the Forum among private citizens, and erected covered walks and booths.

XXXVI. He was also preparing to build a stone wall around the City, when a Sabine war interrupted his plans. And so sudden was the invasion, that they had crossed the Anio before the Roman army was able to march out and stop them, so that the City was thrown into a panic. The first battle was indecisive, with heavy losses on both sides. The enemy then withdrew into their camp, affording the Romans an opportunity to renew their preparations for the war. Tarquinius believed that cavalry was what he chiefly lacked. To the Ramnes, Titienses, and Luceres, the centuries which Romulus had enrolled, he therefore determined to add others, and to give them his own name as a permanent distinction. But since this was a matter in which Romulus had obtained the sanction of augury before acting, it was asserted by Attus Navius, a famous augur of those days, that no change or innovation could be introduced unless the birds had signified their approval. The king's ire was aroused by this, and he is reported to have said, in derision of the science, "Come now, divine seer! Inquire of your augury if that of which I am now thinking can come to pass." When Attus, having taken the auspices, replied that it would surely come to pass, the king said, "Nay, but this is what I was thinking of, that you should cleave a whetstone with a razor. Take them, and accomplish what your birds declare is possible!" Whereupon, they say, the augur, without a sign of hesitation, cut the whetstone in two. There was a statue of Attus standing, with his head covered, on the spot where the thing was done, in the comitium, even at the steps on the left of the senate-house; tradition adds that the whetstone also was deposited in the same place, to be a memorial of that miracle to posterity. However this may be, auguries and the augural priesthood so increased in honor that nothing was afterwards done, in the field or at home, unless the auspices had first been taken: popular assemblies, musterings of the army, acts of supreme importance—all were put off when the birds refused their consent. Neither did Tarquinius at that time make any change in the organization of the centuries of knights. Their numerical strength he doubled, so that there were now eighteen hundred knights, in three centuries. But though enrolled under the old names, the new men were called the "secondary knights," and the centuries are now, because doubled, known as the "six centuries."

XXXVII. When this arm of the service had been enlarged, a second battle was fought with the Sabines. And in this, besides being increased in strength, the Roman army was further helped by a stratagem, for men were secretly dispatched to light a great quantity of firewood lying on the bank of the Anio, and throw it into the river. A favoring wind set the wood in a blaze, and the greater part of it lodged against the boats and piles, where it stuck fast and set the bridge on fire. This was another source of alarm to the Sabines during the battle, and upon their being routed the same thing hindered their flight, so that many of them escaped the Romans only to perish in the stream; while their shields floated down the Tiber toward the City, and, being recognized, gave assurance that a victory had been won almost sooner than the news of it could be brought. In this battle the cavalry particularly distinguished themselves. They were posted on either flank of the Romans, and when the center, composed of infantry, was already in retreat, they are said to have charged from both sides, with such effect that they not only checked the Sabine forces, which were pressing hotly forward as their enemy gave way, but suddenly put them to flight. The Sabines made for the mountains in a scattered rout, and indeed a few gained that refuge. Most of them, as has been said before, were driven by the cavalry into the river. Tarquinius thought it proper to follow up his victory while the other side was panic-stricken; he therefore sent the booty and the prisoners to Rome, and after making a huge pile of the captured arms and setting fire to it, in fulfilment of a vow to Vulcan, pushed forward at the head of his army into the enemy's country. Although defeat had been the portion of the Sabines, and another battle could not be expected to result in better success, still, as the situation allowed no room for deliberation, they took the field with what soldiers they could hastily muster, and being then routed a second time and fairly reduced to extremities, they sued for peace.

XXXVIII. Collatia, and what land the Sabines had on the hither side of Collatia, was taken from them, and Egerius, the son of the king's brother, was left in the town with a garrison. The surrender of the Collatini took place, I understand, in accordance with this formula: the king asked, "Are you the legates and spokesmen sent by the People of Collatia to surrender yourselves and the People of Collatia?" "We are." "Is the People of Collatia its own master?" "It is." "Do you surrender yourselves and the People of Collatia, city, lands, water, boundary marks, shrines, utensils, all appurtenances divine and human, into my power and that of the Roman People?" "We do." "I receive the surrender." Upon the conclusion of the Sabine war Tarquinius returned to Rome and triumphed. He then made war against the Ancient Latins. In this campaign there was no general engagement at any point, but the king led his army from one town to another until he had subdued the entire Latin race. Corniculum, Ficulea Vetus, Cameria, Crustumerium, Ameriola, Medullia, and Nomentum—these were the towns which were captured from the Ancient Latins, or from those who had gone over to the Latins. Peace was then made.

From that moment the king devoted himself to peaceful undertakings with an enthusiasm which was even greater than the efforts he had expended in waging war, so that there was no more rest for the people at home than there had been in the field. For he set to work to encircle the hitherto unfortified parts of the city with a stone wall, a task which had been interrupted by the Sabine war; and he drained the lowest parts of the city, about the Forum, and the other valleys between the hills, which were too flat to carry off the floodwaters easily, by means of sewers so made as to slope down toward the Tiber. Finally, with prophetic anticipation of the splendor which the place was one day to possess, he laid foundations for the temple of Jupiter on the Capitol, which he had vowed in the Sabine war.

XXXIX. At this time there happened in the house of the king a portent which was remarkable alike in its manifestation and in its outcome. The story is that while a child named Servius Tullius lay sleeping, his head burst into flames in the sight of many. The general outcry which so great a miracle called forth brought the king and queen to the place. One of the servants fetched water to quench the fire, but was checked by the queen, who stilled the uproar and commanded that the boy should not be disturbed until he awoke of himself. Soon afterwards sleep left him, and with it disappeared the flames. Then, taking her husband aside, Tanaquil said: "Do you see this child whom we are bringing up in so humble a fashion? Be assured he will one day be a lamp to our dubious fortunes, and a protector to the royal house in the day of its distress. Let us therefore rear with all solicitude one who will lend high renown to the state and to our family." It is said that from that moment the boy began to be looked upon as a son, and to be trained in the studies by which men are inspired to bear themselves greatly. It was a thing easily accomplished, being the will of Heaven. The youth turned out to be of a truly royal nature, and when Tarquinius sought a son-in-law there was no other young Roman who could be at all compared to Servius; and the king accordingly betrothed his daughter to him. This great honor, for whatever cause conferred on him, forbids us to suppose that his mother was a slave and that he himself had been in a state of servitude as a child. I am rather of the opinion of those who say, that on the capture of Corniculum, when Servius Tullius, the chief man of that city, had been slain, his wife, who was great with child, had been recognized amongst the other captive women, and on the score of her unique nobility had been rescued from slavery by the Roman queen, and had brought forth her child at Rome in the house of Priscus Tarquinius; in the sequel this act of generosity led to a growing intimacy between the women, and the boy, as one reared from childhood in the palace, was held in affection and esteem; it was his mother's misfortune, who by the capture of her native town came into the power of its enemies, which gave rise to the belief that Servius was born of a slave woman.

XL. It was now about thirty-eight years since Tarquinius had begun to reign, and not only the king, but the Fathers and the commons too, held Servius Tullius in the very highest honor. Now the two sons of Ancus had always considered it a great outrage that they had been ousted from their father's kingship by the crime of their guardian, and that Rome should be ruled by a stranger whose descent was derived from a race not only remote but actually not even Italian. But their indignation was vastly increased by the prospect that even after Tarquinius' death the sovereignty would not revert to them, but, plunging down to yet baser depths, would fall into the hands of slaves; so that where, a hundred years before, Romulus, a god's son and himself a god, had borne sway, so long as he remained on earth, in that self-same state a slave and the son of a slave woman would be king. It would be not only a general disgrace to the Roman name, but particularly to their own house, if during the lifetime of Ancus' sons it should be open not only to strangers, but even to slaves to rule over the Romans. They therefore determined to repel that insult with the sword. But resentment at their wrong urged them rather against Tarquinius himself than against Servius, not only because the king, if he survived, would be more formidable to avenge the murder than a subject would be, but because if Servius should be dispatched it seemed probable that the kingdom would be inherited by whomsoever else Tarquinius might choose to be his son-in-law. For these reasons they laid their plot against the king himself. Two very desperate shepherds were selected to do the deed. Armed with the rustic implements to which they were both accustomed, they feigned a brawl in the entrance-court of the palace and, making as much noise as possible, attracted the attention of all the royal attendants; then they appealed to the king, until their shouts were heard inside the palace and they were sent for and came before him. At first each raised his voice and tried to shout the other down. Being repressed by the lictor and bidden to speak in turn, they finally ceased to interrupt each other, and one of them began to state his case, as they had planned beforehand. While the king, intent upon the speaker, turned quite away from the other shepherd, the latter lifted his axe and brought it down upon his head. Then, leaving the weapon in the wound, they both ran out of doors.

XLI. The dying Tarquinius had hardly been caught up in the arms of the bystanders when the fugitives were seized by the lictors. Then there was an uproar, as crowds hurried to the scene, asking one another in amazement what the matter was. In the midst of the tumult Tanaquil gave orders to close the palace, and ejected all witnesses. She busily got together the remedies needful for healing a wound, as if there were still hope, taking at the same time other measures to protect herself in case her hope should fail her. Having hastily summoned Servius, she showed him her husband's nearly lifeless body, and grasping his right hand, besought him not to suffer the death of his father-in-law to go unpunished, nor his mother-in-law to become a jest to her enemies. "To you, Servius," she cried, "if you are a man, belongs this kingdom, not to those who by the hands of others have committed a dastardly crime. Arouse yourself and follow the guidance of the gods, who once declared by the token of divine fire poured out upon this head that you should be a famous man. Now is the time for that heaven-sent flame to quicken you! Now wake in earnest! We, too, were foreigners, yet we reigned. Consider what you are, not whence you were born. If your own counsels are benumbed in this sudden crisis, at least use mine." When the shouting and pushing of the crowd could hardly be withstood, Tanaquil went up into the upper storey of the house, and through a window looking out upon the Nova Via—for the king lived near the temple of Jupiter the Stayer—addressed the populace. She bade them be of good cheer: the king had been stunned by a sudden blow; the steel had not sunk deep into his body; he had already recovered consciousness; the blood had been wiped away and the wound examined; all the symptoms were favorable; she trusted that they would soon see Tarquinius himself; meanwhile she commanded that the people should obey Servius Tullius, who would dispense justice and perform the other duties of the king. Servius went forth in the royal robe, accompanied by lictors, and sitting in the king's seat rendered judgment in some cases, while in regard to others he gave out that he would consult the king. In this way for several days after Tarquinius had breathed his last he concealed his death, pretending that he was merely doing another's work, while he was really strengthening his own position; then at last the truth was allowed to be known, from the lamentations which arose within the palace. Servius surrounded himself with a strong guard, and ruled at first without the authorization of the people, but with the consent of the Fathers. The sons of Ancus, upon the arrest of the agents of their crime and the report that the king was alive and that Servius was so strong, had already gone into voluntary exile at Suessa Pometia.

XLII. Servius now took steps to assure his position by private as well as public measures. In order that the sons of Tarquinius might not show the same animosity towards himself which the sons of Ancus had felt towards Tarquinius, he married his two daughters to the young princes, Lucius and Arruns Tarquinius. But he could not break the force of destiny by human wisdom; and jealousy of his power, even among the members of his household, created an atmosphere of treachery and hostility. Most opportune for the tranquil preservation of the existing state of things was a war which was undertaken against the people of Veii—for the truce[48] had now run out—and the other Etruscans. In this war the bravery and good fortune of Tullius were conspicuous; and when he had utterly defeated the vast army of his enemies, he found on returning to Rome that his title to the kingship was no longer questioned, whether he tested the feeling of the Fathers or that of the commons. He then addressed himself to what is by far the most important work of peace: as Numa had established religious law, so Servius intended that posterity should celebrate himself as the originator of all distinctions among the citizens, and of the orders which clearly differentiate the various grades of rank and fortune. For he instituted the census,[49] a most useful thing for a government destined to such wide dominion, since it would enable the burdens of war and peace to be borne not indiscriminately, as heretofore, but in proportion to men's wealth. He then distributed the people into classes and centuries according to the following scale, which was based upon the census and was suitable either for peace or war.

XLIII. Out of those who had a rating of a hundred thousand asses[50] or more he made eighty centuries, forty each of seniors and of juniors; these were all known as the first class; the seniors were to be ready to guard the city, the juniors to wage war abroad. The armor which these men were required to provide consisted of helmet, round shield, greaves, and breast-plate, all of bronze, for the protection of their bodies; their offensive weapons were a spear and a sword. There were added to this class two centuries of mechanics, who were to serve without arms; to them was entrusted the duty of fashioning siege-engines in war. The second class was drawn up out of those whose rating was between a hundred thousand and seventy-five thousand; of these, seniors and juniors, twenty centuries were enrolled. The arms prescribed for them were an oblong shield in place of the round one, and everything else, save for the breast-plate, as in the class above. He fixed the rating of the third class at fifty thousand; a like number of centuries was formed in this class as in the second, and with the same distinction of ages; neither was any change made in their arms, except that the greaves were omitted. In the fourth class the rating was twenty-five thousand; the same number of centuries was formed, but their equipment was changed, nothing being given them but a spear and a javelin. The fifth class was made larger, and thirty centuries were formed. These men carried slings, with stones for missiles. Rated with them were the horn-blowers and trumpeters, divided into two centuries. Eleven thousand was the rating of this class. Those who were assessed at less than this amount, being all the rest of the population, were made into a single century, exempt from military service. When the equipment and distribution of the infantry had been thus provided for, Servius enrolled twelve centuries of knights out of the leading men of the state. He likewise formed six other centuries—three had been instituted by Romulus— employing the same names which had been hallowed to their use by augury. For the purchase of horses they were allowed ten thousand asses each from the state treasury, and for the maintenance of these horses unmarried women were designated, who had to pay two thousand asses each, every year. All these burdens were shifted from the shoulders of the poor to those of the rich. The latter were then granted special privileges: for manhood suffrage, implying equality of power and of rights, was no longer given promiscuously to all, as had been the practice handed down by Romulus and observed by all the other kings; but gradations were introduced, so that ostensibly no one should be excluded from the suffrage, and yet the power should rest with the leading citizens. For the knights were called upon to vote first; then the eighty centuries of the first class: if there were any disagreement there, which rarely happened, it was provided that the centuries of the second class should be called; and they almost never descended so far as to reach the lowest citizens. Nor ought it to cause any surprise that the present organization, which exists since the increase of the tribes to thirty-five, and the doubling of their number in the matter of the junior and senior centuries, does not correspond with the total established by Servius Tullius. For, having divided the City according to its inhabited regions and hills into four parts, he named them "tribes," a word derived, I suppose, from "tribute";[51] for this likewise the same king planned to have apportioned equitably, on the basis of the census; nor had these tribes anything whatever to do with the distribution or the number of the centuries.

XLIV. Upon the completion of the census, which had been expedited by fear of a law that threatened with death and imprisonment those who failed to register, Servius issued a proclamation calling on all Roman citizens, both horse and foot, to assemble at daybreak, each in his own century, in the Campus Martius. There the whole army was drawn up, and a sacrifice of a pig, a sheep, and a bull was offered by the king for its purification. This was termed the "closing of the lustrum," because it was the last act in the enrolment. Eighty thousand citizens are said to have been registered in that census; the most ancient of the historians, Fabius Pictor, adds that this was the number of those capable of bearing arms. To meet the wants of this population it was apparent that the City must expand, and so the king added two hills, the Quirinal and the Viminal, after which he proceeded to enlarge the Esquiline,[52] going there to live himself, that the place might obtain a good reputation. He surrounded the city with a rampart, trenches, and a wall, and so extended the "pomerium." This word is interpreted by those who look only at its etymology as meaning "the tract behind the wall," but it signifies rather "the tract on both sides of the wall," the space which the Etruscans used formerly to consecrate with augural ceremonies, when they proposed to erect their wall, establishing definite limits on either side of it, so that they might at the same time keep the walls free on their inward face from contact with buildings, which now, as a rule, are actually joined to them, and on the outside keep a certain area free from human uses. This space, which the gods forbade men to inhabit or to till, was called "pomerium" by the Romans, quite as much because the wall stood behind it as because it stood behind the wall; and as the city grew, these consecrated limits were always pushed out for as great a distance as the walls themselves were to be advanced.[53]

XLV. When the king had promoted the grandeur of the state by enlarging the city, and had shaped all his domestic policy to suit the demands of peace as well as those of war, he was unwilling that arms should always be the means employed for strengthening Rome's power, and sought to increase her sway by diplomacy, and at the same time to add something to the splendor of the city. Even at that early date the temple of Diana at Ephesus enjoyed great renown. It was reputed to have been built through the cooperation of the cities of Asia, and this harmony and community of worship Servius praised in superlative terms to the Latin nobles, with whom, both officially and in private, he had taken pains to establish a footing of hospitality and friendship. By dint of reiterating the same arguments he finally carried his point, and a shrine of Diana was built in Rome by the nations of Latium conjointly with the Roman People. This was an admission that Rome was the capital—a point which had so often been disputed with force of arms. But though it seemed that the Latins had lost all interest in this contention after the repeated failure of their appeals to war, there was one man amongst the Sabines who thought that he saw an opportunity to recover the empire by a shrewd plan of his own. In the Sabine country, on the farm of a certain head of a family, there was born a heifer of extraordinary size and beauty; a marvel to which the horns afterwards bore testimony, for they were fastened up for many generations in the vestibule of Diana's temple. This heifer was regarded as a prodigy, as indeed it was; soothsayers prophesied that the state whose citizens should sacrifice the animal to Diana would be the seat of empire, and this prediction had reached the ears of the priest of Diana's shrine. On the earliest day which seemed suitable for the sacrifice, the Sabine drove the heifer to Rome, and bringing her to the shrine of Diana, led her up to the altar. There the Roman priest, moved by the great size of the victim, which had been much talked of, and recalling the prophecy, asked the Sabine, "What is this that you are doing, stranger? Would you sacrifice, unpurified, to Diana? Not so! First bathe in a running stream; the Tiber flows by in the bottom of the valley." The stranger, touched by a scruple and wishing to do everything according to ritual, that the prodigy might be answered by the event, at once descended to the Tiber. Meanwhile the Roman offered the heifer to Diana, an act which was exceedingly acceptable to the king and the citizens.

XLVI. Servius had by this time a definite prescriptive right to the supreme power. Still, hearing that the young Tarquinius now and then threw out a hint that he was reigning without the consent of the people, he proceeded to gain the goodwill of the commons by dividing among all the citizens the land obtained by conquest from the enemy; after which he made bold to call upon the people to vote whether he should be their ruler, and was declared king with such unanimity as none of his predecessors had experienced. Yet the circumstance did not lessen Tarquinius' hopes of obtaining the kingship. On the contrary, perceiving that the bestowal of land on the plebeians was in opposition to the wishes of the senate, he felt that he had got an opportunity of vilifying Servius to the Fathers and of increasing his own influence in the senate-house. He was a hot-headed youth himself, and he had at hand, in the person of Tullia his wife, one who goaded on his restless spirit. For the royal house of Rome produced an example of tragic guilt, as others had done,[54] in order that loathing of kings might hasten the coming of liberty, and that the end of reigning might come in that reign which was the fruit of crime. This Lucius Tarquinius—whether he was the son or the grandson of King Tarquinius Priscus is uncertain; but, following the majority of historians, I would designate him son—had a brother, Arruns Tarquinius, a youth of a gentle disposition. These two, as has been said before, had married the two Tullias, daughters of the king, themselves of widely different characters. Chance had so ordered matters that the two violent natures should not be united in wedlock, thanks doubtless to the good fortune of the Roman People, that the reign of Servius might be prolonged and the traditions of the state become established. It was distressing to the headstrong Tullia that her husband should be destitute of ambition and enterprise. With her whole soul she turned from him to his brother; him she admired, him she called a man and a prince: she despised her sister because, having got a man for a mate, she lacked a woman's daring. Their similarity soon brought these two together, as is generally the case, for evil is strongly drawn to evil; but it was the woman who took the lead in all the mischief. Having become addicted to clandestine meetings with another's husband, she spared no terms of insult when speaking of her own husband to his brother, or of her sister to that sister's husband. She urged that it would have been juster for her to be unmarried and for him to lack a wife than for them to be united to their inferiors and be compelled to languish through the cowardice of others. If the gods had given her the man she deserved she would soon have seen in her own house the royal power which she now saw in her father's. It was not long before she had inspired the young man with her own temerity, and, having made room in their respective houses for a new marriage, by deaths which followed closely upon one another, they were joined together in nuptials which Servius rather tolerated than approved.

XLVII. From that moment the insecurity of the aged Tullius and the menace to his authority increased with each succeeding day. For the woman was already looking forward from one crime to another, nor would she allow her husband any rest by night or day, lest the murders they had done before should be without effect. She had not wanted a man just to be called a wife, just to endure servitude with him in silence; she had wanted one who should deem himself worthy of the sovereignty, who bethought him that he was the son of Tarquinius Priscus, who preferred the possession of the kingship to the hope of it. "If you are he," she cried, "whom I thought I was marrying, I call you both man and king; if not, then I have so far changed for the worse, in that crime is added, in your case, to cowardice. Come, rouse yourself! You are not come, like your father, from Corinth or Tarquinii, that you must make yourself king in a strange land; the gods of your family and your ancestors, your father's image, the royal palace, with its throne, and the name of Tarquinius create and proclaim you king. Else, if you have no courage for this, why do you cheat the citizens? Why do you suffer yourself to be looked on as a prince? Away with you to Tarquinii or Corinth! Sink back into the rank of your family, more like your brother than your father!" With these and other taunts she excited the young man's ambition. Nor could she herself submit with patience to the thought that Tanaquil, a foreign woman, had exerted her spirit to such purpose as twice in succession to confer the royal power—upon her husband first, and again upon her son-in-law—if Tullia, the daughter of a king, were to count for nothing in bestowing and withdrawing a throne. Inspired by this woman's frenzy Tarquinius began to go about and solicit support, especially among the heads of the lesser families, whom he reminded of his father's kindness to them, and desired their favor in return; the young men he attracted by gifts; both by the great things he promised to do himself, and by slandering the king as well, he everywhere strengthened his interest. At length, when it seemed that the time for action was now come, he surrounded himself with a body of armed men and burst into the Forum. Then, amidst the general consternation which ensued, he seated himself on the throne in front of the Curia, and commanded, by the mouth of a herald, that the senators should come to King Tarquinius at the senate-house. They at once assembled: some of them already prepared before-hand, others afraid that they might be made to suffer for it if they did not come; for they were astounded at this strange and wonder-ful sight, and supposed that Servius was utterly undone. Tarquinius then went back to the very beginning of Servius' family and abused the king for a slave and a slave-woman's son who, after the shameful death of his own father, Tarquinius Priscus, had seized the power; there had been no observance of the interregnum, as on former occasions; there had been no election held; not by the votes of the people had sovereignty come to him, not with the confirmation of the Fathers, but by a woman's gift. Such having been his birth, and such his appointment to the kingship, he had been an abettor of the lowest class of society, to which he himself belonged, and his hatred of the nobility possessed by others had led him to plunder the leading citizens of their land and divide it amongst the dregs of the populace. All the burdens which had before been borne in common he had laid upon the nation's foremost men. He had instituted the census that he might hold up to envy the fortunes of the wealthy, and make them available, when he chose to draw upon them, for largesses to the destitute.

XLVIII. In the midst of this harangue Servius, who had been aroused by the alarming news, came up and immediately called out in a loud voice from the vestibule of the Curia: "What means this, Tarquinius? With what assurance have you dared, while I live, to convene the Fathers or to sit in my chair?" Tarquinius answered truculently that it was his own father's seat he occupied; that the king's son was a fitter successor to his kingdom than a slave was; that Tullius had long enough been suffered to mock his masters and insult them. Shouts arose from the partisans of each, and the people began to rush into the senate-house; it was clear that he would be king who won the day. Tarquinius was now compelled by sheer necessity to go on boldly to the end. Being much superior to Servius in youth and strength, he seized him by the middle, and bearing him out of the senate-house, flung him down the steps. He then went back into the Curia to hold the senate together. The king's servitors and companions fled. The king himself, half fainting, was making his way home without the royal attendants, when the men whom Tarquinius had sent in pursuit of the fugitive came up with him and killed him. It is believed, inasmuch as it is not inconsistent with the rest of her wickedness, that this deed was suggested by Tullia. It is agreed, at all events, that she was driven in her carriage into the Forum, and nothing abashed at the crowd of men, summoned her husband from the Curia and was the first to hail him king. Tarquinius bade her withdraw from so turbulent a scene. On her way home she had got to the top of the Vicus Cyprius, where the shrine of Diana recently stood, and was bidding her driver turn to the right into the Clivus Urbius, to take her to the Esquiline Hill, when the man gave a start of terror, and pulling up the reins pointed out to his mistress the prostrate form of the murdered Servius. Horrible and inhuman was the crime that is said to have ensued, which the place commemorates—men call it the Street of Crime—for there, crazed by the avenging spirits of her sister and her sister's husband, they say that Tullia drove her carriage over her father's corpse, and, herself contaminated and defiled, carried away on her vehicle some of her murdered father's blood to her own and her husband's penates, whose anger was the cause that the evil beginning of this reign was, at no long date, followed by a similar end.

Servius Tullius had ruled forty-four years, so well that even a good and moderate successor would have found it hard to emulate him. But there was this to enhance his renown, that just and lawful kingship perished with him. Yet, mild and moderate though his sway was, some writers state that he had intended to resign it, as being a government by one man, had not the crime of one of his family interrupted his plans for the liberation of his country.

XLIX. Now began the reign of Lucius Tarquinius, whose conduct procured him the surname of Superbus, or the Proud. For he denied the rites of sepulture to his own father-in-law, asserting that Romulus had also perished without burial. He put to death the leading senators, whom he believed to have favored the cause of Servius and, conscious that a precedent for gaining the kingship by crime might be found in his own career and turned against himself, he assumed a bodyguard. He had indeed no right to the throne but might, since he was ruling neither by popular decree nor senatorial sanction. Moreover, as he put no trust in the affection of his people, he was compelled to safeguard his authority by fear. To inspire terror therefore in many persons, he adopted the practice of trying capital causes[55] by himself, without advisers; and, under the pretext thus afforded, was able to inflict death, exile, and forfeiture of property, not only upon persons whom he suspected and disliked, but also in cases where he could have nothing to gain but plunder. It was chiefly the senators whose numbers were reduced by this procedure, and Tarquinius determined to make no new appointments to the order, that it might be the more despised for its very paucity, and might chafe less at being ignored in all business of state. For this king was the first to break with the custom handed down by his predecessors, of consulting the senate on all occasions, and governed the nation without other advice than that of his own household. War, peace, treaties, and alliances were entered upon or broken off by the monarch himself, with whatever states he wished, and without the decree of people or senate. The Latin race he strove particularly to make his friends, that his strength abroad might contribute to his security at home. He contracted with their nobles not only relations of hospitality but also matrimonial connections. To Octavius Mamilius of Tusculum, a man by long odds the most important of the Latin name, and descended, if we may believe report, from Ulysses and the goddess Circe,[56] he gave his daughter in marriage, and in this way attached to himself the numerous kinsmen and friends of the man.

L. Tarquinius had already won great influence with the Latin nobles, when he gave notice that they should assemble on a certain day at the grove of Ferentina, saying that there were matters of common interest which he wished to discuss. The Latins gathered at daybreak in large numbers; Tarquinius himself, though he did indeed keep the day, arrived but a little while before sundown. There had been much talk in the council all day about various subjects.

Turnus Herdonius of Aricia had inveighed violently against the absent
Tarquinius. He said it was no wonder he had been given the name
of Superbus at Rome—for that was the name by which they already
called him, secretly and in whispers, but still quite generally; could
anything be more overbearing than to flout the whole Latin race as
he was doing then? Their leaders had been summoned from distant
homes, and the very man who had called the council was not there.
He was evidently trying their patience, intending, if they submitted
to the yoke, to use them as his vassals. For who could fail to see that
he was aiming at sovereignty over the Latins? If his own people had
done well to intrust this to him, if indeed it had been intrusted to him
at all, and had not been ravished by foul murder, then it was right
that the Latins also should intrust it to him—nay, not even then, for
he was of foreign birth; but if his own subjects were weary of him,
as men who, one after another, were being made to suffer death,
exile, confiscation, what better prospect was held out to the Latins?
If they were guided by the speaker they would depart every man to
his own home, nor observe the day of meeting more than he who
had proclaimed it was observing it. As these words and others of the
same import were being uttered by the factious and turbulent Latin,
who owed to these qualities his influence amongst his own people,
Tarquinius came up. This was the end of the speech; all turned to
salute Tarquinius. Silence was commanded, and the king, being
advised by those nearest him to excuse himself for having come so
late, declared that he had been chosen arbiter between a father and
his son, and had been delayed by his anxiety to reconcile them. He
added that since this business had used up that day, he would take up
on the morrow the matters which he had meant to bring before them.
They say that Turnus would not suffer even this to go unchallenged,
asserting that there was no question more quickly settled than one
betwixt father and son, for these few words were enough to end it:
"Unless you obey your father it will be the worse for you."

LI. Girding thus against the Roman king, the Arician quitted the
council. Tarquinius was considerably more vexed than he appeared
to be, and at once looked about him for the means of destroying
Turnus, that he might inspire in the Latins the same terror with

which he had broken the spirit of the Romans. And since he could not openly put his man to death by virtue of sovereign right, he charged him with a crime of which he was innocent, and so destroyed him. Through the agency of certain men of the opposite party in Aricia, he bribed a slave of Turnus with gold to allow a large quantity of swords to be brought secretly into his master's lodging. Having accomplished this in a single night, Tarquinius, shortly before dawn, summoned the chief men of the Latins to his quarters, pretending to have received alarming news, and informed them that his tardiness on the preceding day, as though somehow providentially occasioned, had been the means of saving himself and them. For he was told that Turnus was plotting his murder and that of the chief men of the different cities, that he might be sole ruler over the Latins. He would have attacked them the day before in the council, but had postponed the attempt because the summoner of the council, whom he chiefly aimed at, was not there. That was the reason Turnus had railed at him in his absence, for his delay had balked the Arician's expectation. Tarquinius said that he had no doubt, if his information was true, that Turnus would come at dawn, when they had assembled in the council, and would be armed and attended by a band of conspirators. It was said that a great quantity of swords had been carried to his lodging; the falsity or truth of this could be ascertained immediately, and he asked them to go with him to Turnus' quarters. The charge was made plausible both by the aggressive spirit of Turnus and his speech of the day before, and by Tarquinius' delay, since it seemed that the massacre might have been postponed on that account. The nobles went therefore with a disposition to believe the story, but still, if the swords should not be found, they were prepared to conclude the other charges false. As soon as they reached the place they wakened Turnus from his sleep and surrounded him with guards; and having overpowered the slaves, who out of affection for their master would have resorted to force, they proceeded to pull out the hidden swords from every corner of the inn. There was now no doubt that Turnus was caught in the act, and he was cast into chains, while the summons was instantly sent out, amidst intense excitement, for a council of the Latins. There such bitter resentment was aroused by the public display of the swords, that the accused was not permitted to plead his cause, but suffered a new kind of death, being plunged into the source of the Ferentine Water and sunk beneath a wicker crate heaped up with stones.

LII. Tarquinius then called the Latins again to the place of council, and praised them for the punishment which they had justly meted out to the rebellious attempt of Turnus, in view of the treason in which he had just been taken. The king then went on to say that it was in his power to proceed according to an ancient right, since all the Latins, having sprung from Alba, were included in that treaty by which, from the time of Tullus, the whole Alban state, with its colonies, had come under Rome's dominion.[57] But the advantage of all would be better served, he thought, if that treaty were renewed and the good fortune of the Roman people were thrown open to the participation of the Latins, than if they were always to be dreading or enduring the razing of their cities and the devastation of their lands which they had suffered first in Ancus' reign and afterward in that of the speaker's father. It was not difficult to persuade the Latins, although the Roman interest preponderated in this treaty. For the rest, they saw that the chiefs of the Latin name stood with the king and took his view of the matter, and they had just been given a demonstration of the danger they would each incur if they opposed the project. So the treaty was renewed, and the Latin juniors were commanded to present themselves at the grove of Ferentina on a certain day, armed and in full force, as the treaty prescribed. When they had assembled, agreeably to the king's edict, from the different districts, Tarquinius was unwilling that they should have their own leaders, or a separate command, or their own standards; he therefore mingled Latins and Romans in the maniples, making one maniple of two and two of one, and over the maniples thus doubled he put centurions.[58]

LIII. But if the king was unjust in peace, yet he was not a bad general in war. Indeed, he would have equalled in this art the kings who had gone before him, if his degeneracy in other things had not also dimmed his glory here. It was he who began the war with the Volsci which was to last more than two hundred years after his time, and took Suessa Pometia from them by storm. There, having

sold off the booty and raised forty talents of silver,[59] he conceived
the project of a temple of Jupiter so magnificent that it should be
worthy of the king of gods and men, the Roman empire, and the
majesty of the site itself. The money from the captured city he put
aside to build this temple.

He then engaged in an unexpectedly tedious war with Gabii, a
neighboring town. After first assaulting the place in vain, he laid
siege to it, but this attempt was as unsuccessful as the other, for he
was driven off from the walls; and he finally resorted to the policy,
so unlike a Roman, of deceit and trickery. For he pretended to have
given up the war and to be engrossed in laying the foundations of his
temple and in other city works, arranging meanwhile to let Sextus,
who was the youngest of his three sons, desert to Gabii, and there
complain that his father was intolerably cruel to him. His father's
pride, he said, was now diverted from strangers upon his own family.
Even his children were too many to please him, and the solitude
which he had caused in the senate-house he wished to bring to pass
in his own home also, that he might leave no descendant, no heir to
his kingdom. The young man said that he had himself escaped from
amidst the swords and javelins of his father, and had made up his
mind that there was no safety for him anywhere save with the enemies
of Lucius Tarquinius. Let them not delude themselves, he said; the
war which the king pretended to have abandoned was still awaiting
them, and when the chance offered he would attack them unawares.
But if they had no room for suppliants, he was prepared to wander
all over Latium, and thence seek out the Volsci and the Aequi and
the Hernici, till at last he should come to people who knew how to
protect a son from the cruel and wicked tortures inflicted on him by
a father. Possibly he might even discover some enthusiasm for war and
arms against the haughtiest of kings and the most insolent of nations.
When it appeared that if they were indifferent he would leave them
in anger and continue his flight, the Gabini bade him welcome. They
told him not to be surprised if the king had been the same to his
children that he had been to his subjects, to his allies; he would end
by venting his cruelty upon himself if other objects failed him. But
for their own part, they said, they were glad of his coming, and they

believed that in a short time, with his help, the seat of war would be shifted from the gates of Gabii to the walls of Rome.

LIV. Sextus next obtained admission to the Gabian councils of state, where, on all subjects but one, he professed a deference for the opinion of those who had long been citizens of Gabii and were better acquainted with the facts. War, however, he did take it upon himself to urge, again and again; and in so doing he assumed a special competence, as one who was acquainted with the strength of both nations, and knew that the king's pride must necessarily be hateful to all the citizens, since even his children had not been able to put up with it. In this way, little by little, he stirred up the leaders of the Gabini to reopen the war. He would himself take the boldest of the young men and go upon raids and forays. All his words and acts were calculated to deceive, and their ill-grounded confidence so increased that in the end he was chosen commander-in-chief. The war began, and the people had no suspicion of what was going forward. Skirmishes took place between Rome and Gabii, in which, as a rule, the Gabini had the best of it. Thereupon their citizens, both high and low, contended who should be loudest in expressing the belief that in Sextus Tarquinius they had a heaven-sent leader. And the soldiers, seeing him ever ready to share in their dangers and hardships, and ever lavish in distributing the plunder, came to love him so devotedly that the elder Tarquinius was not more truly master in Rome than was his son in Gabii. And so, when Sextus saw that he had acquired strength enough for any enterprise, he despatched one of his own followers to his father in Rome, to ask what the king might please to have him do, since the gods had granted that at Gabii all power in the state should rest with him alone. To this messenger, I suppose because he seemed not quite to be trusted, no verbal reply was given. The king, as if absorbed in meditation, passed into the garden of his house, followed by his son's envoy. There, walking up and down without a word, he is said to have struck off the heads of the tallest poppies with his stick. Tired of asking questions and waiting for an answer, the messenger returned to Gabii, his mission, as he thought, unaccomplished. He reported what he had said himself and what he had seen. Whether from anger, or hatred, or native pride, the king, he said, had not pronounced a single word. As soon as it was clear to Sextus what his father meant and what was the purport of his silent hints, he rid himself of the chief men of the state. Some he accused before the people; against others he took advantage of the odium they had themselves incurred. Many were openly executed; some, whom it would not have looked well to accuse, were put to death in secret. Some were permitted, if they chose, to leave the country; or they were driven into banishment, and once out of the way, their property was forfeited, just as in the case of those who had been put to death. Thence came largesses and spoils, and in the sweetness of private gain men lost their feeling for the wrongs of the nation, until, deprived of counsel and aid, the state of Gabii was handed over unresisting to the Roman king.

LV. Having got possession of Gabii, Tarquinius made peace with the Aequian nation and renewed the treaty with the Etruscans. He next turned his attention to affairs in the city. Here his first concern was to build a temple of Jupiter on the Tarpeian Mount[60] to stand as a memorial of his reign and of his name, testifying that of the two Tarquinii, both kings, the father had made the vow and the son had fulfilled it. And that the site might be free from all other religious claims and belong wholly to Jupiter and his temple, which was building there, he determined to annul the consecration of several fanes and shrines which had been first vowed by King Tatius at the crisis of the battle against Romulus, and had afterwards been consecrated and inaugurated. At the very time when he began this task the gods are said to have exerted their power to show the magnitude of this mighty empire. For whereas the birds permitted that the consecrations of all the other shrines should be rescinded, they refused their consent for the shrine of Terminus. This omen and augury was thus construed: the fact that the seat of Terminus was not moved, and that of all the gods he alone was not called away from the place consecrated to him, meant that the whole kingdom would be firm and steadfast. When this auspice of permanence had been received, there followed another prodigy foretelling the grandeur of their empire. A human head, its features intact, was found, so it is said, by the men who were digging for the foundations of the temple. This appearance plainly foreshowed that here was to be the citadel of the empire and the head of the world, and such was the interpretation of the soothsayers, both those who were in the City and those who were called in from Etruria to consider the matter. This made the king all the more ready to spend money on the work. Hence the Pometian spoils, which had been destined to carry the building up to the roof, barely sufficed for the foundations. This disposes me to believe the statement of Fabius (who is, besides, the earlier writer) that the spoils were only forty talents, rather than Piso's, who writes that forty thousand pounds of silver were put aside for this work. So great a sum of money could not be expected from the booty of a single city of that time, and there is no building, even among those of our own day, for the foundations of which it would not be more than enough.

LVI. Being intent upon completing the temple, the king called in workmen from every quarter of Etruria, and used for this purpose not only the state funds but laborers drawn from the commons. This work was far from light in itself, and was added to their military service. Yet the plebeians felt less abused at having to build with their own hands the temples of the gods, than they did when they came to be transferred to other tasks also, which, while less in show, were yet rather more laborious. I mean the erection of seats in the circus, and the construction underground of the Great Sewer, as a receptacle for all the offscourings of the City, two works for which the new splendor of these days has scarcely been able to produce a match. After making the plebeians toil at these hard tasks, the king felt that a populace which had now no work to do was only a burden to the City; he wished, moreover, by sending out settlers, to extend the frontiers of his dominions. He therefore sent colonists to Signia and Circei, to safeguard the City by land and sea.

While he was thus occupied, a terrible portent appeared. A snake glided out of a wooden pillar, causing fright and commotion in the palace. As for the king himself, his heart was not so much struck with sudden terror as filled with anxious forebodings. Now for public prodigies none but Etruscan soothsayers were wont to be employed, but this domestic apparition, as he regarded it, so thoroughly alarmed him that he determined to send to Delphi, the most famous oracle in the world; and, not daring to trust the oracle's reply to anybody else, he sent two of his sons, through strange lands, as they were then, and over stranger seas, to Greece. Titus and Arruns were the ones who went; and, to bear them company, Lucius Junius Brutus was sent too, the son of Tarquinia, sister of the king, a young man of a very different mind from that which he pretended to bear. Having heard that the leading men of the state, and among them his own brother, had been put to death by his uncle, he determined to leave nothing in his disposition which the king might justly fear, nor anything in his fortune to covet, resolving to find safety in contempt, where justice afforded no protection. He therefore deliberately assumed the appearance of stupidity, and permitted himself and his property to become the spoil of the king; he even accepted the surname Brutus,[61] that behind the screen afforded by this title the great soul which was to free the Roman People might bide its time unseen. He it was who was then taken by the Tarquinii to Delphi, more as a butt than as a comrade; and he is said to have carried a golden staff inclosed within one of cornel wood, hollowed out to receive it, as a gift to Apollo, and a roundabout indication of his own character. When they came there, and had carried out their father's instructions, a desire sprang up in the hearts of the youths to find out which one of them should be king at Rome. From the depths of the cavern this answer, they say, was returned: "The highest power at Rome shall be his, young men, who shall be first among you to kiss his mother." The Tarquinii, anxious that Sextus, who had been left in Rome, might know nothing of the answer and have no share in the rule, gave orders that the incident should be kept strictly secret; as between themselves, they decided by lot which should be first, upon their return to Rome, to give their mother a kiss. Brutus thought the Pythian utterance had another meaning; pretending to stumble, he fell and touched his lips to Earth, evidently regarding her as the common mother of all mortals. They then returned to Rome, where preparations for war with the Rutuli were being pushed with the greatest vigor.

LVII. Ardea belonged to the Rutuli, who were a nation of commanding wealth, for that place and period. This very fact was the cause of the war, since the Roman king was eager not only to enrich himself, impoverished as he was by the splendor of his public works, but also to appease with booty the feeling of the common people; who, besides the enmity they bore the monarch for other acts of pride, were especially resentful that the king should have kept them employed so long as artisans and doing the work of slaves. An attempt was made to capture Ardea by assault. Having failed in this, the Romans invested the place with intrenchments, and began to beleaguer the enemy. Here in their permanent camp, as is usual with a war not sharp but long drawn out, furlough was rather freely granted, more freely however to the leaders than to the soldiers; the young princes for their part passed their idle hours together at dinners and drinking bouts. It chanced, as they were drinking in the quarters of Sextus Tarquinius, where Tarquinius Collatinus, son of Egerius, was also a guest, that the subject of wives came up. Every man fell to praising his own wife with enthusiasm, and, as their rivalry grew hot, Collatinus said that there was no need to talk about it, for it was in their power to know, in a few hours' time, how far the rest were excelled by his own Lucretia. "Come! If the vigor of youth is in us let us mount our horses and see for ourselves the disposition of our wives. Let every man regard as the surest test what meets his eyes when the woman's husband enters unexpected." They were heated with wine. "Agreed!" they all cried, and clapping spurs to their horses were off for Rome. Arriving there at early dusk, they thence proceeded to Collatia, where Lucretia was discovered very differently employed from the daughters-in-law of the king. These they had seen at a luxurious banquet, whiling away the time with their young friends; but Lucretia, though it was late at night, was busily engaged upon her wool, while her maidens toiled about her in the lamplight as she sat in the hall of her house.[62] The prize of this contest in womanly virtues fell to Lucretia. As Collatinus and the Tarquinii approached, they were graciously received, and the victorious husband courteously invited the young princes to his table. It was there that Sextus Tarquinius was seized with a wicked desire to debauch Lucretia by force; not only her beauty, but her proved chastity as well, provoked him. However, for the present they ended the boyish prank of the night and returned to the camp.

LVIII. When a few days had gone by, Sextus Tarquinius, without letting Collatinus know, took a single attendant and went to Collatia. Being kindly welcomed, for no one suspected his purpose, he was brought after dinner to a guest-chamber. Burning with passion, he waited till it seemed to him that all about him was secure and everybody fast asleep; then, drawing his sword, he came to the sleeping Lucretia. Holding the woman down with his left hand on her breast, he said, "Be still, Lucretia! I am Sextus Tarquinius. My sword is in my hand. Utter a sound, and you die!" In affright the woman started out of her sleep. No help was in sight, but only imminent death. Then Tarquinius began to declare his love, to plead, to mingle threats with prayers, to bring every resource to bear upon her woman's heart. When he found her obdurate and not to be moved even by fear of death, he went farther and threatened her with disgrace, saying that when she was dead he would kill his slave and lay him naked by her side, that she might be said to have been put to death in adultery with a man of base condition. At this dreadful prospect her resolute modesty was overcome, as if with force, by his victorious lust; and Tarquinius departed, exulting in his conquest of a woman's honor. Lucretia, grieving at her great disaster, dispatched the same message to her father in Rome and to her husband at Ardea: that they should each take a trusty friend and come; that they must do this and do it quickly, for a frightful thing had happened. Spurius Lucretius came with Publius Valerius, Volesus' son. Collatinus brought Lucius Junius Brutus, with whom he chanced to be returning to Rome when he was met by the messenger from his wife. Lucretia they found sitting sadly in her chamber. The entrance of her friends brought the tears to her eyes, and to her husband's question, "Is all well?" she replied, "Far from it; for what can be well with a woman when she has lost her honor? The print of a strange man, Collatinus, is in your bed. Yet my body only has been violated; my heart is guiltless, as death shall be my witness. But pledge your right hands and your words that the adulterer shall not go unpunished. Sextus Tarquinius is he that last night returned hostility for hospitality, and brought ruin on me, and on himself no less—if you are men—when he worked his pleasure with me." They give their pledges, every man in turn. They seek to comfort her, sick at heart as she is, by diverting the blame from her who was forced to the doer of the wrong. They tell her it is the mind that sins, not the body; and that where purpose has been wanting there is no guilt. "It is for you to determine," she answers, "what is due to him; for my own part, though I acquit myself of the sin, I do not absolve myself from punishment; nor in time to come shall ever unchaste woman live through the example of Lucretia." Taking a knife which she had concealed beneath her dress, she plunged it into her heart, and sinking forward upon the wound, died as she fell. The wail for the dead was raised by her husband and her father.

LIX. Brutus, while the others were absorbed in grief, drew out the knife from Lucretia's wound, and holding it up, dripping with gore, exclaimed, "By this blood, most chaste until a prince wronged it, I swear, and I take you, gods, to witness, that I will pursue Lucius Tarquinius Superbus and his wicked wife and all his children, with sword, with fire, aye with whatsoever violence I may; and that I will suffer neither them nor any other to be king in Rome!" The knife he then passed to Collatinus, and from him to Lucretius and Valerius. They were dumbfounded at this miracle. Whence came this new spirit in the breast of Brutus? As he bade them, so they swore. Grief was swallowed up in anger; and when Brutus summoned them to make war from that very moment on the power of the kings, they followed his lead. They carried out Lucretia's corpse from the house and bore it to the market place, where men crowded about them, attracted, as they were bound to be, by the amazing character of the strange event and its heinousness. Every man had his own complaint to make of the prince's crime and his violence. They were moved, not only by the father's sorrow, but by the fact that it was Brutus who chid their tears and idle lamentations and urged them to take up the sword, as befitted men and Romans, against those who had dared to treat them as enemies. The boldest of the young men seized their weapons and offered themselves for service, and the others followed their example. Then, leaving Lucretia's father to guard Collatia, and posting sentinels so that no one might announce the rising to the royal family, the rest, equipped for battle and with Brutus in command, set out for Rome. Once there, wherever their armed band advanced it brought terror and confusion; but again, when people saw that in the van were the chief men of the state, they concluded that whatever it was it could be no meaningless disturbance. And in fact there was no less resentment at Rome when this dreadful story was known than there had been at Collatia. So from every quarter of the City men came running to the Forum. No sooner were they there than a crier summoned the people before the Tribune of the Celeres,[63] which office Brutus then happened to be holding. There he made a speech by no means like what might have been expected of the mind and the spirit which he had feigned up to that day. He spoke of the violence and lust of Sextus Tarquinius, of the shameful defilement of Lucretia and her deplorable death, of the bereavement of Tricipitinus, in whose eyes the death of his daughter was not so outrageous and deplorable as was the cause of her death. He reminded them, besides, of the pride of the king himself and the wretched state of the commons, who were plunged into ditches and sewers and made to clear them out. The men of Rome, he said, the conquerors of all the nations round about, had been transformed from warriors into artisans and stone-cutters. He spoke of the shameful murder of King Tullius, and how his daughter had driven her accursed chariot over her father's body, and he invoked the gods who punish crimes against parents. With these and, I fancy, even fiercer reproaches, such as occur to a man in the very presence of an outrage, but are far from easy for an historian to reproduce, he inflamed the people, and brought them to abrogate the king's authority and to exile Lucius Tarquinius, together with his wife and children. Brutus himself then enrolled the juniors, who voluntarily gave in their names, and arming them set out for the camp at Ardea to arouse the troops against the king. The command at Rome he left with Lucretius, who had been appointed Prefect of the City by the king, sometime before. During this confusion Tullia fled from her house, cursed wherever she went by men and women, who called down upon her the furies that avenge the wrongs of kindred.

LX. When the news of these events reached the camp, the king, in alarm at the unexpected danger, set out for Rome to put down the revolt. Brutus, who had perceived the king's approach, made a circuit to avoid meeting him, and at almost the same moment, though by different roads, Brutus reached Ardea and Tarquinius Rome. Against Tarquinius the gates were closed and exile was pronounced. The liberator of the City was received with rejoicings in the camp, and the sons of the king were driven out of it. Two of them followed their father, and went into exile at Caere, in Etruria. Sextus Tarquinius departed for Gabii, as though it had been his own kingdom, and there the revengers of old quarrels, which he had brought upon himself by murder and rapine, slew him.

Lucius Tarquinius Superbus ruled for five and twenty years. The rule of the kings at Rome, from its foundation to its liberation, lasted two hundred and forty-four years. Two consuls were then chosen in the centuriate comitia, under the presidency of the Prefect of the City, in accordance with the commentaries of Servius Tullius.[64] These were Lucius Junius Brutus and Lucius Tarquinius Collatinus.

SUMMARY OF BOOK I

A. ARRIVAL OF AENEAS IN ITALY AND HIS DEEDS. REIGN OF ASCANIUS, and after him of the Silvii, at Alba. Romulus and Remus born to Mars by the daughter of Numitor. Amulius killed. The City founded by Romulus. The senate chosen. War with the Sabines. *Spolia opima* dedicated to Jupiter Feretrius. The people divided into wards. The Fidenates and Veientes conquered. Romulus deified.

Numa Pompilius handed on religious rites. The door of Janus' temple closed.

Tullus Hostilius ravaged the country of the Albans. Battle of the triplets. Punishment of Mettius Fufetius. Tullus slain by a thunderbolt.

Ancus Martius conquered the Latins; founded Ostia.

Tarquinius Priscus defeated the Latins; made a circus; conquered the neighboring peoples; built walls and sewers.

The head of Servius Tullius gave forth flames. Servius Tullius conquered the Veientes and divided the people into classes; dedicated a temple to Diana.

Tarquinius Superbus slew Tullius and seized the kingship. Tullia's crime against her father. Turnus Herdonius killed by the machinations of Tarquinius. War with the Volsci. Gabii sacked,[1] in consequence of the fraud of Sextus Tarquinius. The Capitol commenced. The altars of Termo and Juventa could not be moved.[2] Lucretia slew herself. Expulsion of Superbus. The kings reigned 255 years.[3]

B. Having beaten the Latins,[4] he assigned them the Aventine Hill; planted a colony at Ostia; extended the boundaries and revived the ceremonies established by Numa.

It was he who is said to have asked the augur, Attus Navius, to test his skill, whether the thing he was thinking of could be accomplished and, when Attius replied that it could, to have bid him cut a whetstone in two with a razor, which Attius is said forthwith to have done.

He reigned twenty-four years. In his reign Lucumo, son of the Corinthian Demaratus, came from Tarquinii, an Etruscan city, to Rome, and being received into the friendship of Ancus began to bear the name of Tarquinius Priscus, and after the death of Ancus succeeded to the kingship. He added a hundred members to the senate; subjugated the Latins; gave games in the circus; increased the centuries of knights; surrounded the city with a wall; made sewers. He was killed by the sons of Ancus after ruling thirty-eight years.

His successor was Servius Tullius, son of a noblewoman, a captive from Corniculum. It is related that when he was still a babe, lying in the cradle, his head burst into flames. He conducted the first census and closed the lustrum, and it is said that 80,000 were assessed. He enlarged the pomerium; added to the city the Quirinal, Viminal, and Esquiline Hills; and with the Latins erected a temple to Diana on the Aventine. He was killed by Lucius Tarquinius, son of Priscus, on the advice of his own daughter Tullia, after reigning forty-four years.

After him Lucius Tarquinius Superbus seized the kingdom, without the authorization of either Fathers or People. He kept armed men about him to protect him. He waged war with the Volsci, and out of their spoils built a temple to Jupiter on the Capitol. He brought Gabii under his sway by guile. When his sons had gone to Delphi and were consulting the oracle as to which of them should be king in Rome, answer was made that he should reign who should first kiss his mother. This response the princes themselves explained otherwise, but Junius Brutus, who had accompanied them, pretended to fall upon his face, and kissed the earth. And the outcome sanctioned his act. For when Tarquinius Superbus had brought all men to hate him by the violence of his behavior, and finally Lucretia, whose chastity had been violated at night by the king's son Sextus, summoned her father Tricipitinus and her husband Collatinus and, adjuring them not to leave her death unavenged, killed herself with a knife, Tarquinius was expelled, chiefly through the efforts of Brutus, after a reign of twenty-five years. Then the first consuls were chosen, Lucius Junius Brutus and Lucius Tarquinius Collatinus.

Book II

I. The new liberty enjoyed by the Roman people, their achievements in peace and war, annual magistracies, and laws superior in authority to men will henceforth be my theme. This liberty was the more grateful as the last king had been so great a tyrant. For his predecessors so ruled that there is good reason to regard them all as successive founders of parts, at least, of the City, which they added to serve as new homes for the numbers they had themselves recruited.[1] Nor is there any doubt that the same Brutus who earned such honor by expelling the haughty Tarquinius, would have acted in an evil hour for the commonwealth had a premature eagerness for liberty led him to wrest the power from any of the earlier kings. For what would have happened if that rabble of shepherds and vagrants, having deserted their own peoples, and under the protection of inviolable sanctuary having possessed themselves of liberty, or at least impunity, had thrown off their fear of kings only to be stirred by the ruffling storms of tribunician demagogues, breeding quarrels with the senators of a city not their own, before ever the pledges of wife and children and love of the very place and soil (an affection of slow growth) had firmly united their aspirations? The nation would have crumbled away with dissension before it had matured. But it was favored by the mild restraint of the government, which nursed it up to the point where its ripened powers enabled it to bear good fruit of liberty. Moreover you may reckon the beginning of liberty as proceeding rather from the limitation of the consuls' authority to a year than from any diminution of their power compared with that which the kings had exercised. All the rights of the kings and all their insignia were possessed by the earliest consuls; only one thing was guarded against—that the terror they inspired should not be doubled by permitting both to have the rods. Brutus was the first to have them, with his colleague's consent, and he proved as determined in guarding liberty as he had been in asserting it. To begin with, when the people were still jealous of their new freedom, he obliged them to swear an oath that they would suffer no man to be king in Rome, lest they might later be turned from their purpose by the entreaties or the gifts of princes. In the next place, that the strength of the senate might receive an added augmentation from the numbers of that order, he filled up the list of the Fathers, which had been abridged by the late king's butcheries, drawing upon the foremost men of equestrian rank until he had brought the total up to three hundred. From that time, it is said, was handed down the custom of summoning to the senate the Fathers and the Enrolled, the latter being the designation of the new senators, who were appointed.[2] This measure was wonderfully effective in promoting harmony in the state and attaching the plebs to the Fathers.[3]

II. Matters of worship then received attention. Certain public sacrifices had habitually been performed by the kings in person, and that their absence might nowhere be regretted, a "king of sacrifices" was appointed. This priesthood they made subordinate to the pontifex, lest the office, in conjunction with the title, might somehow prove an obstacle to liberty, which was at that time their chief concern. Perhaps the pains they took to safeguard it, even in trivial details, may have been excessive. For the name of one of the consuls, though he gave no other offense, was hateful to the citizens. "The Tarquinii had become too used to sovereignty. It had begun with Priscus; Servius Tullius had then been king; but not even this interruption had caused Tarquinius Superbus to forget the throne or regard it as another's; as though it had been the heritage of his family, he had used crime and violence to get it back; Superbus was now expelled, but the supreme power was in the hands of Collatinus. The Tarquinii knew not how to live as private citizens. Their name was irksome and a menace to liberty." Beginning in this way, with a cautious sounding of sentiment, the talk spread through the entire nation, and the plebs had become anxious and suspicious, when Brutus summoned them to an assembly. There he first of all recited the oath which the people had taken, that they would suffer no king in Rome, nor any man who might be dangerous to liberty. This oath they must uphold, he said, with all their might, nor make light of anything which bore upon it. He spoke with reluctance, on the man's account, nor would he have broken silence unless he had been forced to do so by his love of country. The Roman people did not believe that they had recovered absolute freedom. The royal family, the royal name were not only present in the state, but were actually in authority, an obstacle and a stumbling-block in the way of liberty. "This fear," he cried, "do you yourself remove, Lucius Tarquinius, of your own free will! We are mindful—we confess it—that you drove out the kings; complete the good work you have begun, and rid us of the royal name. Your possessions shall not only be granted you by the citizens, at my instance, but if they are in anyway inadequate they shall be generously increased. Depart our friend, and relieve the state of what is, perhaps, an idle fear. The people are persuaded that with the family of Tarquinius the kingship will vanish from amongst us." The consul was at first prevented from uttering a word by his astonishment at this strange and unexpected turn; then, when he tried to speak, the chief men of the state surrounded him, and with many entreaties made the same request. The others had little influence over him, but when Spurius Lucretius, his superior in years and dignity, and his father-in-law besides, began to urge him, with mingled entreaty and advice, to permit himself to yield to the unanimous wish of his fellow-citizens, Collatinus became alarmed lest when his year of office should have ended, his misfortunes might be increased by the confiscation of his property and the addition of yet other ignominies. He therefore resigned the consulship, and transferring all his possessions to Lavinium, withdrew from the Roman state. In pursuance of a resolution of the senate, Brutus proposed to the people a measure which decreed the exile of all the Tarquinian race. To be his colleague the centuriate comitia, under his presidency, elected Publius Valerius, who had helped him to expel the kings.

III. Although no one doubted that the Tarquinii would presently go to war, their attack was delayed beyond all expectation; while a thing men did not fear at all, to wit a treasonable plot, almost cost Rome her liberty. There were among the young men a number of youths, the sons of families not unimportant, whose pleasures had been less confined under the monarchy, who, being of the same age as the young Tarquinii, and their cronies, had grown used to the untrammelled life of princes. This license they missed, now that all enjoyed equal rights, and they had got into the way of complaining to each other that the liberty of the rest had resulted in their own enslavement. A king was a man, from whom one could obtain a boon, whether it were just or unjust; there was room for countenance and favor; a king could be angry, could forgive, could distinguish between friend and enemy. The law was a thing without ears, inexorable, more salutary and serviceable to the pauper than to the great man; it knew no relaxation or indulgence, if one exceeded bounds; and, inasmuch as man is so prone to blunder, it was dangerous to rely on innocence alone. Thanks to such reflections, they were already infected with disloyalty when envoys from the royal family appeared, who without saying anything about the return of the Tarquinii, sought merely to recover their property. The senate, having given them a hearing, debated the question for several days; for they feared that if they refused to make restitution it would be a pretext for war, if they consented it would be to furnish means and assistance for its prosecution. Meantime the envoys were exerting themselves to a different purpose. Ostensibly seeking to recover the property, they secretly laid their plans for winning back the kingdom; and, as if in furtherance of their apparent object, they went about sounding the disposition of the youthful nobles. To those who gave them a friendly hearing they delivered letters from the Tarquinii, and plotted with them to admit the royal family secretly by night into the City.

IV. The brothers Vitellii and Aquilii were the first to be entrusted with the project. A sister of the Vitellii had married the consul

Brutus, and there were sons of this marriage who were now young men, Titus and Tiberius; these were also admitted by their uncles to a share in the design. There were besides several other young nobles taken into the secret, but their names are lost in antiquity. The senate meantime had acquiesced in the opinion of those who were in favor of giving back the property. This very fact gave the agents of the exiles an excuse for lingering in the City, for the consuls had granted them time for obtaining vehicles with which to carry away the belongings of the royal family. All this time they spent in consultation with the conspirators, whom they urged and at length persuaded to give them letters for the Tarquinii: for otherwise how could the princes be convinced that the statements of their agents regarding matters of such importance were to be relied on? These letters, being given as a pledge of sincerity, furnished clear proof of the crime, For on the eve of the envoys' setting out to rejoin their masters it happened that they were dining at the house of the Vitellii, where the conspirators, having dismissed all witnesses, had much talk together, naturally enough, about their new design. This conversation one of the slaves overheard. He had for sometime perceived what was in the wind, but was waiting for the opportunity which the delivery of the letters to the envoys would provide, that their seizure might make good his accusation. When he saw that the letters had been given, he laid the matter before the consuls. The consuls left their houses, arrested the agents and the conspirators, and, without making any disturbance, completely crushed the plot, being especially careful not to lose the letters. The traitors were thrown into prison forthwith. As for the envoys, it was uncertain for a little while what would be done with them, but, notwithstanding they appeared to have deserved no less than to be treated as enemies, the law of nations nevertheless prevailed.

V. The question of the royal property, which they had before voted to return, was laid before the Fathers for fresh consideration. This time anger won the day. They refused to return it, and refused to confiscate it to the state, but gave it up to the plebeians to plunder, that having had their fingers in the spoils of the princes they might forever relinquish hope of making their peace with them. The land of the Tarquinii, lying between the City and the Tiber, was consecrated to Mars and became the Campus Martius. It happened, they say, that there was then standing upon it a crop of spelt, ripe for the harvest. Since this produce of the land might not, for religious reasons, be consumed, the grain was cut, straw and all,[4] by a large body of men, who were set to work upon it simultaneously, and was carried in baskets and thrown into the Tiber, then flowing with a feeble current, as is usually the case in midsummer. So the heaps of grain, caught in the shallow water, settled down in the mud, and out of these and the accumulation of other chance materials such as a river brings down, there was gradually formed an island. Later, I suppose, embankments were added, and work was done, to raise the surface so high above the water and make it strong enough to sustain even temples and porticoes. When the chattels of the princes had been pillaged, sentence was pronounced and punishment inflicted upon the traitors—a punishment the more conspicuous because the office of consul imposed upon a father the duty of exacting the penalty from his sons, and he who ought to have been spared even the sight of their suffering was the very man whom Fortune appointed to enforce it. Bound to the stake stood youths of the highest birth. But the rest were ignored as if they had been of the rabble: the consul's sons drew all eyes upon themselves. Men pitied them for their punishment not more than for the crime by which they had deserved that punishment. To think that those young men, in that year of all others, when their country was liberated and her liberator their own father, and when the consulship had begun with the Junian family, could have brought themselves to betray all—the senate, the plebs, and all the gods and men of Rome—to one who had formerly been a tyrannical king and was then an enemy exile! The consuls advanced to their tribunal and dispatched the lictors to execute the sentence. The culprits were stripped, scourged with rods, and beheaded, while through it all men gazed at the expression on the father's face, where they might clearly read a father's anguish, as he administered the nation's retribution. When the guilty had suffered, that the example might be in both respects a notable deterrent from crime, the informer was rewarded with money from the treasury, emancipation, and citizenship. He is said to have been the first to be freed by the *vindicta*.[5] Some think that even the word *vindicta* was derived from his name, which they suppose to have been Vindicius. From his time onwards it was customary to regard those who had been freed by this form as admitted to citizenship.

VI. When these occurrences had been faithfully reported to Tarquinius, he was stirred not only by disappointment at the collapse of so great hopes, but also by hatred and anger. He saw that the way was now closed against trickery, and believed it was time to contrive an open war. He therefore went about as a suppliant amongst the cities of Etruria, directing his prayers chiefly to the Veientes and the Tarquinienses. Reminding them that he had come from them and was of the same blood as themselves, and that exile and poverty had followed hard upon his loss of what had been but now great power, he besought them not to let him perish, with his youthful sons, before their very eyes. Others had been called in from abroad to be kings in Rome: he himself, while actually king, and enlarging Rome's sway by war, had been driven out by his next-of-kin in a wicked conspiracy. His enemies, perceiving that no single claimant was fit to be king, had seized and usurped the power amongst themselves, and had given up his goods to be plundered by the people, that none might be without a share in the guilt. He wished to regain his country and his sovereignty, and to punish the ungrateful Romans. Let them succor and support him, and avenge, as well, their own long-standing grievances, the oft-repeated destruction of their armies, and seizure of their lands. This last plea moved the men of Veii, and they cried out with threatenings that they ought, at all events with a Roman for their commander, to wipe out their disgraces and recover what they had lost in war. The Tarquinienses were influenced by his name and kinship: it seemed a fine thing to them that one of their blood should be king in Rome. So it came about that two armies, representing two nations, followed Tarquinius, to regain his kingdom for him and to chastise the Romans. When they had come into Roman territory the consuls went out to meet the enemy: Valerius led the foot in defensive formation; Brutus, with the cavalry, went ahead to scout. In the same fashion the enemy's horse headed their march, commanded by Arruns Tarquinius, the king's son, while the king himself followed with the legions. Arruns, perceiving a long way off by the consul's lictors that it was he, and then, as they drew nearer together, recognizing Brutus more unmistakably by his countenance, blazed with resentment. "Yonder," he cried, "is the man who drove us into exile from our native land. Look! He is himself decked out with our trappings, as he comes proudly on! O gods, avengers of kings, be with us!" Spurring his horse, he charged straight at the consul. Brutus saw that he was the object of the man's attack. In those days it was to a general's credit to take part in the actual fighting, so he eagerly accepted the challenge, and they rushed at one another with such desperation, neither of them taking thought for his own defense if only he might wound his adversary, that each was pierced right through his shield by the other's thrust, and, impaled upon the two spears, they fell dying from their horses. At the same time the rest of the cavalry as well began to fight, and not long after the infantry also appeared. In this battle the advantage was divided, and the fortune of war seemed equally balanced: the right wing on each side was victorious, while the left was defeated. The Veientes, used to being beaten by the Roman troops, were routed and dispersed; the men of Tarquinii, a new enemy, not only stood their ground, but drove back the Roman forces which opposed them.

VII. Yet despite the indecisive character of the battle, so great a panic came over Tarquinius and the Etruscans that they gave up the enterprise for lost, and that same night both armies, the Veientine and the Tarquiniensian, marched off every man to his own home. To the story of this fight common report adds a prodigy: that in the silence of the following night a loud voice was heard coming out of the Arsian forest, which was believed to be the voice of Silvanus, and that this was what he said: "The Tuscans have lost one more man in the battle-line; the Romans are conquerors in the war." At all events the Romans left the field like victors, and the Etruscans like an army that has been defeated. For when it grew light and not a single enemy was to be seen, Publius Valerius the consul gathered up the spoils and returned in triumph to Rome. His colleague's funeral he celebrated with all the pomp then possible; but a far greater honor to the dead man was the general grief, which was particularly conspicuous inasmuch as the matrons mourned a year for him, as for a father, because he had been so spirited an avenger of outraged modesty.

Soon after this the surviving consul, so fickle are the affections of the mob, became unpopular; not only did the people dislike him, but they actually suspected him and made cruel charges against him. It was noised about that he was aspiring to the power of a king, since he had not caused a colleague to be elected in the place of Brutus, and was building a house on the highest part of the Velia, an elevated position of natural strength, men said, which he was converting into an impregnable citadel. The frequency of these remarks and the general acceptance they met with, shamefully unjust as they were, distressed the consul. He summoned the people to a council, and with lowered fasces[6] mounted the speaker's platform. It was a welcome spectacle to the multitude when they beheld the emblems of authority there abased before them, in acknowledgment that the people's majesty and power were superior to the consul's. Then, bidding them attend, the consul extolled the good fortune of his colleague, who, after his country had thrown off the yoke, had held the highest office in her gift, and, fighting for the state, at the height of a reputation as yet untarnished by envy, had met his death. He had himself outlived his glory, and survived to face accusations and ill-will. From being the savior of his country he had sunk to the level of the Aquilii and Vitellii. "Will there never be worth and merit, then," he exclaimed, "so established in your minds that suspicion cannot wrong it? Could I possibly have feared that I, well known as the bitterest enemy of kings, should myself incur the charge of seeking kingly power? Could I have believed that, though I dwelt in the very Citadel and on the Capitol itself, I could be feared by my fellow-citizens? Can so trivial a cause ruin my reputation with you? Does your confidence rest on so slight a foundation that it makes more difference where I am than who I am? There shall be no menace in the house of Publius Valerius to your liberties, Quirites; your Velia shall be safe. I will not only bring my house down on to level ground, but will even place it under a hill, that you may live above me, the citizen whom you suspect. Let those build on the Velia who can better be trusted with men's liberty than can Publius Valerius!" Immediately the materials were all brought down below the Velia, and the house was erected where the temple of Vica Pota is now, at the bottom of the slope.

VIII. Laws were then proposed which not only cleared the consul from the suspicion of seeking kingly power, but took such an opposite turn that they even made him popular and caused him to be styled Publicola, the People's Friend. Above all, the law about appealing from the magistrates to the people, and the one that pronounced a curse on the life and property of a man who should plot to make himself king, were welcome to the commons. When he had carried through these measures alone, that he might enjoy without a rival all the favor arising out of them, he finally held an election to choose a colleague for the unexpired term. The choice fell upon Spurius Lucretius, who by reason of his great age was no longer strong enough for the duties of the consulship, and died within a few days. They elected in Lucretius' place Marcus Horatius Pulvillus. In some ancient authorities I do not find Lucretius given as consul, but Brutus is followed immediately by Horatius; I suppose that because no exploit lent distinction to Lucretius' consulship men forgot it.

The temple of Jupiter on the Capitol had not yet been dedicated. Valerius and Horatius the consuls drew lots to determine which should do it. Horatius received the lot, and Publicola set out to conduct the war against the Veientes. With more bitterness than was reasonable, the friends of Valerius resented that the dedication of so famous a temple should be given to Horatius. They tried in all sorts of ways to hinder it, but their schemes all came to naught. Finally, when the consul's hand was on the doorpost and he was in the midst of his prayers to the gods, they broke in upon the ceremony with the evil tidings that his son was dead, averring that whilst the shadow of death was over his house he could not dedicate a temple. Whether he did not believe the news to be true, or possessed great fortitude, we are not informed with certainty, nor is it easy to decide. Without permitting himself to be diverted from his purpose by the message, further than to order that the body should be buried, he kept his hand upon the doorpost, finished his prayer, and dedicated the temple.

Such were the achievements, at home and in the field, of the first year after the expulsion of the kings.

IX. Next Publius Valerius (for the second time) and Titus Lucretius were made consuls.[7] By this time the Tarquinii had sought refuge with Lars Porsinna, king of Clusium. There they mingled advice and entreaty, now imploring him not to permit them, Etruscans by birth and of the same blood and the same name as himself, to suffer the privations of exile, and again even warning him not to allow the growing custom of expelling kings to go unpunished. Liberty was sweet enough in itself. Unless the energy with which nations sought to obtain it were matched by the efforts which kings put forth to defend their power, the highest would be reduced to the level of the lowest; there would be nothing lofty, nothing that stood out above the rest of the state; there was the end of monarchy, the noblest institution known to gods or men. Porsinna, believing that it was not only a safe thing for the Etruscans that there should be a king at Rome, but an honor to have that king of Etruscan stock, invaded Roman territory with a hostile army. Never before had such fear seized the senate, so powerful was Clusium in those days, and so great Porsinna's fame. And they feared not only the enemy but their own citizens, lest the plebs should be terror-stricken and, admitting the princes into the City, should even submit to enslavement, for the sake of peace. Hence the senate at this time granted many favors to the plebs. The question of subsistence received special attention, and some were sent to the Volsci and others to Cumae to buy up corn. Again, the monopoly of salt, the price of which was very high, was taken out of the hands of individuals and wholly assumed by the government. Imposts and taxes were removed from the plebs that they might be borne by the well-to-do, who were equal to the burden: the poor paid dues enough if they reared children. Thanks to this liberality on the part of the Fathers, the distress which attended the subsequent block-ade and famine was powerless to destroy the harmony of the state, which was such that the name of king was not more abhorrent to the highest than to the lowest; nor was there ever a man in after years whose demagogic arts made him so popular as its wise governing at that time made the whole senate.

X. When the enemy appeared, the Romans all, with one accord, withdrew from their fields into the City, which they surrounded with guards. Some parts appeared to be rendered safe by their walls, others by the barrier formed by the river Tiber. The bridge of piles almost afforded an entrance to the enemy, had it not been for one man, Horatius Cocles; he was the bulwark of defense on which that day depended the fortune of the City of Rome. He chanced to be on guard at the bridge when Janiculum was captured by a sudden attack of the enemy. He saw them as they charged down on the run from Janiculum, while his own people behaved like a frightened mob, throwing away their arms and quitting their ranks. Catching hold first of one and then of another, blocking their way and conjuring them to listen, he called on gods and men to witness that if they forsook their post it was vain to flee; once they had left a passage in their rear by the bridge, there would soon be more of the enemy on the Palatine and the Capitol than on Janiculum. He therefore warned and commanded them to break down the bridge with steel, with fire, with any instrument at their disposal; and promised that he would himself receive the onset of the enemy, so far as it could be withstood by a single body. Then, striding to the head of the bridge, conspicuous amongst the fugitives who were clearly seen to be shirking the fight, he covered himself with his sword and buckler and made ready to do battle at close quarters, confounding the Etruscans with amazement at his audacity. Yet were there two who were prevented by shame from leaving him. These were Spurius Larcius and Titus Herminius, both famous for their birth and their deeds. With these he endured the peril of the first rush and the stormiest moment of the battle. But after a while he forced even these two to leave him and save themselves, for there was scarcely anything left of the bridge, and those who were cutting it down called to them to come back. Then, darting glances of defiance around at the Etruscan nobles, he now challenged them in turn to fight, now railed at them collectively as slaves of haughty kings, who, heedless of their own liberty, were come to overthrow the liberty of others. They hesitated for a moment, each looking to his neighbor to begin the fight. Then shame made them attack, and with a shout they cast their javelins from every side against their solitary foe. But he caught them all upon his shield, and, resolute as ever, bestrode the bridge and held his ground; and now they were trying to dislodge him by a charge, when the crash of the falling bridge and the cheer which burst from the throats of the Romans, exulting in the completion of their task, checked them in mid-career with a sudden dismay. Then Cocles cried, "O Father Tiberinus, I solemnly invoke thee; receive these arms and this soldier with propitious stream!" So praying, all armed as he was, he leaped down into the river, and under a shower of missiles swam across unhurt to his fellows, having given a proof of valor which was destined to obtain more fame than credence with posterity. The state was grateful for so brave a deed: a statue of Cocles was set up in the comitium, and he was given as much land as he could plough around in one day. Private citizens showed their gratitude in a striking fashion, in the midst of his official honors, for notwithstanding their great distress everybody made him some gift proportionate to his means, though he robbed himself of his own ration.

XI. Porsinna, repulsed in his first attempt, gave up the plan of storming the City, and determined to lay siege to it. Placing a garrison on Janiculum, he pitched his camp in the plain by the banks of the Tiber. He collected ships from every quarter, both for guarding the river, to prevent any corn from being brought into the City, and also to send his troops across for plundering, as the opportunity might present itself at one point or another; and in a short time he made all the territory of the Romans so unsafe that not only were they forced to bring all their other property inside the walls, but even their flocks too, nor did anybody dare to drive them outside the gates. This great degree of license was permitted to the Etruscans not so much from timidity as design. For Valerius the consul, who was eager for an opportunity of assailing a large number at once, when they should be scattered about and not expecting an attack, cared little to avenge small aggressions, and reserved his punishment for a heavier blow. Accordingly, to lure forth plunderers, he issued orders to his people that on the following day a large number of them should drive out their flocks by the Esquiline Gate, which was the most remote from the enemy, believing that they would hear of it, since the blockade and famine were causing desertions on the part of faithless slaves. And in fact the enemy did hear of it from a deserter's report, and crossed the river in much greater force than usual, in the hope of making a clean sweep of the booty. Consequently Publius Valerius directed Titus Herminius to lie in ambush with a small force two miles out on the Gabinian Way, and Spurius Larcius with a body of light-armed youths to take post at the Colline Gate, until the enemy should pass, and then to throw themselves between him and the river, cutting off his retreat. Of the two consuls, Titus Lucretius went out by the Naevian Gate with several maniples of soldiers, Valerius himself led out some picked cohorts by way of the Caelian Mount.[8] These last were the first to be seen by the enemy. Herminius had no sooner perceived that the skirmish was begun than he rushed in from his ambush and fell upon the rear of the Etruscans, who had turned to meet Valerius. On the right hand and on the left,[9] from the Naevian Gate and from the Colline, an answering shout was returned. Thus the raiders were hemmed in and cut to pieces, for they were no match for the Romans in fighting strength, and were shut off from every line of retreat. This was the last time the Etruscans roamed so far afield.

XII. The blockade went on notwithstanding. The corn was giving out, and what there was cost a very high price, and Porsinna was beginning to have hopes that he would take the City by sitting still, when Gaius Mucius, a young Roman noble, thinking it a shame that although the Roman People had not, in the days of their servitude when they lived under kings, been blockaded in a war by any enemies, they should now, when free, be besieged by those same Etruscans whose armies they had so often routed, made up his mind that this indignity must be avenged by some great and daring deed. At first he intended to make his way to the enemy's camp on his own account. Afterwards, fearing that if he should go unbidden by the consuls and without anyone's knowing it, he might chance to be arrested by the

Roman sentries and brought back as a deserter—a charge which the state of the City would confirm—he went before the senate. "I wish," said he, "to cross the river, senators, and enter, if I can, the enemy's camp—not to plunder or exact reprisals for their devastations: I have in mind to do a greater deed, if the gods grant me their help." The Fathers approved. Hiding a sword under his dress, he set out. Arrived at the camp, he took up his stand in the thick of the crowd near the royal tribunal. It happened that at that moment the soldiers were being paid; a secretary who sat beside the king, and wore nearly the same costume, was very busy, and to him the soldiers for the most part addressed themselves. Mucius was afraid to ask which was Porsinna, lest his ignorance of the king's identity should betray his own, and following the blind guidance of Fortune, slew the secretary instead of the king. As he strode off through the frightened crowd, making a way for himself with his bloody blade, there was an outcry, and thereat the royal guards came running in from every side, seized him and dragged him back before the tribunal of the king. But friendless as he was, even then, when Fortune wore so menacing an aspect, yet as one more to be feared than fearing, "I am a Roman citizen," he cried; "men call me Gaius Mucius. I am your enemy, and as an enemy I would have slain you; I can die as resolutely as I could kill: both to do and to endure valiantly is the Roman way. Nor am I the only one to carry this resolution against you: behind me is a long line of men who are seeking the same honor. Gird yourself therefore, if you think it worth your while, for a struggle in which you must fight for your life from hour to hour with an armed foe always at your door. Such is the war we, the Roman youths, declare on you. Fear no serried ranks, no battle; it will be between yourself alone and a single enemy at a time." The king, at once hot with resentment and aghast at his danger, angrily ordered the prisoner to be flung into the flames unless he should at once divulge the plot with which he so obscurely threatened him. Whereupon Mucius, exclaiming, "Look, that you may see how cheap they hold their bodies whose eyes are fixed upon renown!" thrust his hand into the fire that was kindled for the sacrifice. When he allowed his hand to burn as if his spirit were unconscious of sensation, the king was almost beside himself with wonder. He bounded from his seat and bade them remove the young man from the altar. "Do you go free," he said, "who have dared to harm yourself more than me. I would invoke success upon your valor, were that valor exerted for my country; since that may not be, I release you from the penalties of war and dismiss you scathless and uninjured." Then Mucius, as if to requite his generosity, answered, "Since you hold bravery in honor, my gratitude shall afford you the information your threats could not extort: we are three hundred, the foremost youths of Rome, who have conspired to assail you in this fashion. I drew the first lot; the others, in whatever order it falls to them, will attack you, each at his own time, until Fortune shall have delivered you into our hands."

XIII. The release of Mucius, who was afterwards known as Scaevola,[10] from the loss of his right hand, was followed by the arrival in Rome of envoys from Porsinna. The king had been so disturbed, what with the hazard of the first attack upon his life, from which nothing but the blunder of his assailant had preserved him, and what with the anticipation of having to undergo the danger as many times more as there were conspirators remaining, that he voluntarily proposed terms of peace to the Romans. In these terms Porsinna suggested, but without effect, that the Tarquinii should be restored to power, more because he had been unable to refuse the princes this demand upon their behalf than that he was ignorant that the Romans would refuse it. In obtaining the return of their lands to the Veientes he was successful; and the Romans were compelled to give hostages if they wished the garrison to be withdrawn from Janiculum. On these terms peace was made, and Porsinna led his army down from Janiculum and evacuated the Roman territory. The Fathers bestowed on Gaius Mucius, for his bravery, a field across the Tiber, which was later known as the Mucian Meadows.

Now when courage had been thus distinguished, even the women were inspired to deeds of patriotism. Thus the maiden Cloelia, one of the hostages, eluded the sentinels, when it chanced that the Etruscans had encamped not far from the bank of the Tiber, and heading a band of girls swam the river and, under a rain of hostile darts, brought them all back in safety to their kinsmen in Rome.

When this had been reported to the king, he was at first enraged and sent emissaries to Rome to demand that the hostage Cloelia be given up, for he made no great account of the others. Then, admiration getting the better of anger, he asserted that her feat was a greater one than those of Cocles and Mucius, and declared that although in case the hostages were not returned he should regard the treaty as broken, yet if she were restored to him he would send her back safe and inviolate to her friends. Both parties kept their word. The Romans returned the pledge of peace, as the treaty required; and the Etruscan king not only protected the brave girl but even honored her, for after praising her heroism he said that he would present her with half the hostages, and that she herself should choose the ones she wished. When they had all been brought out it is said that she selected the young boys, because it was not only more seemly in a maiden, but was unanimously approved by the hostages themselves, that in delivering them from the enemy she should give the preference to those who were of an age which particularly exposed them to injury. When peace had been established the Romans rewarded this new valor in a woman with a new kind of honor, an equestrian statue, which was set up on the summit of the Sacred Way, and represented the maiden seated on a horse.

XIV. This peaceful departure of the Etruscan king from Rome is inconsistent with the custom handed down from antiquity even to our own age, among other formalities observed at sales of booty, of proclaiming "the goods of King Porsinna." Such a practice must either have arisen during the war and have been retained when peace was made, or else have had its origin in some kindlier circumstance than would be suggested by the notice that an enemy's goods were to be sold. The most credible of the traditional explanations is that when Porsinna retired from Janiculum he handed over his camp, well stocked with provisions brought in from the neighboring fertile fields of Etruria, as a gift to the Romans, who were then in a destitute condition after the long siege. These supplies were then sold, lest, if people were given a free hand, they might plunder the camp like an enemy; and they were called the goods of Porsinna rather by way of implying thankfulness for the gift than an auction of the king's property, which was not even in the possession of the Roman People.

On relinquishing his campaign against the Romans, Porsinna was unwilling that he should appear to have led his army into that region to no purpose, and accordingly sent a part of his forces, under his son Arruns, to besiege Aricia. At first the Aricini were paralysed with surprise. Afterwards the auxiliaries whom they called in from the Latin peoples, and also from Cumae, so encouraged them that they ventured to measure their strength with the enemy in the open field. When the battle began, the attack of the Etruscans was so impetuous that they routed the Aricini at the first charge. The Cumaean levies, employing skill to meet force, swerved a little to one side, and when the enemy had swept by them, faced about and attacked them in the rear, with the result that the Etruscans, caught between two lines, almost in the moment of victory, were cut to pieces. A very small number of them, having lost their leader and finding no nearer refuge, drifted to Rome, unarmed and with all the helplessness and the dejected aspect of suppliants. There they were kindly received and were quartered about among the citizens. When their wounds had healed, some departed for their homes to report the hospitality and kindness they had met with, but many were persuaded to remain in Rome by the affection they felt for their hosts and for the City. To these a place of residence was allotted which was afterwards called the Vicus Tuscus.

XV. Spurius Larcius and Titus Herminius were the next consuls, and after them came Publius Lucretius and Publius Valerius Publicola. In the latter year an embassy was sent to Rome for the last time by Porsinna to negotiate for the restoration of Tarquinius to power. To these envoys the senate replied that they would send representatives to the king, and they forthwith dispatched those of the Fathers who were held in the highest esteem. It would not have been impossible, they said, to reply shortly that the royal family would not be received. It was not for that reason that they had preferred to send chosen members of the senate to him rather than to give their answer to his ambassadors in Rome. But they had desired that for all time discussion of that question might be ended, and that where there were so great obligations on both sides there might not be mutual irritation, from the king's seeking that which was incompatible with the liberty of the Roman people, while the Romans, unless they were willing to sacrifice their existence to their good nature, denied the request of a man whom they would not willingly have denied anything. The Roman people were not living under a monarchy, but were free. They had resolved to throw open their gates to enemies sooner than to kings; in this prayer they were all united, that the day which saw the end of liberty in their City might also see the City's end. They therefore entreated him, if he desired the welfare of Rome, to permit her to be free. The king, yielding to his better feelings, made answer: "Since this is your fixed resolve, I will neither importune you with repeated insistence upon a hopeless plea, nor will I deceive the Tarquinii with the hope of aid which it is not in my power to grant. Let them seek elsewhere, whether war or peace be their object, for a place of exile, that nothing may hinder my being at peace with you." His words were followed by yet more friendly deeds. The hostages remaining in his hands he returned, and he gave back the Veientine land which he had taken from the Romans by the treaty made on Janiculum. Tarquinius, cut off from all hope of returning, departed for Tusculum, to spend his exile in the home of his son-in-law, Mamilius Octavius. The Romans enjoyed an unbroken peace with Porsinna.

XVI. The consulship of Marcus Valerius and Publius Postumius. This year a successful war was waged against the Sabines, and the consuls triumphed. More elaborate preparations for war were then made by the Sabines. To confront them, and to prevent any sudden peril arising from Tusculum, in which quarter hostility, though not openly avowed, was none the less suspected, Publius Valerius was made consul for the fourth time and Titus Lucretius for the second. A schism which occurred between the advocates of war and those of peace amongst the Sabines resulted in the transfer of some part of their strength to the Romans. For Attius Clausus, afterwards known at Rome as Appius Claudius, himself a champion of peace, was hard bested by the turbulent war-party, and finding himself no match for them, left Inregillus, with a large band of clients, and fled to Rome. These people were made citizens and given land across the Anio. The "Old Claudian Tribe" was the name used later, when new tribesmen had been added, to designate those who came from this territory.[11] Appius, having been enrolled in the senate, came in a short time to be regarded as one of its leading members. The consuls led an army into the country of the Sabines, and by wasting their fields, and afterwards by a battle, so crushed the enemy's strength that there could be no fear for a long time of any outbreak of hostilities in that region. They then returned to Rome and triumphed. Publius Valerius, universally regarded as the foremost citizen, both in military and in civil qualities, died in the following year, when Agrippa Menenius and Publius Postumius were consuls. He was a man of extraordinary reputation, but so poor that money was wanting for his burial, and it was furnished from the treasury of the state. He was mourned by the matrons as Brutus had been. In the same year two Latin colonies, Pometia and Cora, revolted to the Aurunci. The Aurunci were the first to be attacked. Upon the defeat of the great army which had boldly issued forth to meet the invasion of their territory by the consuls, the whole weight of the Auruncan war fell upon Pometia. After the battle, as well as during its progress, no quarter was given. The slain had somewhat outnumbered the prisoners, and the prisoners were indiscriminately slaughtered. Even the hostages, of whom three hundred had been received, were not spared in the rage of war.[12] This year also a triumph was celebrated at Rome.

XVII. The consuls of the next year, Opiter Verginius and Spurius Cassius, attempted to capture Pometia, first by assault and then by the use of mantlets and other engines. Against their besiegers the Aurunci, rather of an implacable hatred than for any hope or opportunity offered, rushed out, armed with firebrands for the most part, instead of swords, and carried death and flames in all directions. The mantlets were burned, many of their enemies were wounded or slain, and one of the consuls—which one the historians do not add—was seriously wounded, thrown from his horse, and almost killed. The Romans then marched home, defeated. Amongst the many wounded they brought the consul, hovering betwixt life and death. When a short time had elapsed, long enough for healing wounds and recruiting the army, they returned, with heightened resentment and also with augmented forces, to the attack of Pometia. They had repaired their mantlets and the rest of their equipment, and they were already upon the point of sending their men against the walls when the town capitulated. But the fate of the Aurunci was no less awful from their having surrendered their city than if it had been stormed. Their chief men were beheaded, and the rest of the colonists were sold as slaves.[13] The town was razed; its land was sold. The consuls obtained a triumph, more because they had heavily avenged Rome's wrongs than because of the magnitude of the war which they had successfully concluded.

XVIII. The year after had as its consuls Postumius Cominius and Titus Largius. In this year, during the celebration of the games at Rome, the Sabine youths, in a spirit of wantonness, forcibly abducted certain harlots. Men gathered hastily and there was a brawl which was almost a battle, and, trifling as its origin was, it seemed to threaten a fresh outbreak of the war.[14] Besides the Sabine peril, it was generally known that the thirty Latin cities had already conspired, at the instigation of Octavius Mamilius. These grave apprehensions having occasioned a general anxiety, the appointment of a dictator was suggested, for the first time. But there is no general agreement as to the year, or which consuls were distrusted as being of the Tarquinian faction—for this is included in the tradition—or who it was that was first named dictator. In the oldest writers, however, I find it said that Titus Largius was the first to be made dictator, and that Spurius Cassius was master of the horse. They chose men of consular rank, for so the law prescribed which had been passed to regulate the selection of a dictator. I am therefore the more disposed to believe that Largius, a consular, rather than Manius Valerius, the son of Marcus and grandson of Volesus, a man who had not yet held the consulship, was assigned to be the director and superior of consuls; and indeed if men had been specially desirous of choosing the dictator from that family, they would much sooner have selected Marcus Valerius the father, a man of proven worth and an ex-consul.

When they had named a dictator for the first time at Rome, and men saw the axes borne before him, a great fear came over the plebs and caused them to be more zealous in obeying orders. For there was no recourse in this case, as with the consuls, who shared the powers of their office equally, to the assistance of the man's colleague, nor was there any appeal nor any help anywhere but in scrupulous obedience.[15] The Sabines, too, were inspired with fear by the appointment of the dictator, especially since they believed that it was on their account that he had been created. Accordingly they sent legates to treat for peace. When they requested the dictator and the senate to pardon an error committed by young men, the answer was given that to pardon young men was possible, but not old men who contrived one war after another. Nevertheless negotiations for peace were begun, and it would have been granted to the Sabines, could they have made up their minds to guarantee, as the Romans demanded, the sum which had been expended for the war. Hostilities were declared, but a tacit truce preserved a state of peace through the year.

XIX. In the consulship of Servius Sulpicius and Manius Tullius nothing worthy of note occurred. They were succeeded by Titus Aebutius and Gaius Vetusius. During their year of office Fidenae was besieged, Crustumeria taken; Praeneste went over from the Latins to the Romans, and it was no longer possible to postpone the Latin war, which had now been smouldering for several years. Aulus Postumius as dictator,[16] and Titus Aebutius as master of the horse, set out with large forces of infantry and cavalry, and at Lake Regillus, in the territory of Tusculum, met the enemy's advancing column. The Romans had learned that the Tarquinii were with the Latin army, and were so enraged that they could not be withheld from instantly attacking, and the battle itself, in consequence of this report, was fought with a good deal more determination and bitterness than any other had been. For the leaders were not only in the field to direct the engagement with their strategy, but joined battle and fought in their own persons. Almost none of the nobles on either side came off unscathed, except the Roman dictator. Postumius was in the front rank encouraging his men and forming them, when Tarquinius Superbus, though now burdened with years and broken in strength, rode full-tilt against him. But the old man received a thrust in the side, and his followers rushed in and rescued him. Similarly on the other wing, Aebutius, the master of the horse, charged Octavius Mamilius. But the Tusculan commander saw him coming, and he too spurred his horse to the encounter; and so great was the force in their levelled lances as they met, that the arm of Aebutius was transfixed, while Mamilius was struck in the breast. Mamilius was received by the Latins within their second line: Aebutius, being unable to manage a weapon with his wounded arm, retired from the battle. The Latin leader, not a jot discouraged by his wound, urged on the fighting, and, because he saw that his men were in retreat, called up a cohort of Roman exiles, commanded by a son of Lucius Tarquinius,[17] and these, fighting with greater fury on account of the loss of their property and native land, restored the battle for a while.

XX. When the Romans were now beginning to give way in that part of the field, Marcus Valerius, Publicola's brother, espied the young Tarquinius, who was boldly inviting attack in the front rank of the exiles. Valerius found in his brother's glory an additional incentive, and resolving that the family which had the honor of expelling the tyrants should also gain the credit for their death, he dug his spurs into his charger and rode at Tarquinius with levelled spear. The Etruscan drew back within the company of his followers to avoid his desperate antagonist. Valerius was plunging blindly into the exiles' line when one of them attacked him in the flank and ran him through the body. But the rider's wound did not check the career of his horse, and the dying Roman came down in a heap upon the ground with his arms upon him. When the dictator Postumius perceived that so brave a soldier had fallen, that the exiles were advancing boldly at the double, and that his troops were checked and were giving ground, he issued orders to his own cohort, a picked body of men which he kept about his person as a guard, that if they saw any Roman running away they should treat him as an enemy. Being thus between two dangers, the Romans faced about to meet the foe, and the battle-line was formed again. The cohort of the dictator then entered the engagement for the first time. With fresh strength and spirit they attacked the weary exiles and cut them to pieces. Then began another combat between leaders. The Latin general, perceiving that the cohort of the exiles was nearly cut off by the Roman dictator, took a few companies of his reserves and hurried them to the front. As they came marching up, Titus Herminius, the lieutenant, caught sight of them, and in their midst, conspicuous in dress and accoutrements, he saw and recognized Mamilius. Whereupon he hurled himself upon the enemy's commander with so much more violence than the master of the horse had done a little before, that not only did he pierce Mamilius through the side and slay him with a single lunge, but in the act of stripping the body of his antagonist he was himself struck by a hostile javelin, and after being borne off in the moment of victory to the Roman camp, expired just as they began to dress his wound. The dictator then dashed up to the knights and besought them, since the foot-soldiers were exhausted, to dismount and enter the fight. They obeyed: they leaped down from their horses, hastened to the front, and covered the front-rankers with their shields. It restored at once the courage of the foot to see the young nobles on even terms with themselves and sharing in the danger. Then at last the Latins received a check, and their battle-line was forced to yield. The knights had their horses brought up that they might be able to pursue the enemy, and they were followed by the infantry. Then the dictator, neglecting no help, divine or human, is said to have vowed a temple to Castor, and to have promised rewards to the soldiers who should be first and second to enter the camp of the enemy; and so great was the ardor of the Romans, that with a single rush they routed their opponents and took their camp. Such was the battle at Lake Regillus. The dictator and his master of the horse returned to the City and triumphed.

XXI. For the next three years there was neither a stable peace nor war. The consuls Quintus Cloelius and Titus Larcius were followed by Aulus Sempronius and Marcus Minucius. In the latter year a temple to Saturn was dedicated and the Saturnalia was established as a festal day.[18] Next Aulus Postumius and Titus Verginius were made consuls. It was not until this year, according to some authorities I have consulted, that the battle of Lake Regillus was fought. They say that Aulus Postumius, because his colleague was of doubtful loyalty, resigned the consulship, and was then made dictator. One is involved in so many uncertainties regarding dates by the varying order of the magistrates in different lists that it is impossible to make out which consuls followed which, or what was done in each particular year, when not only events but even authorities are so shrouded in antiquity.

At the next election Appius Claudius and Publius Servilius were chosen consuls. This year was marked by the announcement of Tarquinius' death. He died at Cumae, whither he had gone to the court of Aristodemus after the downfall of the Latin cause. These tidings cheered the Fathers and encouraged the plebs. But the Fathers were too inconsiderate, in consequence of their rejoicing at this event; and the plebs, who up to this time had been most studiously deferred to, began to feel the oppression of the nobles. The same year the colony of Signia, which King Tarquinius had planted, was recruited with new colonists and established for the second time. At Rome twenty-one tribes were formed. The temple of Mercury was consecrated on the fifteenth of May.

XXII. With the Volscian race there had been during the Latin war neither peace nor open hostilities; for while the Volsci had raised levies to send to the aid of the Latins, had the Roman dictator not moved quickly, yet the Romans did move quickly, that they might not have to fight both nations in the same battle. Upon this quarrel the consuls led their legions into the country of the Volsci, who, not expecting to be held to account for their design, were surprised and overwhelmed. They had no thought of resisting, and surrendered as hostages three hundred children of the nobility of Cora and Pometia, and so the legions were withdrawn without a conflict. Yet it was not long before the Volsci, being relieved of their alarm, resumed their native duplicity; again they made secret preparations for war, and formed a military alliance with the Hernici, while they also sent out envoys, this way and that, to instigate the Latins to rebellion. But the disaster which had recently befallen the Latins at Lake Regillus so filled them with rage and hate against anyone who advised them to go to war, that they did not even abstain from violating an embassy, but seized the Volsci and brought them to Rome. There they delivered them up to the consuls with the information that the Volsci and the Hernici were preparing to attack the Romans. When this service had been reported to the senate the Fathers were so grateful that they released to the Latins six thousand captives, and referred the question of a treaty, which they had all but refused in perpetuity, to the incoming magistrates.[19] Then, indeed, the Latins rejoiced at the action they had taken, and the advocates of peace were in great repute. They sent a golden crown as a gift to the Capitoline Jupiter. With the envoys who brought the gift came the captives who had been restored to their friends, a vast attendant multitude. Proceeding to the homes of those whom they had severally served, they thanked them for the liberality and consideration which had been shown them in their adversity, and entered into covenants of hospitality with them. Never before had there been so close a union, both official and personal, between the Latin name and the Roman state.

XXIII. But not only was war with the Volsci imminent; the citizens were at loggerheads among themselves, and internal dissensions between the Fathers and the plebs had burst into a blaze of hatred, chiefly on account of those who had been bound over to service for their debts.[20] These men complained loudly that while they were abroad fighting for liberty and dominion they had been enslaved and oppressed at home by fellow-citizens, and that the freedom of the plebeians was more secure in war than in peace, amongst enemies than amongst citizens. This bitter feeling, which was growing spontaneously, the notable calamity of one man fanned into a flame. Old, and bearing the marks of all his misfortunes, the man rushed into the Forum. His dress was covered with filth, and the condition of his body was even worse, for he was pale and half dead with emaciation. Besides this, his straggling beard and hair had given a savage look to his countenance. He was recognized nevertheless, despite the hideousness of his appearance, and the word went round that he had commanded companies; yet other military honors were openly ascribed to him by the compassionate bystanders, and the man himself displayed the scars on his breast which bore testimony to his honorable service in various battles. When they asked the reason of his condition and his squalor, he replied, while the crowd gathered about him much as though it were an assembly, that during his service in the Sabine war not only had the enemy's depredations deprived him of his crops, but his cottage had been burnt, all his belongings plundered, and his flocks driven off. Then the taxes had been levied, in an untoward moment for him, and he had contracted debts. When these had been swelled by usury, they had first stripped him of the farm which had been his father's and his grandfather's, then of the remnants of his property, and finally like an infection they had attacked his person, and he had been carried off by his creditor, not to slavery, but to the prison and the torture-chamber. He then showed them his back, disfigured with the wales of recent scourging. The sight of these things and the man's recital produced a mighty uproar. The disturbance was no longer confined to the Forum, but spread in all directions through the entire City. Those who had been bound over, whether in chains or not, broke out into the streets from every side, and implored the Quirites to protect them. At no point was there any lack of volunteers to join the rising; everywhere crowds were streaming through the different streets and shouting as they hurried to the Forum. Great was the peril of those senators who happened to be in the Forum and fell in with the mob, which would not indeed have stopped short of violence had not the consuls, Publius Servilius and Appius Claudius, hurriedly intervened to put down the insurrection. But the crowd turned on them and displayed their chains and other hideous tokens. These, they cried, were the rewards they had earned, and they bitterly rehearsed the campaigns they had each served in various places. They demanded, in a manner much more threatening than suppliant, that the consuls should convene the senate; and they surrounded the Curia, that they might themselves witness and control the deliberations of the state. The consuls succeeded in collecting only a few of the senators whom chance had thrown in their way. The rest were afraid to enter not only the Curia but even the Forum, and nothing could be done because those present were too few. Whereat the people concluded they were being flouted and put off, and that the missing senators were absent not from accident, nor fear, but with the intent to hinder action, and that the consuls themselves were paltering; nor did they doubt that their misery was made a jest. A little more and not even the majesty of the consuls could have held in check the angry crowd, when the absent Fathers, uncertain whether they should incur more danger by holding back or by coming forward, finally came into the senate, and the required number being at length assembled, not only the senators, but even the consuls themselves were unable to agree. Appius, a headstrong man, was for settling the matter by the exercise of consular authority; when one or two men had been arrested, the others, he said, would calm down. Servilius, more inclined to gentle measures, believed that it was safer, as well as easier, to assuage their fury than to quell it.

XXIV. In the midst of the debate a greater alarm arose from a new quarter, for some Latin horsemen galloped up with the disquieting news that a Volscian army was advancing to attack the City. This report awoke very different feelings—so completely had their dissensions divided the state into two—in the Fathers and the plebs. The commons were jubilant; they said that the gods were taking a hand in punishing the arrogance of the senators. They encouraged one another not to give in their names; it would be better to perish all together than alone. Let the Fathers serve, let the Fathers take up arms, that those might incur the hazards of war who received its rewards. The Curia, on the other hand, was downcast and dismayed. In their twofold fear—of their fellow-citizens and of the enemy—they begged Servilius the consul, whose character appealed more to the people than did that of his colleague, that he would extricate the state from the fearful perils with which it was beset. Thereupon the consul adjourned the senate and went before the people. There he declared that the Fathers were anxious to consult the interests of the plebs, but that their deliberations concerning that very important part—but only a part after all—of the state had been broken off by their fears for the entire nation. It was impossible, when the enemy was almost at the city gates, to consider anything before the war; and even if there should be some slight respite in that regard, it was neither to the credit of the plebs to refuse to arm for their country, unless they should first receive a recompense, nor honorable to the Fathers to be driven by fear into passing measures for the relief of their fellow-citizens which they would have passed later of their own free will. He then confirmed his speech by a proclamation in which he commanded that no one should hold a Roman citizen in chains or durance so that he should not be able to give in his name to the consuls, and that none should seize or sell a soldier's property so long as he was in camp, or interfere with his children or his grand-children. When this edict had been published, the debtors who were present at once enlisted, and from every quarter, all over the City, they hastened from the houses where their creditors no longer had the right to detain them, and rushed into the Forum to take the mili-tary oath. It was a great throng, nor were there any soldiers whose courage and usefulness in the Volscian war were more conspicuous. The consul led his troops against the enemy, and pitched his camp at a short distance from theirs.

XXV. The next night the Volsci, relying on the lack of harmony among the Romans, attacked their camp on the chance that the darkness might encourage desertions or treachery. But the sentries perceived them, the army was roused, and, the signal being given, rushed to arms. Thus the design of the Volsci came to naught, and the remainder of the night was devoted by both armies to sleeping. On the following day at dawn the Volsci filled up the trenches and assaulted the rampart, and soon they were everywhere pulling down the palisades. On every side the consul's men were clamoring for the signal—none more loudly than the debtors. He waited a moment, to test the temper of the soldiers. When there could no longer be any doubt of their great ardor, he finally gave the command for a sortie and released them, eager for the fray. At the very first onset the enemy were routed. While they ran, the foot-soldiers struck at them from behind as long as they could keep up the pursuit; then the horsemen drove them panic-stricken clear to their camp. Soon the camp itself had been surrounded by the legions, and when the Volsci had fled from it in terror, it was taken and plundered. Next day Servilius led his forces to Suessa Pometia, where the enemy had taken refuge, and within a few days took the town and gave it up to be sacked.[21] This yielded some slight relief to the soldiers, who needed it badly. The consul led his army back to Rome, with great honor to himself. As he was setting out on his return thither ambassadors approached him from the Volsci of Ecetra, who were alarmed at their own prospects, in view of the capture of Pometia. A decree of the senate granted them peace, but took away their land.

XXVI. Directly after this the Sabines also caused an alarm at Rome—for it was indeed a turmoil rather than war. One night the City got word that a Sabine army bent on pillage had come as near as the river Anio, and was there plundering and burning farmhouses right and left. The Romans at once dispatched in that direction all their cavalry, under Aulus Postumius, who had been dictator in the Latin war. He was followed by the consul Servilius with a picked body of foot-soldiers. Many stragglers were cut off by the cavalry and, when the column of infantry drew near, no resistance was offered by the Sabine troops. Exhausted not only by their march but by their night of pillage as well, a great part of them had gorged themselves in the farmhouses with food and wine, and had scarcely vigor enough to run away.

A single night having sufficed for hearing of the Sabine war and ending it, men's hopes next day ran high that peace was now assured in every quarter, when legates from the Aurunci appeared before the senate to say that unless the territory of the Volsci were evacuated they should declare war. The Auruncan army had set out from home at the same time with the legates, and the report that it had already been seen not far from Aricia threw Rome into such a state of confusion that it was impossible to bring the matter regularly before the senate, or to return a peaceful answer to a people who had already drawn the sword, while they themselves were also arming. They marched on Aricia in fighting order, joined battle with the Aurunci not far from the town, and in a single engagement finished the war.

XXVII. Having routed the Aurunci, and having been, within a few days, victorious in so many wars, the Romans were looking for the help which the consul had promised and the senate guaranteed, when Appius, partly out of native arrogance, partly to discredit his colleague, began to pronounce judgment with the utmost rigor in suits to recover debts. In consequence, not only were those who had been bound over before delivered up to their creditors, but others were bound over. Whenever this happened to a soldier he would appeal to the other consul. The people flocked to the house of Servilius: it was he who had made them promises; it was he whom they reproached, as each rehearsed his services in the wars and displayed the scars he had received. They demanded that he should either lay the matter before the senate or lend his aid as consul to his fellow-citizens, as general to his soldiers. They moved the consul by this plea, but the situation forced him to temporize, so vehemently was the other side supported, not only by his colleague, but by the entire party of the nobles. And so he steered a middle course, and neither avoided the dislike of the plebs nor gained the goodwill of the Fathers. These considered him a pusillanimous consul and an agitator, while the commons held him to be dishonest; and it was soon apparent that he was as cordially hated as Appius. The consuls had got into a dispute as to which should dedicate the temple to Mercury. The senate referred the case to the people for decision. Whichever consul should, by command of the people, be entrusted with the dedication was to have charge of the corn-supply, to establish a guild of merchants,[22] and perform the solemn rites in the presence of the pontifex. The people assigned the dedication to Marcus Laetorius, a centurion of the first rank—a choice which would readily be understood as intended not so much to honor Laetorius, to whom a commission had been given which was too exalted for his station in life, as to humiliate the consuls. Appius and the Fathers were furious then, if they had not been before; but the plebeians had plucked up heart and threw themselves into the struggle with far more spirit than they had shown at first. For, despairing of help from consuls and senate, they no sooner beheld a debtor being haled away than they flew to his assistance from every side. It was impossible for the consul's decree to be heard above the din and shouting, and when it had been pronounced nobody obeyed it. Violence was the order of the day, and fear and danger had quite shifted from the debtors to the creditors,

who were singled out and maltreated by large numbers in full sight
of the consul. To crown these troubles came the fear of a Sabine
invasion. A levy was decreed, but no one enlisted. Appius stormed
and railed at the insidious arts of his colleague, who, he said, to
make himself popular, was betraying the state by his inactivity; and
to his refusal to give judgment for debt was adding a fresh offense
in refusing to hold the levy as the senate had directed. Nevertheless
the welfare of the state was not wholly forgotten, nor the authority
of the consulate abandoned; he would himself, single-handed, assert
both his own and the senate's majesty. When the usual daily throng
of lawless men was standing about him, he gave orders to seize one
who was a conspicuous leader in their disturbances. The lictors were
already dragging the man away, when he appealed; nor would the
consul have granted the appeal, for there was no question what
the decision of the people would be, had not his obstinacy been with
difficulty overcome, more by the advice and influence of the nobles
than by the popular outcry, so steeled was he to endure men's hate.
From that moment the trouble grew worse each day, and not only
were there open disturbances, but what was far more pernicious,
secret gatherings and conferences. At last the consuls whom the
plebeians so hated went out of office. Servilius had the goodwill of
neither party, but Appius was in high esteem with the senators.

XXVIII. Aulus Verginius and Titus Vetusius then entered upon
the consulship. Whereat the plebs, uncertain what sort of consuls
they would prove to be, held nightly gatherings, some on the
Esquiline and others on the Aventine, lest if they met in the Forum
they might be frightened into adopting ill-considered measures, and
manage all their business rashly and at haphazard. This seemed to
the consuls, as indeed it was, a mischievous practice. They laid the
matter before the Fathers, but their report could not be discussed
in an orderly fashion, so tumultuously was it received, with shouts
from every part of the house and expressions of indignation from
the senators, that a thing which ought to have been settled by an
exercise of consular authority should be invidiously referred by the
consuls to the senate. It was evident that if only there were magistrates in the nation there would have been no assembly in Rome but

the assembly of the people; as it was, the government was broken up into a thousand separate curias and meetings. One single *man*—a more significant word than *consul*—of the type of Appius Claudius, would have dispersed those assemblages in a moment. When the consuls, thus upbraided, asked the Fathers what then they desired them to do, and promised that their conduct of the matter should be no whit less strenuous and stern than the senate wished, it was resolved that they should hold a levy with the utmost severity: it was idleness that made the plebeians lawless. Having adjourned the senate, the consuls mounted the tribunal and cited the young men by name. When no one answered to his name, the crowd, which surrounded the speaker as in a public meeting, declared that it was impossible to deceive the commons any longer; the consuls would never have a single soldier unless a public guarantee were given: liberty must first be restored to every man before arms were given him, that he might fight for his country and his fellow-citizens, not for a master. It was clear to the consuls what the senate had bidden them do; but of all those who had uttered truculent speeches within the walls of the curia they found not one at their side to share their odium, and they saw before them a terrible struggle with the people. Accordingly they thought it best, before proceeding to extremities, to consult the senate a second time. When it met, the youngest senators all rushed up in hot haste to the seats of the consuls, bidding them to abdicate their office and to lay down an authority which they lacked the spirit to support.

XXIX. Having sufficiently weighed both the courses open to them,[23] the consuls finally said: "Lest you should say that you had not been warned, Conscript Fathers, we are on the verge of a great mutiny. We demand that those who are loudest in accusing us of cowardice stand by us while we hold the levy. The most severe amongst you, since such is your pleasure, shall guide our procedure." They returned to the tribunal, and purposely commanded to cite by name one of those who were present. When he stood still without answering, in the midst of a little knot of men who, fearing the possibility of violence, had gathered round him, the consuls sent a lictor to him. The lictor was driven back. Whereupon, with a cry of

"Shame!" the senators who were attending the consul rushed down from the tribunal to assist the lictor. But when the mob turned from the officer, whom they had merely prevented from arresting the man, and assailed the senators, the consuls intervened and checked the brawl, in which no stones had been thrown nor any weapons used, and there were more shouts and expressions of rage than hurts. The senate was convened in confusion, and they deliberated in still greater confusion. Those who had been roughly handled demanded an investigation, and all the more violent members urged the resolution, not only with speeches but with shouts and uproar. When at length their passions had subsided, and the consuls berated them for showing as little sanity in the Curia as the people had shown in the Forum, they began to deliberate in an orderly manner. Three proposals were made. Publius Verginius advised against a general relief: only those who, relying on the promise of Publius Servilius the consul, had fought in the Volscian, Auruncan, and Sabine wars should, he thought, be considered. Titus Largius held that this was no time for merely requiting services; the whole commons was submerged in debt, and the situation could not be remedied unless provision were made for all; indeed, if some were treated in one way and some in another, it would heighten the discontent instead of allaying it. Appius Claudius, naturally harsh, and rendered savage by the hatred of the plebs on the one hand and the praises of the Fathers on the other, said that it was not misery but license that had stirred up so great a hubbub, and that wantonness was what ailed the plebs rather than anger. That was precisely the mischief which the appeal occasioned; for the consuls might threaten but could not command, when those who had shared in the guilt might be constituted the court of appeal. "Come," said he, "let us appoint a dictator, from whom there is no appeal. At once this frenzy which has now set everything ablaze will be stilled. Let anybody strike a lictor then, knowing that the right to scourge and behead him rests with that one man whose majesty he has violated!"

XXX. Many felt, and with reason, that the proposal of Appius was stern and cruel; on the other hand those of Verginius and Largius were inexpedient because of the precedent; particularly that of Largius, since it destroyed all credit. The most reasonable and moderate plan, in its regard for both sides, was held to be that of Verginius. But owing to party spirit and consideration for private interests, things which have always been hurtful to public deliberations and always will be, Appius prevailed, and came very near to being himself appointed dictator, a step which would infallibly have estranged the commons, and that at a most dangerous moment, since the Volsci, the Aequi, and the Sabines were all, as it chanced, up in arms at once. But the consuls and the older senators saw to it that a magistracy rendered formidable by its paramount authority should be committed to a man of gentle disposition, and chose for dictator Manius Valerius, son of Volesus. The plebs, though they perceived that it was against themselves that the creation of a dictator was aimed, still, since it was through a law proposed by a brother of Valerius that they possessed the right of appeal,[24] they had no fear of any harsh or oppressive act on the part of one of that family. An edict which the dictator soon promulgated strengthened their confidence. It conformed essentially to the edict of Servilius; but Valerius and the office he held commanded greater confidence, and, ceasing to struggle, men gave in their names. So large an army had never been enrolled before. Ten legions were embodied; each consul was given three of these, and the dictator had four.

Nor could war be deferred any longer, for the Aequi had invaded Latin territory. Emissaries from the Latins begged the senate either to send them help or permit them to take up arms themselves in defense of their country.[25] It seemed safer that the Latins should be defended without arming them, than that they should be suffered to resume their weapons. Vetusius the consul was dispatched to them, and this ended the pillaging. The Aequi left the fields, and trusting more to situation than to arms, secured themselves on the summits of the ridges. The other consul marched against the Volsci. Lest he too might waste his time, he provoked the enemy, chiefly by ravaging their lands, to bring their camp nearer and do battle with him. In the plain between the camps the two armies formed their lines, each in front of its own stockade. In numbers the Volsci were somewhat superior, and accordingly they came on in a loose and careless order. The Roman consul did not advance, nor did he allow a response to the enemy's shout. He commanded his men to plant their spears in the ground and stand still until the enemy had come to close quarters; then they were to assail them with all their might, and settle the question with the sword. The Volsci, weary with running and shouting, hurled themselves upon the Romans, who seemed to be numb with fear. But when the attackers found that their charge was firmly met and saw the swords flash in their faces, they were no whit less confounded than if they had fallen into an ambush, and turned and fled; and even flight was beyond their strength, since they had been running as they entered the battle. The Romans on the contrary, having stood at ease at the beginning of the fight, were fresh and strong; they readily caught up with the exhausted Volsci, and having taken their camp with a rush, pursued their enemies beyond it to Velitrae, where vanquished and victors burst into the city in one body. More blood was shed there, in the promiscuous slaughter of all sorts of people, than had been in the battle itself. A very few were granted quarter, having come without arms and given themselves up.

XXXI. While these things were going on in the Volscian country, the dictator put to rout the Sabines—by far Rome's most important enemy—and captured their camp. Attacking with his cavalry, he made havoc of their center, which, in extending their wings too widely, they had unduly weakened; and in the midst of the disorder the infantry assailed them. By a single rush the camp was captured and the war ended. From the time of the fight at Lake Regillus no other battle of those days was more famous. The dictator entered the City in triumph. In addition to the customary honors a place was assigned him in the circus, for himself and his descendants, to witness the games, and a curule chair was put there for him.[26] The Volsci, having been conquered, were deprived of the Veliternian land; colonists were sent from the City to Velitrae and a colony was planted. Soon after this there was a battle with the Aequi, though the consul was against it, for it was necessary to approach the enemy from unfavorable ground; but his men accused him of dragging out the campaign in order that the dictator might relinquish his office before their return to the City, and his promises thus come to naught, as the consul's promises had done before. Verginius was thus driven to order an advance at random, up the mountains which confronted him. This ill-advised measure the enemy's cowardice turned into success, for before the Romans had come within a spear's throw, the Aequi, appalled at their audacity, abandoned the camp which they had maintained in a highly defensible position, and threw themselves down into the valleys on the other side. There the Romans gained considerable booty and a bloodless victory.

Though a threefold success had thus been gained in the war, neither senators nor plebeians had been relieved of their anxiety respecting the outcome of affairs at home, so great was the artfulness, as well as influence, with which the money-lenders had laid their plans to baffle not only the commons but even the dictator himself. For after the return of the consul Vetusius, the first business which Valerius brought before the senate was in behalf of the victorious people, that the senate might declare its policy regarding the treatment of those bound over for debt. This resolution having failed to pass, the dictator said: "I do not please you in urging harmony. You will soon wish, I warrant you, that the Roman plebs had men like me for their spokesmen. For my own part I will not be the means of further disappointing my fellow citizens, nor will I be dictator to no purpose. Internal strife and foreign war made this office necessary to the nation; peace has been secured abroad, but at home it is being thwarted; I will play my part as a private citizen rather than as a dictator, when the mutiny breaks out." So saying he left the Curia and laid down his office. It was evident to the people that resentment of their wrongs had caused him to resign the magistracy. And so, as though he had kept his pledge (for it had not been his fault that it was not being carried out), they attended him as he retired to his house with manifestations of favor and approval.

XXXII. Thereupon the senators became alarmed, fearing that if the army should be disbanded there would again be secret gatherings and conspiracies. And so, although the levy had been held by order of the dictator, yet because the men had been sworn in by the consuls they regarded the troops as bound by their oath, and, under the pretext that the Aequi had recommenced hostilities, gave orders to lead the legions out of the City. This brought the revolt to a head. At first, it is said, there was talk of killing the consuls, that men might thus be freed from their oath; but when it was explained to them that no sacred obligation could be dissolved by a crime, they took the advice of one Sicinius, and without orders from the consuls withdrew to the Sacred Mount, which is situated across the river Anio, three miles from the City. This version of the story is more general than that given by Piso, namely that the Aventine was the place of their secession.[27]—There, without any leader, they fortified their camp with stockade and trench, and continued quietly, taking nothing but what they required for their subsistance, for several days, neither receiving provocation nor giving any. There was a great panic in the City, and mutual apprehension caused the suspension of all activities. The plebeians, having been abandoned by their friends, feared violence at the hands of the senators; the senators feared the plebeians who were left behind in Rome, being uncertain whether they had rather they stayed or went. Besides, how long would the seceding multitude continue peaceable? What would happen next if some foreign war should break out in the interim? Assuredly no hope was left save in harmony amongst the citizens, and this they concluded they must restore to the state by fair means or foul. They therefore decided to send as an ambassador to the commons Menenius Agrippa, an eloquent man and dear to the plebeians as being one of themselves by birth.[28] On being admitted to the camp he is said merely to have related the following apologue, in the quaint and uncouth style of that age: In the days when man's members did not all agree amongst themselves, as is now the case, but had each its own ideas and a voice of its own, the other parts thought it unfair that they should have the worry and the trouble and the labor of providing everything for the belly, while the belly remained quietly in their midst with nothing to do but to enjoy the good things which they bestowed upon it; they therefore conspired together that the hands should carry no food to the mouth, nor the mouth accept anything that was given it, nor the teeth grind up what they received. While they sought in this angry spirit to starve the belly into submission, the members themselves and the whole body were reduced to the utmost weakness. Hence it had become clear that even the belly had no idle task to perform, and was no more nourished than it nourished the rest, by giving out to all parts of the body that by which we live and thrive, when it has been divided equally amongst the veins and is enriched with digested food—that is, the blood. Drawing a parallel from this to show how like was the internal dissension of the bodily members to the anger of the plebs against the Fathers, he prevailed upon the minds of his hearers.[29]

XXXIII. Steps were then taken towards harmony, and a compromise was effected on these terms: the plebeians were to have magistrates of their own, who should be inviolable, and in them should lie the right to aid the people against the consuls, nor should any senator be permitted to take this magistracy. And so they chose two "tribunes of the people," Gaius Licinius and Lucius Albinus. These appointed three others to be their colleagues. Amongst the latter, Sicinius, the promoter of the revolt, was one, as all agree; the identity of the other two is less certain. Some hold that there were only two tribunes elected on the Sacred Mount, and that the law of inviolability was enacted there.[30]

During the secession of the plebs Spurius Cassius and Postumus Cominius entered upon their consulship. In this year a treaty was made with the Latin peoples. In order to make this treaty one of the consuls remained in Rome, while the other was dispatched to the Volscian war, and defeated and put to flight the Volsci of Antium. Forcing them to take refuge in the town of Longula, he followed them up and captured the place. Thence he proceeded to take Polusca, another Volscian town, after which he directed a strong attack upon Corioli. There was in camp at that time amongst the young nobles Gnaeus Marcius, a youth of active mind and ready hand, who afterwards gained the surname of Coriolanus. The Romans were laying siege to Corioli and were intent upon the townspeople shut up within the walls, with no thought of danger from any attack which might be impending from without, when they found themselves suddenly assailed by a Volscian army from Antium, and simultaneously by the besieged, who made a sortie from the town. It happened that Marcius was on guard. Taking a picked body of men he not only repelled the sally, but boldly forced his way through the open gate, and having spread carnage through the adjacent part of the town, caught up a firebrand on the spur of the moment, and threw it upon the buildings which overhung the wall. Thereupon the townspeople raised a shout, mingled with such a wailing of women and children as is generally heard at the first alarm. This brought new courage to the Romans and covered the Volsci with confusion—as was natural when the city which they had come to relieve was taken. Thus the men of Antium were routed, and Corioli was won. So completely did the glory of Marcius overshadow the consul's fame, that, were it not for the record on a bronze column of the treaty with the Latins which was struck by Spurius Cassius alone, in the absence of his colleague, men would have forgotten that Postumus Cominius had waged war on the Volsci.

That same year saw the death of Menenius Agrippa, a man who throughout his life had been equally beloved by patricians and plebeians, and who after the secession was even dearer to the commons. This mediator and umpire of civil harmony, this ambassador of the senators to the people, this restorer of the plebs to Rome, did not leave sufficient wealth to pay for a funeral. He was buried by the commons, who contributed a *sextans*[31] each to the cost.

XXXIV. The consuls next chosen were Titus Geganius and Publius Minucius. This year, though there was no war to occasion trouble from without and the breach at home had been healed, another and a much more serious misfortune befell the nation; for first the price of corn went up, from men's failure to cultivate the fields during the withdrawal of the plebs; and this was followed by a famine, such as comes to a beleaguered city. It would have meant starvation for the slaves, at least, and the plebeians, had not the consuls met the situation by sending agents far and wide to buy up corn, not only to Etruria, northwards along the coast from Ostia, and south past the Volsci by sea, all the way to Cumae, but even to Sicily—so far afield had the enmity of Rome's neighbors driven her to seek for help. When grain had been purchased at Cumae the ships were held back by Aristodemus, the tyrant, in satisfaction for the property of the Tarquinii, whose heir he was. Among the Volsci and Pomptini the agents could not even make any purchases, and they were actually in danger from the violence of the people. From the Tuscans corn came in by way of the Tiber, and with this the plebs were kept alive. A disastrous war would have been added to the distresses arising from the scarcity of provisions, had not a grievous pestilence descended upon the Volsci just as they were beginning hostilities. Its ravages so terrified the enemy that even after the worst of it was over they did not fully recover from their fear, and the Romans increased the number of colonists at Velitrae and sent out a new colony to Norba, in the mountains, as a stronghold for the Pomptine country.

Next year, in the consulship of Marcus Minucius and Aulus Sempronius, a large quantity of grain was imported from Sicily, and the senate debated at what price it should be sold to the plebeians. Many thought the time had come for repressing the commons, and resuming the rights which they had violently extorted from the Fathers by secession. Conspicuous among these was Marcius Coriolanus, an enemy to the tribunician power, who said: "If they want corn at the old price let them restore to the senate its ancient rights. Why do I see plebeian magistrates, why do I, after being sent beneath the yoke and ransomed, as it were, from brigands, behold Sicinius in power? Shall I endure these humiliations any longer than I must? When I would not brook Tarquinius as king, must I brook Sicinius? Let him secede now and call out the plebs; the way lies open to the Sacred Mount and the other hills. Let them seize grain from our fields as they did two years ago. Let them enjoy the corn-prices they have brought about by their own madness. I make bold to say that this evil plight will so tame them that they will sooner till the land themselves than withdraw under arms and prevent its cultivation by others." It is not so easy to say whether it would have been right to do this, as it is clear, I think, that it lay within the Fathers' power to have made such conditions for reducing the price of corn as to have freed themselves from the tribunician authority and all the terms which they had unwillingly agreed to.

XXXV. Even the senate deemed the proposal too harsh, and the plebs were so angry that they almost resorted to arms. Starvation, they said, was now being employed against them, as though they were public enemies, and they were being defrauded of their food and sustenance; the imported corn, their only supply, unexpectedly bestowed on them by Fortune, was to be snatched from their mouths unless the tribunes should be delivered up in chains to Gnaeus Marcius, unless he should work his will on the persons of the Roman plebeians; in him a new executioner had risen up against them, who bade them choose between death and slavery. When he came out from the Curia they would have set upon him, had not the tribunes, in the nick of time, appointed a day to try him; whereupon their anger subsided, for every man saw that he was himself made his enemy's judge, and held over him the power of life and death. With contempt at first Marcius heard the threats of the tribunes, alleging that the right to help, not to punish, had been granted to that office, and that they were tribunes not of the Fathers, but of the plebs. But the commons had risen in such a storm of anger that the Fathers had to sacrifice one man to appease them. For all that, they resisted the hatred of their adversaries and called upon the private resources of the several senators, as well as the strength of the entire order. At first they tried, by posting their clients[32] here and there, to frighten persons from coming together for deliberation, in the hope that they might thereby break up their plans. Then they came out in a body—you would have said all the members of the senate were on their trial—and entreated the plebs to release to them one citizen, one senator; if they were unwilling to acquit him as innocent let them give him up, though guilty, as a favor. But when Marcius himself, on the day appointed for the hearing, failed to appear, men's hearts were hardened against him. Condemned in his absence, he went into exile with the Volsci, uttering threats against his country, and even then breathing hostility. When he came among the Volsci they received him with a kindness which increased from one day to the next, in proportion as he allowed a greater hatred of his own people to appear, and was more and more frequently heard to utter both complaints and threats. His host was Attius Tullius, at that time by far the foremost of the Volscian name and ever unfriendly to the Romans. And so, spurred on, the one by his inveterate hatred and the other by fresh resentment, they took counsel together how they might make war on Rome. They believed that it would be no easy matter to induce the Volscian commons to take up the arms which they had so often unluckily essayed; the destruction of their young men in oft-repeated wars, and finally by the plague, had, they supposed, broken their spirit; artifice must be invoked, where hate had grown dull with lapse of time, that they might find some new cause of anger to exasperate men's hearts.

XXXVI. It so happened that at Rome preparations were making to repeat the Great Games.[33] The reason of the repetition was as follows: at an early hour of the day appointed for the games, before the show had begun, a certain householder had driven his slave, bearing a yoke, through the midst of the circus, scourging the culprit as he went. The games had then been begun, as though this circumstance had in no way affected their sanctity. Not long after, Titus Latinius, a plebeian, had a dream. He dreamt that Jupiter said that the leading dancer at the games[34] had not been to his liking; that unless there were a sumptuous repetition of the festival the City would be in danger; that Latinius was to go and announce this to the consuls. Though the man's conscience was by no means at ease, nevertheless the awe he felt at the majesty of the magistrates was too great; he was afraid of becoming a laughing-stock. Heavy was the price he paid for his hesitation, for a few days later he lost his son. Lest this sudden calamity should leave any uncertainty as to its cause in the mind of the wretched man, the same phantom appeared again before him in his dreams, and asked him, as he thought, whether he had been sufficiently repaid for spurning the gods; for a greater recompense was at hand unless he went quickly and informed the consuls. This brought the matter nearer home. Yet he still delayed and put off going, till a violent attack of illness suddenly laid him low. Then at last the anger of the gods taught him wisdom. And so, worn out with his sufferings, past and present, he called a council of his kinsmen and explained to them what he had seen and heard, how Jupiter had so often confronted him in his sleep, and how the threats and anger of the god had been instantly fulfilled in his own misfortunes. Then, with the unhesitating approval of all who were present, he was carried on a litter to the consuls in the Forum; and thence, by their command, to the Curia, where he had no sooner told the same story to the Fathers, greatly to the wonder of them all, when—lo, another miracle! For it is related that he who had been carried into the senate-house afflicted in all his members, returned home, after discharging his duty, on his own feet.

XXXVII. Games of the greatest possible splendor were decreed by the senate, and to see them came, at the suggestion of Attius Tullius, a host of Volsci. Before the beginning of the spectacle Tullius, in pursuance of the plan he and Marcius had formed at home, went to the consuls and told them that he had something of public importance which he wished to discuss with them in private. When the bystanders had been removed, "I am loath," he said, "to tell concerning my countrymen what may discredit them. Still I do not come to charge them with having committed any crime, but to put you on your guard lest they should commit one. The disposition of our people is far more fickle than I could wish. Many disasters have taught us the truth of this, since it is not to our own merit, but to your patience, that we owe our preservation. A great crowd of Volsci is now in Rome; there are games; the citizens will be intent upon the spectacle. I remember what the Sabine youths did in this City on the same opportunity arising; I tremble lest something ill-advised and rash may happen. It has seemed to me that both on our account and on yours I ought to tell you this beforehand, consuls. For my own part I intend to go home at once, lest being on the spot I might be implicated in some act or word and be compromised." With this he departed. The consuls laid before the senate this vague warning which came from so reliable a source. It was the source, as often happens, rather than the story, which induced them to take precautions, even though they might prove superfluous. The senate decreed that the Volsci should leave the City, and heralds were sent about to command them all to depart before nightfall. At first they were stricken with a great alarm, as they hurried this way and that to the houses of their hosts to get their things. But when they had started, their hearts swelled with indignation, that like malefactors and polluted persons, they should have been driven off from the games at a time of festival, and excluded, in a way, from intercourse with men and gods.

XXXVIII. As they journeyed on in an almost unbroken line, Tullius, who had gone ahead, arrived before them at the source of the Ferentina. There, when any of their chief men arrived, he met them with words of complaint and indignation. These leaders, eagerly drinking in the words with which he ministered to their anger, he conducted and, thanks to their influence, the rest of the throng also, to a field which lay below the road. There he launched out upon a speech like a general's harangue. "Though you should forget all else," he cried, "the ancient wrongs done by the Roman People and the disasters that have overtaken the Volscian race, with what feelings, pray, can you bear the insult which this day has brought to us, making our humiliation serve as the opening of their festival? Or did you not feel that they were triumphing over you today? That you furnished a spectacle to everybody when you departed—to the citizens, to the strangers, to all the neighboring nations? That your wives and children were made a mock in the eyes of the world? What of those who heard the words of the herald? What of those who saw us going away? What of those who have met this ignominious procession? What think you they all supposed, but that we were certainly attainted of some sin; that because, were we to be present at the spectacle, we should pollute the games and incur the god's displeasure—for that reason we were being expelled from the seat of the righteous and from their gathering and their council? Moreover, does it not occur to you that we are alive because we hastened to depart? if, indeed, this is a departure and not rather a flight. And this City—do you not regard it as a city of enemies, when if you had delayed there a single day, you would all have had to die? War has been declared upon you, and greatly shall they rue it who have been responsible, if you are men." So, their spontaneous anger fanned to a flame, they dispersed to their several homes, and, every man arousing his own people, they brought about a revolt of the entire Volscian name.

XXXIX. As generals for this war the nations all agreed in choosing Attius Tullius and Gnaeus Marcius, the Roman exile, who inspired rather more hope than did his colleague. This hope he by no means disappointed, so that it was easy to see that Rome's commanders were a greater source of strength to her than her armies were. Marching first to Circei, he drove out the Roman colonists from that city and turned it over, thus liberated, to the Volsci. He took Satricum, Longula, Polusca, and Corioli, places which the Romans had recently acquired. He then recovered Lavinium, and then, passing over by crossroads into the Latin Way, captured in succession Corbio, Vetelia, Trebium, Labici, and Pedum. From Pedum he finally led his army against Rome and, pitching his camp at the Cluilian Trenches, five miles from the city, laid waste the Roman territory from that base, sending out guards with the pillagers to preserve intact the farms of the patricians, whether from anger at the plebs, or to sow dissension between them and the Fathers. And no doubt it would have sprung up, so vehemently did the tribunes seek by their accusations to rouse the already headstrong commons against the nation's leaders, but dread of invasion, the strongest bond of harmony, tended to unite their feelings, however they might suspect and dislike one another. In this one point they were unable to agree, that the senate and the consuls saw no hope anywhere but in arms, while the plebs preferred anything to war. Spurius Nautius and Sextus Furius were now consuls.[35] While they were reviewing their levies and distributing garrisons about the walls and the other places where they had seen fit to place pickets and sentries, a great multitude of people demanding peace first terrified them with their rebellious clamor, and then forced them to call the senate together and propose the sending of envoys to Gnaeus Marcius. The Fathers consented to propose it when they saw that the plebeians were growing discouraged, and ambassadors were sent to Marcius to treat for peace. Stern was the answer they brought back. If the land of the Volsci were restored to them the question of peace could be taken up; if the Romans wished to enjoy the spoils of war without doing anything, he would forget neither the wrong his fellow-citizens had done him nor the kindness of his hosts, but would strive to show that exile had quickened his courage, not broken it. When the same envoys were sent back a second time, they were denied admittance to the camp. Even priests, wearing the appropriate fillets, are said to have gone as suppliants to the enemy's camp, where they were no more able than the envoys had been to alter the determination of Marcius.

XL. Then the married women gathered in large numbers at the house of Veturia, the mother of Coriolanus, and Volumnia, his wife. Whether this was public policy or woman's fear I cannot find out; in any case they prevailed with them that both Veturia, an aged woman, and Volumnia should take the two little sons of Marcius and go with them to the camp of the enemy; and that, since the swords of the men could not defend the City, the women should defend it with their prayers and tears. When they reached the camp, and the word came to Coriolanus that a great company of women was at hand, at first, as might have been expected of one whom neither the nation's majesty could move, as represented in its envoys, nor the awfulness of religion, as conveyed to heart and eye by the persons of her priests, he showed even greater obduracy in resisting women's tears. Then one of his friends, led by Veturia's conspicuous sadness to single her out from amongst the other women, as she stood between her son's wife and his babies, said: "Unless my eyes deceive me, your mother is here and your wife and children." Coriolanus started up like a madman from his seat, and running to meet his mother would have embraced her, but her entreaties turned to anger, and she said: "Suffer me to learn, before I accept your embrace, whether I have come to an enemy or a son; whether I am a captive or a mother in your camp. Is it this to which long life and an unhappy old age have brought me, that I should behold in you an exile and then an enemy? Could you bring yourself to ravage this country, which gave you birth and reared you? Did not your anger fall from you, no matter how hostile and threatening your spirit when you came, as you passed the boundary? Did it not come over you, when Rome lay before your eyes: 'Within those walls are my home and my gods, my mother, my wife, and my children?' So then, had I not been a mother Rome would not now be besieged! Had I no son I should have died a free woman, in a free land! But I can have nothing now to suffer which could be more disgraceful to you or more miserable for myself; nor, wretched though I am, shall I be so for long: it is these you must consider, for whom, if you keep on, untimely death or long enslavement is in store." The embraces of his wife and children, following this speech, and the tears of the entire company of women, and their lamentations for themselves and their country, at last broke through his resolution. He embraced his family and sent them back, and withdrew his forces from before the City. Having then led his army out of Rome's dominions he is said to have perished beneath the weight of resentment which this act caused, by a death which is variously described. I find in Fabius, by far the oldest authority, that Coriolanus lived on to old age. At least he reports that this saying was often on his lips, that exile was a far more wretched thing when one was old. There was no envy of the fame the women had earned, on the part of the men of Rome—so free was life in those days from disparagement of another's glory—and to preserve its memory the temple of Fortuna Muliebris was built and dedicated.[36]

Afterwards the Volsci again invaded Roman soil, in conjunction with the Aequi, but these would no longer put up with Attius Tullius for their general. Whereupon the dispute as to whether the Volsci or the Aequi should furnish a commander for the allied army, led to a quarrel, and this to a bloody battle. There the good fortune of the Roman People destroyed two hostile armies in one struggle, which was no less ruinous than it was obstinately fought.

The consulship of Titus Sicinius and Gaius Aquilius. Sicinius got the Volscian war for his command, and Aquilius that with the Hernici—for they too were up in arms. This year the Hernici were conquered, while the campaign against the Volsci was indecisive.

XLI. Spurius Cassius and Proculus Verginius were then made consuls. A treaty was struck with the Hernici, and two-thirds of their land was taken from them. Of this the consul Cassius proposed to divide one half amongst the Latins and the other half amongst the plebeians. To this gift he wished to add some part of that land which, he charged, was held by individuals, although it belonged to the state. Whereupon many of the Fathers, being themselves in possession of the land, took fright at the danger which threatened their interests. But the senators were also concerned on public grounds, namely, that the consul by his largesses should be building up an influence perilous to liberty. This was the first proposal for agrarian legislation, and from that day to within living memory it has never been brought up without occasioning the most serious disturbances. The other consul resisted the largess, and the Fathers supported him; nor were the commons solidly against him, for to begin with, they had taken offense that the bounty had been made general, being extended to include allies as well as citizens; and again, they often heard the consul Verginius declare in his speeches, as though he read the future, that destruction lurked in the gift proposed by his colleague; that those lands would bring servitude to the men who should receive them, and were being made a road to monarchy. For what reason had there been, he asked, in including the allies and the Latin name, and in restoring to the Hernici, who had been enemies a short time before, a third of the land which had been taken from them, if it were not that these tribes might have Cassius in the room of Coriolanus for their captain? Popular favor now began, to go over to the opponent and vetoer of the land-legislation. Each consul then began, as if vying with the other, to pamper the plebs. Verginius said that he would permit lands to be assigned, provided they were assigned to none but Roman citizens. Cassius, having by his proposed agrarian grants made a bid for the support of the allies and thereby lowered himself in the eyes of the Romans, desired to regain the affection of his fellow-citizens by another donation, and proposed that the money received from the Sicilian corn should be paid back to the people. But this the people spurned, as a downright attempt to purchase regal power; to such an extent did their instinctive suspicion of monarchy render them scornful of his gifts, as if they had possessed a superfluity of everything; and Cassius had no sooner laid down his office than he was condemned and executed, as all authorities agree. There are those who say that his father was responsible for his punishment: that he tried the case in his house, and that, after causing his son to be scourged and put to death, he consecrated to Ceres his personal property, from the proceeds of which a statue was made and inscribed "the gift of the Cassian family." I find in certain authors, and this is the more credible account, that the quaestors Caeso Fabius and Lucius Valerius brought him to trial for treason, and that he was found guilty by judgment of the people and his house pulled down by popular decree. Its site is now the open space in front of the temple of Tellus. But whether it was a domestic or a state trial, he was condemned in the consulship of Servius Cornelius and Quintus Fabius.

XLII. It was not long before the people forgot the anger they had felt against Cassius. The inherent attractiveness of the agrarian legislation appealed to them on its own account, when its author had been removed, and their desire for it was enhanced by the meanness of the Fathers, who after the defeat in that year of the Volsci and the Aequi defrauded the soldiers of their booty. Whatever was taken from the enemy Fabius sold and placed the proceeds in the public treasury. The Fabian name was hateful to the plebs, on the last consul's account; nevertheless the patricians succeeded in procuring the election of Caeso Fabius to that office, along with Lucius Aemilius. This increased the rancor of the plebeians, and by their seditions at home they brought about a foreign war. The war then caused domestic strife to be interrupted, while with one mind and purpose patricians and plebeians met the rebellious Volsci and Aequi and, led by Aemilius, defeated them in a successful action. Yet more of the enemy perished in flight than in the battle, so relentlessly did the cavalry pursue their routed forces. Castor's temple was dedicated the same year, on the fifteenth of July. It had been vowed during the Latin war by Postumius, the dictator. His son, being made duumvir for this special purpose, dedicated it.[37]

The desires of the plebs were this year again excited by the charms of the land-law. The tribunes of the plebs endeavored to recommend their democratic office by a democratic law, while the senators, who thought there was frenzy enough and to spare in the populace, without rewarding it, shuddered at the thought of land-grants and encouragements to rashness. The most strenuous of leaders were at hand for the senatorial opposition, in the persons of the consuls. Their party was therefore victorious and not only won an immediate success but, besides, elected as consuls for the approaching year Marcus Fabius, Caeso's brother, and one whom, on account of the prosecution of Spurius Cassius, the people hated even more, namely, Lucius Valerius. This year also there was a conflict with the tribunes. Nothing came of the legislation, and its supporters fell into contempt, from boasting of a measure which they could not carry through. The Fabii were thenceforward held in great repute, after their three successive consulships, which had all without interruption been subjected to the proof of struggles with the tribunes; accordingly the office, as if well invested, was permitted to remain sometime in that family.[38] War then broke out with Veii, and the Volsci revolted. But for foreign wars there was almost a superabundance of resources, and men misused them in quarrelling amongst themselves. To increase the general anxiety which was now felt, portents implying the anger of the gods were of almost daily occurrence in the City and the country. For this expression of divine wrath no other reason was alleged by the soothsayers, when they had enquired into it both officially and privately, sometimes by inspecting entrails and sometimes by observing the flight of birds, than the failure duly to observe the rites of religion. These alarms at length resulted in the condemnation of Oppia, a Vestal virgin, for unchastity, and her punishment.

XLIII. Quintus Fabius and Gaius Julius were then made consuls. This year there was no less discord at home, and the menace of war was greater. The Aequi took up arms, and the Veientes even made a foray into Roman territory. During the increasing anxiety occasioned by these campaigns Caeso Fabius and Spurius Furius were elected to the consulship. Ortona, a Latin city, was being besieged by the Aequi; while the Veientes, who by this time had their fill of rapine, were threatening to attack Rome itself. These alarms, though they should have restrained the animosity of the plebeians, actually heightened it; and they resumed their custom of refusing service, though not of their own initiative; for it was Spurius Licinius, tribune of the plebs, who, deeming that the moment had come for forcing a land-law on the patricians by the direst necessity, had undertaken to obstruct the preparations for war. But he drew upon his own head all the odium attaching to the tribunician office, nor did the consuls inveigh against him more fiercely than did his own colleagues, and with their help the consuls held a levy. Armies were enlisted for two wars at the same time; the command of one, which was to invade the Aequi, was given to Fabius, while with the other Furius was to oppose the Veientes. Against the Veientes nothing worth recording was accomplished; and in the Aequian campaign Fabius had somewhat more trouble with his fellow-Romans than with the enemy. That one man, the consul himself, preserved the state, which the army in its hatred of the consul would, so far as it was able, have betrayed. For when the consul, besides the many other instances of good generalship which he displayed in preparing for the war and in his conduct of it, had so drawn up the battle-line that a charge of the cavalry alone sufficed to rout the enemy's army, the foot refused to pursue the flying foe; nor could even their own sense of guilt—to say nothing of the exhortation of their hated general, nor even the thought of the immediate disgrace to all, and the danger they must presently incur if the enemy should recover his courage, compel them to quicken their pace, or, if nothing else, to stand in their ranks. Contrary to orders they retreated and returned to their camp, in such dejection that you would have supposed them beaten, now uttering execrations against their leader and now against the efficient services of the horse. Ruinous though their example was, the general found no remedy for it; so true is it that noble minds are oftener lacking in the qualities by which men govern their fellow-citizens than in those by which they conquer an enemy. The consul returned to Rome, having purchased more hatred of his irritated and embittered soldiers than won increase in military fame. Nevertheless the Fathers held out for the retention of the consulship in the Fabian family. Marcus Fabius was the man they elected, and they gave him Gnaeus Manlius as a colleague.

XLIV. This year also had a tribune who advocated a land-law, Tiberius Pontificius. He set out on the same path that Spurius Licinius had trodden, as though Licinius had been successful, and for a time obstructed the levy. The senators were again thrown into consternation, but Appius Claudius told them that the tribunician power had been overcome the year before, actually for the time being, and potentially forever, since a way had been discovered for employing its resources to its own undoing. For there would always be some tribune who would be willing to gain a personal victory over his colleague, and obtain the favor of the better element, while doing the nation a service. There would be a number of tribunes, if a number should be needed, who would be ready to help the consuls; and a single one was enough, though opposed to all the rest. Only let the consuls, and the leading senators as well, make a point of winning over, if not all, at any rate some of the tribunes to the state and the senate. Acting on the instructions of Appius, the Fathers began as a class to address the tribunes in a courteous and kindly manner; and those who were of consular rank, when it happened that any of them had any private claim upon an individual tribune, brought it about, in part by personal influence, in part by political, that those officials were disposed to use their powers for the good of the state; and four of them, as against one who would have hindered the general good, assisted the consuls to hold the muster.

The army then set out for a war with the Veientes, to whose help forces had rallied from every quarter of Etruria, not so much roused by goodwill towards the men of Veii as by hopes that civil discord might effect the downfall of the Roman state. And indeed the leading men in the councils of all the Etrurian peoples were wrathfully complaining that there would be no end to the power of the Romans unless factional quarrels should set them to fighting amongst themselves. They asserted that this was the only poison, the only decay which had been found to work upon opulent states, so as to make great empires transitory. For a long time the Romans had withstood this evil, thanks partly to the prudence of the senate, partly to the patience of the plebs; but they had now come to a crisis. Two states had been created out of one: each faction had its own magistrates, its own laws. At first, though they had a way of fiercely opposing the levies, yet when war began they had obeyed their generals. No matter what the condition of things in the City, so long as military discipline held it had been possible to make a stand; but now the fashion of disobeying magistrates was following the Roman soldier even to his camp. In their latest war, when the army was already drawn up for battle, and at the very instant of conflict, they had with one accord actually handed over the victory to the conquered Aequi, had deserted their standards, had left their general on the field, and had returned, against his orders, to their camp. Assuredly if her enemies pressed forward they could vanquish Rome by means of her own soldiers. There needed nothing more than to make a declaration and a show of war; Fate and the gods would of their own will do the rest. Such were the hopes which had led the Etruscans to take up arms, after many a shifting hazard of defeat and victory.

XLV. The Roman consuls also felt that they had nothing else to dread but their own forces and their own arms. The recollection of the heinous example set in the last war deterred them from offering battle in a situation where they would be in danger from two armies at the same time. Accordingly they kept within their camp, restrained by the thought of so grave a peril: time and circumstances would perhaps assuage the anger of the men and bring them to their senses. Their enemies the Veientes and the other Etruscans were for that reason the more in haste to act; they attempted to provoke the Romans to fight, at first by riding up to their camp and challenging them to come out, and finally, when they gained nothing by this, by shouting insults both at the consuls themselves and at the army. They said that their pretended want of harmony amongst themselves had been resorted to in order to conceal their fear, and that the consuls distrusted the courage of their men even more than their loyalty; it was a strange kind of mutiny where armed men were silent and inactive. To these taunts they added others upon the newness of their race and origin, partly false and partly true. This abuse, noisily uttered beneath the very rampart and the gates, was endured unconcernedly enough by the consuls. But the inexperienced rank and file, stirred now by indignation and now by shame, were diverted from the thought of their domestic troubles; they were unwilling that their enemies should go unpunished; they were unwilling that the patricians, that the consuls should obtain a success; hatred of the foe contended in their bosoms with hatred of their fellow-citizens. At length the former feeling got the upper hand, so proud and insolent was the jeering of the enemy. They gathered in crowds at the praetorium,[39] demanded battle, requested that the signal should be given. The consuls, as though considering the matter, put their heads together and conferred for a long time.

They desired to fight, but it was needful to keep back their desire and conceal it, that by opposition and delay they might stimulate to fury the already eager soldiery. The men were therefore told that the thing was premature, that the time for battle had not yet come; that they must keep within the camp. Then the consuls issued an order to abstain from fighting, declaring that if any man fought without orders they should treat him as an enemy. Dismissed with these words, the less inclination the soldiers discovered in the consuls the greater became their own eagerness for the fray. They were still further exasperated by the enemy, who were much bolder even than before, when the consuls' determination not to fight became known: it was clear that they could insult the Romans with impunity; their soldiers were not trusted with weapons, the affair would culminate in absolute mutiny, and the end of the Roman power had come. Relying on these convictions, they charged up to the gates, flung gibes at their defenders, and scarcely refrained from assaulting the camp. At this the Romans could no longer brook their insults; from all over the camp they came running to the consuls. There were no more cautious requests, preferred through the chief centurions, but on all sides arose a general clamor. The time was ripe; nevertheless the consuls hung back. Then Fabius, when his colleague, beginning to fear mutiny, was on the point of yielding to the growing tumult, commanded silence by a trumpet-blast and said: "I know, Gnaeus Manlius, that these men have the power to conquer, but their will to do so I know not; and for this they are themselves to blame. I am therefore resolved and determined not to give the signal unless they swear that they will return victorious from this engagement. Once, in a battle, the soldiers betrayed a Roman consul: they will never betray the gods." There was a centurion named Marcus Flavoleius, who had been among the foremost in demanding battle. "I will return victorious from the field, Marcus Fabius," he cried, and invoked the wrath of Father Jupiter, Mars Gradivus, and the other gods, if he failed to keep his vow. The same pledge was then taken in order by the entire army, each man invoking its penalties upon himself. When they had sworn, the signal sounded. They armed and entered the fight, angry and confident. Now let the Etruscans fling their taunts! Now—they all cried—now, when they were armed, let the lip-bold enemy face them! On that day they all showed splendid courage, both commoners and nobles, but the Fabian name was especially distinguished. In the course of many political struggles they had estranged the plebs, and they resolved to regain their goodwill in that battle.

XLVI. The line was drawn up, nor did the Veientes and the Etruscan levies shun the encounter. They felt almost certain that the Romans would no more fight with them than they had fought with the Aequi. That they might even be guilty of some greater enormity, exasperated as they were, and possessed of a critical opportunity, was not too much to hope. But it turned out quite otherwise. For there had never been a war when the Romans went into battle with a keener hostility—so embittered had they been, on the one hand by the enemy's insults, on the other by the procrastination of the consuls. The Etruscans had barely had time to deploy when their enemies, who in the first excitement had rather cast their javelins at random than fairly aimed them, were already come to sword-strokes at close quarters, where fighting is the fiercest. The Fabian clan was conspicuous among the foremost, a spectacle and encouragement to their fellow-citizens. One of them, the Quintus Fabius who had been consul three years before, was leading the attack on the closely marshalled Veientes, when a Tuscan, exulting in his strength and skill at arms, caught him unawares in the midst of a crowd of his enemies and drove his sword through his breast. As the blade was withdrawn Fabius fell headlong upon his wound. It was but the fall of one man, but both armies felt it; and the Romans were giving way at that point, when Marcus Fabius the consul leaped over the prostrate corpse and, covering himself with his target, cried, "Was this your oath, men, that you would return to your camp in flight? Do you then fear the most dastardly of foes more than Jupiter and Mars, by whom you swore? But I, though I have sworn no oath, will either return victorious or fall fighting here by you, Quintus Fabius!" To this speech of the consul Caeso Fabius, consul of the year before, made answer, "Think you that your words will persuade them to fight, brother? The gods will persuade them, by whom they have sworn. And let us, as is meet for nobles, as is worthy of the name of Fabius, kindle by fighting rather than by exhortation the courage of our soldiers!" With that the two Fabii rushed into the press with levelled spears and carried the whole line forward with them.

XLVII. Thus the fortune of the day was retrieved in one part of the field. On the other wing Gnaeus Manlius the consul was urging on the fight with no less vigor, when almost the same thing happened. For as Quintus Fabius had done on the other flank, so here the consul Manlius was personally leading the attack upon the enemy, whom he had almost routed, for his soldiers followed him valiantly, when he was severely wounded and retired from the fighting line. His men believed him to be dead, and faltered; and they would have yielded the position, had not the other consul ridden up at a gallop, with some few troops of horse, and calling out that his colleague was alive, and that he himself had defeated and routed the other wing and was come to help them, in that way put a stop to their wavering. Manlius also showed himself among them, helping to restore the line; and the soldiers, recognizing the features of their two consuls, plucked up courage. At the same time the battle-line of the enemy was now less strong, for, relying on their excess of numbers, they had withdrawn their reserves and dispatched them to storm the Roman camp. There, having forced an entrance without encountering much opposition, they were frittering away their time, their thoughts more taken up with the booty than with the battle, when the Roman reserves, which had been unable to withstand the first onset, sent word to the consuls how things stood, and then closed up their ranks, returned to the praetorium, and of themselves resumed the battle. Meanwhile Manlius the consul had ridden back to the camp, and by posting men at all the gates had cut off the enemy's egress. In desperation at this turn the Etruscans had been inflamed to the point rather of madness than of recklessness. For when, as they rushed in whatever direction there seemed a prospect of escape, they had made several charges to no purpose, one band of youths made a dash at the consul himself, whose arms made him conspicuous. Their first discharge of javelins was parried by the soldiers who surrounded him, but after that there was no withstanding their violence. The consul fell, mortally wounded, and all about him fled. The Etruscans grew more reckless than before; the Romans were driven, quaking with terror, right across the camp, and their case would have been desperate, had not the lieutenants caught up the body of the consul and opened a way for the enemy by one of the gates. By that they burst forth, and escaping in a disordered column, fell in the way of the other, the victorious consul, where they were again cut to pieces, and dispersed in all directions. A victory of great importance had been won, but it was saddened by the death of two so famous men. The consul therefore made answer to the senate, when it would have voted him a triumph, that if the army could triumph without its general, its services in that war had been so remarkable that he would readily grant his consent; as for himself, when his family was in mourning for the death of Quintus Fabius his brother, and the state was half orphaned by the loss of the other consul, he would not accept a laurel which was blighted with national and private sorrow. No triumph ever celebrated was more famous than was his refusal to accept a triumph, so true is it that a season-able rejection of glory sometimes but increases it. The consul then solemnized, one after the other, the funerals of his colleague and his brother, and pronounced the eulogy of each; but while yielding their meed of praise to them, he gained for himself the very highest praises. Nor was he unmindful of that policy which he had adopted in the beginning of his consulship, of winning the affections of the plebs, but billeted the wounded soldiers on the patricians, to be cared for. To the Fabii he assigned the largest number, nor did they anywhere receive greater attention. For this the Fabii now began to enjoy the favor of the people, nor was this end achieved by aught but a demeanor wholesome for the state.

XLVIII. The senators were now therefore not more forward than the plebeians in choosing Caeso Fabius to be consul, along with Titus Verginius. On taking office his first concern was neither war nor the raising of troops nor anything else, save that the prospect of harmony which had been already partly realized should ripen at the earliest possible moment into a good understanding between the patricians and the plebs. He therefore proposed at the outset of his term that before one of the tribunes should rise up and advocate a land-law, the Fathers themselves should anticipate him by making it their own affair and bestowing the conquered territory upon the plebs with the utmost impartiality; for it was right that they should possess it by whose blood and toil it had been won. The senators scorned the proposal, and some even complained that too much glory was spoiling and dissipating that vigorous intellect which Caeso had once possessed. In the sequel there were no outbreaks of strife and faction in the City, but the Latins were plagued with incursions of the Aequi. Thither Caeso was dispatched with an army, and passed over into the Aequians' own country to lay it waste. The Aequi retired to their towns and kept within their walls. For this reason there was no memorable battle.

But the Veientes inflicted a defeat on the Romans owing to the rashness of the other consul; and the army would have been destroyed if Caeso Fabius had not come, in the nick of time, to its rescue. Thenceforward there was neither peace nor war with the Veientes, but something very like freebooting. In the face of the Roman legions they would retreat into their city; when they perceived the legions to be withdrawn they would make raids upon the fields, evading war by a semblance of peace, and peace in turn by war. Hence it was impossible either to let the whole matter go or to end it. Other wars, too, were immediately threatening—like the one with the Aequi and the Volsci, who would observe peace only so long as the suffering involved in their latest defeat was passing away, or were soon to be begun, by the always hostile Sabines and all Etruria. But the enmity of the Veientes, persistent rather than perilous, and issuing in insults oftener than in danger, kept the Romans in suspense, for they were never permitted to forget it or to turn their attention elsewhere. Then the Fabian clan went before the senate, and the consul said, speaking for the clan: "A standing body of defenders rather than a large one is required, Conscript Fathers, as you know, for the war with Veii. Do you attend to the other wars, and assign to the Fabii the task of opposing the Veientes. We undertake that the majesty of the Roman name shall be safe in that quarter. It is our purpose to wage this war as if it were our own family feud, at our private costs: the state may dispense with furnishing men and money for this cause." The thanks of the Fathers were voted with enthusiasm. The consul came out from the senate-house, and escorted by a column of the Fabii, who had halted in the vestibule of the curia while awaiting the senate's decision, returned to his house. After receiving the command to present themselves armed next day at the consul's threshold, they dispersed to their homes.

XLIX. The news spreads to every part of the City and the Fabii are lauded to the skies. Men tell how a single family has taken upon its shoulders the burden of a state, how the war with Veii has been turned over to private citizens and private arms. If there were two other clans of equal strength in the City, the one might undertake the Volsci, the other the Aequi, and the Roman People might enjoy the tranquillity of peace, while all the neighboring nations were being subdued. On the following day the Fabii arm and assemble at the designated place. The consul, coming forth in the cloak of a general,[40] sees his entire clan drawn up in his vestibule, and being received into their midst gives the order to march. Never did an army march through the City less in number or more distinguished by the applause and the wonder of men: three hundred and six soldiers, all patricians, all of one blood, no one of whom you would have rejected as a leader, and who would have made an admirable senate in any period, were going out to threaten the existence of the Veientine nation with the resources of a single house. They were followed by a throng partly made up of people belonging to them, their kinsmen and close friends, whose thoughts were busy with no mean matters, whether of hope or of fear, but with boundless possibilities; partly of those who were moved with concern for the commonwealth, and were beside themselves with enthusiasm and amazement. "Go," they cry, "in your valor, go with good fortune, and crown your undertaking with success as great!" They bid them look forward to receiving consulships at their hands for this work, and triumphs, and all rewards and all honors. As they pass by the Capitol and the citadel and the other temples, they beseech whatever gods present themselves to their eyes and their thoughts to attend that noble band with blessings and prosperity, and restore them soon in safety to their native land and their kindred. Their prayers were uttered in vain. Setting out by the Unlucky Way,[41] the right arch of the Porta Carmentalis, they came to the river Cremera, a position which seemed favorable for the erection of a fort.

Lucius Aemilius and Gaius Servilius were then chosen consuls. And so long as nothing more than plundering was afoot the Fabii were not only an adequate garrison for the fort, but in all that region where the Tuscan territory marches with the Roman they afforded universal security to their own countrymen and annoyance to the enemy, by ranging along the border on both sides. Then came a brief interruption to these depredations, while the men of Veii, having called in an army from Etruria, attacked the post on the Cremera, and the Roman legions, led thither by Lucius Aemilius the consul, engaged them in a pitched battle; though in truth the Veientes had scarcely time to draw up a battle-line, for at the first alarm, while the ranks were falling in behind the standards and the reserves were being posted, a division of Roman cavalry made a sudden charge on their flank and deprived them of the power not only of attacking first, but even of standing their ground. And so they were driven back upon Saxa Rubra, where they had their camp, and sued for peace. It was granted, but their instinctive fickleness caused them to weary of the pact before the Roman garrison was withdrawn from the Cremera.

L. Again the Fabii were pitted against the people of Veii. No preparations had been made for a great war, yet not only were raids made upon farming lands, and surprise attacks upon raiding parties, but at times they fought in the open field and in serried ranks; and a single clan of the Roman People often carried off the victory from that most mighty state, for those days, in all Etruria. At first the Veientes bitterly resented this; but they presently adopted a plan, suggested by the situation, for trapping their bold enemy, and they even rejoiced as they saw that the frequent successes of the Fabii were causing them to grow more rash. And so they now and then drove flocks in the way of the invaders, as if they had come there by accident; and the country folk would flee from their farms and leave them deserted; and rescuing parties of armed men, sent to keep off pillagers, would flee before them in a panic more often feigned than real. By this time the Fabii had conceived such scorn for the enemy that they believed themselves invincible and not to be withstood, no matter what the place or time. This confidence so won upon them that on catching sight of some flocks at a distance from the Cremera, across a wide interval of plain, they disregarded the appearance here and there of hostile arms, and ran down to capture them. Their rashness carried them on at a swift pace past an ambuscade which had been laid on both sides of their very read. They had scattered this way and that and were seizing the flocks, which had dispersed in all directions, as they do if terrified, when suddenly the ambush rose up, and enemies were in front and on every side of them. First the shout which echoed all along the Etruscan line filled them with consternation, and then the javelins began to fall upon them from every quarter; and as the Etruscans drew together and the Romans were now fenced in by a continuous line of armed men, the harder the enemy pressed them the smaller was the space within which they themselves were forced to contract their circle, a thing which clearly revealed both their own fewness and the vast numbers of the Etruscans, whose ranks were multiplied in the narrow space. The Romans then gave up the fight which they had been directing equally at every point, and all turned in one direction. Thither, by dint of main strength and arms, they forced their way with a wedge. Their road led up a gentle acclivity. There they at first made a stand; presently, when their superior position had afforded them time to breathe and to collect their spirits after so great a fright, they actually routed the troops which were advancing to dislodge them; and a handful of men, with the aid of a good position, were winning the victory, when the Veientes who had been sent round by the ridge emerged upon the crest of the hill, thus giving the enemy the advantage again. The Fabii were all slain to a man, and their fort was stormed. Three hundred and six men perished, as is generally agreed; one, who was little more than a boy in years,[42] survived to maintain the Fabian stock, and so to afford the very greatest help to the Roman People in its dark hours, on many occasions, at home and in the field.

LI. When this disaster befel, Gaius Horatius and Titus Menenius had begun their consulship. Menenius was at once sent out to confront the Etruscans, elated by their victory. Again the Roman arms were unsuccessful, and Janiculum was taken by the enemy. They would also have laid siege to Rome, which was suffering not only from war but from a scarcity of corn—for the Etruscans had crossed the Tiber—had not the consul Horatius been recalled from the Volscian country; and so nearly did that invasion approach the very walls of the City that battles were fought first at the temple of Hope, where the result was indecisive, and again at the Colline Gate. There, although the advantage to the Roman side was but slight, still the engagement restored their old-time spirit to the troops and made them the better soldiers for the battles that were to come.

Aulus Verginius and Spurius Servilius were made consuls. After the defeat the Veientes had suffered in the last fight, they avoided a battle and took to pillaging. From Janiculum, as from a citadel, they sent out expeditions far and wide into the territory of the Romans; there was no security anywhere for flocks or country-folk. After a time they were caught by the same trick with which they had caught the Fabii. Having pursued the flocks which had been driven out here and there on purpose to lure them on, they plunged into an ambush, and as their numbers exceeded those of the Fabii so did their losses. This disaster threw them into a violent rage, which proved the cause and the beginning of a greater reverse. For they crossed the Tiber in the night and assaulted the camp of the consul Servilius. There they were routed with heavy losses and regained Janiculum with difficulty. Forthwith the consul himself crossed the Tiber and fortified a camp beneath the hill. Next day at dawn, partly because he was emboldened by the successful battle of the day before, but more because the want of corn drove him to the rashest kind of measures, provided only they were speedy, he was so reckless as to lead his army up Janiculum to the enemy's camp, and after suffering a more disgraceful repulse than he had administered the day before, owed his own rescue and that of his army to the arrival of his colleague. Caught between two lines, the Etruscans turned their backs first on one and then on the other, and were cut down with great slaughter. Thus the Veientine invasion was defeated by a lucky temerity.

LII. There came to the City with the return of peace a relaxation in the corn-market; for not only was grain imported from
Campania, but now that each had ceased to fear for his own future
want, men brought out the stores which they had concealed. As a
consequence of plenty and idleness a spirit of license again began
to affect men's minds, and they began to seek at home for the old
troubles which were no longer to be met with abroad. The tribunes
roused the plebs to madness with their usual poison, a land-law.
The Fathers resisted, but the tribunes incited the people against
them, not as a body merely, but as individuals. Quintus Considius
and Titus Genucius, the proposers of the agrarian measure, cited
Titus Menenius to appear for trial.[43] He had incurred the dislike
of the plebs owing to the loss of the outpost on the Cremera, when
he as consul had occupied a permanent camp not far away; and
this unpopularity was his undoing, though the senators exerted
themselves in his behalf no less than they had done for Coriolanus,
and though the favor enjoyed by his father Agrippa had not yet
passed away. In respect to the penalty the tribunes showed restraint;
though they had charged him with a capital offense, they fixed the
fine of the condemned at two thousand *asses*. But it cost him his life;
they say that he could not endure the shame and grief, and from
this cause fell ill and died.

Another man was then put upon his trial, namely Spurius
Servilius. He had laid down the consulship and been succeeded by
Gaius Nautius and Publius Valerius, when he was cited, in the very
beginning of the year, by the tribunes Lucius Caedicius and Titus
Statius. Unlike Menenius, he did not meet the attacks of the tribunes
with entreaties, preferred by himself or the senators, but with high
confidence in his innocence and popularity. He, too, was accused
in connection with the battle against the Etruscans at Janiculum.
But the fiery courage of the man had not been more in evidence
in the nation's hour of peril than it was then in his own, and he
confuted not only the tribunes but the plebs, upbraiding them, in
a daring speech, with the condemnation and death of Menenius,
to whose father, he declared, the plebs formerly owed their restoration and the possession of those very magistrates and laws which

were the tools of their cruelty. This boldness swept away the danger. He was helped, too, by Verginius, his colleague, who, being called as a witness, shared his own credit with Servilius. But the trial of Menenius stood him in even better stead, so great a revulsion of feeling had set in.

LIII. Domestic strife was at an end; but war broke out with the Veientes, with whom the Sabines had united their arms. Publius Valerius the consul was dispatched to Veii with an army to which had been added auxiliaries from the Latins and the Hernici. He at once advanced upon the Sabine camp, which had been established in front of the walls of their allies, and threw the enemy into such confusion that, while they were running out in small groups, someone way and some another, to repel the attack of the Romans, he captured the gate against which he had directed his first assault. What followed within the stockade was a massacre rather than a battle. The sounds of confusion in the camp penetrated even to the city, and the frightened inhabitants ran hastily to their weapons, as though Veii had been surprised. Some went to the rescue of the Sabines, others assailed the Romans, who were wholly preoccupied with the camp. For a moment the Romans were disconcerted and thrown into disorder; then they, too, faced both ways and made a stand, and the horse which the consul sent into the fight dispersed and routed the Etruscans. In one and the same hour two armies, two of the greatest and most powerful neighboring nations, were defeated.

While these victories were being won at Veii, the Volsci and the Aequi had encamped on Latin soil, and had laid waste the country. These the Latins, acting independently, with the assistance of the Hernici, but without either general or aid from Rome, despoiled of their camp. Immense booty, in addition to property of their own which they recovered, fell into their hands. Nevertheless a consul, Gaius Nautius, was sent from Rome against the Volsci. The precedent, I suppose, of allies waging wars, without a Roman commander and army, by means of their own forces and their own strategy, was not welcome. There was no species of disaster or indignity which was not visited upon the Volsci, yet they could not be forced into giving battle.

LIV. Lucius Furius and Gaius Manlius were the next consuls. To Manlius fell the command against the Veientes. But there was no war; a truce for forty years was granted, at their solicitation, and corn and a money-indemnity were exacted of them. The foreign peace was immediately succeeded by quarrels at home. The land-law with which the tribunes goaded the plebs excited them to the pitch of madness. The consuls, not a jot intimidated by the condemnation of Menenius, not a jot by the danger of Servilius, resisted the measure with the utmost violence. As their term expired, Gnaeus Genucius, a plebeian tribune, haled them to trial.

Lucius Aemilius and Opiter Verginius entered upon the consulship. Vopiscus Julius I find given as consul in certain annals, instead of Verginius. This year—whoever its consuls were—Furius and Manlius went about among the people as men accused, in garments of mourning, seeking out the younger patricians, as well as the plebeians. They advised them, they warned them to forbear from office-holding and the administration of the public business; as for the consular fasces, the purple-bordered toga, and the curule chair, these they should regard in no other light than as the pageantry of burial; for splendid insignia, like the fillets placed on victims, doomed the wearer to death. But if the consulship was so alluring to them, let them recognize at once that it had been fettered and enslaved by the might of the tribunes; that the consul, as though an attendant upon those officials, must be subject in all he did to their beck and call; if he should bestir himself, if he should show consideration for the patricians, if he should believe that the state comprised any other element than the plebs—let him call to mind the exile of Gnaeus Marcius, the condemnation of Menenius and his death. Fired by these speeches, the senators began to hold councils, no longer publicly, but in private, where the people could not learn their plans. In these deliberations there was but one guiding principle, that by fair means or foul the defendants must be got off. The more truculent a suggestion was, the greater was the favor it evoked, and an agent was not wanting for the most daring crime. Well then, on the day of the trial the plebeians were in the Forum, on tiptoe with expectation. At first they were filled with amazement because the tribune did not come down;[44] then, when at length his delay began to look suspicious, they supposed he had been frightened away by the nobles, and fell to complaining of his desertion and betrayal of the people's cause; finally, those who had presented themselves at the tribune's vestibule brought back word that he had been found dead in his house. When this report had spread through all the gathering, the crowd, like an army which takes to flight at the fall of its general, melted away on every side. The tribunes were particularly dismayed, for the death of their colleague warned them how utterly ineffectual to protect them were the laws that proclaimed their sanctity. Nor did the senators place a proper restraint upon their satisfaction; so far, indeed, was anyone from repenting of the guilty deed that even the innocent desired to be thought its authors, and men openly asserted that chastisement must be employed to curb the power of the tribunes.

LV. Immediately following this pernicious victory a levy was proclaimed, which the timorousness of the tribunes allowed the consuls to push through without ever a veto. But this time the commons were fairly roused to anger, more by the silence of the tribunes than by the consuls' power. They declared that it was all up with their liberty; that men had gone back to their old ways; that with Genucius the tribunician power had suffered death and burial. They must adopt another course and other plans to resist the patricians; but the only way was this: that the plebs should undertake their own defense, since they had no one else to help them. Twenty-four lictors were all the retinue of the consuls, and even these were plebeians. Nothing was more contemptible or weaker, if there were any to contemn; it was every man's own imagination that made them great and awe-inspiring. They had incited one another with arguments of this sort when the consuls sent a lictor to arrest Volero Publilius, a plebeian, who, on the ground that he had been a centurion, denied their right to make him a common soldier.[45] Volero called upon the tribunes. When no one came to aid him, the consuls gave orders to strip the man and get out the rods. "I appeal," cried Volero, "to the people, since the tribunes would rather a Roman citizen should be scourged with rods before their eyes than themselves be murdered in their beds by you." But the more boldly he shouted the more roughly the lictor fell to tearing off his clothes and stripping him. Then Volero, who was himself a powerful man and was helped by those he had called to his assistance, beat off the lictor and, choosing the place where the uproar of his sympathisers was the angriest, plunged into the thick of the crowd, calling out, "I appeal, and implore the protection of the plebs; help, citizens! Help, fellow-soldiers! It is useless for you to wait for the tribunes, who themselves stand in need of aid from you." In their excitement men made ready as if to fight a battle, and it was evident that anything might happen, that nobody would respect any right, whether public or private. The consuls, exposed to this furious tempest, were quickly convinced of the insecurity of majesty when unaccompanied with force. The lictors were roughly handled and their rods were broken, while the consuls themselves were driven out of the Forum into the Curia, with no means of knowing how far Volero might use his victory. Afterwards, when the uproar began to die away, they summoned the Fathers into the senate-house and complained of the insults they had suffered, the violence of the plebs, and Volero's outrageous conduct. Though many daring opinions were expressed, the wishes of the older men prevailed, who had no mind to a conflict between an angry senate and a reckless plebs.

LVI. Volero, having been taken into favor by the plebs, was at the next election made plebeian tribune for that year which had Lucius Pinarius and Publius Furius for consuls. And contrary to the expectation of all, who believed that he would employ his tribuneship in persecuting the consuls of the preceding year, he set the general welfare above his private grievance, and without attacking the consuls by so much as a word, brought a bill before the people providing that plebeian magistrates should be chosen in the tribal assembly.[46] It was no trivial matter which he proposed under this form, which at first sight appeared so harmless, but one that completely deprived the patricians of the power of using their clients' votes to select what tribunes they liked. This measure was extremely welcome to the plebs; the Fathers opposed it with all their might, yet the only effectual resistance—to wit, a veto by some member of the tribunician college—neither consuls nor nobles were sufficiently influential to command. Nevertheless the legislation, which its very importance rendered difficult, was drawn out by party strife to the end of the year. The plebs re-elected Volero tribune: the senators, thinking the quarrel was sure to proceed to extremities, made Appius Claudius, son of Appius, consul, a man whose unpopularity with the plebs and hostility towards them went back to the struggles between their fathers. For colleague they gave him Titus Quinctius.

The new year was no sooner begun than discussion of the law took precedence of everything else, and it was urged not only by its author, Volero, but by his colleague Laetorius as well, whose advocacy of it was at once fresher and more acrimonious. He was emboldened by the great reputation he enjoyed as a soldier, since no one of that generation surpassed him in physical prowess. While Volero spoke of nothing but the law, and forbore to inveigh against the consuls' persons, Laetorius launched out into an arraignment of Appius and his family, as most cruel and arrogant towards the Roman plebs. But when he strove to show that the patricians had elected, not a consul, but an executioner, to harass and torture the plebeians, the inexperienced tongue of the soldier was inadequate to express his audacity and spirit. Accordingly when words began to fail him he cried, "Since speech is not so easy for me, Quirites, as it is to make good what I have spoken, be at hand tomorrow. I will either die here in your sight or carry through the law." The tribunes were the first on the scene next day, and possessed themselves of the rostra;[47] the consuls and nobles took their stand in the assembly, with the purpose of obstructing the passage of the law. Laetorius ordered the removal of all but those who were voting. The youthful nobles stayed where they were and would not give way at the officer's behest. Then certain of them were ordered by Laetorius to be seized. The consul Appius declared that the tribune had no authority over anybody but a plebeian, seeing that he was not a magistrate of the people, but of the plebs; and even if he were, he could not, consistently with the custom of the Fathers, command the removal of anyone, by virtue of his authority, since the formula ran thus: "If it seems good to you, depart, Quirites." It was an easy matter to throw Laetorius into a passion by these contemptuous remarks about his rights. It was therefore in a blaze of anger that the tribune dispatched his attendant to the consul; while the consul sent his lictor to the tribune, crying out that Laetorius was a private citizen, without power, and no magistrate; and the tribune would have been mishandled, had not the whole assembly rallied fiercely to his support against the consul, while men rushed into the Forum from all over the City, in an excited throng. Still, Appius was obstinately holding out, despite the fury of the tempest, and a sanguinary battle would have ensued, if Quinctius, the other consul, had not entrusted the senators of consular rank with the task of getting his colleague out of the Forum, by force, if they could not achieve it otherwise; while he himself now appealed to the raging populace with soothing entreaties, and now besought the tribunes to dismiss the council. Let them give their anger time: time would not rob them of their power, but would add wisdom to their strength; the Fathers would be subject to the people, and the consul to the Fathers.

LVII. It was hard for Quinctius to still the plebs; much harder for the senators to quiet the other consul. At length the council of the plebs was adjourned, and the consuls convened the senate. At this meeting alternating hope and fear gave rise to conflicting opinions. But in proportion as their passions cooled with the lapse of time and gave way to deliberation, their minds more and more revolted from the struggle; insomuch that they passed a vote of thanks to Quinctius, because it was due to him that the quarrel had been abated. They desired Appius to be content that the majesty of the consul should be no greater than was compatible with harmony in the state, pointing out that while tribunes and consuls were each striving to carry things his own way there was no strength left in the nation at large, and the commonwealth was torn and mangled, the question being rather in whose power it was than how it might be safe. Appius, on the other hand, called gods and men to witness that the state was being betrayed through cowardice, and abandoned; that it was not the consul who was failing the senate, but the senate the consul; that harder terms were being accepted than had been accepted on the Sacred Mount. Nevertheless he was borne down by the senate's unanimity and held his peace. The law was passed without opposition.

LVIII. Then for the first time tribunes were elected in the tribal assembly. That their number was also increased by three, as if there had been only two before, is stated by Piso. He also gives the names of the tribunes: Gnaeus Siccius, Lucius Numitorius, Marcus Duillius, Spurius Icilius, Lucius Maecilius.

While Rome was thus distracted, the Volsci and the Aequi began war. They had laid waste the fields in order that the plebeians, if they should secede, might find a refuge with them.[48] Then, when the matter was settled, they withdrew their camp. Appius Claudius was sent against the Volsci; to Quinctius fell the command against the Aequi. In his conduct in the field Appius displayed the same violence that he had shown in Rome, and it now had freer play because it was not hampered by the tribunes. He hated the plebs with a hatred that surpassed his father's: What? Had he been beaten by them? Was it in his consulship, who had been chosen as pre-eminently fitted to resist the tribunician power, that a law had been passed which former consuls had prevented, with less effort and by no means so much hope of success on the part of the patricians? His wrath and indignation at this thought drove his fierce spirit to torment the army with a savage exercise of authority. Yet he was unable by any violence to subdue them, so deeply had their spirits drunk of opposition. Sloth, idleness, neglect, and obstinacy were in all they did. Neither shame nor fear restrained them. If he wished the column to advance more rapidly they deliberately retarded their pace; if he stood by to encourage their work, they would all relax the industry they had manifested of their own accord. In his presence they sunk their gaze; as he passed by they cursed him under their breath; till that proud spirit, which the hatred of the plebs had never broken, was at times disturbed. After exhausting every species of severity without effect, he would have no more to do with the men; the centurions, he said, had corrupted the army, and he sometimes sneeringly dubbed them "tribunes of the plebs" and "Voleros."

LIX. Everyone of these circumstances was known to the Volsci, and they pressed their enemy the harder, hoping that the Roman army would exhibit the same spirited opposition to Appius which it had evinced towards the consul Fabius. But Appius found his men far more unruly than had Fabius; for not only were they unwilling to conquer, as the Fabian army had been, but they wished to be conquered. Being drawn out into battle-order, they basely fled and sought their camp; nor did they make a stand until they saw the Volsci advancing against their fortifications and inflicting a disgraceful slaughter upon their rearguard. This compelled them to exert themselves and fight, with the result that the enemy was dislodged from the stockade in the moment of victory. Yet it was evident enough that the capture of their camp was the only thing at which the Roman soldiers balked, and that elsewhere they rejoiced at their own defeat and ignominy. These things in no wise daunted the haughty spirit of Appius. But when he would have gone further and have vented his rage upon the army, and was issuing orders for an assembly, the lieutenants and tribunes gathered hurriedly about him and warned him upon no account to seek a test of his authority, when its effectiveness all depended on the goodwill of those obeying it. The men, they reported, were saying that they would not go to be harangued, and everywhere voices were overheard demanding that the camp be removed from Volscian territory. The victorious enemy had a little while before been almost in their gates and on their wall, and a great disaster was not merely to be apprehended, but was openly hovering before their eyes. Giving way at last, since the soldiers were gaining nothing but a postponement of their punishment, he relinquished the idea of an assembly, and commanded a march for the following day. At daybreak he caused the signal for departure to be sounded on the trumpet. At the very instant when the column was getting clear of the camp, the Volsci, as though set in motion by the same signal, fell upon their rear. Thence the confusion spread to the van, and the panic so disordered the standards and the ranks that it was impossible either to hear commands or to form a line. Nobody thought of anything but flight, and so demoralised was the rout, as the men escaped over fallen bodies and discarded weapons, that the enemy sooner ceased to pursue than the Romans to flee. When at last the soldiers had been collected from their scattered flight, the consul, who had followed his men in a vain attempt to call them back, pitched his camp on friendly soil. Then he summoned an assembly and soundly rated them, not without reason, as an army which had been false to military discipline and had deserted its standards. Asking them all in turn where their arms and where their standards were, he caused the unarmed soldiers and the standard-bearers who had lost their standards, and in addition to these the centurions and the recipients of a double ration[49] who had quitted their ranks, to be scourged with rods and beheaded; of the remaining number every tenth man was selected by lot for punishment.

LX. To contrast with all this, in the Aequian campaign there subsisted between consul and soldiers an emulation of goodwill and kindness. Not only was it natural to Quinctius to be more gentle, but the unfortunate harshness of his colleague had given him the more reason to be content with his own disposition. Against this complete harmony between commander and army the Aequi ventured no opposition, but suffered their enemies to devastate their fields at will; and in fact no previous war had ever yielded a larger booty from that country. This was all given to the troops, and to the spoils were added encomiums, which are no less efficacious than rewards in rejoicing a soldier's heart. Not only their leader, but for their leader's sake the Fathers, too, were looked upon with greater kindness by the army when they returned. They declared that to them the senate had given a parent, to the other army a tyrant.

Varying fortune in war, grievous discord at home and in the field, had characterized the year just ended; but it was chiefly distinguished by the tribal assembly, a matter more important because the men had won a victory in the struggle which they had undertaken than in its practical results; for the loss of dignity to the assembly itself, caused by the removal from it of the patricians, was greater than the gain in strength by the plebeians or the loss of it by the Fathers.

LXI. A stormier year succeeded, under the consuls Lucius Valerius and Titus Aemilius, partly owing to strife between the classes about the land-law, partly to the trial of Appius Claudius. He was the bitterest opponent of the law, and was upholding the claim of those who had possession of the public domain as if he had been a third consul, when Marcus Duillius and Gnaeus Siccius lodged an accusation against him. Never before had a defendant whom the plebs so detested been brought to trial before the people, burdened as he was with men's hatred, both of himself and of his father. The patricians, for their part, had not lightly put forth such exertions in behalf of any man. They felt that the champion of the senate and the guardian of their own dignity, who had stood firm against all sorts of tribunician and plebeian outbreaks, though he had possibly gone too far in the heat of the struggle, was being exposed to the angry commons. Alone amongst the Fathers, Appius Claudius himself regarded tribunes, plebs. and his own trial with perfect unconcern. He was not one whom the threats of the plebeians or the entreaties of the senate could ever prevail upon, I do not say to put on mourning, or to seek men out with appeals for mercy, but even to soften and subdue in a slight degree the accustomed sharpness of his tongue, though it was before the people he must plead. There was the same expression on his countenance, the same arrogance in his glance, the same fire in his speech; so markedly, in fact, that a great part of the plebs feared Appius no less when a defendant than they had feared him as consul. Once only did he plead his cause, in the tone he had been wont to use on all occasions, namely, that of a prosecutor; and so completely did his firmness overwhelm the tribunes and the commons that they themselves voluntarily adjourned the trial to a later day, and then allowed the affair to drag. The interval was not very long, but before the appointed day came round Appius fell sick and died. When his eulogy was being pronounced, the tribunes of the plebs attempted to interfere, but the plebs were not willing that the funeral-day of so great a man should be defrauded of the customary honors. They listened to his praises with as great goodwill, now he was dead, as they had heard the living man accused, and attended his burial in crowds.

LXII. The same year Valerius the consul, having marched with an army against the Aequi, was unable to entice the enemy into a battle, and directed an assault upon their camp. This was foiled by an awful storm that descended upon them with hail and claps of thunder.

Their amazement was soon increased, on the signal for retreat being given, by the reappearance of so tranquil and cloudless a sky, that, as though some god had defended the camp, they scrupled to attack it a second time, and directed all their hostility towards devastating the fields. The other consul, Aemilius, conducted a campaign in the Sabine country. There, too, the enemy kept within his walls, and the Romans laid waste his fields. Afterwards, by setting fire not only to farmhouses but even to the villages, where the people lived close together, they aroused the Sabines, who, having met the pillagers and fought a drawn battle with them, next day withdrew their camp to a safer position. This seemed to the consul a sufficient pretext for leaving the enemy, as conquered, and he retired ere the campaign had fairly begun.

LXIII. While these wars were going on and there was still discord at home, Titus Numicius Priscus and Aulus Verginius were elected consuls. It was clear that the plebs would endure no further postponement of the land-law, and were preparing to use violent measures, when the approach of a Volscian army was announced by the smoke which rose from burning farmhouses and by the flight of the country people. By this circumstance the insurrection, which was already matured and on the point of breaking out, was repressed. The consuls, being at once commanded to do so by the senate, led the young men out of the City to the war, a policy which diminished the restlessness of the plebeians who were left behind. As for the enemy, they did no more than cause the Romans a needless panic, and hastily retreated. Numicius marched to Antium against the Volsci, Verginius against the Aequi. In the Aequian campaign an ambush nearly resulted in a severe defeat for the Romans, but the courage of the soldiers restored the day, which the carelessness of the consul had almost lost. The Volscian expedition was better directed: the enemy were routed in the first engagement and driven in flight to Antium, a very opulent city for those days. This place the consul did not venture to assail, but he captured from the Antiates another town, named Caeno, of far less wealth. While the Aequi and Volsci kept the Roman armies busy, the Sabines advanced clear to the gates of the City on a plundering raid. A few days after this they themselves had to confront two armies, for both the consuls indignantly invaded their borders, and they suffered greater losses than they had themselves inflicted.

LXIV. Towards the close of the year there was a brief season of peace, but, as always on other occasions, a peace distracted by the strife of patricians and plebeians. The angry plebs refused to take part in the consular elections:[50] by the votes of the patricians and their clients Titus Quinctius and Quintus Servilius were chosen consuls. They experienced a year like the preceding one: dissensions, to begin with, then a foreign war and tranquillity. The Sabines executed a rapid march across the Crustuminian plains, bringing fire and sword to the country about the river Anio. When almost at the Colline Gate and the City walls they were beaten back, yet they carried off immense spoils of men and cattle. Servilius the consul pursued them with an army, and though he could not overtake the column itself on ground which was suitable for offering battle, he devastated the country so extensively as to leave nothing untouched by the ravages of war, and returned with many times the plunder which the Romans had lost. Operations in the Volscian country, too, were very successful, thanks both to the general and to his soldiers. First, there was a pitched battle in the open field, with enormous numbers killed and wounded on both sides. The Romans indeed, whose fewness made them feel their loss more sensibly, would have fallen back, had it not been for a salutary falsehood told by the consul, who shouted that the enemy were running away on the other wing, and so aroused the spirits of his troops. The Romans charged and, believing themselves to be conquering, they conquered. The consul feared lest by pressing the enemy too hard he might cause a renewal of the struggle. He therefore gave the signal for the recall. For a few days both sides rested, as if they had tacitly agreed on a truce. Meanwhile a great force of men came in from all their tribes to the camp of the Volsci and Aequi. They made no question but that the Romans, if they had perceived them, would retreat in the night, and accordingly at about the third watch[51] they came to attack the camp. Quinctius stilled the tumult which the sudden alarm had raised, and bidding the soldiers remain quietly in their tents, led out a cohort of Hernici to an outpost, and mounting trumpeters and buglers upon horses, ordered them to blow their instruments in front of the rampart and keep the enemy in suspense till daybreak. For the remainder of the night all was so peaceful in camp that the Romans were even able to sleep. But the Volsci, beholding armed foot-soldiers, whom they supposed to be more numerous than they were, and to be Romans; and hearing the stamping and neighing of the horses, which were infuriated not only at finding unaccustomed riders on their backs, but also by the blare of the trumpets, were kept on the alert in anticipation of an attack.

LXV. As soon as it was light, the Romans, who were fresh and had enjoyed a good sleep, were led out into line of battle. The Volsci, weary from standing and from loss of sleep, were driven back at the first assault; though it was rather a retreat than a rout, for behind them were hills, to which, under cover of the first line, they withdrew safely and in good order. The consul ordered a halt when his army reached rising ground. The infantry could hardly be restrained, noisily demanding permission to press on after the fleeing enemy. Still more ardent were the cavalry. They swarmed about the general, and shouted that they were going on before the standards. While the consul was hesitating, feeling certain of the valor of his troops but doubtful of the ground, the men cried out that they were going, and instantly made good their word. Planting their spears in the ground, that they might be the lighter for the ascent they went up at a run. The Volsci, having discharged their javelins at the first onset, picked up the stones which lay about under their feet, and flung them at their enemies as they mounted. Confused by this rain of missiles from above, the left wing of the Romans was nearly overwhelmed, and had already begun to retreat, when the consul, reproaching them at once with rashness and with cowardice, succeeded in shaming them out of their fear. First they made a resolute stand; then, after holding their ground and returning blow for blow, they even dared to press forward and, renewing their cheers, set their line in motion; then with another rush they struggled upward and scaled the height; and they were just emerging upon the summit of the ridge, when the enemy turned and fled. Running at full speed, and almost in one body, the pursued and the pursuers reached the Volscian camp, which was captured in the panic. Those of the Volsci who succeeded in escaping made for Antium, and to Antium marched the Roman army also. After a blockade of a few days the place surrendered; the besiegers had not delivered any new attack, but the Volsci had lost heart from the moment of their unsuccessful battle and the capture of their camp.

Summary of Book ii

Brutus bound the people with an oath to allow no one to reign in Rome. Tarquinius Collatinus, his colleague, who had incurred suspicion because of his relationship to the Tarquinii, he forced to abdicate the consulship and withdraw from the state. He ordered the king's goods to be plundered, and consecrated his land to Mars. It was named the Campus Martius. Certain noble youths—among them his own sons and his brother's—he beheaded, because they had conspired to bring back the kings. To the slave who gave the information, a man called Vindicius, he gave his freedom; from his name came the word *vindicta*. Having led an army against the princes, who had collected forces from Veii and Tarquinii and begun a war, he fell in the battle, together with Arruns, the son of Superbus, and the matrons mourned for him a year. Publius Valerius the consul proposed a law about appealing to the people. The Capitol was dedicated. Porsenna, king of Clusium, made war in behalf of the Tarquinii and came to Janiculum, but was prevented from crossing the Tiber by the bravery of Horatius Cocles, who, while the others were cutting down the Sublician Bridge, kept the Etruscans at bay, single-handed, and when the bridge had been destroyed, threw himself armed into the river and swam across to his fellows. Another example of courage was exhibited by Mucius. Having entered the camp of the enemy with the purpose of killing Porsenna, he slew a secretary, whom he had taken for the king. Being arrested, he placed his hand upon the altar, where sacrifice had been made, and suffering it to be burned off, declared that there were three hundred others as determined as himself. Overcome with astonishment at their daring, Porsenna proposed terms of peace and, having taken hostages, relinquished the war. One of the hostages, the maiden Cloelia, evaded the sentinels and swam across the Tiber to her people. She was given up to Porsenna, but was restored by him with marks of honor, and was presented with an equestrian statue. Aulus Postumius the dictator fought a successful battle against Tarquinius Superbus, who was advancing with an army of Latins. Appius Claudius came over from the Sabines to the Romans. On this account the Claudian tribe was added and the number of tribes was increased to twenty-one. The plebs, after seceding to the Sacred Mount because of those who had been enslaved for debt, were induced by the advice of Menenius Agrippa to cease from their rebellion. The same Agrippa when he died was buried, owing to his poverty, at the state's expense. Five plebeian tribunes were elected. The Volscian town of Corioli was captured by the valiant efforts of Gnaeus Marcius, who acquired from this circumstance the name of Coriolanus. Titus Latinius, a man of the plebs, was warned in a dream to inform the senate regarding certain offenses against religion. Having neglected to do it, he lost a son and was paralysed in his feet. When he had been carried to the senate in a litter and had revealed these same matters, he recovered the use of his feet and returned to his house. When Gnaeus Marcius Coriolanus, who had been driven into exile and had been made general of the Volsci, had led a hostile army nearly to Rome, and when the envoys who had been sent to him at first and afterwards the priests had vainly besought him not to make war upon his native land, his mother Veturia and his wife Volumnia persuaded him to withdraw. For the first time a land-law was proposed. Spurius Cassius, the ex-consul, charged with aspiring to be king, was condemned and put to death. Opillia, a Vestal Virgin, was buried alive for unchastity. The neighboring Veientes being a troublesome rather than a dangerous enemy, the Fabian family asked to be allowed to carry on that war, and dispatched thither 306 armed men, who were all but one killed by the enemy at the Cremera. When Appius Claudius the consul had sustained a defeat at the hands of the Volsci, owing to the contumacy of his army, he caused every tenth soldier to be scourged to death. It contains besides campaigns against the Volsci, the Hernici, and the Veientes, and the quarrels between the patricians and the plebs.

BOOK III

I. AFTER THE CAPTURE OF ANTIUM, TITUS AEMILIUS AND QUINTUS Fabius were elected consuls. This was that Fabius who had been the sole survivor of his family destroyed at the Cremera.[1] In his former consulship Aemilius had already supported the assignment of land to the plebs. Consequently, when he entered a second time upon the office, not only had the agrarians begun to have hopes of a law, but the tribunes, who had often tried to carry the measure against the opposition of the consuls, now took it up in the belief that with the cooperation of a consul it could certainly be made good; and the consul continued of the same mind. The possessors of the land, comprising a large proportion of the patricians, complained that the head of the state was openly supporting tribunician policies and making himself popular by a generosity exhibited at other men's expense; they thus diverted the resentment awakened by the whole affair from the tribunes to the consul. A bitter struggle was impending, when Fabius, by a proposal which neither side found injurious, set the matter right. Under the leadership and auspices of Titus Quinctius, as he pointed out, a considerable territory had been conquered the year before from the Volsci; Antium, a well-situated maritime city, could be made the seat of a colony; in this way the plebs would obtain farms without causing the landholders to complain, and the state would be at harmony. This suggestion was adopted. As commissioners for distributing the land Fabius appointed Titus Quinctius, Aulus Verginius, and Publius Furius, and it was ordered that those who

wished to receive grants should give in their names. There at once
appeared the fastidiousness which usually attends abundance, and
so few persons enrolled that Volscian colonists were added to fill out
the number; the rest of the populace preferred demanding land at
Rome to receiving it elsewhere. The Aequi begged Quintus Fabius,
who had invaded their country, to grant them peace; and broke it
themselves by a sudden raid on Latin territory.

II. Quintus Servilius, being sent against the Aequi in the following year—when he and Spurius Postumius were consuls—made a
permanent camp in the Latin country, where the army was attacked
by a pestilence which deprived it of the power to act. The war
dragged on into its third year, the consulship of Quintus Fabius
and Titus Quinctius. To Fabius was given the command against the
Aequi, without the customary drawing of lots, since he had been
victorious over them and had granted them peace. Setting out in the
full expectation that the glory of his name would bring the enemy
to terms, he sent envoys to their national council and bade them
announce that Quintus Fabius the consul said that he had brought
peace from the Aequi to Rome, and was then bringing war from
Rome to the Aequi in the same right hand, now armed, which he had
formerly given them in friendship. Whose faithlessness and perjury
were responsible for this, the gods were even then witnesses, and
would presently punish the offenders. Yet however that might be,
he would himself prefer that the Aequi should even now freely
repent, instead of suffering the penalties of war. If they did so,
they could count on a safe refuge in the clemency they had already
proved; but if they rejoiced in perjury, it was rather with the angry
gods than with their enemies that they would be at war. So far were
these words from having the slightest effect on anyone, that the
envoys narrowly escaped violation, and an army was dispatched to
Algidus against the Romans. On the arrival of this news at Rome, the
insult, rather than the danger, brought the other consul out from
the City. And so two consular armies approached the enemy, drawn
up in line of battle, that they might instantly engage them. But since
it happened to be near the end of the day, a man called out to them
from an outpost of the enemy, "This, Romans, is making a parade

of war, not waging it. When night is about to fall, you draw up your battle-line; we need more hours of daylight for the struggle which is close at hand. Tomorrow at sunrise form your battle-line again; there will be opportunity for fighting, never fear!" Galled by these words the troops were led back to their camp to await the morrow; the night would be a long one, they felt, that must intervene before the combat. Meanwhile they refreshed themselves with food and sleep. When it grew light next morning, the Roman army took the field, sometime before the enemy. At last the Aequi too came out. The battle raged fiercely on both sides, for the Romans fought with exasperation and hatred, while the Aequi were conscious that the danger in which they were involved was due to their own fault, and this, with their despair of ever being trusted again, incited them to the last degree of daring and exertion. Nevertheless they were unable to withstand the attack of the Romans. And yet, when they had been defeated and had fallen back to their own territory, the warlike soldiers, their spirit as little inclined to peace as ever, complained against their generals for having staked the cause on a pitched battle, a species of fighting in which the Romans excelled; the Aequi, they said, were better at pillaging and raiding, and a number of scattered bands could make war more effectively than the great mass of a single army.

III. Leaving a garrison, therefore, in their camp, they crossed the Roman border in so headlong an incursion as to carry terror even to the City. Moreover, the unexpectedness of the inroad added to the alarm, for nothing could have been apprehended less than that an enemy who was defeated and almost shut up in his camp should be thinking of a raid; and the country people who in their fright came tumbling in through the gates told not of pillaging nor of small bands of raiders, but, exaggerating everything in their senseless fear, cried out that whole armies of the enemy were close at hand and rushing on the City in a serried column. The very vagueness of these rumors led to further exaggeration as the bystanders passed them on to others. The running and shouting of men as they called "To arms!" was almost like the panic in a captured city. It chanced that the consul Quinctius had returned from Algidus to Rome. This circumstance allayed men's fears, and when the confusion had been stilled, he indignantly reminded them that the enemy they dreaded had been conquered, and posted watches at the gates. He then convened the senate, and in accordance with a resolution which the Fathers passed, proclaimed a suspension of the courts.[2] After that he set out to defend the frontier, leaving Quintus Servilius as prefect of the City, but did not meet with the enemy in the field. The other consul campaigned with great success. Knowing where the enemy would come, he fell upon them when they were weighed down with the booty which incumbered their advancing column, and caused them bitterly to rue their pillaging. But few of them escaped the ambush, and the spoils were all recovered. So the suspension of the courts, which had lasted four days, was lifted on the return of the consul Quinctius to the City.

The census was then taken and Quinctius solemnized the concluding purification. There are said to have been registered 104,714 citizens, besides orphans and widows. In the Aequian country there was no memorable action after that; the people retired to their towns, and permitted their farms to be burnt and ravaged. The consul made a number of forays with his army throughout the enemy's territory, and returned to Rome with great renown and huge spoils.

IV. The next consuls were Aulus Postumius Albus and Spurius Furius Fusus. (Some writers spell the name Fusius instead of Furius, which I note lest anybody should regard as a substitution of one man for another what is really only a matter of names.)[3] There was no doubt but that one consul would make war on the Aequi, and these accordingly appealed to the Ecetranian Volsci for help. It was eagerly granted them—such was the rivalry between these nations in inveterate hatred of Rome—and the most vigorous preparations were made for war. The Hernici perceived, and warned the Romans, that Ecetra had gone over to the Aequi. Suspicion already rested on the colony of Antium, on the ground that a large body of men, escaping from the place at the time of its capture, had taken refuge with the Aequi; and in fact they fought with the greatest spirit all through the Aequian war; afterwards, when the Aequi had been shut up in their towns, this company dispersed, returned to Antium, and won over the colonists, who were even then at heart disloyal to the Romans. The plot was not yet ripe when their proposed defection was reported to the senate, and the consuls were instructed to summon the leaders of the colony to Rome and inquire what was going on. These men made no objection to coming, but on being introduced into the senate by the consuls returned such answers to the questions they were asked that they were under a stronger suspicion when dismissed than they had been on their arrival.

War was from that moment regarded as certain. Spurius Furius, one of the consuls, having received that command, set out against the Aequi. In the country of the Hernici he found the enemy engaged in marauding, and being ignorant of their strength, because they had never all been seen together, rashly offered battle with an army which was no match for theirs in numbers. At the first attack he was repulsed and withdrew into his camp. Nor did this end his danger, for both that night and the following day his camp was so vigorously hemmed in and assaulted that not even a messenger could be got off to Rome. The Hernici reported the defeat and blockade of the consul and his army, striking such terror into the hearts of the senators that they passed a decree which has always been held to signify the direst necessity: that Postumius, the other consul, should be commissioned to see to it that the republic took no hurt.[4] It was deemed wisest that the consul himself should remain in Rome, to enroll all who were capable of bearing arms; and that a proconsul, Titus Quinctius, should be sent, with an army of the allies, to relieve the camp. In order to fill out this army the Latins and the Hernici and the colony of Antium were commanded to furnish Quinctius with "emergency-men," as they used then to term hastily levied auxiliaries.

V. There was much manœuvring during the days that followed, and many attacks were delivered in one place or another, for the enemy, having a preponderance of numbers, set about harassing the Roman forces in many places, with the expectation that they would prove unequal to all the demands that were made upon them; at the same time that they were besieging the camp, a part of their army was sent to devastate the Roman fields and to attack the City itself, should an opportunity offer. Lucius Valerius was left to defend the City, while the consul Postumius was sent out to protect the frontier from pillage. There was no relaxation anywhere of vigilance or effort; watches were set in the City, outposts were established before the gates, and troops were posted on the walls; and, as was necessary in the midst of such confusion, the courts were suspended for several days. In camp meanwhile the consul Furius, having begun by submitting tamely to the blockade, caught the Aequi off their guard, and made a sortie by the decuman gate.[5] He might have pursued the enemy, but stopped for fear the camp might be assailed from the opposite quarter. The lieutenant Furius, a brother of the consul, was carried a good way off by his charge, nor did he observe, in the ardor of pursuit, either that his friends were retiring or that the enemy were moving up to attack him in the rear. His retreat was thus cut off, and after repeated but unsuccessful attempts to force his way back to the camp, he perished, fighting bravely. The consul too, upon learning that his brother was surrounded, set his face towards the battle and plunged into the midst of the mellay, with more rashness than prudence; for he received a wound, and was barely rescued by the men about him. This misfortune dismayed his own troops and quickened the courage of the enemy, who were so inspirited by the death of the lieutenant and the wounding of the consul that from that moment no force could withstand them, and the Romans were driven into their camp and again besieged, being no match for their opponents either in confidence or strength. The very existence of the army would have been imperilled, had not Titus Quinctius come up with the foreign troops, the Latins and Hernici. He found the Aequi intent on the Roman camp, and truculently displaying the head of the lieutenant. Attacking them in the rear, while the besieged, in answer to a signal he had given them from afar, were making a sally from the camp, he intercepted a large body of them. There was less carnage but a more headlong rout in the case of the Aequi who were in Roman territory. These men were dispersed and collecting booty when they were attacked by Postumius at several points where he had opportunely stationed troops. The pillagers, fleeing in a disordered crowd, fell in with Quinctius, who was returning from his victory with the wounded consul; whereupon the consular army splendidly avenged the consul's wound and the slaughter of the lieutenant and his cohorts. Heavy losses were inflicted and sustained on both sides at that time. It is hard to make a trustworthy statement, in a matter of such antiquity, as to just how many fought and how many fell; yet Valerius Antias ventures to specify the totals, saying that the Romans lost five thousand eight hundred in the country of the Hernici; that of the Aequian marauders who were roaming about and pillaging within the Roman borders two thousand four hundred were slain by Aulus Postumius, the consul; and that the rest of the expedition, which stumbled upon Quinctius as they were driving off their booty, got off by no means so lightly, for their killed amounted, so he says, with minute particularity, to four thousand two hundred and thirty.

When the army had returned to Rome, and the suspension of the courts was ended, the heavens were seen to blaze with numerous fires, and other portents either were actually seen or were due to the illusions of the terror-stricken observers. To avert these alarms a three days' season of prayer was ordered, and during this period all the shrines were crowded with a throng of men and women beseeching the pardon of the gods. After that the cohorts of the Latins and the Hernici were thanked by the senate for their energetic service and sent home. A thousand men from Antium who had come too late to help, when the battle was over, were dismissed, almost in disgrace.

VI. The elections were then held, and Lucius Aebutius and Publius Servilius were chosen consuls. On the first of August, then the beginning of the year, they entered office.[6] It was the sickly season, and chanced to be a year of pestilence both in the City and in the country, for beasts as well as men; and the people increased the virulence of the disease, in their dread of pillage, by receiving flocks and country-folk into the City. This conflux of all kinds of living things distressed the citizens with its strange smells, while the country-people, being packed into narrow quarters, suffered greatly from the heat and want of sleep; and the exchange of ministrations and mere contact spread the infection. The Romans could scarce endure the calamities which pressed hard upon them, when suddenly envoys from the Hernici appeared, announcing that the Aequi and the Volsci had joined forces and established a camp in their territory, from which base they were devastating their land with an enormous army. Not only did the reduced numbers of the senate show their allies that the nation was prostrated by the pestilence, but they also returned a melancholy answer to their suit, that the Hernici, namely, with the help of the Latins, must defend their own possessions; for the City of Rome, in a sudden visitation of divine displeasure, was being ravaged by disease; if there should come any respite from their suffering, they would help their friends, as they had done the year before and on every other occasion. The allies departed, bearing home, in return for their sad tidings, a reply that was even sadder, since it meant that their people must sustain by themselves a war which they could hardly have sustained with the powerful assistance of the Romans. No longer did the enemy confine themselves to the country of the Hernici; they proceeded thence to invade the Roman fields, which had been made desolate even without the violence of war. Encountering no one there, not even an unarmed man, and passing through a country wholly destitute not only of defenders but also of cultivation, they came to the third milestone on the Gabinian Way.

Death had taken Aebutius, the Roman consul; for his colleague Servilius there was little hope, though he still breathed; the disease had attacked most of the leading men, the greater part of the senators, and almost all of military age, so that their numbers were not only insufficient for the expeditions which so alarming a situation called for, but were almost too small for mounting guard. The watchmen's duty was performed by those of the senators themselves whose years and strength admitted of it; the rounds were made and the watches supervised by the plebeian aediles;[7] into their hands had passed the supreme control, and the majesty of consular authority.

VII. In this helpless plight, without a leader and without strength, the commonwealth was saved by its tutelary gods and the good fortune of the City, which inspired the Volsci and Aequi with the spirit of plunderers rather than of soldiers. For they were so far from entertaining any hope of approaching, not to speak of capturing, the walls of Rome, and the distant sight of her roofs and beetling hills so damped their ardor, that the entire army began to murmur, and to ask why they should waste their time in desolate and abandoned fields, where bodies of beasts and men lay rotting and there was no booty, when they might be invading an unspoiled country, the land of Tusculum, abounding in wealth; so they suddenly pulled up their standards, and passed by crossroads through the Labican fields to the hills of Tusculum, and on that point all the impetus and fury of the war converged. Meanwhile the Hernici and Latins, moved not by pity alone but by shame, if they should fail to oppose the common enemy, advancing in force against the City of Rome, and should bring no assistance to their besieged allies, united their armies and proceeded to the City. Failing to find the enemy there, but following the report and traces of his march, they met him as he was coming down from the Tusculan valley into that of Alba. There they engaged the invaders on far from equal terms, and their loyalty to their friends was for the moment not attended with success.

In Rome the ravages of the disease were no less fatal than those of the sword had been amongst her allies. The surviving consul died; and death took other famous men, the augurs Marcus Valerius and Titus Verginius Rutulus, and the head curio,[8] Servius Sulpicius; as for the base rabble, the violence of the plague stalked at large amongst them; until the senate, finding no help in man, sent the people to the gods in prayer, commanding them to take their wives and children and supplicate Heaven for forgiveness. Thus summoned by the state's authority to do what each was impelled to by his own distress, they crowded all the shrines. Everywhere were prostrate matrons, sweeping the floors of the temples with their hair, while they besought the angry gods to grant them pardon and end the pestilence.

VIII. After that, little by little, whether it was that the gods had been persuaded to forgive or that the sickly season was now past, those whose disease had run its course began to regain their health; and men's thoughts now turned to the commonwealth. Several interregna had expired, when Publius Valerius Publicola, three days after being made interrex, declared the election to the consulship of Lucius Lucretius Tricipitinus and Titus Veturius Geminus—or Vetusius, if that was his name.[9] On the 11th of August they took office, the nation being by that time so strong that it was able not only to defend itself, but even to assume the offensive. Accordingly, when the Hernici reported that the enemy had crossed their borders, they were promptly offered assistance. Two consular armies were enlisted; Veturius was sent to carry the war into the country of the Volsci; while Tricipitinus, having been appointed to secure the territory of the allies from inroads, proceeded no further than the land of the Hernici. Veturius in his first battle defeated and routed his opponents; Lucretius, while encamped among the Hernici, was eluded by a company of raiders, who marched over the mountains of Praeneste and thence down into the campagna; there they laid waste the Praenestine and Gabinian fields; and from the latter district turned towards the hills about Tusculum. The City of Rome itself received a great fright, more on account of the surprise than from any lack of resources for defense. Quintus Fabius was in charge of the City. Arming the young men and disposing his defenses, he made everything secure and tranquil. And so the enemy, having laid hold of the plunder in their immediate neighborhood, did not venture to approach Rome, but making a detour, set out towards home. The farther they got from the hostile City the less was their anxiety, till they came unexpectedly upon Lucretius the consul, who having already marked their line of march, had drawn up his troops and was eager to fight. The spirits of the Romans were therefore prepared for their task, while the enemy were stricken with a sudden panic on being attacked, though by somewhat inferior numbers. The Romans completely routed the great multitude, and driving them into deep valleys, from which escape was difficult, surrounded them. There the Volscian name was almost blotted out. Thirteen thousand four hundred and seventy fell in the battle and the flight, seventeen hundred and fifty were taken alive, and twenty-seven military standards were brought in, as I find recorded in certain annals; and though there may be some exaggeration of the numbers, it was beyond question a great slaughter. The victorious consul, in possession of enormous spoils, returned to the permanent camp he had occupied before. Then the consuls encamped together, and the Volsci and Aequi united their shattered forces. The ensuing battle was the third of that year. Fortune bestowed the victory where she had done before; the enemy were routed, and even lost their camp.

IX. Rome was thus restored to her former condition, and the success of the campaign at once occasioned disturbances in the City. Gaius Terentilius Harsa was tribune of the plebs that year. Thinking that the absence of the consuls afforded the tribunes an opportunity for action, he employed some days in complaining to the people of the pride of the patricians, and inveighed especially against the authority of the consuls, as a thing excessive and intolerable in a free state. For it was only in name, he said, that it was less hateful than that of a king; in reality it was almost crueler, since in place of one master they had now got two, who possessed an unregulated and unlimited power, and while free themselves and without restraint, brought to bear all the terrors of the law and all its punishments upon the plebs. That they might not forever have this license, he was about to propose a law providing for the appointment of five men to write out the statutes pertaining to the consular power;[10] such authority over them as the people had granted the consuls they should enjoy, but they should not make a law of their own whims and caprices. When this measure had been promulgated, the Fathers were alarmed lest they might be humbled, in the absence of the consuls; the prefect of the City, Quintus Fabius, convened the senate, and attacked the measure and its author himself with such bitterness that if both the consuls had been present to outface the tribune there was nothing they could have added to his threats and denunciations. Terentilius, he said, had laid an ambush and watching his opportunity had attacked the state. If the angry gods had given them a tribune like him the year before, when they were suffering from war and disease, it would have been impossible to save the situation. Finding both consuls dead, the citizens plague-stricken, and confusion everywhere, he would have proposed a law to do away with consular government, and would have led the Volsci and the Aequi to besiege the City. Pray what did he desire? Was he not at liberty, if the consuls had committed any act of pride or cruelty against a citizen, to call them into court and accuse them where the judges would be the very men against one of whom the injury had been done? It was not the authority of the consul but the power of the tribune that he was making hateful and intolerable; this power had been reconciled and brought into harmony with the senate, but was now being degraded again to its former evil state. Yet he would not supplicate Terentilius to abandon the course on which he had embarked. "It is you other tribunes," he cried, "whom we beg to reflect, as a matter of the last importance, that your power was obtained for the purpose of assisting individuals, not for the destruction of us all; that you were elected tribunes of the plebs, not enemies of the senate. To us it is a source of sorrow, to you of odium, that the state should be attacked in the absence of its defenders. You will be diminishing, not your authority, but your unpopularity, if you plead with your colleague to postpone the question, as it stands, until the arrival of the consuls. Even the Aequi and the Volsci, when disease last year had carried off the consuls, refrained from pressing a cruel and pitiless war against us." The tribunes pleaded with Terentilius, and the measure having been ostensibly postponed, but in reality killed, the consuls were immediately summoned.

X. Lucretius returned with vast spoils and far greater glory; and this he increased, on his arrival, by exposing all the booty in the Campus Martius, where it lay for three days, that every man might identify and carry off what belonged to him. The other things, for which no owner appeared, were sold. That the consul had earned a triumph all agreed; but the matter was put off, for the tribune was urging his law, and this was a question of more importance in the eyes of Lucretius. The measure was debated several days, not only in the senate but before the people. Finally the tribune gave way to the majesty of the consul and desisted. The general and his army then received their meed of honor; Lucretius triumphed over the Volsci and the Aequi, and his own legions followed the triumphal chariot. The other consul was permitted to enter the City in an ovation,[11] without soldiers.

In the following year the Terentilian law was brought up again by the entire college and menaced the new consuls, to wit, Publius Volumnius and Servius Sulpicius. This year the heavens were seen to blaze, and the earth was shaken with a prodigious quake. That a cow had spoken—a thing which had found no credence the year before—was now believed. Among other portents there was even a rain of flesh, which is said to have been intercepted by vast numbers of birds flying round in the midst of it; what fell to the ground lay scattered about for several days, but without making any stench. The two commissioners for sacred rites consulted the Sibylline Books, where it was predicted that there was danger to come from a concourse of foreigners, lest they attack the highest places of the City, and blood be shed; amongst other things was a warning to avoid factions. The tribunes charged them with trying to hinder their law, and a violent struggle was impending; when lo! That the same cycle of events might recur each year—the Hernici announced that the Volsci and the Aequi, despite the losses they had sustained, were again fitting out their armies; that Antium was the center of the enterprise; that at Ecetra Antian colonists were holding public meetings; and that the Antiates were the head and sinews of the war. After listening to this report, the senate decreed a levy, and directed the consuls to divide between them the direction of the war, so that one might operate against the Volsci, the other against the Aequi. The tribunes openly and loudly protested in the Forum that the Volscian war was a prearranged farce, and that the nobles had employed the Hernici to act a part in it: they no longer used manhood even, to suppress the liberty of the Roman People, but cajoled and tricked them. Inasmuch as the almost total destruction of the Volsci and Aequi made it incredible that they should be going to war on their own initiative, new enemies were trumped up, and a loyal and neighboring colony was traduced. It was against the innocent Antiates that war was being declared; it was being waged against the Roman plebeians, whom the consuls would load with arms and lead out of the City in hot haste, exiling and banishing citizens to avenge themselves upon the tribunes. By these means—and they need not think that anything else had been intended—the law was already defeated, unless, while the situation was still intact, while they were at home, while they still wore the toga, they should guard themselves against expulsion from the City and submitting to the yoke. If they proved courageous, help would not be wanting; the tribunes were all of one mind. There was no fear of foreign foes, no danger; the gods had seen to it the previous year that they might defend their liberties in safety. To this purport the tribunes.

XI. But the consuls, on the other hand, had placed their chairs in full sight of the tribunes, and began to hold the levy. The tribunes hastened to the place, drawing the people after them. A few were cited, as if by way of a test, and immediately a riot began. As often as a lictor arrested a man on the consul's order, a tribune would command that he be released; in every case it was not a man's right that determined his conduct, but the confidence he had in his strength; and one had to make good by force what one meant to do.

Precisely as the tribunes had borne themselves in preventing the levy, so did the senators in blocking the law, which was brought forward everyday the comitia could be held.[12] The quarrel broke out when the tribunes had ordered the people to separate,[13] since the patricians would not permit themselves to be removed. And yet the older nobles for the most part took no share in an affair which was not to be guided by wisdom, but had been committed to rashness and impudence. To a considerable extent the consuls too kept aloof, lest they should expose their dignity to some affront in the general confusion.

There was a young man, Caeso Quinctius, emboldened not only by his noble birth but also by his great stature and physical strength; and to these gifts of the gods he had himself added many honors in the field, and also forensic eloquence, so that no citizen was held to be readier, whether with tongue or with hand. When this man had taken his place in the midst of the band of senators, towering above his fellows as though wielding all the might of dictators and consuls in his voice and strength of body, he would sustain unaided the attacks of the tribunes and the fury of the rabble. His leadership often drove the tribunes from the Forum and ignominiously routed the plebeians; the man who crossed his path came off bruised and stripped; so that it was clear that if things were allowed to go on in this way the law was beaten. Finally, when the other tribunes had already been pretty well cowed, one of their college named Aulus Verginius summoned Caeso to stand trial on a capital charge.[14] The man's fierce nature was rather aroused by this than terrified; and he continued all the more bitterly to resist the law, to harry the plebs, and to assail the tribunes as if in actual warfare. The accuser permitted the defendant to storm, and to fan the flames of popular resentment, while furnishing fresh materials for the charges which he intended to bring against him; meanwhile he continued to urge the law, not so much from any hope of carrying it as to provoke Caeso to recklessness. In these circumstances it was Caeso alone, as being a suspected character, who got all the blame for many a rash word and act which proceeded from the young aristocrats. Nevertheless the law continued to meet resistance. And Aulus Verginius kept saying to the plebeians: "I suppose you see now, Quirites, that you cannot at the same time have Caeso for a fellow-citizen and obtain the law you desire? And yet why do I say *law*? It is *liberty* he is thwarting; in all the Tarquinian house was no such arrogance. Wait till this man becomes consul or dictator, whom you see lording it over us while a private citizen, by virtue of his strength and impudence!" There were many who agreed with him; they complained of the beatings they had received, and freely urged the tribune to see the business through.

XII. The day of the trial now drew near, and it was clearly the general opinion that liberty depended on Caeso's condemnation. Then at last he was obliged, though greatly disdaining such a course, to sue for the support of individuals. He was accompanied by his friends, the chief men of the state. Titus Quinctius Capitolinus, who had thrice been consul, rehearsed the many honors which had come to himself and his family, and declared that neither in the Quinctian clan nor in the Roman state had there ever been such native qualities, so early ripening into manly worth; Caeso had been his best soldier, and had often fought under his own eyes. Spurius Furius testified that Caeso had been sent to him by Quinctius Capitolinus, and had come to his aid when he was in a dangerous plight; that there was no single person whose services he considered to have been more effectual in saving the day. Lucius Lucretius, the consul of the year before, in the splendor of his new-won renown, shared his glory with Caeso, told of the young man's combats, and recounted his wonderful exploits on raids or in the field of battle; he earnestly advised the people to prefer that a distinguished youth, endowed with every advantage of nature and of fortune, and sure to be an important factor in the affairs of any state which he might join, should rather be their own than the citizen of another nation. Those qualities in him which gave offense, impetuosity and rashness, were diminishing each day, as he grew older: that in which he was deficient, namely prudence, was daily increasing. They should suffer a man of his greatness—his worth maturing as he outlived his faults—to grow old in the possession of his citizenship. The young man's father, Lucius Quinctius, surnamed Cincinnatus, was among his advocates. He did not dwell on Caeso's praises, lest he should add to his unpopularity; but, craving indulgence for his errors and his youth, he begged them to acquit the son as a favor to the father, who had offended no man either in word or deed. But some turned away from the petitioner, through either embarrassment or fear; while others complained of the injuries which Caeso had inflicted on themselves or their friends, and showed by their harsh replies how they meant to vote.

XIII. There was one charge, besides the general dislike of him, which bore hard upon the accused. Marcus Volscius Fictor, who had been a tribune of the plebs a few years before, had certified that shortly after the epidemic had been in the City he had fallen in with a band of young men swaggering through the Subura.[15] There a brawl had arisen, and his elder brother, who had not yet fully recovered from the disease, had been felled by a blow from Caeso's fist; he had been picked up half-alive and carried home, and his death, Volscius considered, had resulted from this hurt; yet under the consuls of previous years he had been unable to avenge that wicked crime. As Volscius shouted out this story, men became so excited that Caeso had nearly perished by the fury of the people. Verginius gave orders to seize the fellow and throw him into prison. The patricians resisted force with force. Titus Quinctius cried out that a man who had been charged with a capital crime and whose day of trial was at hand ought not to suffer violence, uncondemned and unheard. The tribune answered that he did not propose to punish him uncondemned, but that he should keep him in prison notwithstanding, till the day of trial, that the Roman People might have it in their power to punish a homicide. The other tribunes, on being appealed to,[16] asserted by a compromise their prerogative of protection: they forbade the imprisonment of the accused, but declared it to be their pleasure that he be produced for trial, and that money be pledged to the people in the event of a failure to produce him. How great a sum was proper to be guaranteed was a doubtful point; it was referred to the senate, and Caeso was detained in custody till the Fathers could be consulted. They voted that sureties should be furnished, and fixed the responsibility of one surety at 3,000 asses; how many sureties should be given they left the tribunes to determine. They decided on ten, and with this number of sureties the accuser admitted the accused to bail. Caeso was the first that ever gave sureties to the people. Being allowed to leave the Forum, he departed that night and went into exile amongst the Etruscans. On the day of trial, when it was pleaded that he had gone into voluntary exile, Verginius nevertheless attempted to hold the comitia, but an appeal was taken to his colleagues, who dismissed the assembly.[17] The money was exacted from Caeso's father without pity, so that he was obliged to sell all that he had and live for sometime on the other side of the Tiber,[18] like one banished, in a certain lonely hovel.

XIV. This trial and the promulgation of the law[19] kept the citizens in a turmoil: from foreign wars there was a respite. The tribunes, assuming that the rebuff sustained by the patricians in Caeso's exile had given themselves the victory, believed the law to be as good as passed; and so far as the older senators were concerned, they had indeed relinquished their grasp upon the government; but the juniors, especially those who had been of Caeso's fellowship, grew more bitter against the plebs, and their courage ran as high as ever. Yet they greatly promoted their cause by tempering their fury with a kind of moderation. At the first attempt after Caeso's exile to pass the law, they were organized and ready, and fell upon the tribunes with a great army of clients, as soon as the tribunes gave them an excuse by attempting to remove them; in such wise that no single patrician came off with any conspicuous share of glory or unpopularity, and the plebeians complained that a thousand Caesos had sprung up in the place of one. During the intervening days on which the tribunes took no action about the law, nothing could have been more peaceable or quiet than these same youths. They would salute plebeians courteously, converse with them, invite them to their houses, assist them in the courts, and permit the tribunes themselves to hold their other assemblies without interruption. They never displayed arrogance towards anyone, either openly or in private, except when the law came up; at other times they were democratic. By avoiding so much as an offensive word, to say nothing of any sort of violence, they managed little by little, with gentleness and tact, to disarm the hostility of the plebs. By such arts the law was evaded for an entire year. And yet not only did the tribunes carry through their other measures without opposition, but they were even re-elected for the following twelvemonth.

XV. The state was less distracted when the consuls Gaius Claudius, the son of Appius, and Publius Valerius Publicola assumed control. No new difficulty had come in with the new year; anxiety to pass the law on the one side, and on the other the dread of having to accept it, occupied the thoughts of the citizens. The more the younger patricians tried to ingratiate themselves with the plebs, the more sharply were they opposed by the tribunes, who endeavored by bringing charges against their adversaries to make the plebeians suspect them: A conspiracy had been formed; Caeso was in Rome; plans had been laid to kill the tribunes and massacre the plebs; the elder patricians had intrusted the younger men with the task of abolishing the tribunician power from the commonwealth, that the state might have the same aspect it had worn before the occupation of the Sacred Mount. Also men feared the Volsci and Aequi, whose attack was by this time almost a regular and stated custom of annual recurrence; and a new and unexpected danger sprang up nearer home. Exiles[20] and slaves to the number of twenty-five hundred, led by Appius Herdonius, the Sabine, came by night and seized the Capitol and the Citadel. They at once put to the sword those in the Citadel who refused to conspire and take up arms with them. Some escaped in the confusion and ran down terror-stricken into the Forum. Alternating cries were heard, "To arms!" and "The enemy is in the City!" The consuls were afraid either to arm the plebs or to leave them unarmed, not knowing whence this sudden attack upon the City had come, whether from without or from within, from the hatred of the plebs or the treachery of slaves. They tried to still the uproar, and sometimes by their efforts made it the greater; for the trembling, panic-stricken multitude could not be controlled by authority. Nevertheless they gave out arms, not to everybody, but only so far as to insure, in the uncertainty regarding their foe, that there should be a fairly dependable defense for any emergency. Filled with concern, and wondering who their enemy was and what his numbers, they employed the rest of the night in disposing pickets at suitable points throughout the City. Then came daylight and disclosed the nature of the war and its leader. From the Capitol Herdonius was calling the slaves to freedom; he had undertaken, he said, the cause of all the wretched, that he might bring back to their native land the exiles who had been wrongfully expelled, and release the slaves from their heavy yoke; he had rather this were done with the approval of the Roman people: if there were no hope in that quarter, he would call in the Volsci and the Aequi and leave no desperate measure unattempted.

XVI. The situation became clearer to the senators and the consuls. Still, besides the dangers with which they were publicly threatened, they were afraid that this might be a ruse of the Veientes or the Sabines, and that while there were so many enemies within the City, Sabine and Etruscan levies might presently combine for an invasion;[21] or again that their perpetual foes, the Volsci and Aequi, might come, not as before to lay waste their fields, but to the City, which they would regard as already partly captured. Men's fears were many and various; above all the rest stood out their dread of the slaves. Everybody suspected that he had an enemy in his own household, whom it was safe neither to trust, nor, from want of confidence, to refuse to trust, lest his hostility should be intensified; and it seemed hardly possible that even cooperation between the classes should arrest the danger. So greatly did other evils overtop and threaten to engulf them that no one feared the tribunes or the plebeians; that seemed a milder mischief, and springing up, as it always did, when other troubles were quieted, appeared now to have been lulled to sleep by the foreign peril. But in fact it bore down almost more heavily than anything else upon their sinking fortunes. For so frenzied were the tribunes that they asserted it was no war which had taken possession of the Capitol, but an idle mimicry of war, got up to divert the minds of the plebeians from thinking about the law; the patricians' friends and retainers would depart, when the passing of the law showed them how useless had been their insurrection, even more silently than they had come. They then convened an assembly to carry the measure through, having called the people away from their service as soldiers. Meantime the consuls were holding a meeting of the senate, where more fear of the tribunes was manifested than the night-attack of the enemy had caused.

XVII. On being informed that the men were laying down their arms and quitting their posts, Publius Valerius left his colleague to keep the senate together, and hurrying from the Curia sought out the tribunes in their meeting-place.[22] "What means this, tribunes?" he exclaimed, "Are you going to overturn the state under the leadership and auspices of Appius Herdonius? Has he who could not arouse the slaves been so successful in corrupting you? With the enemy over your heads can you choose to quit your arms and legislate?" Then, turning to the crowd, he continued: "If you feel no concern, Quirites, for your City, or for yourselves, yet fear your gods, whom the enemy hold captive. Jupiter Optimus Maximus, Queen Juno, and Minerva, and the other gods and goddesses, are beleaguered; a camp of slaves is in possession of the tutelary deities of your country; does this seem to you a healthy polity? All these foes are not merely within our walls, but in the Citadel, above the Forum and the Curia; the people meanwhile are assembled in the Forum, and in the Curia sits the senate; as when peace reigns supreme, the senator gives voice to his opinion, the other Quirites vote. Should not every patrician and plebeian, the consuls, the tribunes, gods, and men, all have drawn the sword and helped; have rushed upon the Capitol; have brought liberty and peace to that most august house of Jupiter Optimus Maximus? Father Romulus, grant thou to thy descendants that spirit in which thou didst aforetime regain thy Citadel from these same Sabines, when they had captured it with gold; bid them advance by that road where thou didst lead, and thy army followed. Lo, I the consul will be the first, so far as mortal can emulate a god, to follow in thy footsteps!" He ended by announcing that he drew his sword and called to arms all the Quirites; if any hindered, he should no longer remember consular authority, nor tribunician power, nor the guarantees of sanctity; whoever the man, wherever he might be, on the Capitol, in the Forum, he should hold him a public enemy. Since the tribunes forbade them to arm against Appius Herdonius, let them order an attack on Publius Valerius the consul; he would not fear to deal with tribunes as the founder of his family[23] had dealt with kings. It was evident that there would soon be an appeal to force, and that the enemy would be afforded the spectacle of mutiny among the Romans. Yet it was equally impossible for the law to be carried and for the consul to go up into the Capitol. Night put an end to the struggle. The tribunes retired as darkness fell, fearing the armed strength of the consuls. When the instigators of insurrection were once out of the way, the Fathers went about among the plebs, and mingling with the different groups, talked to them in a strain adapted to the crisis. They warned them to have a care into what straits they brought the nation: It was not between patricians and plebeians that the conflict lay; patricians and plebeians alike, the Citadel of the City, the temples of the gods, and the guardian deities of the state and of private citizens, were being surrendered to enemies. Such were the means employed in the Forum to allay dissension. Meanwhile the consuls, lest Sabine or Veientine enemies might be afoot, had set out to make the round of the gates and walls.

XVIII. That same night Tusculum received tidings of the capture of the Citadel, the seizure of the Capitol, and the general disorder in the City. Lucius Mamilius was then dictator at Tusculum. He at once convoked the senate; and having introduced the messengers, expressed an earnest conviction that they ought not to wait till ambassadors should come from Rome requesting help; her perilous and critical situation spoke for itself—the gods of their alliance and the obligations of their treaty called on them to act. Heaven would never bestow on them an equal opportunity to earn the gratitude of so powerful and so near a state, by doing it a service. The senate resolved to help. The young men were enrolled, and arms were issued. As they marched towards Rome in the early dawn, the Tusculans, who were seen a long way off, were taken for enemies; it looked like an invasion of the Aequi or the Volsci. When the alarm proved groundless, they were received into the City, and marched in column down into the Forum. There they found Publius Valerius, who had left his colleague to protect the gates and was marshalling his army. The personal influence of the man had prevailed. He had assured the people that when the Capitol should be won back and peace restored in the City, if they would permit him to point out to them the mischief which lurked in the law the tribunes were proposing, he would remember his forefathers and the surname with which he had, as it were, inherited from those forefathers the charge of caring for the people, nor would he interfere with the council of the plebs. Following him as their leader, despite the idle efforts of the tribunes to restrain them, they advanced up the Clivus Capitolinus, accompanied by the troops from Tusculum. It was a contest between the allies and the citizens, which should obtain the honor of recovering the Citadel. The leader of each party urged on his followers. The enemy now began to quake with fear, having no great confidence in anything but their position. As they stood there quaking, the Romans and their allies assailed them. They had already burst into the vestibule of the temple, when Publius Valerius was killed, as he was directing the attack in the van. Publius Volumnius, a former consul, saw him fall. Charging his men to cover up the body, he threw himself into the consul's place. In the ardor and enthusiasm of the soldiers so important an event passed unnoticed; and they had won the victory before they realized that they were fighting without their leader. Many of the exiles stained the temples with their blood; many were taken alive; Herdonius was slain. Thus the Capitol was regained. The captives, according as they were free or slave, paid the penalty appropriate in each case to their condition; the Tusculans were thanked; the Capitol was purged and ceremonially purified. It is said that the plebeians flung their coppers into the consul's house, that he might be given a grander funeral.[24]

XIX. When peace had been established, the tribunes began to urge the patricians to fulfill the promise made by Publius Valerius; and to urge Gaius Claudius to absolve the manes of his colleague from deceit, and allow the law to be discussed. The consul refused to permit discussion of the law, until he should have accomplished the election of a colleague. These disputes continued up to the time

when the comitia met to fill the vacant consulate. In December,
thanks to extraordinary zeal on the part of the patricians, Lucius
Quinctius Cincinnatus, Caeso's father, was declared consul, to enter
upon the office at once. The plebs were filled with dismay at the
prospect of a consul incensed against themselves and strong in
the favor of the senate, his own worth, and his three sons, none of
whom was inferior to Caeso in courage, while they surpassed him in
using wisdom and restraint when the need arose. Cincinnatus, having
taken up the magistracy, harangued the people incessantly from the
tribunal; yet was no more vehement in repressing the plebs than
in castigating the senate. It was owing, he declared, to the apathy
of that order that the tribunes of the plebs, whose tenure was now
become permanent, exercised such a tyranny of speech and accusation as might be expected in a disordered household, but not in the
public affairs of the Roman People. With his son Caeso, manhood,
steadfastness, and all the qualities which honor youth in war and in
civil life had been driven from Rome and put to rout. Garrulous,
seditious, sowers of discord, obtaining office—by the most wicked
practices—for a second and even a third term, the tribunes led as
lawless a life as kings. "*Did Aulus Verginius*," he cried, "because he was
not in the Capitol, deserve less punishment than Appius Herdonius?
Nay, somewhat more, if one were disposed to be fair. Herdonius had
one thing to his credit: by professing himself an enemy, he as good
as warned you to arm; the other, denying the existence of a war,
took away your arms and exposed you unprotected to your slaves and
exiles. And did you—without offense to Gaius Claudius and the dead
Publius Valerius be it said, did you carry your standards against the
Capitoline Hill before clearing these enemies out of the Forum? I am
ashamed in the sight of gods and men. When foes were in the Citadel,
foes in the Capitol, when the captain of slaves and exiles, profan-
ing everything, was quartered in the very shrine of Jupiter Optimus
Maximus, it was Tusculum—not Rome—where the first sword was
drawn. It was a question whether Lucius Mamilius, the Tusculan
general, or Publius Valerius and Gaius Claudius, the consuls, would
free the Roman Citadel; and we who until then did not allow the
Latins to touch their weapons, even in their own defense, though

they had an enemy within their borders, had now, unless the Latins had armed of their own free will, been taken captive and destroyed. Is this, tribunes, what you mean by helping the plebs, to deliver them over unarmed to be slaughtered by the enemy? Why, if the humblest man belonging to your plebs, a part of the people which you have sundered, as it were, from the rest and made a country of your own and a state apart, if one of these, I say, had announced that his slaves had armed and seized his house, you would have thought yourselves bound to help him; was Jupiter Optimus Maximus, beset by the swords of exiles and slaves, too mean to merit any man's assistance? And do these tribunes demand that they be held sacred and inviolable, in whose eyes the very gods are neither the one nor the other? So! Weighed down with crimes against gods and men you assert that you will carry through your law this year! Then, by Heaven, it was an evil day for the nation when I was chosen consul, far more evil than when Publius Valerius the consul fell, if indeed you carry it! First of all then, Quirites," he concluded, "I and my colleague are resolved to lead the legions against the Volsci and the Aequi. We are somehow fated to enjoy the favor of the gods in larger measure when warring than when at peace. How dangerous these peoples would have been, had they known that the Capitol was seized by exiles, we may more profitably conjecture from the past than ascertain by trying it."

XX. The consul's speech had moved the plebs, and the senators took courage, believing that the state was on its feet again. The other consul, more spirited in cooperation than invention, had been quite willing that his colleague should take the lead in initiating such weighty measures; but in carrying them out he claimed for himself a share of the duties of the consulship. Then the tribunes, jeering at what they termed the idle words of Cincinnatus, proceeded to inquire how the consuls were going to lead out an army, when no one would permit them to hold a levy. "But we have no need of a levy," said Quinctius, "for when Publius Valerius gave arms to the people for the recovery of the Capitol, they all made oath that they would assemble at the bidding of the consul and not depart without his order. We therefore command that all you who took the oath report tomorrow, armed, at Lake Regillus." Whereupon the tribunes, seeking to release the people from their obligation, resorted to a quibble: Quinctius had been a private citizen at the time when they bound themselves by the oath. But there had not yet come about that contempt for the gods which possesses the present generation; nor did everybody seek to construe oaths and laws to suit himself, but rather shaped his own practices by them. Accordingly the tribunes, as there was no prospect of thwarting the design, concerned themselves with retarding the departure; the more so since a story was about that the augurs had been commanded to present themselves at Lake Regillus, there to inaugurate a place where the auspices could be taken and matters brought before the people, to the end that whatever had been enacted at Rome—thanks to the violence of the tribunes—might there be repealed by the comitia; everybody, they said, would vote as the consuls wished; for there was no appeal when one was more than a mile from the City, and the tribunes, if they should come there, would be subjected, amongst the rank and file of the citizens, to the consular authority. These were terrifying rumors, but far the greatest terror that preyed upon their spirits was this, that Quinctius repeatedly declared that he would hold no consular election; the disease of the commonwealth was not one that could be cured by ordinary remedies; the nation needed a dictator, that whoever went about to disturb the state might learn that the dictatorship knew no appeal.

XXI. The senate was in the Capitol. Thither came the tribunes with the troubled plebs. The multitude loudly besought protection, now of the consuls, now of the senators. Yet they could not move the consul from his purpose, until the tribunes had promised that they would submit to the authority of the Fathers. The consul then brought up the demands of the tribunes and the plebs, and the senate resolved that neither should the tribunes proceed with the law that year, nor the consuls lead the army out of the City; that as regarded the future, it was the sense of the senate that for magistrates to succeed themselves and for the same tribunes to be re-elected was contrary to the general welfare. The consuls acquiesced in the authority of the Fathers; the tribunes, in spite of the protests of the consuls, were returned to office. Then the patricians also, that they might yield in no respect to the plebs, would themselves have re-elected Lucius Quinctius consul. At no time during the entire year did the consul express himself with greater vehemence. "Can I wonder," he cried, "if your influence with the people, Conscript Fathers, is unavailing? You yourselves impair it, when, because the people have disregarded the senate's resolution regarding successive terms, you desire to disregard it yourselves, that you may not lag behind the multitude in rashness; as if to be more inconstant and more lawless were to possess more power in the state. For surely it is more fickle and light-minded to nullify one's own decrees and resolutions, than those of others. Pattern yourselves, Conscript Fathers, after the thoughtless crowd; and do you, who ought to set others an example, err rather by the example of those others, than permit them to follow yours and do right. But I, with your leave, will not imitate the tribunes, nor suffer myself to be named consul against the senate's resolution. As for you, Gaius Claudius, I urge that you too restrain the Roman People from this lawlessness; and for my own part be assured I shall not feel that your action has stood in the way of my election, but that my renown has gained by my refusal of the office, and that the odium which threatened me from its continuation has been removed." They then united in an edict that no one should vote for Lucius Quinctius for consul; if any man should do so they would disregard his vote.

XXII. The consuls elected were Quintus Fabius Vibulanus (for the third time) and Lucius Cornelius Maluginensis. The census was taken that year, but there were scruples against performing the lustral sacrifice, on account of the seizure of the Capitol and the slaying of the consul.

The consulship of Quintus Fabius and Lucius Cornelius was a stormy one from the very beginning of the year. The tribunes egged on the plebs; the Latins and the Hernici reported that a great attack was being launched by the Volsci and the Aequi, and that Volscian levies were already at Antium. There was much apprehension too lest the colony itself should revolt; and the tribunes were hardly prevailed upon to allow the war to have precedence.[25] Then the consuls divided the commands, appointing Fabius to take the legions to Antium, and

Cornelius to defend Rome, lest some part of the enemy, in accordance with the Aequian custom, should make a foray. The Hernici and the Latins were bidden to furnish soldiers, as by treaty bound; two-thirds of the army were allies, one-third citizens. When the allies had reported on the appointed day, the consul encamped outside the Porta Capena. Thence, after purifying the army, he set out for Antium, and took up a position at no great distance from the town and the standing camp of the enemy. There the Volsci, not daring to give battle—for the Aequian army had not yet come up—sought to protect themselves, without fighting, behind their rampart. The next day Fabius, instead of mingling allies and citizens in one line of battle, drew up the three nations in three separate armies, about the enemy's works, taking the center himself with the Roman legions. He then commanded them all to wait for the signal, that the allies might act with the citizens in beginning the fight, and in retreating, if he should sound the recall. He also stationed the cavalry belonging to each division behind its first line. Advancing thus in three sections he surrounded the camp, and attacking sharply on every side, dislodged the Volsci, who were unable to sustain his charge, from their intrenchments. Passing over these, he drove the frightened rabble before him in one direction and cleared the camp of them. As they dispersed in flight, the cavalry, who had found it difficult to surmount the rampart and had hitherto been mere spectators of the battle, having now a clear field before them played their part in the victory by cutting off the fugitives. Great was the slaughter inflicted on the enemy as they attempted to escape, both in the camp and outside the works; but the booty was still greater, since they had barely been able to carry away their arms. If the forests had not covered the flight, their army would have been utterly destroyed.

XXIII. While this battle was being fought near Antium, the Aequi had sent forward the flower of their troops, and by a surprise attack at night, had captured the Tusculan citadel. The rest of their army they stationed at a short distance from the walls of the town, in order to induce the enemy to extend his forces. The news of these events being speedily carried to Rome and thence to the camp at Antium, had the same effect upon the Romans as if it had been announced that the Capitol was taken, so fresh in their recollection was the service done them by the Tusculans, and so strongly did the similarity of the risk which their allies now ran seem to call for repayment of the assistance they had given. Letting everything else go, Fabius quickly conveyed the plunder of the camp to Antium, and leaving there a moderate garrison, hastened by forced marches to Tusculum. The soldiers were allowed to take nothing but their arms and such bread as happened to be at hand;[26] supplies were sent them from Rome by the consul Cornelius. The fighting at Tusculum lasted for some months. With a part of his army the consul laid siege to the camp of the Aequi; a part he had given to the Tusculans to use in recovering the citadel. The place could never be entered by assault; but the enemy were finally driven out by hunger. Having thus reduced them to extremities, the Tusculans took away their arms, and stripping them to the tunic, sent them under the yoke. As they were ignominiously fleeing homeward, the Roman consul overtook them on Mount Algidus, and slew them, every man. The victor led his army back to Columen—this is the name of a place[27]—and went into camp. The other consul too, now that the defeat of the enemy had removed all danger from the walls of Rome, set out himself from the City. Thus at two points the consuls invaded the enemy's borders, and with keen rivalry devastated the lands of the Volsci on the one hand, and those of the Aequi on the other. I find in a good many writers that the Antiates revolted that same year; and that Lucius Cornelius the consul conducted the war and took the town. I should not venture to affirm it for a certainty, since there is no mention of the matter in the older historians.

XXIV. This war was no sooner finished, than the patricians were alarmed by one waged against them at home, by the tribunes, who cried out that the army was dishonestly kept afield—a trick intended to frustrate the passage of the law; which, notwithstanding, they had undertaken and proposed to carry through. Still, Lucius Lucretius, the prefect of the City, obtained the postponement of any action by the tribunes until the consuls should have come. There had also arisen a new cause for disquiet. Aulus Cornelius and Quintus Servilius, the quaestors, had summoned Marcus Volscius to trial, on the charge that he had been guilty of undoubted perjury against Caeso. For it was becoming generally known, from many witnesses, first, that the brother of Volscius after having once fallen ill had not only never appeared in public, but had not even got up from his sick-bed, where he had died of a wasting disease which lasted many months; and secondly, that within the period to which Volscius, in his testimony, had referred the crime, Caeso had not been seen in Rome; for those who had served with him affirmed that he had often during that time been in their company at the front, without taking any furlough. To prove this contention, many persons offered Volscius to refer the question of fact to a private arbitrator. Since he did not dare proceed to arbitration, all these things, pointing in one direction, made the condemnation of Volscius as certain as that of Caeso had been made by Volscius' evidence. The tribunes delayed matters by refusing to allow the quaestors to hold an assembly for his trial until one should first have been held to consider the law. So both affairs dragged on till the arrival of the consuls. When they had entered the City in triumph[28] with their victorious army, nothing was said about the law, and many people thought the tribunes had been daunted. But the tribunes were seeking a fourth term of office—for the end of the year was now at hand—and had diverted their efforts from the law to the contest for the election. And though the consuls strove quite as vehemently against the re-election of the incumbents to the tribuneship, as if a law were being urged which had been promulgated to curtail their own majesty, the contest resulted in victory for the tribunes.

That same year the Aequi sought and obtained peace. The census, which had been begun the year before, was completed; and this, they say, was the tenth lustral sacrifice performed since the founding of the City. There were enrolled 117,319 citizens. This year the consuls won great renown, at home and in the field; not only had they brought about peace with other nations, but at home also, though the state was not yet harmonious, yet it was less troubled than at other times.

XXV. Lucius Minucius and Gaius Nautius were chosen to be the next consuls, and inherited the two causes left over from the preceding year. As before, the consuls obstructed the passage of the law, and the tribunes the trial of Volscius; but the new quaestors were men of superior force and influence. Marcus Valerius, son of Manius, and grandson of Volesus, shared the magistracy with Titus Quinctius Capitolinus, who had thrice been consul. Capitolinus, since it was beyond his power to restore Caeso to the Quinctian family and the greatest of her young men to the state,[29] waged war, as justice and loyalty demanded, on the false witness who had deprived an innocent man of the power to plead his cause. Verginius was the most active amongst the tribunes in working for the law. The consuls were allowed two months' time to inspect the measure, that having explained to the people what hidden mischief was being proposed they might then permit them to vote. The granting of this breathing-space brought tranquillity to the City. But the Aequi did not suffer it to remain long at rest; breaking the treaty which they had made with the Romans the year before, they intrusted the command of their forces to Cloelius Gracchus, at that time by far the most eminent man in their state. Under this man's leadership they invaded the territory of Labici, and from there the territory of Tusculum, with fire and sword, and, loaded with booty, pitched their camp on Algidus. To this camp came Quintus Fabius, Publius Volumnius, and Aulus Postumius, envoys from Rome, to complain of the wrongs done and demand restitution, as provided in the treaty. The Aequian general bade them recite the message of the Roman senate to the oak, saying that he would meantime attend to other matters. (The oak, a mighty tree, overhung head-quarters and with its dense shade afforded a cool resting-place.) Thereupon one of the envoys said, as he departed, "Let both this sacred oak and whatever gods there are hear that the treaty has been broken by you; and let them attend now to our complaints and presently support our arms, when we shall avenge the simultaneous violation of the rights of gods and men." On the return of the envoys to Rome, the senate ordered one consul to lead an army to Algidus, against Gracchus, and to the other assigned the task of devastating the territories of the Aequi. The tribunes sought in their usual fashion to prevent the levy, and might perhaps have held out against it to the end; but suddenly a fresh alarm supervened.

XXVI. A great body of Sabines made a hostile incursion almost to the walls of Rome, wasting the fields and terrifying the citizens. Thereupon the plebeians willingly enlisted, and despite the unavailing protests of the tribunes, two large armies were enrolled. One of these Nautius led against the Sabines. Pitching his camp at Eretum, he sent out little expeditions, chiefly nocturnal raiding parties, and so liberally repaid on their own fields the depredations of the Sabines, that the Roman territories in comparison seemed scarcely to have been touched by war. Minucius had neither the same good fortune nor equal spirit in conducting his campaign; for he encamped not far from the enemy, and without having suffered any considerable defeat, kept timidly within his breastworks. When the enemy perceived this, their audacity was heightened, as is usually the case, by their opponents' fear, and they attacked the camp by night. Failing to accomplish anything by open force, they next day surrounded the place with earthworks; but before these could be thrown up on every side of the camp and so shut off all egress, five horsemen were sent out through the enemy's outposts and carried to Rome the news that the consul and his army were beleaguered. Nothing more surprising or unlooked-for could have happened. And so the alarm and consternation were as great as if it had been the City, not the camp, which the enemy were investing. They sent for the consul Nautius; but deeming him unequal to their defense, and resolving to have a dictator to restore their shattered fortunes, they agreed unanimously on the nomination of Lucius Quinctius Cincinnatus.

What followed merits the attention of those who despise all human qualities in comparison with riches, and think there is no room for great honors or for worth but amidst a profusion of wealth. The sole hope of the empire of the Roman People, Lucius Quinctius, cultivated a field of some four acres[30] across the Tiber, now known as the Quinctian Meadows, directly opposite the place where the dockyards are at present. There he was found by the representatives of the state. Whether bending over his spade as he dug a ditch, or ploughing, he was, at all events, as everybody agrees, intent upon some rustic task. After they had exchanged greetings with him, they asked him to put on his toga, to hear (and might good come of it to himself and the republic!) the mandates of the senate. In amazement he cried, "Is all well?" and bade his wife Racilia quickly fetch out his toga from the hut. When he had put it on, after wiping off the dust and sweat, and came forth to the envoys, they hailed him Dictator, congratulated him, and summoned him to the City, explaining the alarming situation of the army. A boat was waiting for him, provided by the state; and as he reached the other side his three sons came out to receive him; after them came his other kinsmen and friends; and after them the greater part of the senate. Attended by this throng and preceded by his lictors he was escorted to his house. The plebeians too were gathered in great numbers; but they were by no means so rejoiced at the sight of Quinctius, because they thought that not only was his authority excessive, but that the man was even more dangerous than the authority itself. That night nothing more was done than to keep a watch in the City.

XXVII. On the following day the dictator, coming before dawn into the Forum, named as his master of the horse Lucius Tarquitius, a man of patrician birth, but one who had served as a foot-soldier because of poverty, though in war he had been esteemed by far the best of the Roman youth. With his master of the horse the dictator appeared before the people; proclaimed a suspension of the courts; ordered the shops to be closed all over the City; and forbade anybody to engage in any private business. He then commanded all those who were of military age to come armed, before sunset, to the Campus Martius, bringing each enough bread to last five days, and twelve stakes;[31] those who were too old for war he ordered to prepare food for their neighbors who were soldiers, while the latter were getting their arms in order and looking for stakes. So the young men ran this way and that in search of stakes, and everyone took them from the nearest source, nor was anyone interfered with; and all presented themselves promptly as the dictator had commanded. Then, having drawn up their column so as to be ready for fighting as well as for marching, if need were, the dictator himself led the legions, the master of the horse his cavalry. In each division were spoken such words of encouragement as the occasion called for: Let them mend their pace; there was need of speed, that they might reach the enemy's camp in the night; a consul and a Roman army were being besieged, and it was now the third day of their investment; what each night or day might bring forth was uncertain; a single instant was often the turning-point of a great event. The soldiers also, in complaisance to their commanders, cried out to one another, "Make haste, standard-bearer!" "Follow me, men!" At midnight they came to Algidus, and perceiving that they were now close to the enemy, halted.

XXVIII. Then the dictator, having ridden about and observed, as well as he could for the night, the extent of the camp and its shape, directed the military tribunes to make the soldiers throw down their packs in one place, and return, with arms and stakes, to their proper ranks. They did as he commanded. Then, keeping the order of the march, he led out the whole army in a long column and surrounded the enemy's camp, commanding that at a given signal the troops should all raise a shout, and that after shouting every man should dig a trench in front of his own position and erect a palisade. The signal followed close on the announcement. The men did as they had been bidden. Their cheer resounded on all sides of the enemy, and passing over their camp, penetrated that of the consul; in the one it inspired panic, in the other great rejoicing. The Romans, congratulating one another that it was their fellow-citizens who shouted, and that help was at hand, on their own part began to threaten the enemy with attacks from their pickets and outposts. The consul said that they ought to act without delay; the shout not only signified that their friends were come, but that they had begun to fight; and it would be surprising if they were not already assailing the enemy's camp from without. He accordingly bade his men stand to arms and follow him. It was night when they entered the battle; with a cheer they gave the legions of the dictator to know that on their side as well the issue had been joined. The Aequi were already preparing to resist the work of circumvallation, when the attack was begun upon their inner line. Lest a sortie should be made through the midst of their camp, they turned their backs on those who were entrenching, and faced the attacking forces; and, leaving the others free to work all night, they fought till break of day with the soldiers of the consul. At early dawn they had already been shut in by the dictator's rampart, and were scarcely maintaining the battle against one army. Then the troops of Quinctius, who had at once, on completing the works, resumed their weapons, assailed the rampart of the Aequi. Here was a new battle on their hands, and the other not yet in the least abated. At this, hard-driven by a double danger, they turned from fighting to entreaties, and on the one hand implored the dictator, on the other the consul, not to make the victory a massacre, but to take their arms and let them go. The consul referred them to the dictator, who in his anger added ignominy to their surrender. He commanded that Cloelius Gracchus, their commander, and the other captains, be brought to him in chains, and that the town of Corbio be evacuated. He said that he did not require the blood of the Aequi; they might go; but, that they might at last be forced to confess that their nation had been defeated and subdued, they should pass beneath the yoke as they departed. A yoke was fashioned of three spears, two being fixed in the ground and the third laid across them and made fast. Under this yoke the dictator sent the Aequi.

XXIX. Having taken possession of the enemy's camp, which abounded in all sorts of supplies—for he had sent them out with nothing but their tunics—he gave all the booty to his own troops exclusively, rebuking the consular army and the consul himself in these terms: "You shall have no share, soldiers, in the spoils of that enemy to whom you almost fell a spoil; and you, Lucius Minucius, until you begin to have the spirit of a consul, shall command these legions as my lieutenant." So Minucius abdicated the consulship, and remained, as he was ordered to do, with the army.[32] But so tame and submissive was the temper of this army now towards a better commander, that, considering rather the benefit they had received at his hands than the humiliation, they voted the dictator a golden chaplet of a pound in weight, and when he departed, saluted him as their protector. At Rome the senate, being convened by Quintus Fabius, the prefect of the City, commanded Quinctius to enter the gates in triumph, with the troops that accompanied him. Before his chariot were led the generals of the enemy; the military standards were borne on ahead; after them came the soldiers, laden with booty. It is said that tables were spread before all the houses, and the troops,

feasting as they marched, with songs of triumph and the customary jokes, followed the chariot like revellers. On that day Lucius
Mamilius the Tusculan was granted citizenship, with the approval
of all.[33] Cincinnatus would at once have resigned his office, had
not the trial of Marcus Volscius, the false witness, caused him to delay.
The awe in which the tribunes held the dictator prevented them from
interfering with the trial. Volscius was condemned and went into
exile at Lanuvium. On the sixteenth day Quinctius surrendered
the dictatorship which he had received for six months. During that
period the consul Nautius fought a successful engagement at Eretum
with the Sabines, who in addition to the devastation of their fields
now suffered this new disaster. Fabius was sent to Mount Algidus to
succeed Minucius. At the close of the year there was some agitation
for the law on the part of the tribunes; but since two armies were
abroad, the senators insisted that no proposal should be laid before
the people; the plebs were successful in electing the same tribunes
for the fifth time. It is said that wolves were seen on the Capitol,
pursued by dogs; because of which prodigy the Capitol was purified.
Such were the events of this year.

XXX. The next consuls were Quintus Minucius and Marcus
Horatius Pulvillus. At the beginning of the year, though foreign relations were peaceful, at home there were dissensions, inspired by the
same tribunes and the same law; and they would have proceeded to
even greater lengths—so inflamed were men's passions—had it not
been announced, as if designedly, that the garrison at Corbio had
perished in a night-attack made by the Aequi. The consuls convoked
the senate, and were directed to make a summary levy and lead the
army to Mount Algidus. From that moment the quarrel over the law
was laid aside, and a fresh dispute arose, concerning the levy; in this
consular authority was in a fair way to be defeated, by the help of the
tribunes, when a new alarm was reported: that a Sabine army bent
on pillage had descended upon the Roman fields, and was thence
approaching the City. This was such staggering news that the tribunes
permitted the enrolment of troops; yet not without having obtained
an agreement that since they had themselves been baffled for five
years,[34] and the existing tribunate was an insufficient protection to

the plebs, ten tribunes should in future be elected. To this the patricians were compelled to agree, only stipulating that they should not thereafter see the same men tribunes. The tribunician election was held immediately, lest when the war was over this promise too might be broken, as the others had been. In the thirty-sixth year from the first plebeian tribunes ten men were elected, two from each class,[35] and it was enacted that they should be chosen thus thereafter. The levy was then held, and Minucius marched against the Sabines, but did not find the enemy. Horatius, after the Aequi, having put the garrison at Corbio to the sword, had also captured Ortona, fought a battle with them on Mount Algidus, killed many men, and drove off the enemy, not only from Algidus, but from Corbio and Ortona. Corbio he razed because of its betrayal of the garrison.

XXXI. Marcus Valerius and Spurius Verginius succeeded to the consulship. Affairs were quiet both at home and abroad; but there was a shortage in the corn-supply, due to excessive rains. A law was passed opening up the Aventine to settlement. The same tribunes of the plebs were returned; and in the following year, when Titus Romilius and Gaius Veturius were consuls, they took occasion to urge the law in all their speeches: They were ashamed, they said, of the futile increase in their numbers, if this measure was to lie disregarded during their own two years of office, precisely as it had done throughout the five preceding years. Just when this agitation was at its height, there came a disquieting report from Tusculum that the Aequi were in Tusculan territory. Men were ashamed, in view of the recent service of that nation, to delay in sending aid. Both consuls were dispatched with an army; and finding the enemy on their usual ground, Mount Algidus, they there engaged them. Above seven thousand of the enemy were slain; the rest were put to flight; and immense spoils were taken. These the consuls sold, owing to the impoverished condition of the treasury. Nevertheless, their action made them unpopular with the army, and it also furnished the tribunes with an occasion for impeaching the consuls before the plebs. Accordingly when they laid down their office and Spurius Tarpeius and Aulus Aternius became consuls, they were brought to trial; Romilius by Gaius Calvius Cicero, a plebeian

tribune, Veturius by Lucius Alienus, an aedile of the plebs. Both
were condemned, greatly to the indignation of the patricians;
Romilius was fined 10,000 asses, Veturius 15,000. And yet this disaster to their predecessors did not diminish the energy of the new
consuls; they said that it was possible that they should themselves
be condemned, but that it was not possible that the plebs and the
tribunes should carry their law. Then the tribunes, discarding
the law, which, in the time it had been before the people, had lost
its vitality, began to treat more moderately with the patricians: Let
them at last put an end, they said, to these disputes; if the plebeian
measure were not agreeable to them, let them permit framers of
laws to be appointed jointly from both the plebs and the nobility,
that they might propose measures which should be advantageous
to both sides, and secure equal liberty.[36] The patricians did not
reject the principle; but they declared that no one should propose
laws unless he were a patrician. Since they were agreed in regard
to the laws, and only differed about the mover, they sent Spurius
Postumius Albus, Aulus Manlius, and Publius Sulpicius Camerinus
on a mission to Athens, with orders to copy the famous laws of
Solon, and acquaint themselves with the institutions, customs, and
laws of the other Greek states.

XXXII. No foreign wars disturbed the quiet of that year; but
even more quiet was the year that followed, when Publius Curiatius
and Sextus Quinctilius were consuls, for the tribunes preserved an
unbroken silence. This was due in the first place to their waiting
for the commissioners who had gone to Athens, and for the foreign
laws; in the second place two terrible misfortunes had come at
the same time, famine and pestilence, baneful alike to men and
beasts. The fields were left untenanted; the City was emptied by
incessant funerals; many distinguished families were in mourning. The flamen of Quirinus, Servius Cornelius, died, and the
augur Gaius Horatius Pulvillus, in whose place the augurs elected
Gaius Veturius, the more eagerly because of his condemnation
by the plebs. Death took the consul Quinctilius, and four tribunes
of the plebs. The numerous losses made it a gloomy year; but Rome's
enemies did not molest her.

The next consuls were Gaius Menenius and Publius Sestius Capitolinus. In this year likewise there was no foreign war, but disturbances arose at home. The commissioners had now returned with the laws of Athens. The tribunes were therefore the more insistent that a beginning should be made at last towards codification. It was resolved to appoint decemvirs, subject to no appeal, and to have no other magistrates for that year. Whether plebeians should be permitted a share in the work was for sometime disputed; in the end they yielded to the patricians, only bargaining that the Icilian law about the Aventine and the other sacred laws[37] should not be abrogated.

XXXIII. In the three hundred and second year from the founding of Rome the form of the polity was changed again, with the transfer of supreme authority from consuls to decemvirs, even as before it had passed from kings to consuls. It was not so remarkable a change, because it did not last long. For the luxuriant beginnings of this magistracy took on too rank a growth; and in consequence it soon died down, and the custom was resumed of entrusting to two men the name and authority of consuls. The decemvirs chosen were Appius Claudius, Titus Genucius, Publius Sestius, Lucius Veturius, Gaius Julius, Aulus Manlius, Publius Sulpicius, Publius Curiatius, Titus Romilius, and Spurius Postumius. To Claudius and Genucius, the consuls-elect for that year, the new office was given in compensation for the other; and to Sestius, one of the consuls of the year before, because he had brought the measure before the senate against his colleague's will.[38] Next to these were honored the three envoys who had gone to Athens, not only that the office might serve to reward them for so distant a mission, but also in the belief that their knowledge of foreign laws would be useful in compiling a new code. The other four filled up the number. It is said that old men were chosen for the last places, that they might make a less vigorous opposition to the measures proposed by the rest. The guiding hand in the whole magistracy was that of Appius, thanks to the favor of the plebs; and so novel a character had he assumed, that from being a harsh and cruel persecutor of the plebs, he came out all at once as the people's friend, and caught at every breath of popularity.[39] Sitting each one day in ten they administered justice to the people. On that day he who presided in court had twelve fasces;[40] his nine colleagues were each attended by a single orderly. And while they maintained an unparalleled harmony amongst themselves—a unanimity sometimes prejudicial to the governed, they treated others with the utmost fairness. As proof of their moderation, it will suffice to note a single example. Though they had been chosen to a magistracy from which there was no appeal, yet when a corpse was found buried in the house of Publius Sestius, a patrician, and produced before the assembly, and the man's guilt was as clear as it was heinous, Gaius Julius the decemvir summoned Sestius to trial, and appeared before the people to prosecute a man of whose guilt he was the lawful judge, surrendering his own prerogative that he might add to the liberty of the people what he subtracted from the power of the magistracy.

XXXIV. While this prompt justice, as pure as though derived from an oracle, was being meted out impartially by the decemvirs to the highest and the lowest, they were also busily engaged in framing laws. Men's expectations were running high, when they set up ten tables, and summoning the people to assemble, commanded them—with a prayer that the result might be prosperous, favorable, and fortunate, for the commonwealth, for themselves, and for their children—to go and read the proposed statutes. They themselves, they said, so far as the capacities of ten men could forecast the event, had equalized the rights of all, both high and low; but there was greater efficacy in the capacities and counsels of many. Let them consider each single point in their own minds, then discuss it with their fellows, and lastly state in public what excess or shortcoming there was in the several articles; the Roman People should have only such laws as their unanimity might fairly be considered not only to have passed, but to have proposed. When it appeared that the laws had been sufficiently amended, in the light of the opinions that men expressed concerning each separate section, the centuriate comitia met and adopted the Laws of the Ten Tables; which even now, in this great welter of statutes piled one upon another, are the fountain-head of all public and private law. Afterwards the opinion was general that there lacked two tables, by the addition of which a corpus, so to speak, of all the Roman law could be rounded out. The hope of filling this lack made people desirous, when election day drew near, of choosing decemvirs again. The plebs, besides the fact that they hated the name of consul quite as much as that of king, had already ceased to require even the help of the tribunes, since the decemvirs yielded to one another when an appeal was taken.[41]

XXXV. But when the comitia for the election of decemvirs had been announced to take place in four-and-twenty days,[42] there was a great outburst of canvassing; even the chief men in the state—from fear, I doubt not, that if they left the field this great power might fall into unworthy hands—solicited men's votes and humbly begged for an office which they had themselves opposed with all their influence, from those plebeians with whom they had contended. The risk of losing his position, at his time of life, and after holding the offices he had held, acted as a spur to Appius Claudius. One would not have known whether to reckon him among the decemvirs or the candidates. He was at times more like one who sought a magistracy than like one who exercised it. He vilified the nobles; praised all the most insignificant and low-born candidates; and surrounding himself with former tribunes, like Duillius and Icilius, bustled about the Forum, and through them recommended himself to the plebs; till even his colleagues, who had been singularly devoted to him until then, looked askance at him and wondered what this could mean. It was evident there could be nothing genuine about it; so proud a man would certainly not be affable for nothing; excessive self-abasement and mingling with private citizens were not so much the marks of one who was in haste to retire from office as of one who sought the means of re-election. Open opposition to his desires being more than they dared venture, they endeavored by a show of complaisance to lessen its intensity; and unanimously appointed him, as their youngest colleague, to preside at the election. This was a trick, that he might be unable to declare himself elected, a thing which none but tribunes of the plebs (and even there the precedent was most vicious) had ever done. But Appius, strange as it may seem, having promised, with a prayer for Heaven's blessing, to convene the comitia, turned the obstacle into an opportunity. He effected by collusion[43] the defeat of the two Quinctii, Capitolinus and Cincinnatus, of his uncle Gaius

Claudius, a steadfast champion of the aristocratic cause, and of other citizens of the same exalted rank; and declared the election of decemvirs who were no match for these men in excellence. His own name he announced among the first, a thing which good citizens condemned with as perfect unanimity, now it was done, as they had before believed he would not dare to do it. With him were elected Marcus Cornelius Maluginensis, Marcus Sergius, Lucius Minucius, Quintus Fabius Vibulanus, Quintus Poetelius, Titus Antonius Merenda, Caeso Duillius, Spurius Oppius Cornicen, Manius Rabuleius.[44]

XXXVI. Appius now threw off the mask he had been wearing, and began from that moment to live as his true nature prompted him. His new colleagues too he commenced, even before they entered upon office, to fashion after his own character. Everyday they met together without witnesses. The tyrannical designs which they there adopted they matured in secret. They now no longer sought to conceal their pride; they were difficult of access, and surly towards those who sought to speak with them. Thus they carried matters until the Ides of May,[45] at that time the traditional date for beginning a term of office. So then, when they had taken up their duties, they signalized the first day of their administration by a terrible threat. For whereas the former decemvirs had kept to the rule that only one should have the fasces, and that this regal emblem should pass from one to another in rotation, so that each should have his turn, they suddenly appeared in public, every man with his twelve fasces. A hundred and twenty lictors crowded the Forum, and before them, bound up in the rods, they carried axes. And indeed the decemvirs explained that there had been no reason for removing the axe, since the office to which they had been chosen was without appeal. They seemed like ten kings; and the terror they inspired, not only in the humblest citizens but in the leaders of the senate, was intensified by the belief that the decemvirs were merely seeking a pretext and an opening for bloodshed, so that if anybody should pronounce a word in praise of liberty, either in the senate or before the people, the rods and axes might instantly be made ready, were it only to frighten the rest. For besides that there was no help in the people, the right of appeal having been taken away, they had further agreed not to interfere with each other's decisions; whereas their predecessors had allowed their judgments to be revised upon appeal to one of their colleagues; and certain cases which might have been held to be within their own competence they had referred to the people. For a brief period the terror was shared equally by all; but little by little its full force began to fall upon the plebs. The patricians were left unmolested; humbler folk were dealt with arbitrarily and cruelly. It was all a question of persons, not of causes, with the decemvirs, since influence held with them the place of right. They concocted their judgments in private, and pronounced them in the Forum. If anybody sought redress from another decemvir, he came away regretting that he had not accepted the decision of the first. Moreover a report had got out, though it was not vouched for, that they had not only conspired for present wrongdoing but had ratified with an oath a secret agreement amongst themselves not to call an election, but by means of a perpetual decemvirate to hold the power they had once for all acquired.

XXXVII. The plebeians then fell to searching the countenances of the patricians, and would catch at the breath of freedom in that quarter where they had so feared enslavement as to have reduced the state to its present plight. The leading senators hated the decemvirs and hated the plebs. They could not approve of the things that were being done; still they believed them to be not undeserved. They had no desire to help those who in their greedy rush for liberty had fallen upon servitude, preferring that their wrongs should even be multiplied, that disgust at their actual situation might in the end arouse a longing for the two consuls and the former status of affairs. And now the greater part of the year had passed, and the two tables of laws had been added to the ten of the year before; nor was there any further business to make the decemvirate necessary to the republic, so soon as those statutes too should have been enacted in the centuriate assembly. People were anxiously looking forward to the time when the comitia for the election of consuls should be announced. The plebeians felt only one concern: how were they ever going to restore the tribunician power (their bulwark of liberty) which had been suspended? Meanwhile there was no mention of an election. And the decemvirs, who had at first exhibited themselves to the plebs in the society of former tribunes, because this had been thought a recommendation to the people, had now assumed a retinue of young patricians. Their bands blocked the tribunals. They bullied the plebs and plundered their possessions; for success attended the strong, no matter what they coveted. And now they ceased even to respect a man's person; some they scourged with rods, others they made to feel the axe; and, that cruelty might not go unrequited, they bestowed the victim's property upon his slayer. Corrupted by these wages, the young nobles not only made no stand against wrong-doing, but frankly showed that they preferred license for themselves to liberty for all.

XXXVIII. The Ides of May came. Without causing any magistrates to be elected, the decemvirs, now private citizens, appeared in public with no abatement either of the spirit with which they exercised their power or the insignia which proclaimed their office. But this was unmistakable tyranny. Men mourned for liberty as forever lost; nor did anyone arise, or seem likely to do so, in its defense. And not only had the people themselves lost heart; but they had begun to be despised by the neighboring nations, who could ill brook the existence of imperial power where there was no liberty.[46] The Sabines made an incursion with a large force into Roman territory, which they everywhere laid waste. Having safely driven off their booty, comprising men and beasts, they withdrew their army, which had ranged far and wide, to Eretum. There they established a camp, hoping that the want of harmony at Rome would interfere with the levying of troops. Not only the messengers who came, but the flight of the country-people, who thronged the City, inspired a feeling of dismay. The decemvirs considered what they had best do; for they were left in the lurch by the hatred of the patricians on the one side and of the plebs on the other. Moreover Fortune sent an additional alarm. The Aequi came from another quarter and encamped on Algidus, and from there raided the lands of Tusculum. Tusculan envoys brought tidings of these acts, and besought protection. The fright which this occasioned drove the decemvirs, now that the City was hemmed in between two simultaneous wars, to consult the senate. They ordered the Fathers to be summoned to the Curia, though they were not ignorant how great a storm of unpopularity was brewing: the devastation of the land and the dangers which impended would be laid by everybody at their doors; and this would lead to an attempt being made to abolish their magistracy, unless they presented a united resistance, and by sharply exercising their power upon the few really daring spirits, put a stop to the efforts of the rest. When the crier's voice was heard in the Forum, calling the senators to meet the decemvirs in the Curia, it was like an innovation, so long had they disregarded the custom of consulting the senate, and it aroused the attention of the plebs, who wondered what in the world could have happened, that after so long an interval they should be reviving a forgotten usage; the enemy and the war deserved men's gratitude, if anything whatever was being done which was usual in a free state. Men looked about in every corner of the Forum to discover a senator, and seldom recognized one anywhere; then their glances rested on the Curia and the decemvirs sitting there alone. Meantime the decemvirs themselves explained the Fathers' failure to assemble as owing to the universal detestation of their rule; the commons as due to their having no authority, being private citizens, to convoke the senate: a beginning, it seemed, was already being made towards the recovery of freedom, if the plebs would join with the senate; and if, even as the Fathers were refusing, when summoned, to attend the session, so they, for their part, would reject the levy. Such were the murmurs of the plebs. Of senators there was scarce one in the Forum, and there were but few in the City. In their resentment at the situation they had withdrawn to their farms and were absorbed in their private affairs, disregarding those of the nation; for they felt that they were secure from insult only so far as they removed themselves from contact and association with their tyrannical masters. When on being cited they failed to appear, officers were sent round to their houses, for the double purpose of exacting fines and of ascertaining whether their recalcitrancy were deliberate. They reported that the senators were in the country. This was more pleasing to the decemvirs than if they had announced that the Fathers were in town and repudiated their authority. They commanded them all to be summoned, and proclaimed a meeting of the senate for the following day. This session was somewhat better attended than they had themselves expected. Whereupon the plebs concluded that liberty had been betrayed by the senators, since those who had already gone out of office and were mere private citizens, save for the force they exercised, were obeyed by them as though they had the authority to command.

XXXIX. But their obedience in coming to the senate-house was greater, we are told, than their submissiveness in the expression of their views. It is related that Lucius Valerius Potitus, after Appius Claudius had proposed his motion and before the senators were called upon in order for their opinions, demanded leave to speak on the state of the nation; and when the decemvirs tried with threats to prevent his doing so, stirred up a violent commotion by declaring that he would go before the plebs. With equal spirit, it is said, did Marcus Horatius Barbatus enter the dispute, calling them ten Tarquinii, and warning them that the Valerii and the Horatii had been leaders in the expulsion of the kings.[47] Nor was it the name, said he, which had then disgusted men, since by this name Jupiter was duly called; and Romulus, the founder of the City; and the successive kings; and it had even been retained for religious rites as a solemn title.[48] No, it was the pride and violence of the king which men had hated in those days; and if these qualities had then been intolerable in a king, or the son of a king, who would endure them in so many private citizens? Let them beware lest by denying men freedom of speech in the Curia they should set them a-talking outside the Curia as well. He could not see, he continued, how, as a private citizen, he was less entitled to assemble the people for a speech than they were to convene the senate. When they liked they might learn by making the experiment how much stronger indignation was in the vindication of a man's own liberty than was ambition in defense of unjust power. The decemvirs talked of a Sabine war, as if any war were more important to the Roman People than war with those who, though they had been appointed to propose statutes, had left no law in the state; who had done away with elections, with annual magistracies, with the succession of new governors—the only means of equalizing liberty; and who, though private citizens, had the rods and the power of kings. Following the expulsion of the kings there had been patrician magistrates; later, after the secession of the plebs, plebeian magistrates had been elected. Of what party, he asked, were they? Of the popular party? Pray what had they done through the agency of the people? Of the aristocratic party? When they had held no meeting of the senate for close upon a year, and were now so conducting it as to suppress discussion of the national welfare? Let them not trust too much to other men's fears; the things men were enduring now seemed more grievous to them than the things they feared.

XL. While Horatius was thus declaiming, the decemvirs were at a loss to know how far they could afford either to resent or to overlook it; nor could they make out what the upshot was likely to be. But Gaius Claudius, the uncle of Appius the decemvir, made a speech, approaching more nearly to entreaty than expostulation, in which he implored him in the name of his own brother's and his father's departed spirits to remember rather the civil society in which he had been born than the wicked compact he had entered into with his colleagues. This he begged much more for Appius' own sake than for the sake of the nation; indeed the nation would demand its rights in spite of the decemvirs, if they did not accord them voluntarily; but a great struggle usually aroused great passions, and he shuddered to think what these might lead to. Although the decemvirs wished to prevent discussion of anything but the subject they had introduced, they were ashamed to interrupt Claudius, who accordingly brought his speech to a conclusion, with the proposal that the senate should take no action. Everybody accepted this as meaning that Claudius held the decemvirs to be private citizens; and many of consular rank signified their approval, without discussion. Another motion, ostensibly harsher, but in reality somewhat less drastic, directed the patricians to assemble and proclaim an interrex. For by passing any measure whatsoever they declared those who presided over the senate to be magistrates; whereas they had been rated as mere citizens by him who advised the senate against adopting any resolution. Thus the cause of the decemvirs was already collapsing, when Lucius Cornelius Maluginensis, brother of Marcus Cornelius the decemvir, who had purposely been reserved to be the last speaker among the ex-consuls, defended his brother and his brother's colleagues by feigning anxiety about the war. He said he wondered by what fatality it had come about that the decemvirs were being attacked solely, or at least chiefly, by those who had sought election to that office; or why it was that during the many months in which the state had been at peace nobody had raised the question whether regular magistrates were at the head of affairs, and only now, when the enemy were almost at their gates, were men sowing political dissension; unless it was because they thought that in troubled waters it would be harder to discern what was going on. For the rest, was it not right that when men's attention was taken up with the larger concern, all prejudgment of so important a matter should be eliminated? He therefore proposed, concerning the charge brought by Valerius and Horatius that the official term of the decemvirs had expired on the day before the Ides of May, that they should first conclude the impending wars and restore the state's tranquillity, and then refer the question to the senate for settlement; and that Appius Claudius should at once make up his mind to recognize that he must explain, regarding the comitia which he had held for the election of decemvirs—being one himself—whether they were chosen for one year or until the missing laws should be enacted.[49] For the present he thought they should pay no attention to anything but the war. If the current rumors about it seemed to them to be false, and if they supposed that not only the couriers but the Tusculan envoys also had brought them idle stories, he suggested that they send out scouts to investigate and return with more certain information. But if they trusted both couriers and envoys, a levy should be held at the earliest possible moment; and the decemvirs should lead the armies whither it seemed good to each of them, giving precedence to no other business.

XLI. The younger senators were about to force this motion through on a division, when Valerius and Horatius, in a second and more impassioned outburst, demanded that they be permitted to speak about the state of the nation. They would address the people, they said, if they were restrained by a faction from speaking in the senate; for neither could private citizens prevent them, whether in the senate-house or in an assembly, nor would they yield to the emblems of a fictitious authority. Thereupon Appius, thinking the moment was at hand when, unless he opposed their violence with equal boldness, his authority was doomed, cried out, "It will be safer not to utter a word except on the subject of debate!" And when Valerius asserted that he would not be silenced by a mere citizen, he sent a lictor to arrest him. Valerius was imploring the citizens for help, from the threshold of the Curia, when Lucius Cornelius, throwing his arms about Appius, and feigning to be concerned for the other man,[50] stopped the quarrel. At his request Valerius was permitted to say what he wished. But liberty went no further than speech; the decemvirs made good their design. Even the ex-consuls and the elder senators, in consequence of their lingering hatred of the tribunician power, which they thought the plebs regretted much more keenly than they did the authority of the consuls, almost preferred that at some later time the decemvirs should voluntarily abdicate than that hatred of them should lead to another rising of the plebs. If gentle measures should restore the government to the consuls, without any popular outcry, they might, either through the intervention of wars, or through the moderation of the consuls in the exercise of their power, bring the plebeians to forget the tribunes.

The senators permitted in silence the proclamation of a levy. The young men answered to their names, since the authority of the decemvirs was without appeal. When the legions were enrolled, the decemvirs settled among themselves who ought to go to the front and who command the armies. Chief among the ten were Quintus Fabius and Appius Claudius. The war at home seemed more important than that abroad. The violence of Appius was, they thought, more adapted to quell disturbances in the City; while Fabius was of a character deficient in steady rectitude rather than actively bad. For this man, once preeminent in civil and in military affairs, had been so altered by the decemvirate and by his colleagues that he chose rather to be like Appius than like himself. To him was intrusted the war in the Sabine country, and Manius Rabuleius and Quintus Poetelius were given him as colleagues. Marcus Cornelius was sent to Mount Algidus, with Lucius Minucius, Titus Antonius, Caeso Duillius, and Marcus Sergius. Spurius Oppius they assigned to Appius

Claudius, to help him in looking out for the City; and they gave them the same powers as had been exercised by the entire board.

XLII. The business of the nation was managed no better in the field than at home. The only fault of the generals was that they had made the citizens detest them; the rest of the blame belonged to the soldiers, who, that nothing might anywhere prosper under the command and auspices of the decemvirs, permitted themselves to be beaten, to their own disgrace and that of their commanders. Their armies were routed, both by the Sabines near Eretum, and on Algidus by the Aequi. From Eretum they fled in the silence of the night, and intrenched themselves near the City, between Fidenae and Crustumeria, on elevated ground. When the enemy followed them up, they nowhere ventured to fight in the open field, but defended themselves by the position and their rampart, not by bravery and arms. The disgrace on Algidus was worse, and a worse disaster was sustained; even the camp was lost, and stripped of all their baggage, the soldiers fled to Tusculum, to subsist by the loyalty and compassion of their hosts, which nevertheless did not fail them. To Rome came such alarming reports that the patricians, laying aside now their hatred of the decemvirs, voted to establish watches in the City, and commanded all who were of an age to bear arms to guard the walls and do outpost duty before the gates. They decreed that arms should be dispatched to Tusculum, and reinforcements, and that the decemvirs should descend from the Tusculan citadel and hold their troops in camp; that the other camp should be transferred from Fidenae to Sabine territory, so that by taking the offensive they might frighten the enemy into abandoning his design to besiege the City.

XLIII. To the disaster suffered at the hands of the enemy the decemvirs added two shameful crimes, one committed in the field, the other at home. Lucius Siccius[51] was serving in the Sabine campaign. Taking advantage of the hatred entertained for the decemvirs, he would scatter hints, in secret conversations with the common soldiers, that they should elect tribunes and secede. So the generals sent him to look out a place for an encampment; and instructed the men whom they assigned to share his expedition to set upon him when they had got to a suitable spot, and kill him. He died not unavenged. For he laid about him, and several of the assassins fell, for he was very strong, and though surrounded, defended himself with a courage equal to his strength. The others reported at the camp that they had fallen into an ambuscade, and that Siccius had perished, fighting valiantly, and with him certain soldiers. At first their report was believed; afterwards a cohort set out, by permission of the decemvirs, to bury the slain; and finding that none of the bodies there had been despoiled, and that Siccius lay armed in the midst, with all the bodies facing him, while the enemy had left no dead nor any indication of having withdrawn, they brought back the corpse, and declared that Siccius had certainly been murdered by his own men. The camp was ablaze with indignation, and it was resolved that Siccius should be carried to Rome forthwith; but the decemvirs made haste to give him a military funeral at the public cost. The soldiers sorrowed greatly at his burial, and the worst reports were current about the decemvirs.

XLIV. This outrage was followed by another, committed in Rome, which was inspired by lust and was no less shocking in its consequences than that which had led, through the rape and the death of Lucretia, to the expulsion of the Tarquinii from the City and from their throne; thus not only did the same end befall the decemvirs as had befallen the kings, but the same cause deprived them of their power. Appius Claudius was seized with the desire to debauch a certain maiden belonging to the plebs. The girl's father, Lucius Verginius, a centurion of rank, was serving on Algidus, a man of exemplary life at home and in the army. His wife had been brought up in the same principles, and his children were being trained in them. He had betrothed his daughter to the former tribune Lucius Icilius, an active man of proven courage in the cause of the plebeians. She was a grown girl, remarkably beautiful, and Appius, crazed with love, attempted to seduce her with money and promises. But finding that her modesty was proof against everything, he resolved on a course of cruel and tyrannical violence. He commissioned Marcus Claudius, his client, to claim the girl as his slave, and not to yield to those who demanded her liberation, thinking that the absence of the maiden's father afforded an opportunity for the wrong. As Verginia was entering the Forum—for there, in booths, were the elementary schools—the minister of the decemvir's lust laid his hand upon her, and calling her the daughter of his bond-woman and herself a slave, commanded her to follow him, and threatened to drag her off by force if she hung back. Terror made the maiden speechless, but the cries of her nurse imploring help of the Quirites quickly brought a crowd about them. The names of Verginius her father and of her betrothed Icilius were known and popular. Their acquaintance were led to support the girl out of regard for them; the crowd was influenced by the shamelessness of the attempt. She was already safe from violence, when the claimant protested that there was no occasion for the people to become excited; he was proceeding lawfully, not by force. He then summoned the girl to court. She was advised by her supporters to follow him, and they went before the tribunal of Appius. The plaintiff acted out a comedy familiar to the judge, since it was he and no other who had invented the plot: The girl had been born, said Marcus, in his house, and had thence been stealthily conveyed to the home of Verginius and palmed off upon him as his own; he had good evidence for what he said, and would prove it even though Verginius himself were judge, who was more wronged than he was; meanwhile it was right that the hand-maid should follow her master. The friends of the girl said that Verginius was absent on the service of the state; he would be at hand in two days' time if he were given notice of the matter; it was unjust that a man should be involved in litigation about his children when away from home; they therefore requested Appius to leave the case open until the father arrived, and in accordance with the law he had himself proposed, grant the custody of the girl to the defendants,[52] nor suffer a grown maiden's honor to be jeopardized before her freedom should be adjudicated.

XLV. Appius prefaced his decision by saying that it was evident how much he favored liberty from that very law which the friends of Verginius made the pretext for their claim; but the law would afford liberty a sure protection only if it varied neither with causes nor with persons; for in the case of others who were claimed as free, the demand was legal, since anyone might bring an action: in the case of one who was under the authority of a father there was no one else to whom the master ought to yield the custody; accordingly he decreed

that the father should be summoned, and that meanwhile the claimant should not relinquish his right, but should take the girl in charge
and guarantee that she should be produced at the coming of him
who was called her father.[53]

Against the injustice of the decree, though many murmured
their disapproval, there was not a single man who dared to stand
out; when Publius Numitorius, the girl's great-uncle,[54] and her lover
Icilius, arrived on the scene. When a path had been opened for
them through the throng, since the crowd believed that the intervention of Icilius would be particularly effectual in resisting Appius,
the lictor cried that the case had been decided, and as Icilius began
to protest, attempted to thrust him aside. Even a placid nature
would have been incensed by so violent an insult. "You must use iron
to rid yourself of me, Appius," he cried, "that you may carry through
in silence what you desire should be concealed. This maiden I am
going to wed; and I intend that my bride shall be chaste. So call
together all your colleagues' lictors too; bid them make ready
rods and axes: the promised wife of Icilius shall not pass the night
outside her father's house. No! If you have taken from the Roman
plebs the assistance of the tribunes and the right of appeal, two
citadels for the defense of liberty, it has not therefore been granted
to your lust to lord it over our children and our wives as well! Vent
your rage upon our backs and our necks: let our chastity at least be
safe. If that shall be assailed, I will call on the Quirites here present
to protect my bride, Verginius will invoke the help of the soldiers
in behalf of his only daughter, and all of us will implore the protection of gods and men; nor shall you ever repeat that decree of yours
without shedding our blood. I ask you, Appius, to consider earnestly
whither you are going. Let Verginius decide what to do about his
daughter, when he comes; but of one thing he may rest assured: if
he yields to this man's claim, he will have to seek a husband for her.
As for me, in defense of the freedom of my bride I will sooner die
than prove disloyal."

XLVI. The crowd was deeply moved and a conflict appeared to be
imminent. The lictors had surrounded Icilius, but had nevertheless
gone no further than to threaten him, since Appius declared that it

was not a question of Verginia's defense by Icilius, but of a turbulent fellow, who even now breathed the spirit of the tribunate, seeking an opportunity to stir up strife. He would furnish him no excuse for it that day; but that he might know now that the concession had not been made to his own wantonness but to the absent Verginius, to the name of father, and to liberty, he would not pronounce judgment that day nor deliver a decision; he would request Marcus Claudius to waive his right and suffer the girl to remain at large until the morrow; but unless the father should appear the next day, he gave notice to Icilius and to those like Icilius that the proposer of his law would not fail to support it, nor the decemvir be wanting in firmness; and in any case he should not call together his colleagues' lictors to repress the instigators of sedition, but rest content with his own.

The time for accomplishing the wrong having been postponed, the girl's supporters went apart by themselves, and decided that first of all the brother of Icilius and the son of Numitorius, active young men, should proceed straight to the City gate and make all possible haste to the camp, to summon Verginius; for the maiden's safety turned on her protector's being at hand in time. They set out the moment they got their orders, and galloping their horses, carried the message through to the father. When the claimant of the girl pressed Icilius to furnish the sureties required of her guarantor, and Icilius said that it was precisely that which he was considering (though he was doing his best to consume time, that the messengers who had been dispatched to the camp might get a start on the way), the people began on every side to raise their hands, and every man of them to indicate his readiness to go bail for Icilius. And Icilius said, with tears in his eyes, "I am grateful to you; tomorrow I will use your services; of sureties I now have enough." So Verginia was surrendered, on the security of her kinsmen. Appius waited a little while, that he might not appear to have sat for this case only, and when nobody applied to him—for all other matters were forgotten in men's concern over this, he went to his house and wrote to his colleagues in camp that they should grant no furlough to Verginius, and should even detain him in custody. His base design was too late, as it deserved to be; Verginius had already got his leave, and had set out in the fore-part of the night, nor was it until early the next morning that the letters for detaining him were delivered, to no purpose.

XLVII. But in the City, as the citizens at break of day were standing in the Forum, agog with expectation, Verginius, dressed in sordid clothes and leading his daughter, who was also meanly clad and was attended by a number of matrons, came down into the market place with a vast throng of supporters. He then began to go about and canvass people, and not merely to ask their aid as a favor, but to claim it as his due, saying that he stood daily in the battle-line in defense of their children and their wives; that there was no man of whom more strenuous and courageous deeds in war could be related—to what end, if despite the safety of the City those outrages which were dreaded as the worst that could follow a city's capture must be suffered by their children? Pleading thus, as if in a kind of public appeal, he went about amongst the people. Similar appeals were thrown out by Icilius; but the women who attended them were more moving, as they wept in silence, than any words. In the face of all these things Appius hardened his heart—so violent was the madness, as it may more truly be called than love, that had overthrown his reason—and mounted the tribunal. The plaintiff was actually uttering a few words of complaint, on the score of having been balked of his rights the day before through partiality, when, before he could finish his demand, or Verginius be given an opportunity to answer, Appius interrupted him. The discourse with which he led up to his decree may perhaps be truthfully represented in some-one of the old accounts, but since I can nowhere discover one that is plausible, in view of the enormity of the decision, it seems my duty to set forth the naked fact, upon which all agree, that he adjudged Verginia to him who claimed her as his slave. At first everybody was rooted to the spot in amazement at so outrageous a proceeding, and for a little while after the silence was unbroken. Then, when Marcus Claudius was making his way through the group of matrons to lay hold upon the girl, and had been greeted by the women with wails and lamentations, Verginius shook his fist at Appius and cried, "It was to Icilius, Appius, not to you that I betrothed my daughter; and it was for wedlock, not dishonor, that I brought her up. Would you have men imitate the beasts of the field and the forest in promiscuous gratification of their lust? Whether these people propose to tolerate such conduct I do not know: I cannot believe that those who have arms will endure it."

The claimant of the maiden was being forced back by the ring of women and supporters who surrounded her, when silence was commanded by a herald; (XLVIII) and the decemvir, crazed with lust, declared that he knew, not only from the abusive words uttered by Icilius the day before and the violence of Verginius, which he could prove by the testimony of the Roman People, but also from definite information, that all through the night meetings had been held in the City to promote sedition. Accordingly, having been aware of the approaching struggle, he had come down into the Forum with armed men, not that he might do violence to any peaceable citizen, but to coerce, conformably to the dignity of his office, those who would disturb the nation's peace. "You will therefore," he cried, "best be quiet! Go, lictor, remove the mob and open a way for the master to seize his slave!" When he had wrathfully thundered out these words, the crowd parted spontaneously and left the girl standing there, a prey to villainy. Then Verginius, seeing no help anywhere, said, "I ask you, Appius, first to pardon a father's grief if I have somewhat harshly inveighed against you; and then to suffer me to question the nurse here, in the maiden's presence, what all this means, that if I have been falsely called a father, I may go away with a less troubled spirit." Permission being granted, he led his daughter and the nurse apart, to the booths near the shrine of Cloacina, now known as the "New Booths," and there, snatching a knife from a butcher, he exclaimed, "Thus, my daughter, in the only way I can, do I assert your freedom!" He then stabbed her to the heart, and, looking back to the tribunal, cried, "'Tis you, Appius, and your life I devote to destruction with this blood!" The shout which broke forth at the dreadful deed roused Appius, and he ordered Verginius to be seized. But Verginius made a passage for himself with his knife wherever he came, and was also protected by a crowd of men who attached themselves to him, and so reached the City gate. Icilius and Numitorius lifted up the lifeless body and showed it to the people, bewailing the crime of Appius, the girl's unhappy beauty, and the necessity that had constrained her father. After them came the matrons crying aloud, "Was it on these terms that children were brought into the world? Were these the rewards of chastity?"—with such other complaints as are prompted at a time like this by a woman's anguish, and are so much the more pitiful as their lack of self-control makes them the more give way to grief. The men, and especially Icilius, spoke only of the tribunician power; of the right of appeal to the people which had been taken from them; and of their resentment at the nation's wrongs.

XLIX. The wildest excitement prevailed amongst the people, occasioned in part by the atrocity of the crime,[55] in part by the hope of improving the opportunity to regain their liberty. Appius first commanded that Icilius be summoned; then, on his resisting, that he be arrested; and at last, when the crowd would not allow his attendants to approach the man, he headed a band of patrician youths in person, and advancing through the mob, bade them drag his enemy off to prison. By this time Icilius was supported not only by the populace but by the leaders of the populace as well, Lucius Valerius and Marcus Horatius, who, forcing the lictor back, declared that if Appius proceeded legally, they would protect Icilius from the prosecution of a mere citizen; if he sought to make use of violence, there too they would be a match for him. This led to a desperate struggle. The decemvir's lictor now made a rush at Valerius and Horatius; his rods were broken by the mob. Appius mounted the platform; Horatius and Valerius followed him. To them the crowd listened; the decemvir's voice they drowned with noise. And now, as though vested with authority, Valerius was commanding the lictors to withdraw from one who was a private citizen; when Appius, broken in spirit and fearing for his life, covered up his head and sought refuge in a house near the Forum, unobserved by his opponents. Spurius Oppius, wishing to assist his colleague, burst into the Forum from the other quarter. He saw that authority had been overcome by force. Distracted then by the suggestions which came from every side, and timidly agreeing first with one and then with another of his many advisers, he ended by ordering the senate to be summoned. This course, inasmuch as a great proportion of the patricians appeared to disapprove of the decemvirs' acts, afforded hopes that the senators would end their power, and so quieted the multitude. The senate decided that the plebs must not be provoked, and that it was even more necessary to see to it that the arrival of Verginius in the army should not occasion any turbulence.

L. Accordingly certain of the younger senators were dispatched to the camp, which was then on Mount Vecilius, and carried word to the decemvirs that they must employ all their resources to keep the troops from mutiny. There Verginius aroused a greater commotion than he had left in Rome. For besides that he was seen approaching attended by a body of nearly four hundred men, who had joined him when he left the City, in their anger and resentment at the affair, the weapon in his hand and the gore with which he was spattered drew the attention of the entire camp upon him. Then too the appearance of togas in the camp, in many places, produced the effect of a greater company of civilians than were actually there. Being asked what the matter was, Verginius wept, and for a long time answered never a word; at length, when the bustle and confusion of the gathering had subsided and silence had ensued, he gave an orderly account of all that had taken place. Then, lifting up his hands in an attitude of prayer, and addressing the crowd as his fellow-soldiers, he besought them not to attribute to him the crime of which Appius Claudius stood guilty, nor to repudiate him as one who had murdered his child. To him the life of his daughter had been dearer than his own, if she had been permitted to live pure and chaste; when he saw her being carried off like a slave to be dishonored, thinking it better to lose his children by death than by outrage, he had been impelled by pity to an act of seeming cruelty; nor would he have survived his daughter, had he not hoped to avenge her death by the help of his fellow-soldiers. They too had daughters, sisters, and wives; the lust of Appius Claudius had not been extinguished with the life of Verginia, but its lawlessness would be proportioned to its impunity. In the calamity of another they had been given a warning to be on their guard against similar wrongs. So far as he was concerned, his wife had been taken from him in the course of nature, his daughter, because she could no longer have lived chaste, had died a pitiful but an honorable death; for the lust of Appius there was now no longer in his house any scope; from other forms which his violence might take he would defend his own person with no less spirit than he had shown in defense of his daughter; the others must look out for themselves and for their own children. As Verginius spoke these words in a loud voice, the multitude signified with responsive shouts that they would not forget his sufferings nor fail to vindicate their liberty. And the civilians, mingling with the crowd, repeated the same complaints and told them how much more shameful the thing would have appeared if they could have seen it instead of hearing about it; at the same time they reported that the decemvirate was already overthrown at Rome; and on the arrival of later tidings, to the effect that Appius had almost lost his life and had gone into exile, they induced the troops to raise the cry "To arms!" and to pluck up their standards and set out for Rome. The decemvirs, troubled alike by what they saw and by what they heard had taken place in Rome, rushed through the camp, one this way, another that, to still the rising. And so long as they mildly remonstrated, they got no answer; but if one of them tried to use his authority, they told him that they were men, and armed. They marched in column to the City and took possession of the Aventine, urging the plebeians, as often as they fell in with one, to make an effort to regain their liberty and to elect plebeian tribunes. Save this, no violent proposals were heard. The senate was convened by Spurius Oppius. It was resolved that no harsh action should be taken, seeing that occasion for the mutiny had been given by themselves.[56] Three delegates of consular rank, Spurius Tarpeius, Gaius Julius, and Publius Sulpicius, were dispatched in the name of the senate to inquire by whose orders the men had deserted the camp, and what they meant, who with arms had seized the Aventine, and, abandoning the enemy, had captured their native City. The men were at no loss for an answer: what they lacked was someone to make it, since they had as yet no definite leader, nor did individuals quite dare to single themselves out for enmity. But the crowd called out in unison that they should send them Lucius Valerius and Marcus Horatius, to whom they would intrust their reply.

LI. After the delegates had been dismissed, Verginius reminded the soldiers that they had been thrown into confusion a few

minutes before, over a matter of no very great importance, because
the multitude had been without a head; and although a very good
answer had been returned, yet this had been due rather to their
happening to feel alike about the matter than to a concerted plan.
He recommended that ten men should be chosen to have supreme
command, and that they should be styled, by a military title,
tribunes of the soldiers. When they would have tendered Verginius
himself the first appointment to this office, he replied, "Reserve
your good opinion of me till my own affairs and yours are in a
better plight; to me no honor can be agreeable while my daughter
is unavenged; nor is it well for you, with the state in such confusion,
to be led by those who are most exposed to hatred. If I can render
any service, it shall not be less because I am a private citizen." So
they chose ten military tribunes.

Nor was the army in the Sabine country inactive. There too,
at the instigation of Icilius and Numitorius, a secession from the
decemvirate was brought about; men's anger on being reminded
of the murder of Siccius being no less violent than that which was
kindled in them by the new story of the maiden whose dishonor had
been so foully sought. Icilius, on hearing that military tribunes
had been elected on the Aventine, feared lest the City comitia might
take their cue from the comitia of the soldiers[57] and elect the same
men to be tribunes of the plebs, for he was experienced in the ways
of the people; and having designs upon that office himself, he saw
to it, before they marched to the City, that the same number of men,
vested with equal power, were chosen by his own army. They entered
Rome under their standards, by the Colline Gate, and marched
right through the midst of the City to the Aventine. There they
joined the other army, and directed the twenty military tribunes to
appoint two of their number to exercise supreme command. Marcus
Oppius and Sextus Manilius were appointed.

The Fathers were alarmed about the state; but, though the senate
held daily sessions, they spent more time in recriminations than in
deliberating. Siccius' murder was cast in the teeth of the decemvirs,
as well as the lust of Appius, and their disgraces in the field. It was
decided that Valerius and Horatius should go to the Aventine. They

agreed to go only on condition that the decemvirs would put off the insignia of that magistracy which they had already ceased to hold the year before. The decemvirs, complaining that they were being deprived of their office, asserted that they would not lay down their authority until after the enactment of the laws which had been the reason of their appointment.

LII. Having learned from Marcus Duillius, who had been a plebeian tribune, that nothing was coming of the endless bickerings of the senate, the commons quitted the Aventine for the Sacred Mount, since Duillius assured them that not until the patricians beheld the City deserted would they feel any real concern; the Sacred Mount would remind them of the firmness of the plebs, and they would know whether it were possible or not that affairs should be reduced to harmony without the restoration of the tribunician power. Marching out by the Via Nomentana, then called Ficulensis, they pitched their camp on the Sacred Mount, having imitated the good behavior of their fathers and made no depredations. Following the army came the plebeian civilians; nor did anyone who was of an age to go hold back. They were attended a little way forth by their wives and children, who inquired pathetically to whose protection they were leaving them, in that City where neither chastity nor liberty was sacred.

Now that all Rome was desolate with an unwonted loneliness, and there was nobody in the Forum but a few old men, and it appeared, particularly when the Fathers had been summoned to the senate-house, quite deserted, there were many others besides Horatius and Valerius who remonstrated. "What will you wait for, Conscript Fathers?" they cried out. "If the decemvirs persist in their obstinacy, will you suffer everything to go to wrack and ruin? Pray what is that authority, decemvirs, to which you cling with such tenacity? Is it to roofs and walls you will render judgment? Are you not ashamed that your lictors should be seen in the Forum in almost larger numbers than the other citizens? What do you mean to do if the enemy should come to the City? What if, by and bye, the plebs, finding us unmoved by their secession, come with sword in hand? Do you wish the downfall of the City to be the end of your rule? And yet, either we must have no plebs, or we must have plebeian tribunes. We will sooner dispense with patrician magistrates than they with plebeian. It was a new and untried power when they extorted it from our fathers: now that they have once been captivated by its charm, they would be even less willing to forgo it, especially when we on our side do not so temper the exercise of our authority that they stand in no need of help." As these reproaches were flung at them from every quarter, the decemvirs were overborne by the consensus of opinion and gave assurances that they would submit, since it was thought best, to the authority of the senate. They had but this one request to make—which was also a warning, that their persons might be protected from men's hate, and that their blood might not be the means of accustoming the plebs to punish senators.

LIII. Valerius and Horatius were then sent to bring back the plebs and adjust all differences, on such terms as might seem good to them; and they were also instructed to secure the decemvirs against the anger and violence of the people. Having proceeded to the camp, they were received with great rejoicings by the plebs, as undoubted champions of liberty both in the beginning of the disturbance and in the sequel. In recognition of this they were thanked on their arrival, Icilius speaking on behalf of the multitude. And it was Icilius too who, when terms were discussed and the commissioners inquired what the plebeïans demanded, made such requests, in pursuance of an understanding already reached before the arrival of the envoys, that it was apparent they based their hope more on equity than on arms. For the recovery of the tribunician power and the appeal were the things they sought—things which had been the help of the plebs before the election of decemvirs; and that it should not be held against any man that he had incited the soldiers or the people to recover their liberties by secession. Only in regard to the punishment of the decemvirs was their demand a harsh one; for they thought it just that the decemvirs should be delivered up to them, and threatened to burn them alive. To these proposals the commissioners replied: "The demands which have been prompted by your judgment are so right that they ought to have been accorded you voluntarily; for you seek in them guarantees of liberty, not of a license to make attacks on others. But your anger calls for pardon rather than indulgence, seeing that hatred of cruelty is driving you headlong into cruelty, and almost before you are free yourselves you are wishing to lord it over your adversaries. Will the time never come when our state shall rest from punishments visited either by the patricians on the Roman plebs or by the plebs on the patricians? A shield is what you need more than a sword. It is enough and more than enough for a lowly citizen when he lives in the enjoyment of equal rights in the state, neither inflicting an injury nor receiving one. Even if you are one day to make yourselves dreaded, when you have got back your magistrates and laws and possess authority to put us on trial for our lives and fortunes, you shall then give judgment in accord with the merits of each particular case: for the present it is enough to regain your liberty."

LIV. When the people all consented that they should do as they saw fit, the envoys assured them that they would settle matters and presently return. So they departed and explained to the Fathers the demands of the plebs. The other decemvirs, when they found that, contrary to their expectation, no mention was made of any punishment of themselves, made no objection to anything: Appius, hard-hearted, knowing himself peculiarly unpopular, and measuring other men's hatred of himself by his own of them, exclaimed, "I am not unaware of the lot which threatens me. I perceive that the attack upon us is only being postponed till arms are handed over to our adversaries. Hatred must have its offering of blood. I too am willing to relinquish the decemvirate." A decree was passed by the senate that the decemvirs should abdicate the magistracy at the earliest possible moment; that Quintus Furius, the Pontifex Maximus,[58] should hold an election of plebeian tribunes; and that no one should be made to suffer for the secession of the soldiers and the plebs.

Having so decreed the senate adjourned and the decemvirs went before the people and laid down their office, to the great delight of all. These events were reported to the plebs, the envoys being accompanied by all the people left in the City. The multitude was met by another joyful throng from the camp, and they exchanged congratulations on the restoration of freedom and harmony to the state. The commissioners addressed the people as follows: "Prosperity, favor, and good fortune to you and the Republic! Return to your native

City, to your homes, to your wives, and your children; but let the
self-restraint you have shown here, where no man's farm has been
violated, though so many things were useful and necessary to so
great a multitude, be preserved when you return to the City. Go to
the Aventine, whence you set out. There in the auspicious place where
you first laid the foundations of your liberty, you shall choose tribunes
of the plebs. The Pontifex Maximus will be at hand to hold the election." With loud applause and great alacrity the people showed their
approval of all that had been said. They pulled up their standards
from the place and set out for Rome, vying with those whom they met
in joyful demonstrations. Armed, they proceeded in silence through
the City to the Aventine. There the Pontifex Maximus at once held the
comitia, and they elected tribunes of the plebs; first of all Lucius
Verginius; then Lucius Icilius and Publius Numitorius, Verginia's
great-uncle,[59] the instigators of the secession; then Gaius Sicinius,
son of the man who is related to have been the first plebeian tribune
chosen on the Sacred Mount; and Marcus Duillius, who had filled the
tribuneship with distinction before the decemvirs were appointed,
and had not failed the plebs in their contentions with the decemvirs.
Then, more by reason of their promise than for any deserts of theirs,
they elected Marcus Titinius, Marcus Pomponius, Gaius Apronius,
Appius Villius, and Gaius Oppius. As soon as they had taken office,
Lucius Icilius proposed to the people, and they so voted, that no man
should suffer for the secession from the decemvirs. Immediately a
bill that consuls should be elected subject to appeal was offered by
Marcus Duillius and was carried. These matters were all transacted
by the council of the plebs, in the Flaminian Meadows, which men
now call the Flaminian Circus.

LV. Then, through an interrex, they elected to the consulship
Lucius Valerius and Marcus Horatius, who at once assumed office.
Their administration was favorable to the people, without in any
way wronging the patricians, though not without offending them;
for whatever was done to protect the liberty of the plebs they
regarded as a diminution of their own strength. To begin with, since
it was virtually an undecided question whether the patricians were
legally bound by plebiscites, they carried a statute in the centuriate

comitia enacting that what the plebs should order in the tribal organization should be binding on the people—a law which provided the
rogations of the tribunes with a very sharp weapon. Next they not
only restored a consular law about the appeal, the unique defense
of liberty, which had been overthrown by the decemviral power, but
they also safeguarded it for the future by the solemn enactment of
a new law, that no one should declare the election of any magistrate
without appeal, and that he who should so declare might be put to
death without offense to law or religion, and that such a homicide
should not be held a capital crime. And having sufficiently strengthened the plebs, by means of the appeal on the one hand and the
help of the tribunes on the other, they revived, in the interest of
the tribunes themselves, the principle of their sacrosanctity (which
was a thing that had now come to be well-nigh forgotten) by restoring certain long-neglected ceremonies; and they rendered those
magistrates inviolate, not merely on the score of religion but also by
a statute, solemnly enacting that he who should hurt the tribunes of
the plebs, the aediles,[60] or the decemviral judges[61] should forfeit his
head to Jupiter, and that his possessions should be sold at the temple
of Ceres, Liber, and Libera. Expounders of the law deny that anyone
is sacrosanct by virtue of this statute, but maintain that the man who
has injured any of these officials is solemnly forfeited to Jupiter;
hence the aedile may be arrested and imprisoned by the greater
magistrates, an act which, though it be unlawful—for he is thereby
injured who, according to this statute, may not be injured, is nevertheless a proof that the aedile is not regarded as sacrosanct; whereas
the tribunes are sacrosanct in consequence of the ancient oath taken
by the plebs, when they first created this magistracy.[62] There were
some who taught that by this same Horatian law the consuls also
were protected, and the praetors, inasmuch as they were created
under the same auspices as the consuls; for the consul was called
"judge." But this interpretation is refuted by the fact that it was not
yet the custom in those days for the consul to be called "judge," but
"praetor." Such were the consular laws. The practice was also instituted by the same consuls that the decrees of the senate should be
delivered to the aediles of the plebs at the temple of Ceres. Up to

that time they were wont to be suppressed or falsified, at the pleasure of the consuls. Marcus Duillius, the tribune of the plebs, then proposed to the plebs, and they so decreed, that whosoever should leave the plebs without tribunes and whosoever should declare the election of a magistrate without appeal should be scourged and beheaded. All these measures, though they were passed against the will of the patricians, were yet not opposed by them, since, so far, no one person had been singled out for attack.

LVI. Then, when the tribunician power and the liberty of the plebs were firmly established, the tribunes, believing that it was now safe to proceed against individuals and that the time was ripe for doing so, selected Verginius to bring the first accusation and Appius to be defendant. When Verginius had cited Appius to appear, and the latter, attended by a crowd of young patricians, had come down into the Forum, there was instantly revived in the minds of all the recollection of that most wicked power, as soon as they caught sight of the man himself and his satellites. Then Verginius said, "Oratory was invented for doubtful matters; and so I shall neither waste time in arraigning before you the man from whose cruelty you freed yourselves with arms, nor shall I suffer him to add to his other crimes the impudence of defending himself.[63] I therefore pardon you, Appius Claudius, all the impious and wicked deeds which you dared, during two years, to heap one upon another; on one charge only, unless you shall name a referee to establish your innocence of having illegally assigned custody of a free person to him who claimed her as his slave, I shall order you to be taken to prison." Neither in the protection of the tribunes nor in the decision of the people had Appius anything to hope; yet he called upon the tribunes, and when none of them would stay proceedings, and he had been arrested by an officer, he cried, "I appeal." The sound of this word, the one safeguard of liberty, coming from that mouth by which, shortly before, a free person had been given into the custody of one who claimed her as a slave, produced a hush. And while the people muttered, each man to himself, that there were gods after all, who did not neglect the affairs of men; and that pride and cruelty were receiving their punishment, which though late was nevertheless not light—that he was appealing who had nullified appeal; that he was imploring the protection of the people who had trodden all the rights of the people under foot; that he was being carried off to prison, deprived of his right to liberty, who had condemned the person of a free citizen to slavery—the voice of Appius himself was heard amidst the murmurs of the assembly, beseeching the Roman People to protect him. He reminded them of the services his forefathers had rendered the state in peace and in war; of his own unfortunate affection for the Roman plebs, in consequence of which he had given up his consulship—in order to make the laws equal for all—with great offense to the patricians; of the laws he had himself drawn up,[64] which were still standing while their author was being dragged off to prison. For the rest, when he should be given an opportunity to plead his cause, he would try what would come of his own peculiar services and shortcomings; at present he asked that, in accordance with the common right of citizenship, he be permitted, being a Roman citizen and under accusation, to speak, and to be judged by the Roman People. He did not so fear men's malice as to have no hope in the justice and pity of his fellow citizens. But if he was to be imprisoned, his cause unheard, he appealed once more to the tribunes of the plebs, and warned them not to imitate those whom they hated. And if the tribunes should confess that they were bound by the same agreement which they charged the decemvirs with having entered into, not to hear an appeal, he still appealed to the people, and invoked the laws, both consular and tribunician, which had been enacted concerning appeals that very year. For who, he asked, should make an appeal, if a man who had not been condemned, whose cause had not been heard, might not do so? What humble plebeian would find protection in the laws, if they afforded none to Appius Claudius? His own case would show whether the new statutes had established tyranny or freedom, and whether the appeal to the tribunes and that to the people against the injustice of magistrates had been merely a parade of meaningless forms, or had been really granted.

LVII. Against this plea Verginius asserted that Appius Claudius alone was beyond the pale of the laws and of the rights of citizens and men. He bade his hearers look on the tribunal, the stronghold of all crimes, where that man, as perpetual decemvir, deadly foe to their fortunes, their persons, and their lives, threatening them all with rods and axes, despising gods and men, backed by executioners instead of lictors, had began to turn his thoughts from rapine and murder to lust; and, in full sight of the Roman People, had torn a free maiden from her father's arms, as though she had been a captive taken in war, and bestowed her as a gift upon his pimp and client; the tribunal where, by his tyrannical decree and wicked judgments, he had armed a father's right hand against his daughter; where, as they were lifting up the body of the dying girl, he had ordered her betrothed and her uncle to be haled to prison—more moved by the disappointing of his pleasure than by her death. For Appius too had been built that prison which he was wont to call the home of the Roman plebs. Accordingly, though he should again and repeatedly appeal, he would himself again and repeatedly challenge him to prove before a referee that he had not adjudged a free citizen to the custody of one who claimed her as a slave. Should he refuse to go before a referee, he bade him be led to gaol, as one found guilty. Though none raised his voice in disapproval, there were yet profound misgivings on the part of the plebs when he was cast into prison, since they saw in the punishment of so great a man a sign that their own liberty was already grown excessive. The tribune appointed a day for the continuance of the trial.

Meanwhile from the Latins and the Hernici came envoys to congratulate the Romans upon the harmony subsisting between the patricians and the plebs; and to commemorate it they brought a gift for Jupiter Optimus Maximus, to the Capitol. This was a golden crown, of no great weight, for their states were not rich, and they observed the worship of the gods with piety rather than magnificence. From these same envoys came the information that the Aequi and the Volsci were making strenuous preparations for war. The consuls were therefore bidden to divide the commands between them. To Horatius fell the campaign against the Sabines; to Valerius that against the Aequi.[65] When they had proclaimed a levy for these wars, the plebs showed so much goodwill that not only the juniors but also a great number of volunteers who had served their time presented themselves for enrolment, with the result that not alone in numbers but in the quality of the troops as well, owing to the admixture of veterans, the army was stronger than usual. Before they left the City, the consuls had the decemviral laws, which are known as the Twelve Tables, engraved on bronze, and set them up in a public place. Some authors say that the aediles, acting under orders from the tribunes, performed this service.

LVIII. Gaius Claudius, who loathed the wickedness of the decemvirs and was particularly offended by his nephew's insolence, had retired to Regillus, the ancient seat of his family. He was advanced in years, but he returned to Rome to beg for the pardon of the man whose vices he had fled. In sordid garments, accompanied by his clansmen and clients, he went about the Forum, soliciting the support of one citizen after another, beseeching them that they would not seek to brand the Claudian race with the shame of being held to merit imprisonment and chains. A man whose portrait-mask would be held in the highest honor by coming generations, the framer of statutes and the founder of Roman law, lay in prison among night-prowling thieves and banditti. Let them turn their minds from wrath, for a moment, to consider and reflect upon the matter; and let them sooner forgive one man, at the entreaty of so many Claudii, than scorn, in their hatred of one, the prayers of many. He was doing this, he said, out of regard to his family and his name; nor had there been any reconciliation between him and the man whose adversity he sought to succor. By courage they had got back their liberty; by showing mercy they had it in their power to establish harmony between the orders. There were some whom he moved, more by his family-loyalty than by the cause of the man for whom he pleaded. But Verginius begged them rather to pity himself and his daughter, and to hearken, not to the entreaties of the Claudian family, whose province it was to tyrannize over the plebs, but instead to those of Verginia's relations, the three plebeian tribunes, who had been appointed to help the plebs but were themselves imploring the plebs to protect and comfort them. Men found more reason in his tears. And so Appius, cut off from hope, did not wait for the appointed day to come, but killed himself.

Immediately thereafter Publius Numitorius caused the arrest of Spurius Oppius, who stood next in point of unpopularity, because he had been in the City when the unjust verdict was pronounced by his colleague. Yet a wrong which Oppius committed was more responsible for men's bitterness towards him than the one which he failed to prevent. A witness was produced who, after enumerating his twenty-seven campaigns, during which he had eight times received special decorations, which he wore in full sight of the people, tore open his tunic and exhibited his back, scored by the rods, professing that if the defendant could name any crime of which he had been guilty, he would suffer him without complaining, private citizen though he was, to vent his rage upon him a second time. Oppius too was led to prison, and before the day of trial he there put an end to his life. The property of Claudius and that of Oppius was confiscated by the tribunes. Their colleagues in the decemvirate went into exile, and their possessions were forfeited. Marcus Claudius also, the claimant of Verginia, was cited and condemned, but at the instance of Verginius himself the extreme penalty was remitted; and being allowed to depart, he went into exile at Tibur. And so the manes of Verginia, who was more fortunate after her death than she had been while alive, after ranging through so many houses in quest of vengeance, were finally at peace; for no guilty man remained.

LIX. A great fear had come over the patricians, and the bearing of the tribunes was now just what that of the decemvirs had been, when Marcus Duillius, a tribune of the plebs, placed a salutary check upon their excessive power. "Our own liberty," he declared, "and the exaction of penalties from our enemies have gone far enough; I shall therefore this year allow no one to be arraigned or thrown into gaol. For on the one hand it is not good to rake up old offenses, already blotted out of memory, now that recent crimes have been expiated by the punishment of the decemvirs; and on the other hand we have a guarantee that no wrong will be attempted that could call for the intervention of tribunician authority, in view of the unceasing care both consuls take to protect your liberty." It was this moderation on the tribune's part which first relieved the patricians of their fear. It also increased their dislike of the consuls, since the latter had been so wholly devoted to the plebs that the safety and independence of the patricians had been dearer to a plebeian magistracy than to their own, and their opponents had grown sated with punishing them before the consuls evinced any intention of opposing their license. And there were many who said that the senate had shown a want of resolution in having voted for the measures proposed by the consuls; and indeed there was no doubt that in the troubled state of public affairs they had yielded to the times.

LX. The consuls, having set affairs in order in the City and established the position of the plebs, departed to their respective commands. Valerius, facing the armies of the Aequi and Volsci, which had already effected a junction on Mount Algidus, deliberately postponed engaging them; had he risked an immediate decision, it is likely—such was the difference in spirit between the Romans and the enemy, in consequence of the godless dealings of the decemvirs— that the struggle would have cost him a severe defeat. He established his camp a mile from the enemy and kept his men within the works. The enemy repeatedly drew up their troops in fighting order on the ground between the camps, and challenged the Romans to come out and engage them; but no one answered them. At length, weary with standing and waiting, to no purpose, for the battle, the Aequi and Volsci concluded that the Romans had virtually yielded them the victory; and marched off to pillage, some against the Hernici, others against the Latins, leaving behind what was rather a garrison for the camp than a sufficient force for giving battle. On perceiving this the consul repaid the fear he had previously been made to feel, and forming a line of battle, himself provoked the enemy. Since they declined the combat, conscious of their want of strength, the Romans felt an immediate access of courage, and regarded their opponents, cowering behind the palisade, as beaten men. After standing in line all day intent on fighting, the Romans withdrew at nightfall. And they, on their side, were full of hope, as they ate their evening meal; but the enemy's spirits were by no means so high, and they sent out couriers far and wide, in great alarm, to recall the marauders. The nearest of these hastened back; but those who were farther afield could not be found. As soon as it was light, the Romans sallied from their camp, intending to assault the rampart, unless the enemy gave battle. So, when the day was now far spent and the enemy made no move, the consul ordered an advance. The Roman line having got in motion, the Aequi and Volsci were ashamed that their victorious armies should depend for protection upon stockades, instead of valor and the sword. Accordingly they too demanded of their leaders, and received, the signal to attack. A part had already passed out through the gates and the rest were following in good order, each man coming out into his proper place; when the Roman consul, not waiting till the enemy's line should be strongly posted in full force, advanced to the charge. The attack, which he delivered before their troops had all been brought out, and when those who had been were insufficiently deployed, found little more than a surging mob of men, who as they hurried this way and that cast anxious looks at one another and wished for their missing friends. The shouting and the fury of the onset increased their agitation, and at first they fell back; then, when they had collected their wits and on every side heard their officers wrathfully demanding if they meant to yield to troops whom they had beaten, they rallied and held their own.

LXI. The consul, on the other side, bade the Romans remember that on that day they were for the first time fighting as free men for a free Rome. They would be conquering for themselves, not that they might become the spoil of decemvirs in the hour of victory. It was no Appius who was commanding them, but the consul Valerius, descendant of liberators of the Roman People, and himself their liberator. Let them show that in previous battles it had been the fault of the generals, not of the soldiers, that they had failed to win. It would be disgraceful to have shown more courage in facing their fellow citizens than in facing the enemy, and to have been more fearful of enslavement at home than abroad. No one's chastity but Verginia's had been in danger while they were at peace, no citizen but Appius had been possessed of a dangerous lust; but if the fortune of war turned against them, the children of all of them would be in danger from all those thousands of enemies; yet he would not utter an omen which neither Jupiter nor Mars their Father would suffer to come home to a City founded with such auspices. He reminded them of the Aventine and the Sacred Mount, that they might bring back an undiminished power to the spot where liberty had a few months before been won, and might show that the nature of Rome's soldiers was the same after the expulsion of the decemvirs that it had been before they were elected, and that equality before the law had not lessened the courage of the Roman People. Having pronounced these words amid the standards of the infantry, he hastened to the cavalry. "Come, young men," he cried, "surpass the foot-soldiers in daring as you do in honor and in rank! At the first encounter the infantry have forced the enemy back; now that they are repulsed, do you give rein to your horses and drive them from the field. They will not sustain the shock; even now they are rather hesitating than resisting." Clapping spurs to their horses they charged the enemy, already disordered by the infantry-attack, and penetrating his lines, dashed through to the rear; while another division made a detour over unoccupied ground, and finding the enemy everywhere in flight turned most of them back from their camp and frightened them off by riding across their course. The infantry and the consul himself swept on into the camp in the full tide of battle, and took possession of it. The enemy's losses in men were great, but in booty were even greater.

The report of this battle having been brought not only to Rome but also to the Sabine country and the other army, was celebrated in the City with rejoicings, and in the camp inspired the soldiers with a desire to emulate the glorious achievement. Horatius had already accustomed them, by practice in raids and skirmishes, to be self-reliant, instead of dwelling on the disgrace they had incurred under the leadership of the decemvirs; and small engagements had encouraged the highest hopes of the general outcome. Nor were the Sabines backward—emboldened as they were by their victory of the year before—with challenges and threats. Why, they asked, did the Romans waste their time advancing swiftly in small companies, like brigands, and as hurriedly retreating; thus dissipating in many little combats the issues of one pitched battle? Why did they not attack in line and suffer fortune to decide the matter once for all?

LXII. Besides the fact that they had of themselves accumulated a good store of confidence, the Romans were also kindled with indignation. The other army, they said, would presently be returning victorious to the City; they themselves were actually being insulted and reviled by the enemy; but when should they be a match for him, if they were not at that moment? When the consul became aware how the soldiers were murmuring in the camp, he called them together. "Soldiers," said he, "you have heard, I suppose, how matters have gone on Algidus. The army has proved to be such as it was fitting that the army of a free people should be. By my colleague's strategy and the bravery of his men a victory has been won. As for me, my strategy and my courage will be what you make them yourselves. It is within our power either to prolong the war with advantage or to bring it to a speedy and successful end. If it is to be prolonged, I shall seek to increase your hopes and courage from day to day by the same course of training I have begun; if your spirits are already high enough and you wish the war to be decided, come, give a shout here in the camp, to show your goodwill and your courage, like the cheer you will raise in the battle!" The shout was given with great alacrity, and the consul promised, invoking good fortune on the enterprise, that he would do as they wished and lead them forth to battle on the morrow. The rest of the day they spent in making ready their arms.

Next day, as soon as the Sabines saw the Romans forming, they came out themselves, for they had long been eager to fight. It was a battle such as takes place when both armies are confident; for the glory of the one was ancient and unbroken, and the other was exalted by its recent unaccustomed victory. Moreover the Sabines employed a stratagem to increase their strength; for when they had marshalled a front of equal extent with the Roman, they held two thousand men in reserve to hurl against their opponent's left, as soon as the battle should be under way. These troops, attacking in flank, had almost encompassed that wing, and were beginning to overpower it; when the cavalry of the two legions, numbering about six hundred, leaped down from their horses and rushed to the front, where their comrades were already giving ground. There they made a stand against the foe and at the same time roused the courage of the infantry, first by sharing the danger on equal terms, and then by causing them to feel ashamed. They felt humiliated that the cavalry should be fighting in their own fashion and in that of infantry too, and that the infantry should not be as good as the horsemen, even when these were dismounted.

LXIII. They therefore renewed the battle which on their flank had been given up, and advanced again into the position from which they had retreated, and in a trice the fighting was not merely even, but the Sabine wing had begun to yield. The horsemen, under cover of the ranks of infantry, regained their mounts. Then they galloped across to the other wing, announcing the victory to their friends; and at the same time they made a charge against the enemy, who were already panic-stricken, as they might well be when the stronger of their wings had been defeated. No other troops showed more conspicuous courage in that battle. The consul looked out for every contingency, commended the brave, and upbraided any who fought listlessly. Being rebuked they would at once begin to acquit themselves like men, shame proving as powerful an incentive to them as praise to the others. With a fresh cheer all along the line the Romans made a concerted effort and drove the enemy back, and from that moment there was no resisting the violence of their onset. The Sabines fled in confusion through the fields and left their camp to be plundered by their foes. There the Romans won back not the possessions of their allies, as on Algidus, but their own which had earlier been lost to them through the raids on their lands.

Though a double victory had been gained in two separate battles, the senate was so mean as to decree thanksgivings in the name of the consuls for one day only. The people went unbidden on the second day also in great numbers, to offer up thanks to the gods; and this unorganized and popular supplication was attended with an enthusiasm which almost exceeded that of the other. The consuls had arranged to approach the City within a day of one another, and summoned the senate out into the Campus Martius. While they were there holding forth on the subject of their victories, complaints were made by leading senators that the senate was being held in the midst of the army on purpose to inspire fear. And so the consuls, to allow no room for the accusation, adjourned the senate from that place to the Flaminian Meadows, where the temple of Apollo is now, and which was called even then Apollo's Precinct. When the Fathers, meeting there, refused with great unanimity to grant a triumph, Lucius Icilius the plebeian tribune laid the issue before the people. Many came forward to dissuade them, and Gaius Claudius was particularly vehement. It was a triumph, he said, over the patricians, not Rome's enemies, which the consuls desired; they were seeking a favor in return for personal services they had done the tribune, not an honor in requital of valor. Never before had a triumph been voted by the people; the decision whether this honor had been deserved had always rested with the senate; not even the kings had infringed the majesty of the highest order in the state; let not the tribunes so dominate all things as not to suffer the existence of any public council; if each order retained its own rights and its own dignity, then, and only then, would the state be free and the laws equal for all. After many speeches had been made to the same purpose by the other older members of the senate, all the tribes voted in favor of the motion. Then, for the first time, a triumph which lacked the authorization of the senate was celebrated at the bidding of the people.[66]

LXIV. This victory of the tribunes and the commons had nearly resulted in a dangerous abuse; for the tribunes conspired together to obtain their re-election, and, that their own ambition might be less conspicuous, to procure as well the return to office of the consuls. Their pretext was the solidarity of the patricians, which had operated, by injurious treatment of the consuls, to break down the authority of the tribunes of the plebs. What would happen if, ere the laws were firmly established, the new tribunes should be assailed through the agency of consuls belonging to the patricians' own party? For there would not always be consuls like Valerius and Horatius, who preferred the liberty of the plebs to their own interests. By a fortunate chance in this emergency the superintendence of the elections fell by lot to none other than Marcus Duillius, a far-seeing man who perceived that the re-election of the magistrates would be fraught with odium. But when he asserted that he would not consider the candidacy of any of the former tribunes, his colleagues vehemently insisted that he should receive the suffrages of the tribes without restriction, or else resign the presidency of the election to his fellow-tribunes, who would conduct the voting in accordance with the law rather than the desires of the patricians. A controversy having thus arisen, Duillius summoned the consuls before the benches of the tribunes and asked them what course they meant to pursue in the consular elections; and finding, by their replying that they should have new consuls chosen, that he had got in them popular supporters of his unpopular policy, he went with them before the assembly. When the consuls, on being there brought forth to the people and asked what they would do if the Roman People, mindful of their help in the recovery of liberty at home and remembering their military successes, should again elect them to office, declined to alter their determination, Duillius first praised the consuls for persisting to the end in their unlikeness to the decemvirs, and then held the election. And after five tribunes had been chosen and no other candidates obtained a majority of the tribes, on account of the eagerness with which the nine incumbents openly sought re-election, he dismissed the assembly, nor did he afterwards convene it for an election. He declared that the law had been satisfied, which, without anywhere prescribing the number, provided only that the tribunate should not be left vacant; and directed that those who had been elected should co-opt colleagues. He recited too the formula of the announcement, in which the following words occurred: "If I shall call for your suffrages for ten tribunes of the plebs; if for any reason you shall elect today less than ten tribunes of the plebs, then let those whom the elected tribunes co-opt as their colleagues be as legally tribunes of the plebs as those whom you shall this day have chosen to that office." Having persevered to the end in denying that the state could have fifteen plebeian tribunes,[67] and having defeated the cupidity of his colleagues, Duillius laid down his magistracy, approved by patricians and plebs alike.

LXV. The new tribunes of the plebs consulted the wishes of the nobles in the co-optation of colleagues; they even chose two who were patricians and ex-consuls, Spurius Tarpeius and Aulus Aternius.[68] The new consuls, Spurius Herminius and Titus Verginius Caelimontanus, being specially devoted neither to the cause of the patricians nor to that of the plebs, enjoyed a peaceful year both at home and abroad. Lucius Trebonius, a tribune of the commons, being angry with the patricians, because, as he said, he had been defrauded by them in the co-optation of the tribunes and had been betrayed by his colleagues,[69] proposed a law that he who called upon the Roman plebs to elect tribunes should continue to call upon them until he should effect the election of ten; and he so baited the nobles during his year of office as even to gain the surname of *Asper,* or "the Truculent."

Next, Marcus Geganius Macerinus and Gaius Julius became consuls, and assuaged the strife of the tribunes with the young nobles, without censuring those magistrates or sacrificing the dignity of the patricians. They withheld the plebs from sedition by suspending a levy which had been decreed with a view to making war on the Volsci and the Aequi, averring that so long as the City was quiet their foreign relations were likewise entirely peaceful; that it was discord in Rome which made other nations take heart. The pains they were at to maintain peace were also productive of internal harmony. But the one order was always taking advantage of the moderation of the other; the plebs were tranquil, but the younger patricians began to insult them. When the tribunes attempted to assist the lowly, at first their services were of little effect; and later they did not even escape violence themselves, especially in the last months of their term, since not only were wrongs committed through cabals of the more powerful, but the effectiveness of every magistrate rather languished, as a rule, in the latter part of the year. By this time the plebs had ceased to count upon the tribunate, unless they could have tribunes like Icilius; for two years they had had mere names. The elder patricians, for their part, though they thought their young men too headstrong, yet preferred, if moderation must be left behind, that the excess of spirits should be on their side rather than with their adversaries. So difficult is it to be moderate in the defense of liberty, since everyone, while pretending to seek fair-play, so raises himself as to press another down; while insuring themselves against fear, men actually render themselves fearful to others; and having defended ourselves from an injury, we proceed—as though it were necessary either to do or suffer wrong—to inflict injury upon our neighbor.

LXVI. Titus Quinctius Capitolinus (for the fourth time) and Agrippa Furius were then made consuls. They experienced neither domestic sedition nor foreign war, but were threatened with both. The strife between citizens could now no longer be repressed, since tribunes and plebs alike were inflamed against the patricians, and the trial of one or another of the nobles was continually embroiling the assemblies in new quarrels. At the first disturbance in these meetings the Aequi and Volsci took up arms, as though they had received a signal, and also because their leaders, being eager for plunder, had convinced them that the Romans had found it impossible, the year before, to carry out the levy which they had proclaimed, since the plebs were no longer amenable to authority; and that this had been the reason why armies were not dispatched against themselves. Lawlessness was breaking down their martial traditions, nor was Rome any longer a united nation; all the hostility and quarrelsomeness they had formerly entertained towards other nations was now being turned against themselves; the wolves[70] were blinded with mad rage at one another, and there was now an opportunity to destroy them. Combining their armies, they first desolated the country of the Latins, and then, when it appeared that there was no one in that region to punish them, they carried their marauding, amidst the triumphant rejoicings of the advocates of war, to the very walls of Rome, in the direction of the Esquiline Gate, where they insolently exhibited to the inhabitants of the City the devastation of their lands. After they had withdrawn unmolested, and driving their booty before them had marched to Corbio, the consul Quinctius summoned the people to an assembly.

LXVII. There he spoke, as I understand, to the following effect: "Although I am conscious, Quirites, of no wrong-doing, nevertheless it is with great shame that I have come to this assembly to confront you. To think that you know, to think that future generations will be told, that the Aequi and the Volsci, but now scarce a match for the Hernici, have in the fourth consulship of Titus Quinctius approached the walls of the City of Rome—with impunity, and armed! We have now for a long time been living under such conditions that my mind could foresee nothing good; yet had I known that such a disgrace

was in store for this year, of all others, I should have shunned it even
at the cost of exile or of death, in default of other means of escaping
office. So! Had they been men whose swords were there at our gates,
Rome might have been captured in my consulship! I had enjoyed
honors enough, I had had enough, and more than enough, of life;
death should have come to me in my third consulship. For whom,
pray, did the most dastardly of our enemies feel such contempt? For
us, the consuls, or for you, Quirites? If the fault is ours, deprive us
of authority we do not merit; and if that is not enough, then punish
us to boot: if yours, may neither god nor man seek to punish your
sins, Quirites; only may you yourselves repent of them! It was not
cowardice in you that they despised, nor was it their own courage
in which they put their trust; in truth they have been too often
beaten and routed, despoiled of their camps, stripped of their lands,
and sent under the yoke, not to know both themselves and you: it
was the discord betwixt the classes, and the quarrels—poison of
this City—between the patricians and the plebs that roused their
hopes, as they beheld our greed for power and yours for liberty;
your disgust at the patrician magistracies and ours at the plebeian.
In Heaven's name what would you have? You conceived a longing
for tribunes of the plebs; for the sake of harmony we granted them.
You desired decemvirs; we allowed them to be elected. You grew
exceedingly weary of the decemvirs; we compelled them to abdicate.
When your resentment against them persisted in their retirement
to private life, we permitted men of the highest birth and the most
distinguished careers to suffer death and exile. Again you desired
to choose tribunes of the plebs, and chose them; to appoint consuls
of your own faction, and though we saw that this was unfair to the
patricians, we beheld even the patrician magistracy presented to
the plebs. That you should enjoy the support of tribunes and the
right of appeal to the people; that the decrees of the plebs should
be made binding upon the patricians; that on the pretext of equalizing the laws our rights should be trodden under foot—all this we
have endured and are now enduring. What end will there be to our
dissensions? Will a time ever come when we can have a united City?
Will a time ever come when this can be our common country? We,

the beaten party, accept the situation with more equanimity than do you, the victors. Is it not enough that we must fear you? It was against us that the Aventine was taken; against us that the Sacred Mount was occupied; we have seen the Esquiline almost captured by the enemy, and the Volscian mounting our rampart. The enemy found none to drive him back; against us you show your manhood; against us you have drawn the sword."

LXVIII. "Come now, when you have laid siege to the senate-house here, and rendered the Forum unsafe, and filled the gaol with our leading men, go out in that same valorous spirit beyond the Esquiline Gate; or if your courage is not equal even to that, behold from the walls how your fields have been laid waste with fire and sword, how your cattle are being driven off, while far and wide the smoke is rising from burning buildings. 'But,' you may say, 'it is the community that suffers by these things: the fields are burned; the City is besieged; the glory of the war rests with the enemy.' How now? In what plight are your private interests? Every man of you will presently be getting from the country a report of his personal losses. Pray what resources do you command for supplying the want of these things? Shall the tribunes restore and make good to you your losses? Resounding words they will pour forth to your hearts' content, and accusations against prominent men, and laws one after another, and assemblies; but from those assemblies there was never one of you returned home the better off in circumstances or in fortune. Has ever one of you carried aught back to wife and children but animosities, complaints, and quarrels, both public and private? from which you always fly for refuge, not to your own bravery and innocence, but to the help of others. But, by Hercules! When you used to serve under us, the consuls, instead of under tribunes, and in camp instead of in the Forum; when your shout was raised in the battle-line, not the assembly, and caused not the Roman nobles but the enemy to shudder; in those days, I say, you were wont to capture booty, to strip the enemy of his lands, and crowned with success and glory—for the state no less than for yourselves—to return in triumph to your homes and your household gods; now you suffer the foe to load himself with your riches and depart. Hold fast to your assemblies and live your lives in the Forum; you shall still be pursued by the necessity of that service which you seek to evade. It was hard to march against the Aequi and Volsci; the war is before your gates. If it is not driven back, it will soon be within the walls and will scale Citadel and Capitol and pursue you into your homes. Last year the senate commanded that an army should be levied and led out to Algidus: we are still sitting idly at home, scolding each other like so many women, rejoicing in the temporary peace, and not perceiving that we shall soon be paying for this brief repose with a war many times: as great. I know that there are other things more pleasant to hear; but even if my character did not prompt me to say what is true in preference to what is agreeable, necessity compels me. I could wish to give you pleasure, Quirites, but I had far sooner you should be saved, no matter what your feeling towards me is going to be. It has been ordained by nature that he who addresses a crowd for his own selfish ends should be more acceptable to it than he whose mind regards nothing but the general welfare; unless perhaps you suppose that it is for your sakes that the public flatterers—I mean your courtiers of the plebs, who will suffer you neither to be at war nor to keep the peace—are exciting you and urging you on. Once thoroughly aroused you are a source of political advancement or of profit to them; and because they see that so long as the orders are harmonious they themselves count for nothing anywhere, they had rather lead an evil cause than none. If you are capable at last of feeling a disgust for these things, and are willing to resume your fathers' and your own old-fashioned manners, in place of these new-fangled ones, I give you leave to punish me as you like, if within a few days I have not defeated and routed these devastators of our fields, stripped them of their camp, and shifted this alarm of war which now dismays you from our gates and walls to the cities of our enemies."

LXIX. Rarely has the speech of a popular tribune been more agreeable to the plebs than was at that time this speech by the sternest of consuls. Even the young men, who amid such alarms were wont to regard a refusal to enlist as their sharpest weapon against the nobles, began to look forward to war and arms. And the flight of the country-people and the presence of those who had been plundered while on their farms and wounded, and who reported worse outrages than those which met the eyes of the citizens, filled all Rome with resentment. When the senate had met, then in truth all turned to Quinctius, whom they looked on as the sole champion of Roman majesty. The foremost senators declared that his speech had been worthy of the consular authority, worthy of the many consulships he had held in the past, worthy of his whole life, crowded as it had been with honors which, often as he had received them, he had still oftener deserved. Other consuls had either flattered the plebs by betraying the dignity of the patricians, or by harshly inforcing the rights of their order had exasperated the populace while seeking to subjugate them; Titus Quinctius had spoken without forgetting the dignity of the patricians, or the harmony of the orders, or—what was particularly important—the existing crisis. They begged him and his colleague to undertake the guidance of the state; they besought the tribunes to unite with the consuls in a single-minded effort to repel their enemies from the walls of the City, and to cause the plebs to yield obedience to the patricians in so alarming a situation; the appeal to the tribunes came, they said, from their common country, which implored their assistance for its wasted fields and its well-nigh beleaguered City. By general consent a levy was proclaimed and held. The consuls announced in the assembly that there was no time to consider excuses; that all the juniors should present themselves at dawn of the following day in the Campus Martius; that they would take time when the war was over to listen to the excuses of those who had failed to hand in their names; and that any man whose excuse they did not approve would be treated as a deserter. Next day the entire body of young men appeared. The cohorts each chose their own centurions, and two senators were put in command of every cohort. We are told that all these measures were carried out so promptly that the standards were fetched from the treasury by the quaestors that very day, and being carried to the Campus Martius, headed the line of march from the mustering ground at ten o'clock in the morning; and the newly recruited army, with the voluntary escort of a few cohorts of veterans, encamped over night at the tenth mile-stone.[71] The following day brought the enemy into view, and the

Roman camp was established close to theirs, near Corbio. On the third day, the Romans being urged on by indignation, and the enemy, who had so often revolted, by the consciousness of their guilt and by despair, no attempt was made to delay the battle.

LXX. Although the two consuls were of equal authority in the Roman army, yet they made an arrangement which is extremely advantageous in the administration of important measures, by which Agrippa yielded the supreme command to his colleague. The latter, thus preferred, responded courteously to the ready self-effacement of the other by admitting him to a share in his plans and his achievements, and treating him as an equal, despite his inferiority. In the battle-line Quinctius held the right wing, Agrippa the left; to Spurius Postumius Albus, the lieutenant, they gave the center in charge; and the other lieutenant, Publius Sulpicius, they put in command of the horse. The infantry on the right fought brilliantly, and were vigorously resisted by the Volsci. Publius Sulpicius broke through the enemy's center with his cavalry. He might have returned to the Roman side the way he went, before the enemy could reform their broken ranks; but it seemed better to assail them in the rear. It would have been but the work of a moment to charge them from behind and throw them into confusion between the two attacks; but the Volscian and Aequian cavalry met him with his own kind of troops and held him in check for some little while. Thereupon Sulpicius cried out that there was no time for hesitation; they were surrounded and cut off from their fellows, unless they put forth all their might and disposed of the enemy's cavalry. Nor was it enough to rout them and let them get safely off; they must destroy them, horse and man, that none might ride back into the battle or renew the fight. It would be impossible, he said, for their cavalry to resist his men, when the close ranks of their infantry had given way before them. His words did not fall upon deaf ears. With a single rush the Romans routed the entire body of cavalry. Hurling great numbers of them from their horses, they transfixed men and steeds with their javelins. This ended the cavalry-battle. Then they fell upon the hostile infantry, and sent off gallopers to announce their success to the consuls, where the enemy's line was already beginning to give way.[72] The tidings at once aroused fresh ardor in the conquering Romans and filled the faltering Aequi with confusion. It was in the center that their defeat began, where the attack of the troopers had thrown their ranks into disorder; then the left wing began to fall back before the consul Quinctius. The Romans experienced most difficulty on the right; there Agrippa, young, active, and courageous, perceiving that the battle was everywhere going better than on his own front, snatched the standards from the men who bore them, and began to carry them forward himself, and even to fling some of them into the press of the enemy. The disgrace with which his soldiers were thus threatened spurred them to the attack, and the victory was extended to every part of the line. A message then came from Quinctius, saying that he had beaten the enemy and was already threatening their camp, but did not wish to storm it until he knew that the fight had been decided on the left wing also; if Agrippa had already defeated his opponents, let him bring up his troops, that the entire army might enter together into possession of the spoils. The victorious Agrippa accordingly joined his victorious colleague, with mutual congratulations, in front of the enemy's camp. Its handful of defenders was speedily put to flight, and the Romans burst into the entrenchments without encountering resistance. The consuls led their army back to the City laden with a vast quantity of booty, as well as with the goods which they had lost by the pillage of their fields but had now recovered. I do not find either that the consuls themselves asked for a triumph or that one was offered them by the senate; nor is there any record of the reason why they despised the honor or did not hope for it. The best conjecture I myself can offer, after so long an interval of time, is this: since the consuls Valerius and Horatius, who besides beating the Volsci and Aequi had also attained renown by bringing the Sabine war to a successful conclusion, had been refused a triumph by the senate, they were ashamed to ask for that distinction in recompense of an achievement only half as great, lest even if it should be granted, it might seem that account had been taken rather of persons than of deserts.

LXXI. The glory of defeating the enemy was sullied by a shameful judgment given by the people in Rome regarding the boundaries of her allies. The men of Aricia and those of Ardea had often gone to war over a territory which both cities claimed. Exhausted by the many defeats which each had experienced, they referred their quarrel to the Roman People for decision. When they had come to plead their cause, and a popular assembly had been granted them by the magistrates, they argued their respective claims with great vehemence. The testimony had already been taken, and the time had come for the tribes to be summoned and the people to give their votes, when Publius Scaptius, an aged plebeian, arose and said: "If I am permitted, consuls, to speak concerning the nation's interests, I will not suffer the people to go wrong in this matter." The consuls declared that he was an untrustworthy fellow and ought not to be listened to, and when he protested noisily that the public cause was being betrayed, they ordered him to be removed; whereat he appealed to the tribunes. The tribunes, as almost always happens, were swayed by the crowd, instead of swaying it, and, to please the greedy ears of the plebs, gave Scaptius leave to say what he wished. He therefore began, and said that he was eighty-two years old and had fought in the army, in that district which was under discussion, not as a youth, but as one already in his twentieth year of service at the time of the campaign before Corioli. Hence it came that he was telling them of a matter forgotten with the lapse of years, but fixed in his own memory, namely that the disputed land had been a part of the territory of Corioli, and had consequently, on the capture of that town, become, by right of conquest, the property of the Roman People. He marvelled, he said, at the effrontery with which the men of Ardea and Aricia hoped to deprive the Roman People—whom they had made the judge, in place of being the owner—of a territory over which they had never exercised any authority so long as the state of Corioli was intact. He had himself but a little while to live; yet he had not been able to convince himself that, having as a soldier done his part to conquer the land, he should not defend it, even in his old age, with the only weapon left him, to wit his voice. He earnestly counselled the people not to condemn their own cause from an unreasonable motive of propriety.

LXXII. When the consuls had perceived that Scaptius was listened to not only in silence but actually with approval, they called on gods and men to witness that a great outrage was being perpetrated, and sent for the leaders of the senate. With them they went about among the tribes and implored them not to be guilty of an act which, utterly wrong in itself, would establish a precedent that was even worse, by diverting to their own possession, as judges, the property in dispute; and that too when, even if it were right that a judge should be concerned for his own advantage, they would by no means gain so much by the seizure of the land as they would lose by the wrongful estrangement of their allies. For reputation at least and trustworthiness were things the loss of which was beyond all reckoning. Was this to be the report carried home by the envoys? Was this to be noised abroad and come to the ears of allies and enemies? What grief it would cause the former, and what joy the latter! Did they suppose that Scaptius, a meddling old hanger-on of assemblies, would be held responsible for this by the neighboring nations? It would be a famous thing for Scaptius to have inscribed beneath his portrait, but the Roman People would be playing a rôle of chicanery and of usurpation of the claims of others. For what umpire in a private suit would have thought of awarding to himself the object of litigation? Even Scaptius, though he had already outlived all sense of shame, would not do that. These arguments were loudly urged both by the consuls and by the Fathers; but they were less convincing than men's cupidity, or than Scaptius, who had aroused it. The tribes, being called upon to vote, decided the territory to be public land belonging to the Roman People. Nor is it denied that such would have been the verdict if recourse had been had to another court; but in the circumstances the excellence of the cause did not in the slightest degree extenuate the disgrace of the judgment, which seemed no less scandalous and harsh to the Roman senators than to the men of Aricia and Ardea. The remainder of the year passed without disturbances in either domestic or foreign relations.

Summary of Book III

THERE WERE QUARRELS ABOUT LAND-LAWS. THE CAPITOL WAS SEIZED by exiles and slaves; who were slain and the Capitol recovered. The census was taken twice. By the earlier enumeration there were returned 8714[1] citizens, besides male and female wards; by the second 117,219. After a defeat had been sustained at the hands of the Aequi, Lucius Quintius Cincinnatus, being appointed dictator, was summoned to the control of the war while engaged in working on his farm. He defeated the enemy and sent them under the yoke. The number of tribunes was increased to ten in the 36th year from the election of the first ones. After the laws of Athens had been searched out and brought to Rome by envoys, decemvirs with consular powers were chosen, without any other magistrates, to draw up and publish them. It was in the 302nd year after the founding of Rome that the power was transferred from consuls to decemvirs, as it had formerly been from kings to consuls. When the decemvirs had posted up ten tables of laws, after such moderation in the conduct of their office that it had been voted to continue the same magistracy for another year, they added two tables to the ten; and after many insolent acts refused to lay down their authority, but retained it for a third year, till the lust of Appius Claudius put an end to their hated dominion. Having fallen in love with the maiden Verginia, he suborned an agent to claim her as his slave, and obliged her father Verginius to act. Seizing a knife from the nearest stall, he slew his daughter, since there was no other way to keep her from falling into the hands of the man who meditated her dishonor. By this great wrong the plebeians were roused to action, and occupying the Aventine, forced the decemvirs to abdicate. Of these, Appius, who had been most guilty, was flung into prison; the rest were exiled. The book contains also successful campaigns against the Sabines and the Volsci, and a discreditable judgment rendered by the Roman People, who, being chosen umpire between the Ardeates and the Aricini, awarded to themselves the territory in dispute.

BOOK IV

I. Marcus Genucius and Gaius Curtius succeeded these men as consuls. It was a year of quarrels both at home and abroad. For at its commencement Gaius Canuleius, a tribune of the plebs, proposed a bill regarding the intermarriage of patricians and plebeians which the patricians looked upon as involving the debasement of their blood and the subversion of the principles inhering in the *gentes,* of families; and a suggestion, cautiously put forward at first by the tribunes, that it should be lawful for one of the consuls to be chosen from the plebs, was afterwards carried so far that nine tribunes proposed a bill giving the people power to choose consuls as they might see fit, from either the plebs or the patriciate. To carry out this last proposal would be, in the estimation of the patricians, not merely to give a share of the supreme authority to the lowest of the citizens, but actually to take it away from the nobles and bestow it on the plebs. The Fathers therefore rejoiced to hear that the people of Ardea had revolted because of the unjust decision which deprived them of their land; that the men of Veii had ravaged the Roman frontier; and that the Volsci and Aequi were murmuring at the fortification of Verrugo;[1] so decidedly did they prefer even an unfortunate war to an ignominious peace. Accordingly they made the most of these threats, that the proposals of the tribunes might be silenced amidst the din of so many wars; and ordered levies to be held and military preparations to be made with the utmost energy, and if possible, even more strenuously than had been done when Titus Quinctius was consul. Thereupon

Gaius Canuleius curtly proclaimed in the senate that it was in vain the consuls sought to frighten the plebs out of their concern for the new laws; and, declaring that they should never hold the levy, while he lived, until the plebs had voted on the measures which he and his colleagues had brought forward, at once convened an assembly.

II. At one and the same time the consuls were inciting the senate against the tribune, and the tribune was arousing the people against the consuls. The consuls declared that the frenzy of the tribunes could no longer be endured; the end had now been reached, and there was more war being stirred up at home than abroad. This state of things was, to be sure, as much the fault of the senators as of the plebs, and the consuls were as guilty as the tribunes. That tendency which a state rewarded always attained the greatest growth; it was thus that good men were produced, both in peace and in war. In Rome the greatest reward was given to sedition, which had, therefore, ever been held in honor by all and sundry. Let them recall the majesty of the senate when they had taken it over from their fathers, and think what it was likely to be when they passed it on to their sons, and how the plebs could glory in the increase of their strength and consequence. There was no end in sight, nor would be, so long as the fomenters of insurrection were honored in proportion to the success of their projects. What tremendous schemes had Gaius Canuleius set on foot! He was aiming to contaminate the *gentes* and throw the auspices, both public and private, into confusion, that nothing might be pure, nothing unpolluted; so that, when all distinctions had been obliterated, no man might recognize either himself or his kindred.[2] For what else, they asked, was the object of promiscuous marriages, if not that plebeians and patricians might mingle together almost like the beasts? The son of such a marriage would be ignorant to what blood and to what worship he belonged; he would pertain half to the patricians, half to the plebs, and be at strife even with himself. It was not enough for the disturbers of the rabble to play havoc with all divine and human institutions: they must now aim at the consulship. And whereas they had at first merely suggested in conversations that one of the two consuls should be chosen from the plebeians,[3] they were now proposing a law that the people should elect consuls at its pleasure from patriciate or plebs. Its choice would without doubt always fall upon plebeians of the most revolutionary sort, and the result would be that they would have consuls of the type of Canuleius and Icilius. They called on Jupiter Optimus Maximus to forbid that a power regal in its majesty should sink so low. For their parts, they would sooner die a thousand deaths than suffer so shameful a thing to be done. They felt certain that their forefathers too, had they divined that all sorts of concessions would make the commons not more tractable but more exacting, and that the granting of their first demands would lead to others, ever more unjust, would rather have faced any conflict whatsoever than have permitted such laws to be imposed upon them. Because they had yielded then, in the matter of the tribunes, they had yielded a second time; it was impossible there should be any settlement of the trouble, if in one and the same state there were both plebeian tribunes and patricians; one thing or the other must go, the patriciate or the tribunate. It was better late than never to oppose their rashness and temerity. Were they to be suffered with impunity first to sow discord and stir up neighboring wars, and then to prevent the state from arming and defending itself against the wars they had raised themselves? When they had all but invited in the enemy, should they refuse to allow the enrolment of armies to oppose that enemy; while Canuleius had the hardihood to announce in the senate that unless the Fathers permitted his laws to be received, as though he were a conqueror, he would forbid the levy? What else was this than a threat that he would betray his native City to attack and capture? How must that speech encourage, not the Roman plebs, but the Volsci, the Aequi, and the Veientes! Would they not hope that, led by Canuleius, they would be able to scale the Capitol and the Citadel? Unless the tribunes had robbed the patricians of their courage when they took away their rights and their dignity, the consuls were prepared to lead them against criminal citizens sooner than against armed enemies.

III. At the very time when these opinions were finding expression in the senate, Canuleius held forth in this fashion in behalf of his laws and in opposition to the consuls: "How greatly the patricians despised you, Quirites, how unfit they deemed you to live in the City, within the same walls as themselves, I think I have often observed before, but never more clearly than at this very moment, when they are rallying so fiercely against these proposals of ours. Yet what else do we intend by them than to remind our fellow citizens that we are of them, and that, though we possess not the same wealth, still we dwell in the same City they inhabit? In the one bill we seek the right of intermarriage, which is customarily granted to neighbors and foreigners—indeed we have granted citizenship, which is more than intermarriage, even to defeated enemies; in the other we propose no innovation, but reclaim and seek to exercise a popular right, to wit that the Roman People shall confer office upon whom it will. What reason is there, pray, why they should confound heaven and earth; why they should almost have attacked me just now in the senate; why they should declare that they will place no restraint on force, and should threaten to violate our sacrosanct authority? If the Roman People is granted a free vote, that so it may commit the consulship to what hands it likes, if even the plebeian is not cut off from the hope of gaining the highest honors—if he shall be deserving of the highest honors—will this City of ours be unable to endure? Is her dominion at an end? When we raise the question of making a plebeian consul, is it the same as if we were to say that a slave or a freedman should attain that office? Have you any conception of the contempt in which you are held? They would take from you, were it possible, a part of this daylight. That you breathe, that you speak, that you have the shape of men, fills them with resentment. Nay, they assert, if you please, that it is sinning against Heaven to elect a plebeian consul. Tell me, if we are not admitted to consult the Fasti[4] or the Commentaries of the Pontiffs,[5] are we therefore ignorant of what all men, even foreigners, know, viz. that the consuls succeeded to the place of the kings, and possess no jot nor tittle of right or dignity that belonged not to the kings before? Come! Would you believe the story was ever heard how Numa Pompilius—not only no patrician, but not even a Roman citizen—was sent for from the country of the Sabines, and reigned at Rome, by command of the people and with the senators' consent? And again, how Lucius Tarquinius, who was not even of Italian stock—not to mention Roman—being the son of Demaratus of Corinth, and an immigrant from Tarquinii, was made king, while the sons of Ancus were still living? And how after him Servius Tullius, son of a captive woman from Corniculum, who had nobody for his father and a bond-woman for his mother, held the royal power by his innate ability and worth? For why should I speak of Titus Tatius the Sabine, with whom Romulus himself, the Father of the City, shared his sovereignty? Well then, so long as men despised no family that could produce conspicuous excellence, the dominion of Rome increased. And are you now to scorn a plebeian consul, when our ancestors were not above accepting alien kings, and when the City was not closed against the meritorious foreigner, even after the expulsion of the kings? The Claudian family at least we not only received from the Sabine country, after the kings had been driven out, and gave them citizenship, but even admitted them to the number of patricians. Shall the son of a stranger become patrician and then consul, but a Roman citizen, if plebeian, be cut off from all hope of the consulship? Do we not believe it possible that a bold and strenuous man, serviceable both in peace and in war, should come from the plebs, a man like Numa, Lucius Tarquinius, or Servius Tullius? Or shall we refuse, even if such an one appear, to let him approach the helm of state? Must we rather look forward to consuls like the decemvirs, the vilest of mortals, who nevertheless were all of patrician birth, than to such as shall resemble the best of the kings, new men though they were?"

IV. "But," you will say, "from the time the kings were expelled no plebeian has ever been consul." Well, what then? Must no new institution be adopted? Ought that which has not yet been done—and in a new nation many things have not yet been done—never to be put in practice, even if it be expedient? There were neither pontiffs nor augurs in the reign of Romulus; Numa Pompilius created them. There was no census in the state, no registration of centuries and classes; Servius Tullius made one. There had never been any consuls; when the kings had been banished, consuls were elected. Neither the power nor the name of dictator had ever been known; in the time of our fathers they began. Plebeian tribunes, aediles, and quaestors, there were none; men decided to have them. Within the past ten years we have elected decemvirs for drawing up the laws, and removed them from the commonwealth. Who can question that in a city founded for eternity and of incalculable growth, new powers, priesthoods, and rights of families and individuals, must be established? Was not this very provision, that patricians and plebeians might not intermarry, enacted by the decemvirs a few years since, with the worst effect on the community and the gravest injustice to the plebs? Or can there be any greater or more signal insult than to hold a portion of the state unworthy of intermarriage, as though it were defiled? What else is this but to suffer exile within the same walls and banishment? They guard against having us for connections or relations, against the mingling of our blood with theirs. Why, if this pollutes that fine nobility of yours—which many of you, being of Alban or of Sabine origin, possess not by virtue of race or blood, but through co-optation into the patriciate, having been chosen either by the kings, or, after their expulsion, by decree of the people—could you not keep it pure by your own private counsels, neither taking wives from the plebs nor permitting your daughters and sisters to marry out of the patriciate? No plebeian would offer violence to a patrician maiden: that is a patrician vice. No one would have compelled anybody to enter a compact of marriage against his will. But let me tell you that in the statutory prohibition and annulment of intermarriage between patricians and plebeians we have indeed at last an insult to the plebs. Why, pray, do you not bring in a law that there shall be no intermarrying of rich and poor? That which has always and everywhere been a matter of private policy, that a woman might marry into whatever family it had been arranged, that a man might take a wife from that house where he had engaged himself, you would subject to the restraint of a most arrogant law, that thereby you might break up our civil society and make two states out of one. Why do you not enact that a plebeian shall not live near a patrician, nor go on the same road? That he shall not enter the same festive company? That he shall not stand by his side in the same Forum? For what real difference does it make if a patrician takes a plebeian wife, or a plebeian a patrician? What right, pray, is invaded? The children of course take the father's rank. There is nothing we are seeking to gain from marriage with you, except that we should be accounted men and citizens. Neither have you any reason to oppose us, unless you delight in vying with each other how you may outrage and humiliate us.

V. Finally I would ask, is it you, or the Roman People, who have supreme authority? Did the banishment of the kings bring you dominion, or to all men equal liberty? Ought the Roman People to be permitted, if it so desire, to enact a law; or shall you, as each proposal is brought up, proclaim a levy by way of penalty, and so soon as I, the tribune, begin to summon the tribes to vote, shall you, the consul, at once administer the oath to those of military age and march them out to camp, with threats against the plebs and with threats against the tribune? How would it be if you had not twice[6] already proved how little those threats of yours are worth against the unanimous will of the plebs? I suppose it was consideration for our good that made you refrain from fighting? Or was this rather the reason there was no strife, because the stronger side was also the more moderate? Neither will there be any struggle now, Quirites; they will always test your courage; but will never put your strength to the proof. And so the commons are ready, consuls, for those wars you deal in, be they feigned or genuine, if you give them back their right of inter-marriage, and make this a single state at last; if you enable them to coalesce, to unite, to merge with you in domestic alliances; if the hope of attaining honors is held out to strenuous men and brave; if they are granted a share in the partnership of government; if, in the enjoyment of equal liberty, they are allowed to govern and obey in turn, with the annual change of magistrates. If anyone shall prevent these reforms, you may talk of wars, and multiply them in the telling; but nobody will give in his name, nobody will take up arms, nobody will fight for haughty masters with whom he has no association in the honors of the state nor in the marriages of private life.

VI. When the consuls had come forth to the people and set speeches had given place to wrangling, the tribune demanded what reason there was why a plebeian should not be chosen consul; to whom Curtius replied, with truth perhaps, yet, in the circumstances, to little purpose, "because no plebeian has the auspices, and that is the reason the decemvirs have forbidden intermarriages, lest the auspices should be confounded by the uncertain standing of those born of them." At this the plebs fairly blazed with indignation, because it was declared that they could not take auspices, as though they were hated by the immortal gods; nor was the controversy ended—for the plebeians had got a most energetic champion in their tribune, and rivalled him themselves in determination, until at last the patricians were beaten, and allowed the law regarding intermarriage to be passed, chiefly because they thought that so the tribunes would either wholly give over their contention for plebeian consuls or would postpone it until after the war, and that the plebs meantime, contented with the right to intermarry, would be ready to submit to the levy.

But since Canuleius was grown so great through his victory over the patricians and the favor of the plebs, the other tribunes were encouraged to take up the quarrel; and they fought for their measure with the utmost violence, hindering the levy, though the rumors of war increased from day to day. The consuls, since they were powerless to do anything through the senate when the tribunes interposed their veto,[7] held councils of their leading men in private. It was clear that they must submit to be conquered either by the enemy or by their fellow citizens. Of all the consulars only Valerius and Horatius[8] took no part in their deliberations. Gaius Claudius spoke in favor of arming the consuls against the tribunes; the Quinctii, both Cincinnatus and Capitolinus, were opposed to bloodshed and to injuring those whom they had acknowledged by a solemn treaty with the plebs to be inviolable. The upshot of these consultations was this, that they permitted military tribunes with consular authority to be chosen indifferently from the patriciate and the plebs,[9] but made no change in the election of consuls. With this decision both tribunes and commons were content. An election was called, for choosing three tribunes with consular powers. No sooner was it proclaimed than everybody who had ever spoken or acted in a seditious manner, especially those who had been tribunes, fell to canvassing voters and bustling about all over the Forum in the white robes of candidates; so that the patricians, what with despair of obtaining office now that the plebs were so wrought up, and what with scorn if they must share its administration with these fellows, were deterred from standing. At last, however, they were compelled by their leaders to compete, lest they might seem to have surrendered the control of the commonwealth. The outcome of this election showed how different are men's minds when struggling for liberty and station from what they are when they have laid aside their animosities and their judgment is unbiassed; for the people chose all the tribunes from among the patricians, quite satisfied that plebeians should have been allowed to stand. Where shall you now find in one single man that moderation, fairness, and loftiness of mind, which at that time characterized the entire people?

VII. In the year three hundred and ten from the founding of Rome, military tribunes for the first time took office in place of consuls. Their names were Aulus Sempronius Atratinus, Lucius Atilius,[10] and Titus Cloelius. During their administration domestic harmony insured peace abroad, as well. (Some say that on account of a war with Veii, which broke out in addition to the war with the Aequi and Volsci and the revolt of the men of Ardea, two consuls were unable to cope with so many wars at once, and therefore three military tribunes were created. These writers say nothing of the promulgation of a law about the election of consuls from the plebs, but record that the three tribunes enjoyed the authority and insignia[11] of consuls.) Still, the power of that magistracy was not yet upon a firm footing, for three months after they had taken up their office they laid it down, the augurs having decreed that there had been a flaw in their election, because Gaius Curtius, who had presided over the assembly, had not properly selected the ground for the tent.[12]

Ambassadors from Ardea came to Rome, complaining of the injustice done them, and with such fairness that it was evident that if they were granted redress, through the restoration of their land, they would abide by the treaty and remain friendly. The senate replied that the judgment of the people could not be rescinded by them, not only because they had no precedent or authority for such action, but also because they had regard to the harmony between the orders. If the Ardeates would bide their time and leave the senate to decide upon a remedy for the injury done them, the day would come when they would be glad that they had controlled their anger, and they would learn that the senators had been equally concerned that no wrong should be done them and that what had been done should be speedily redressed. So the ambassadors, having said that they would refer the whole matter to their people, were courteously dismissed.

The patricians, since the state was without any curule magistrate, met and chose an interrex. A dispute whether consuls or military tribunes should be appointed kept the state in an interregnum for several days. The interrex and the senate held out for the election of consuls; the plebeian tribunes and the plebs were for military tribunes. Victory rested with the senators, not only because the plebs gave up the idle contest whether they should confer this honor or that upon the patricians, but also because the leaders of the plebs preferred an election in which they would not be reckoned candidates to one in which they would be passed over as unworthy. The tribunes, too, of the plebs relinquished the unavailing contest in favor of the leaders of the patricians. Titus Quinctius Barbatus, as interrex, declared the election of Lucius Papirius Mugillanus and Lucius Sempronius Atratinus. In their consulship the treaty with the Ardeates was renewed; and in this lies the proof that these men were consuls that year, although their names are found neither in the ancient annals[13] nor in the lists of magistrates;[14] I suppose that, because there were military tribunes in the beginning of the year, the consuls who were elected in their place were passed over as if the tribunes had been in power throughout the year. Licinius Macer testifies that the names of these consuls were given both in the treaty with Ardea and in the Linen Rolls in the temple of Moneta.[15] Things were quiet both abroad and at home, despite the numerous alarms which neighboring states had caused.

VIII. This year, whether it had tribunes only or tribunes succeeded by consuls, was followed by one which had consuls about whom there is no question. These were Marcus Geganius Macerinus, for the second time, and Titus Quinctius Capitolinus, for the fifth time. This same year saw the adoption of the censorship, an institution which originated in a small way but afterwards grew to such dimensions that it was invested with the regulation of the morals and discipline of the Romans. The distribution of honor and ignominy amongst the senate and the centuries of the knights was controlled by this magistracy, while jurisdiction over public and private sites, together with the revenues of the Roman People, were entirely subject to its discretion. What first gave rise to the office was this: the people had not been rated for many years and the census could not be postponed; yet the consuls, when so many nations threatened war, had no time for this work. The subject was brought up in the senate, where it was held that the task, which was a laborious one and beneath the dignity of a consul, required its own proper magistrates, who should have a staff of clerks, assume the custody of the records, and regulate the form of the census. The senators, though it was a small matter, nevertheless gladly welcomed the suggestion, in order that there might be more patrician magistracies in the administration of the state. They thought even then, I imagine, as afterwards proved to be the case, that it would not be long before the consequence of those who held the office would lend authority and dignity to the office itself. The tribunes also, regarding it as a necessary rather than a showy service, as in those days it actually was, did not hold out against the plan, lest they might seem to be vexatiously obstinate even in trifles. The principal men in the state scorned the office, and the taking of the census was, by the votes of the people, committed to Papirius and Sempronius (whose consulship is questioned), that they might round out their incomplete year of office with this magistracy. They were called censors from their function.

IX. While these things were going on in Rome, there came envoys from Ardea begging the Romans in the name of their ancient alliance, renewed by the recent treaty, to send help to their city, which was on the brink of ruin. For the enjoyment of peace, which they had most wisely preserved with the Roman People, had been denied them, owing to civil war. This is said to have had its cause and origin in the rivalry of factions, which have been and will be fraught with destruction to more nations than foreign wars, or famine and pestilence, or whatsoever other scourges men attribute, as the most desperate national calamities, to the wrath of Heaven. A maiden of plebeian family who was famous for her beauty had two youthful suitors. One was of her own class and relied on the approval of her guardians, who were themselves of the same standing. The other was a noble, captivated solely by her good looks, who was supported by the favor of the optimates,[16] which resulted in the introduction of party strife into the household of the girl herself. The noble was preferred by the mother, who wished her daughter to make as grand a match as possible. The guardians, mindful even in a matter like this of political interests, held out for their fellow plebeian. When the dispute could not be settled privately, a suit was instituted. After listening to the pleas of the mother and the guardians, the magistrates decreed that the mother should have power to decide as she saw fit about the marriage. But violence was stronger than they; for the guardians, after openly addressing a crowd of their own party in the market place, on the injustice[17] of the decision, collected a party and carried the girl off from her mother's house. To confront them an even more warlike band of nobles gathered, under the leadership of the injured and indignant youth, and a desperate battle followed. The plebs were routed, bat, unlike the Roman plebs, having armed and withdrawn from their city and encamped upon a certain hill, they sallied forth, sword and torch in hand, to sack the farms of the nobles. They even prepared to besiege the city itself, for the entire body of artizans, even those who had hitherto had no part in the quarrel, had been called out by the hope of plunder; nor was there wanting any form of the horrors of war, as though the nation had been infected with the madness of the two young men who sought a fatal marriage in the ruin of their country. Neither side saw that there had been enough of war and arms at home; the optimates called upon the Romans to relieve their beleaguered city; the plebeians sent for the Volsci to help them capture Ardea. The Volsci, with the Aequian Cluilius for their leader,[18] were the first to reach Ardea, and threw up intrenchments against the walls of their enemies. When the news was brought to Rome, Marcus Geganius the consul immediately set out with an army. When three miles from the enemy he chose a place for his camp; and as the day was now fast drawing to a close, ordered his soldiers to refresh themselves. Then in the fourth watch he marched out, and commencing a contravallation, made such speed that at sunrise the Volsci perceived that they were more securely hemmed in by the

Romans than was the city by themselves; and on one side the consul had thrown out a work to join the walls of Ardea, in order that his friends in the town might be enabled to come and go.[19]

X. The Volscian commander, who had maintained his men up to that time not out of a store provided in advance, but with corn taken from day to day in pillaging the country-side, was no sooner shut in by the rampart than he found himself all at once destitute of everything. He therefore invited the consul to a parley, and said that if the Roman general had come for the purpose of raising the siege, he would lead the Volscians off. The consul replied that it was for the conquered to accept terms, not to make them; the Volsci had consulted their own pleasure in coming to attack the allies of the Roman People; it would be otherwise with their departure. He ordered them to surrender their general, to lay down their arms, and, confessing themselves defeated, to yield to his authority; if they did not, he would be their determined enemy, whether they attempted to go or to stay, and would rather bring back to Rome a victory over the Volsci than a treacherous peace with them. The Volsci, testing the small hope that arms held out to them—for all other hope had been cut off—fought, not to speak of other disadvantages, in a position that was unfavorable for battle and still more unfavorable for flight; and being cut to pieces on every side, left off fighting and fell to entreaties; and after giving up their general and handing over their weapons, were sent under the yoke, with a single garment each, and so dismissed, overwhelmed with shame and disaster. But on their encamping not far from the city of Tusculum, the Tusculans, upon an old grudge, attacked them in their defenseless state, and exacted so heavy a penalty that they scarce left any to report the massacre. The Roman commander, finding Ardea distracted by sedition, composed its troubles by beheading the ringleaders of the revolt and confiscating their property to the public treasury of the Ardeates. The townsmen thought that the great service which the Roman People had thus rendered them had cancelled the injustice of the judgment,[20] but the Roman senate felt that something still remained to do in order to wipe out that reminder of the national greed. The consul returned to the City and triumphed, making Cluilius, the leader of the Volsci, walk before his chariot, and displaying the spoils which he had taken from the hostile army, before sending them under the yoke.

It is no easy thing to do, but the consul Quinctius equalled in civil life the fame of his armed colleague; for so well did he maintain domestic peace and concord, by tempering the law to high and low, that the Fathers regarded him as a strict consul, and the plebs as mild enough. He held his own, too, with the tribunes, more by his personal influence than by contending with them. Five consulships administered on the self-same principles, and a life which had been throughout of consular dignity, made the man himself almost more revered than his office. Hence there was no talk of military tribunes while these men were consuls.

XI. Marcus Fabius Vibulanus and Postumus Aebutius Cornicen were elected to the consulship. These men, perceiving that they succeeded to a period of great renown for civil and military achievements, and that nothing made the year so memorable in the eyes of neighboring peoples, both allies and enemies, as the earnestness with which the Romans had come to the assistance of the Ardeates in their dangerous crisis, were the more concerned to erase completely from men's minds the disgrace of the judgment. They accordingly caused the senate to decree that inasmuch as the citizens of Ardea had been reduced by domestic troubles to a small number, colonists should be enrolled to defend that city against the Volsci. This was the form in which the decree was drawn up and published,[21] that the plebs and the tribunes might not perceive that a plan was on foot for rescinding the judgment; but the senators had privately agreed that they would enroll as colonists a much larger proportion of Rutulians than Romans, and that no land should be parcelled out except that which had been sequestered by the infamous decision, nor a single clod assigned there to any Roman until all the Rutulians had been provided for. Thus the land reverted to the Ardeates. As triumvirs for establishing the colony at Ardea they appointed Agrippa Menenius, Titus Cloelius Siculus, Marcus Aebutius Helva. These men not only had a far from popular service to perform, and offended the plebs by assigning to the allies land which the Roman People had adjudged to be its own; but failed to satisfy even the great patricians, because they had done nothing to conciliate any man's goodwill. They therefore avoided vexatious attacks before the people—where the tribunes had already summoned them for trial—by remaining in the colony, which bore witness to their integrity and justice.

XII. There was peace at home and abroad during this and the following year, when Gaius Furius Paculus and Marcus Papirius Crassus were consuls. The games which the decemvirs had vowed in pursuance of a decree of the senate, during the secession of the plebs from the patricians, were that year celebrated. Occasion for dissension was sought in vain by Poetelius, who though he had got himself elected plebeian tribune for the second time, by proclaiming that he would carry through these very measures, was unsuccessful in forcing the consuls to lay before the senate a proposal for assigning land to the plebs; and when, after a hard struggle, he obtained a vote of the senate to determine whether consuls or tribunes should be elected, the decision was for consuls. Men only laughed when the tribune threatened to hold up the levy, for the neighboring peoples were quiet, and war and warlike preparations were alike uncalled for.

To this tranquil period succeeded the consulship of Proculus Geganius Macerinus and Lucius Menenius Lanatus, a year conspicuous for numerous deaths and dangers, for seditions, famine, and for the yoke of sovereignty, to which, won over by largesses, men almost bowed their necks. The one thing lacking was foreign war, and if that had been added to their burden they could hardly have held out, though all the gods had aided them. The troubles began with a dreadful famine, whether because the season was unfavorable for crops, or that the attraction of assemblies and city-life had left the fields uncultivated; for both explanations have been given. The patricians accused the plebeians of idleness, and the tribunes of the plebs accused the consuls now of dishonesty, now of carelessness. In the end they brought the plebs, with no opposition on the senate's part, to elect Lucius Minucius prefect of the corn-supply. He was destined, while filling this magistracy, to be more successful in safe-guarding liberty than in discharging the duties of his office, although in the end he also earned and received both gratitude and glory for relieving the scarcity. For although he had dispatched to neighboring peoples many embassies by land and sea without result—save that a little corn was brought in from Etruria—he found that he had not materially improved the supply. He then fell back upon the plan of distributing the shortage. He forced men to declare their stocks of corn and to sell the surplus above the requirements of a month; he deprived the slaves of a portion of their daily ration; he brought charges against the dealers and exposed them to the anger of the people; and by this bitter inquisition rather revealed than alleviated the scarcity, so that many of the plebeians lost hope, and sooner than suffer torment by prolonging their existence, covered up their heads[22] and threw themselves into the Tiber.

XIII. Then Spurius Maelius, of the equestrian order,[23] a man for those times very rich, undertook to do a useful thing in a way that set a very bad example and had a motive still worse. For having bought up corn in Etruria with his own money, through the agency of friends and clients there—which very circumstance had hindered, I can well believe, the public efforts to bring down prices—he set about distributing it gratis. The plebeians were captivated by this munificence; wherever he went, conspicuous and important beyond the measure of a private citizen, they followed in his train; and the devotion and hope he inspired in them gave him no uncertain assurance of the consulship. He himself, so insatiable of fortune's promises is the heart of man, began to cherish a loftier and less allowable ambition; and since even the consulship would have to be wrested from unwilling nobles, considered how he might be king: nothing else, he felt, would adequately reward him for his elaborate schemes and the toil and moil of the great struggle he must make. The consular election was now at hand, and found him with his plans not yet fully ripened. For the sixth time Titus Quinctius Capitolinus was chosen consul, a most unsuitable man for the purposes of a would-be revolutionary. For colleague he was given Agrippa Menenius, surnamed Lanatus; and Lucius Minucius either was reappointed prefect of the corn-supply or had been named for an indefinite period, so long as the situation should require; for authorities do not agree, but the name of the prefect is entered in the Linen Rolls among the magistrates for both years. This Minucius was discharging the same function in his public capacity which Maelius had undertaken to perform as a private citizen, and the same sort of men[24] were coming and going in both their houses. Thus Minucius discovered the affair and reported to the senate that weapons were being collected at the house of Maelius, that he was haranguing people there, and that they were certainly contriving a kingdom; the time for executing the plot was not yet fixed; all else had been agreed upon: the tribunes had been bribed to betray liberty, and the leaders of the mob had been assigned their parts. He said that he had withheld his report of these things almost longer than was safe, that he might not become voucher for anything of an uncertain or trivial nature. On hearing this the leaders of the senate loudly blamed the consuls of the year before because they had suffered these donations and plebeian gatherings to take place in a private house, and the new consuls because they had waited till information of so grave a crime was laid before the senate by the prefect of the corn-supply, though it wanted a consul not only to report it but to punish it; but Quinctius said that the consuls were blamed unjustly, for, constrained by the laws of appeal, which had been enacted in order to break down their authority, they had by no means so much power in their office as they had will to punish so heinous an offense in the way it deserved. There was need, he continued, of a man, and one who was not only brave, but free and unfettered by the laws. He would therefore name Lucius Quinctius dictator; there was a spirit whose stature was equal to that great power. Despite the universal approval of this step, Quinctius at first refused, and asked what they meant by exposing him at the end of his life to so fierce a struggle. Then, when men called out on every side that there was not only more wisdom but more courage in that old man's heart than in all the rest and loaded him with not unmerited compliments, and when the consul would not recede from his purpose, at length Cincinnatus uttered a prayer to the immortal gods that they would not suffer his old age to bring harm or shame to the republic in so perilous a case, and was pronounced dictator by the consul. He then himself named Gaius Servilius Ahala his master of the horse.

XIV. The next day, after disposing guards at several points he went down into the Forum, where the novel and surprising sight drew upon him the attention of the plebs. The followers of Maelius and their leader himself perceived that it was against them that the force of that high authority was aimed; while those who knew nothing of the plans for setting up a king asked what outbreak or what sudden war had called for the majesty of a dictator or for Quinctius (now past his eightieth year) to direct the state. Then Servilius, the master of the horse, being sent by the dictator to Maelius, said: "The dictator summons you." When Maelius, trembling, asked what he wanted, Servilius replied that he must stand his trial and clear himself of a charge which Minucius had lodged against him with the senate. Then Maelius drew back into the crowd of his retainers, and at first, glancing this way and that, attempted to avoid the issue; but finally, when the attendant, being so commanded by the master of the horse, would have led him away, he was torn from his grasp by the bystanders and fled, calling on the Roman plebs to protect him, declaring that he was overthrown by a plot of the patricians because he had acted kindly by the commons, and begging them to help him in his extremity and not permit him to be murdered before their eyes. While he was screaming out these appeals, Servilius Ahala overtook and slew him; then, bespattered with his blood and guarded by a company of young nobles, he returned to the dictator and reported that Maelius, having been summoned to appear before him, had repulsed the attendant and was rousing up the populace when he received the punishment he had deserved. Whereat the dictator exclaimed, "Well done, Gaius Servilius; you have delivered the commonwealth!"

XV. Then, as the crowd was in a turmoil, not knowing what to think of the deed, he bade convoke them to an assembly. There he asserted that Maelius had been justly slain, even though he had been innocent of plotting to make himself king, since he had been cited before the dictator by the master of the horse and had not obeyed. He himself, he said, had sat to hear the cause, and if the hearing had been concluded Maelius would have prospered as his cause deserved; but, planning violence to avoid undergoing trial, he had been repressed by violence. Neither would it have been right to deal with Maelius as with a citizen. The man had been born amongst a free people enjoying rights and laws, in a City from which he knew that the kings had been banished, and how in that very year the king's nephews,[25] sons of the consul who had freed his country, had, on the exposure of a compact they had made to bring the princes back to Rome, been beheaded by their father's orders. He knew that in this City the consul Tarquinius Collatinus had been commanded, out of hatred for the name he bore, to lay down his office and go into exile; that here, some years after, Spurius Cassius[26] had been punished for aiming at royalty; that here, but lately, the decemvirs had been visited with confiscation, banishment, and death, because of kingly arrogance. Yet in this same City a Spurius Maelius had conceived the hope of reigning. And who was this fellow? To be sure, no nobility, no honors, no merits, opened wide the road to tyranny for any man; nevertheless the Claudii[27] and Cassii had been encouraged by consulships and decemvirates, by their own honors and those of their forefathers, and by the splendor of their families, to aim at forbidden heights; Spurius Maelius, a rich corn-dealer, a man who might have desired but ought scarcely to have hoped to become a plebeian tribune, had flattered himself that for a couple of pounds of spelt he had purchased the liberty of his fellow citizens; he had imagined that by flinging food to them he could entice into slavery a people who had conquered all their neighbors, so that a state which could scarce have stomached him as a senator would endure him for its king, having the insignia and authority of Romulus its founder, who was descended from the gods and had returned to them. This ought to be regarded as a thing no less monstrous than wicked; nor was his blood sufficient expiation, unless the roof and walls within which such madness had been conceived should be demolished, and the goods which had been tainted with the offer of them as the price to buy a tyranny be confiscated; he therefore bade the quaestors sell those goods and place the proceeds in the public treasury.

XVI. Quinctius then commanded the man's house to be pulled down, that the bare site might commemorate the frustration of his wicked purpose. The place was named Aequimaelium.[28] Lucius Minucius was presented with an ox and a gilded statue outside the Porta Trigemina, without opposition even on the part of the plebs, since Minucius divided the corn of Maelius among them at the price of one *as* the peck. I find it stated by some historians that this Minucius went over from the patricians to the plebeians, and being co-opted an eleventh tribune of the plebs, allayed the rebellious feeling which arose from the killing of Maelius; but it is hardly credible that the patricians should have permitted the number of tribunes to be increased, and that this precedent, of all others, should have been introduced by a patrician; or that the plebs, having once obtained this concession, should not have held fast to it, or at least have tried to do so. But what proves more conclusively than anything the falsity of the inscription on his portrait is this, that it was enacted by law a few years before that the tribunes might not co-opt a colleague.[29] Quintus Caecilius, Quintus Junius, and Sextus Titinius were the only members of the college of tribunes who had not supported the law conferring honors on Minucius, and had never ceased to accuse now Minucius, now Servilius, before the plebs, and to complain of the unmerited death of Maelius. So they forced through a measure providing that military tribunes should be elected instead of consuls, not doubting that for some of the six places—for this was now the number that might be filled—plebeians would be chosen, if they would promise to avenge the death of Maelius. The plebeians, though they had been aroused that year by many different commotions, elected no more than three tribunes with consular powers, and among these Lucius Quinctius, son of Cincinnatus, from whose dictatorship men were trying to derive the odium for inspiring a mutiny. Aemilius Mamercus, a man of the highest standing, was ahead of Quinctius in the voting; Lucius Julius was elected third.

XVII. During the term of these magistrates, Fidenae, a Roman colony, revolted to Lars Tolumnius and the Veientes. To their defection they added a worse crime, for when Gaius Fulcinius, Cloelius Tullus, Spurius Antius, and Lucius Roscius, Roman envoys, came to inquire the reason of this new policy, at the command of Tolumnius they put them to death. Some persons seek to palliate the king's act, saying that an ambiguous expression of his upon a lucky throw of dice, which made him seem to order them to kill the envoys, was heard by the Fidenates and was responsible for the men's death. But it is quite incredible that the king on being interrupted by the

Fidenates, his new allies, come to consult him about a murder that would violate the law of nations, should not have withdrawn his attention from the game, and that the attribution of the crime to a mistake did not come later. It is easier to believe that he wished the people of Fidenae to be involved by the consciousness of so heinous a deed, that it might be impossible for them to hope for any reconciliation with the Romans. The envoys who had been slain at Fidenae were honored, at the public cost, with statues on the Rostra.[30] With the Veientes and Fidenates, not only because they were neighboring peoples, but also in consequence of the nefarious act with which they had begun the war, a bitter struggle now impended.

Accordingly, out of regard for the general welfare, the plebeians and their tribunes kept quiet, and raised no opposition to the election as consuls of Marcus Geganius Macerinus (for the third time) and Lucius Sergius Fidenas. I suppose that the name was given him from the war which he then waged; for he was the first who fought a successful battle on this side the Anio with the king of the Veientes; but he gained no bloodless victory, and so there was more grief for the citizens who were lost than rejoicing over the defeat of the enemy; and the senate, as is usual in an alarming situation, commanded the appointment of a dictator, Mamercus Aemilius. He named as his master of the horse a man who had been his colleague the year before, when they had both been military tribunes with consular authority, namely Lucius Quinctius Cincinnatus, a young man worthy of his father. To the troops, which the consuls levied were added veteran centurions experienced in war, and the losses of the last battle were made good. The dictator bade Titus Quinctius Capitolinus and Marcus Fabius Vibulanus follow him as his lieutenants. The high authority of the dictatorship, in the hands of one who was equal to it, drove the enemy out of Roman territory and across the Anio. They withdrew their camp and pitched upon the hills between Fidenae and the Anio; nor did they descend into the plains until the forces of the Faliscans had come to their support. Then, and not till then, did the Etruscans encamp before the walls of Fidenae. The Roman dictator likewise went into camp not far off, on the banks of both rivers, at their confluence, and threw up a rampart between his army and the enemy, where he was able to span the interval with intrenchments.[31] Next day he formed up in line of battle.

XVIII. The enemy were of several minds. The Faliscans, chafing under service performed away from home[32] and fairly self-confident, demanded battle: the Veientes and Fidenates anticipated greater success from a prolongation of the war. Tolumnius, though the views of his own followers were more agreeable to him, announced that he would fight on the following day, lest the Faliscans might not tolerate a protracted campaign. The dictator and the Romans were encouraged at the enemy's reluctance; and the next day, on the soldiers threatening that they would at once attack the camp and the city, unless the enemy came to an engagement, both armies marched out in line of battle into the plain between the two camps. The Veientes, having men to spare, dispatched a party round the mountains to assail the camp of the Romans during the engagement. The army of the three nations was so drawn up that the Veientes held the right wing, the Faliscans the left, and the Fidenates formed the center. The dictator advanced on the right, against the Faliscans, and Quinctius Capitolinus on the left, to meet the Veientes; while the master of the horse, with the cavalry, led the attack on the center. For a brief moment all was hushed and still; since the Etruscans were resolved not to begin fighting unless they were forced, and the dictator kept looking back to the Citadel of Rome, that the augurs might thence make him a signal, as they had arranged to do, the moment the omens were propitious. As soon as he descried the signal, he first sent his cavalry against the enemy, cheering as they charged; and the infantry followed with a furious attack. At no point could the Etruscan legions withstand the onset of the Romans; their horse made the chief resistance, and of all their horse by far the bravest was the king himself, who rode against the Romans, as they scattered in every direction for the pursuit, and prolonged the struggle.

XIX. There was at that time among the cavalrymen a tribune of the soldiers named Aulus Cornelius Cossus, a man of strikingly handsome person and no less distinguished for courage and strength. Proud of his name, which was very famous when it came to him, he left to his descendants one still greater and more glorious. This man, seeing how Tolumnius, wherever he charged, brought confusion to the Roman squadrons, and recognizing him, conspicuous in his royal dress, as he galloped swiftly up and down the line, exclaimed, "Is this the breaker of human leagues, the violater of the law of nations? I will speedily offer him up as a sacrificial victim, if only it is the will of Heaven that there should be aught sacred on this earth, to the manes of the envoys!" Clapping spurs to his charger and levelling his spear, he made for his one enemy. Having struck and unhorsed his man, he himself leaped quickly to the ground by the help of his lance, and as the king struggled to his feet flung him back with the boss of his shield, and plunging the spear again and again into his body, pinned him to earth. Then stripping the spoils from the corpse and cutting off the head, he bore it victoriously on the point of his spear and drove the enemy before him, panic-stricken at the sight of their slain king. Thus even the cavalry was routed, which alone had made the issue of the contest doubtful. The dictator pressed on after the flying legions, and pursuing them to their camp cut them to pieces. Large numbers of the Fidenates escaped, thanks to their knowledge of the ground, into the mountains. Cossus crossed the Tiber with his cavalry, and from the fields of the Veientes brought a vast quantity of booty back to town. During the battle there was also fighting at the Roman camp with a part of the forces of Tolumnius which he had dispatched against it, as has been said before. Fabius Vibulanus first manned the rampart with a cordon of defenders; and then, when the attention of the enemy was fixed on the wall, sallied out of the Porta Principalis, on the right,[33] with his reserves,[34] and fell suddenly upon them. In consequence of the panic thus occasioned, though the slaughter was less, because fewer were engaged, yet the rout was quite as complete as in the battle-line.

XX. Having been everywhere victorious, the dictator, as decreed by the senate and ratified by the people, returned to the City in triumphal procession. By far the greatest spectacle in the triumph was Cossus, bearing the spoils of honor of the slain king, while the soldiers sang rude verses about him, comparing him to Romulus. The spoils he fastened up as an offering, with solemn dedication, in the temple of Jupiter Feretrius, near the spoils of Romulus, which had been the first to be called *opima,* and were at that time the only ones. Cossus had drawn the gaze of the citizens away from the car of the dictator upon himself, and the honors of that crowded festival were virtually his alone. The dictator, at the people's behest, presented to Jupiter: on the Capitol a golden chaplet of a pound in weight, from the public treasury.

Following all previous historians, I have stated that Aulus Cornelius Cossus was a military tribune when he brought the second spoils of honor to the temple of Jupiter Feretrius. But besides that only those are properly held to be "spoils of honor" which one commander has taken from another commander, and that we know no "commander" but him under whose auspices the war is waged, the very words inscribed upon the spoils disprove their account and mine, and show that it was as consul that Cossus captured them. Having heard from the lips of Augustus Caesar, the founder or renewer of all the temples, that he had entered the shrine of Jupiter Feretrius, which he repaired when it had crumbled with age, and had himself read the inscription on the linen breast-plate, I have thought it would be almost sacrilege to rob Cossus of such a witness to his spoils as Caesar, the restorer of that very temple.[35] Where the error in regard to this matter lies, in consequence of which such ancient annals and also the books of the magistrates, written on linen and deposited in the temple of Moneta, which Licinius Macer cites from time to time as his authority, only give Aulus Cornelius Cossus as consul (with Titus Quinctius Poenus) seven years later, is a matter on which everybody is entitled to his opinion. For there is this further reason why so famous a battle could not be transferred to the later year, that the consulship of Cossus fell within a period of about three years when there were no wars, owing to a pestilence and a dearth of crops, so that certain annals, as though death-registers, offer nothing but the names of the consuls. The third year after Cossus' consulship saw him military tribune with consular powers, and in the same year he was master of the horse, in which office he fought another famous cavalry-engagement. Here is freedom for conjecture, but in my opinion it is idle; for one may brush aside all theories when the man who fought the battle, after placing the newly won spoils in their sacred resting-place, testified in the presence of Jupiter himself, to whom he had vowed them, and of Romulus—witnesses not to be held lightly by a forger—that he was Aulus Cornelius Cossus, consul.[36]

XXI. When Marcus Cornelius Maluginensis and Lucius Papirius Crassus were consuls, armies invaded the country of the Veientes and the Faliscans and drove off booty consisting of men and flocks; they nowhere encountered their enemies in the fields nor met with any opportunity to give them battle; still, they besieged no cities, for a pestilence attacked the people. And seditions were attempted at home, but not brought about, by Spurius Maelius, tribune of the plebs, who, imagining that the popularity of his name would enable him to stir up trouble, had appointed a day for the prosecution of Minucius, and had also proposed a law for confiscating the goods of Servilius Ahala, maintaining that Maelius had been circumvented by Minucius with false accusations, and flinging it up to Servilius that he had killed a citizen who had not been condemned. These charges were even less regarded by the people than was their author. But the increasing virulence of the disease gave concern, and so did certain alarms and prodigies; in particular that it was frequently announced that farm-buildings had been thrown down by earthquakes. A supplication was therefore offered up by the people under the direction of the duumviri.[37]

The pestilence was worse next year, when Gaius Julius (for the second time) and Lucius Verginius were the consuls, and caused such fears and ravages in the City and the country that not only did no one go out beyond the Roman marches to pillage, nor either patricians or plebs have any thought of waging war, but the men of Fidenae, who at first had kept to their mountains or their city walls, actually came down into Roman territory, bent on plunder. Then, when they had called in an army from Veii—for the Faliscans could not be driven into renewing the war either by the calamity of the Romans or the entreaties of their allies, the two peoples crossed the Anio and set up their standards not far from the Colline Gate. The consternation in the City was therefore no less than in the fields; the consul Julius disposed his troops on the rampart and walls, and Verginius took counsel with the senate in the temple of Quirinus.

It was resolved that Quintus Servilius, whose surname some give as Priscus, others as Structus, should be appointed dictator. Verginius delayed till he could consult his colleague; then, with his consent, he that night named the dictator, who appointed as his master of the horse Postumus Aebutius Helva.

XXII. The dictator commanded everybody to be outside the Colline Gate at break of day. All those who were able to bear arms were at hand. The standards were taken out of the treasury and brought to the dictator. While this was going on, the enemy withdrew to a more elevated position. Thither the dictator marched under arms, and not far from Nomentum joined battle with the Etruscan forces and put them to rout. From there he drove them into the city of Fidenae, which he surrounded with a rampart; but could not capture it with scaling-ladders, since it was a lofty, well-fortified town, nor accomplish anything by blockade, for they not only had corn enough for their necessities, but in fact were lavishly supplied with it from stores which they had collected in advance. In despair therefore alike of storming the place and of forcing it to surrender, the dictator, operating in a region which was familiar from its nearness to Rome, began, on the farthest side of the city, which was least guarded because its peculiar character made it the safest of all, to drive a mine into the citadel. He himself, advancing against the city from widely separated points—with his army in four divisions, that they might relieve one another in the attack—by fighting continuously day and night distracted the enemy's attention from the work, until a tunnel had been dug through the hill and a passage-way constructed up into the citadel; when the Etruscans, intent on groundless alarms and unmindful of their real danger, were apprised by the shouts of the enemy above their heads that their city had been taken.

In that year Gaius Furius Paculus and Marcus Geganius Macerinus the censors approved a public building erected in the Campus Martius, and the census of the people was taken there for the first time.

XXIII. That the same consuls were re-elected the following year (Julius for a third and Verginius for a second term) I find stated by Licinius Macer: Valerius Antias and Quintus Tubero give Marcus Manlius and Quintus Sulpicius as the consuls for that year. For the rest, in spite of the great discrepancy in their statements, both Tubero and Macer cite the authority of the Linen Rolls; neither writer dissembles the fact that the elder historians had recorded that there were military tribunes for that year. Licinius sees fit to follow without hesitation the Linen Rolls: Tubero is uncertain where the truth lies. With all the other matters which are shrouded in antiquity this question too may be left undecided.[38]

There was great alarm in Etruria in consequence of the capture of Fidenae. Not only were the people of Veii terrified by the fear of a similar disaster, but the Faliscans too remembered that they had commenced the war in alliance with the Fidenates, although they had not supported them in their revolt. Accordingly when the two states, sending envoys round amongst the twelve cities, had obtained their consent to have a council proclaimed for all Etruria at the shrine of Voltumna, the senate, feeling that they were threatened with a great outbreak in that quarter, ordered that Mamercus Aemilius be again named dictator. By him Aulus Postumius Tubertus was appointed master of the horse, and preparations for war were set about as much more energetically than on the last occasion, as the danger from all Etruria was greater than it had been from two cities.

XXIV. This affair ended a good deal more quietly than anybody had anticipated. It was reported by merchants[39] that the Veientes had been refused assistance and had been told that having embarked on the war at their own discretion they must prosecute it with their own forces nor seek the alliance of those in their adversity with whom they had not shared the prospect of success. Whereupon the dictator, that his appointment might not have been for nothing, was desirous, being deprived of the means of winning military renown, of accomplishing some peaceful achievement to signalize his dictatorship. He therefore laid his plans to weaken the censorship, either thinking its powers excessive, or troubled less by the greatness of the office than by its long duration. So, calling an assembly, he said that the immortal gods had undertaken to manage the foreign relations of the state and to make everything safe: he himself would do what needed to be done within the City, and would defend the liberty of the Roman People. Now the greatest safeguard was that great powers should not be long-continued, but that a limit of time should be imposed on them, since no limit of jurisdiction could be. Other magistracies were tenable for one year, the censorship for five. It was a serious matter for the same man to have authority over people for so many years, in a great part of their affairs. He announced that he should propose a law that the censorship might not last longer than a year and a half. With vast enthusiasm on the part of the people the law was next day enacted, and Mamercus exclaimed, "That you may have positive proof, Quirites, how little I approve prolonged authority, I lay down my dictatorship." Thus, having resigned his own magistracy and assigned a limit for the other, he was escorted to his home by the people, with striking manifestations of rejoicing and goodwill. The censors, in their indignation that Mamercus had abridged a magistracy of the Roman People, removed him from his tribe, and assessing him at eight times his former tax, disfranchised him.[40] This they say Mamercus bore with great fortitude, having regard rather to the cause of his humiliation than to the humiliation itself. The leading patricians, though they had opposed the curtailment of the jurisdiction of the censorship, were offended by this example of censorial ruthlessness, since each of them perceived that he should be subjected to the censor for a longer period and more frequently than he should hold the censor's office. The people at any rate are said to have been so enraged that no man's influence but that of Mamercus himself could have shielded the censors from their violence.

XXV. The tribunes of the plebs by persistent opposition prevented the consular elections from taking place. At last, when matters had been brought almost to an interregnum, they succeeded in their contention that military tribunes with consular powers should be chosen. Though they hoped their victory would be rewarded by the choice of a plebeian, they were disappointed: all those who were elected were patricians, Marcus Fabius Vibulanus, Marcus Folius, Lucius Sergius Fidenas. An epidemic that year afforded a respite from other troubles. A temple was vowed to Apollo in behalf of the people's health. The duumviri did many things by direction of the Books[41] for the purpose of appeasing the angry gods and averting the plague from the people. Nevertheless the losses were severe, both in the City and the country, and men and cattle were stricken without distinction. They even feared that famine would succeed the epidemic, since the farmers were down with the disease. They therefore sent to Etruria and the Pomptine district, and to Cumae, and finally to Sicily itself, for corn. Nothing was said about consular elections; military tribunes with consular authority were chosen as follows: Lucius Pinarius Mamercus, Lucius Furius Medullinus, Spurius Postumius Albus—all patricians.

This year the violence of the disease was mitigated, and there was no risk of a dearth of corn, since precautions had been taken in advance. Schemes for instigating war were discussed in the councils of the Volsci and Aequi, and in Etruria at the shrine of Voltumna. There the enterprise was put over for a year, and it was decreed that no council should convene before that date, though the Veientes complained—without effect—that Veii was threatened with the same destruction as had overtaken Fidenae.

Meanwhile in Rome the leaders of the plebs, who had now for a long time, while there was peace with other nations, been thwarted in their hopes of attaining to greater honors, began to appoint meetings at the houses of the plebeian tribunes. There they considered their plans in secret; they complained that they were held in such contempt by the plebs that although military tribunes with consular powers had been elected for so many years, no plebeian had ever been admitted to that office. Their ancestors had shown great foresight in providing that no patrician should be eligible for the plebeian magistracies; otherwise they would have been obliged to have patricians as tribunes of the plebs, so contemptible did they appear, even to their own class, being no less despised by the commons than by the nobles. Others exonerated the plebs and threw the blame upon the patricians: it was owing to their artful canvassing that the plebeians found the road to office blocked; if the plebs might have a breathing-spell from the mingled prayers and menaces of the nobles, they would think of their friends when they went to vote, and to the protection they had already won would add authority.[42] It was resolved in order to do away with canvassing, that the tribunes[43] should propose a law forbidding anyone to whiten his toga, for the purpose of announcing himself a candidate.[44] This may now appear a trivial thing and one scarcely to be considered seriously, but at that time it kindled a furious struggle between the patricians and the plebs. Yet the tribunes prevailed and carried their law; and it was clear that the plebeians in their irritated mood would support the men of their own order. That they might not be at liberty to do so, the senate decreed that consuls should be elected.

XXVI. The reason alleged was a sudden outbreak of hostilities on the part of the Aequi and Volsci, which the Latins and the Hernici had reported. Titus Quinctius Cincinnatus, son of Lucius—the same who is given the added surname Poenus, and Gnaeus Julius Mento were made consuls. Nor was the fear of war deferred. After a levy, held under a *lex sacrata*[45] which was their most effective means of collecting soldiers, strong armies marched out from both nations and met on Algidus, where the Aequi encamped in one place and the Volsci in another, and their generals took more pains than ever before to intrench, and to drill their men. For this reason the report occasioned the more dismay in Rome. The senate resolved that a dictator should be appointed, since, though often beaten, those nations had renewed the war with greater efforts than at any previous time, and a considerable proportion of the young Romans had been carried off by the plague. Above all, men were frightened by the wrong-headedness of the consuls, their want of harmony between themselves, and their opposition to each other in all their plans. Some writers say that these consuls were defeated on Algidus, and that this was the reason of the dictator's being named. Thus much is clear: though they might differ in other matters, they were agreed on one thing, to oppose the wishes of the Fathers for the appointment of a dictator; until, as the reports grew more and more alarming, and the consuls refused to be guided by the senate, Quintus Servilius Priscus, a man who had filled with distinction the highest offices, cried out, "To you, tribunes of the plebs, since matters have come to an extremity, the senate appeals, that in this great national crisis you may compel the consuls, by virtue of your authority, to name a dictator." Hearing this the tribunes felt that an opportunity had come for increasing their power; they conferred apart, and then announced, in behalf of the college, that they were resolved that the consuls should obey the senate; if they persisted further to oppose the unanimous opinion of that most honorable order, they should command them to be put in prison. The consuls preferred to be defeated by the tribunes rather than by the senate. They declared that the senators had betrayed the rights of the highest office in the state and had ignominiously surrendered the consulship to the tribunician power, since apparently it was possible for the consuls to be subjected to the official compulsion of a tribune, and even—what could a private citizen fear more than that? be carried off to gaol. It was determined by lot—for the colleagues had not been able to agree even about this—that Titus Quinctius should name the dictator. He appointed Aulus Postumius Tubertus, his father-in-law, a man of the sternest authority; and by him Lucius Julius was chosen master of the horse. At the same time a levy was proclaimed and a cessation of legal business, and it was ordered that nothing else should be done in all the City but prepare for war. The examination of those who claimed exemption from military service was put over till after the war, and so even those whose cases were uncertain were disposed to give in their names.[46] Men were required also of the Hernici and the Latins, and in both instances the dictator was zealously obeyed.

XXVII. These measures were all carried out with great dispatch. Gnaeus Julius the consul was left behind to protect the city; and Lucius Julius, the master of the horse, to meet the sudden demands which arise in war, that the troops might not be hampered in camp by the want of anything that they might need. The dictator, repeating the words after Aulus Cornelius the pontifex maximus, vowed to celebrate great games[47] if he succeeded in quelling the outbreak, and, dividing his army with the consul Quinctius, set out from Rome and came to the enemy. Seeing that the opposing forces occupied two camps with a little space between, the Roman generals followed their example and encamped about a mile from the enemy, the dictator nearer to Tusculum and the consul to Lanuvium. Thus the four armies in their four intrenchments had in their midst a field of sufficient extent not merely for small preliminary skirmishes but even for drawing up lines of battle on both sides. Nor from the moment the Romans had pitched their camp near that of the enemy did they once cease skirmishing; and the dictator was well content that his men should match their strength against their adversaries, and by trying the outcome of these contests come, little by little, to count upon a general victory. The enemy in consequence abandoned all hope of success in a regular battle and attacked the consul's camp at night, committing their cause to the hazard of a dangerous enterprise. The shout which suddenly broke out aroused not only the consul's sentries and after them his entire army, but the dictator as well. When circumstances required instant action, the consul proved to be wanting neither in resolution nor in judgment. With a part of his soldiers he reinforced the guards at the gates; with a part he lined the palisade. In the other camp, with the dictator, there was less confusion and a correspondingly clearer perception what was needful to be done. Reinforcements were immediately sent to the consul's camp, under Spurius Postumius Albus the lieutenant: the dictator himself, taking a part of his forces, marched by a slight detour to a place absolutely screened from the fighting, that he might thence strike the enemy unawares as he faced the other way. The lieutenant Quintus Sulpicius he put in charge of the camp; to the lieutenant Marcus Fabius he assigned the cavalry, but ordered him not to move his command till daybreak, as it would be hard to control in the confusion of the night. Everything that any wise and active general could have commanded and carried out in such a situation was duly commanded and carried out by him; but an unusual proof of judgment and daring and one which reflects no ordinary credit upon him was this, that he actually attacked the enemy's camp (from which, as he ascertained, they had marched out with more than half their troops), dispatching Marcus Geganius with some chosen cohorts on that service. This officer found his foes absorbed in the issue of the dangerous work undertaken by their fellows, and with no thought for themselves, neglecting their sentinels and outguards; he attacked them, captured their camp almost before they fully realized that they were assailed, and sent up a prearranged signal of smoke, on seeing which the dictator cried out that the enemy's camp was taken and bade spread the news.

XXVIII. By this time the day was breaking and everything could be seen. Fabius had delivered a charge with his cavalry; the consul had made a sally from the camp against the enemy, who were already wavering; while the dictator, on the other side of the field, attacking the supports and the second line, had fallen upon the foe from every side, as they wheeled about to meet the wild shouts and sudden onsets, with his victorious foot and horse. Accordingly, being now hemmed in on every side, the enemy would have suffered to a man the penalty of their rebellion, had not Vettius Messius, a Volscian more distinguished by his deeds than by his birth, called out in a clear voice to his men, who were already crowding together in a circle, "Are you going to offer yourselves up here to the weapons of the enemy, defenseless and unavenged? To what end then are you armed, or why without provocation did you make war, turbulent in peace and sluggards in the field? What hope is there while you stand here? Do you think that some god will protect you and deliver you from this plight? It is your swords must make a way for you! Come, where you see me go before, there you must follow, if you would look on homes, parents, wives and children! It is not a wall or rampart that blocks your path, but armed men like yourselves. In courage you are their equals; in necessity, which is the last and chiefest weapon, you are the better men." So he spoke, and acted on the word. Renewing their shouts they followed after, and hurled themselves against the Romans where the cohorts of Postumius Albus had confronted them. And they forced the victors to give ground, until the dictator came up, as his men were already falling back, and the fighting all centered on that spot. On one single warrior, Messius, hung the fortunes of the enemy. Many were the wounds on either side, and great was the slaughter everywhere. Now even the Roman leaders were bleeding as they fought. Only Postumius left the battle, struck by a stone that broke his head. A wounded shoulder could not drive the dictator from so critical a fight; nor would Fabius retire for a thigh almost pinned to his horse; nor the consul for an arm that was hewn away.

XXIX. Messius pressed on with a band of courageous youths over the slain bodies of his enemies, and reached the Volscian camp, which had not yet been taken; and on that point the entire battle converged. The consul, after pursuing his opponents clear up to the rampart, assailed the camp itself and the palisade; and thither from another part of the field the dictator brought up his troops. The assault was no less vigorous than the battle had been. They say that the consul even cast his standard into the stockade, to make his men the more eager in the charge, and that in seeking to recover it they made the first breach. The dictator too had breached the rampart and had already carried the fighting into the camp. Then the enemy began on every hand to throw down their arms and surrender. Finally the camp itself was captured, and the enemy were all sold into slavery, except the senators. A portion of the booty was restored to the Latins and the Hernici, on their identifying it as their own; a part was sold at auction by the dictator; who then left the consul in command of the camp and returning himself in triumph to the City laid down his office. The memory of the noble dictatorship assumes a sombre hue in a tradition that Aulus Postumius' son, who, tempted by an opportunity of fighting to advantage, had left his post unbidden, was in the hour of his victory beheaded by his father's orders. One is loath to believe this story, and the diversity of opinion allows one to reject it. It is an indication of its falsity that we speak of Manlian,[48] not Postumian discipline, whereas he who had first established so rigorous a precedent would himself have received that notorious stigma of cruelty. Besides, Manlius was given the surname *Imperiosus*—"the Despotic"—while Postumius received no such grim distinction.

Gnaeus Julius the consul dedicated the temple of Apollo in the absence of his colleague, without drawing lots. Quinctius resented this, when he had dismissed his army and returned to the City; but his complaint of it in the senate was without effect.

To the history of a year famous for its great events, is appended a statement—as though the incident was then regarded as of no importance to the Roman state—that the Carthaginians, destined to be such mighty enemies, then for the first time sent over an army into Sicily to assist one of the factions in the domestic quarrels of the Sicilians.[49]

XXX. An effort was made in the City by the tribunes of the plebs to procure the election of military tribunes with consular powers, but it was unsuccessful. Lucius Papirius Crassus[50] and Lucius Julius were chosen consuls. The Aequi, through their envoys, sought a treaty from the senate. Instead of granting a treaty, the senate suggested that they surrender; but they asked and obtained a truce for eight years. The Volscian commonwealth, in addition to the disaster it had suffered on Algidus, had become involved in quarrels and seditions, in consequence of an obstinate struggle between the advocates of peace and those of war. The Romans everywhere enjoyed peace. A law concerning the valuation of fines was most welcome to the people. Having learned through the treachery of a member of the college that the tribunes were drawing one up, the consuls anticipated their action and themselves proposed it.[51]

The next consuls were Lucius Sergius Fidenas (for the second time) and Hostius Lucretius Tricipitinus. Nothing noteworthy was done this year. They were succeeded in the consulship by Aulus Cornelius Cossus and Titus Quinctius Poenus, who was elected for the second time. The Veientes made inroads into Roman territory. It was rumored that certain young men of Fidenae had shared in the pillaging. The investigation of this report was intrusted to Lucius Sergius, Quintus Servilius, and Mamercus Aemilius; and certain men were banished to Ostia, because it was not clear why they had been away from Fidenae during those days. A number of settlers were added to the colony, and land was assigned them which had belonged to men who had fallen in the war. A drought that year caused great suffering. Not only did the skies provide too little rain, but the earth as well was deficient in native moisture and could hardly supply the perennial streams. In some cases the failure of the sources caused the dry springs and brooks to be lined with cattle perishing of thirst; others were carried off by a mange, and their diseases were by contact communicated to mankind. At first they attacked country people and slaves; then the City was infected. And not only were men's bodies smitten by the plague, but a horde of superstitions, mostly foreign, took possession of their minds, as the class of men who find their profit in superstition-ridden souls introduced strange sacrificial rites into their homes, pretending to be seers; until the public shame finally reached the leading citizens, as they beheld in every street and chapel outlandish and unfamiliar sacrifices being offered up to appease Heaven's anger. The aediles were then commissioned to see to it that none but Roman gods should be worshipped, nor in any but the ancestral way.

Revenge on the men of Veii was postponed till the following year, when Gaius Servilius Ahala and Lucius Papirius Mugillanus were consuls. Even then a religious scruple prevented the immediate declaration of war and dispatch of armies; they resolved that fetials must first be sent to require restitution. Not long before there had been a battle with the Veientes near Nomentum and Fidenae, and this had been followed not by peace but by a truce. Its time had now run out, and indeed the enemy had begun to fight again before its expiration; nevertheless fetials were sent; yet their words, when they sought reparation after taking the customary oath,[52] were not attended to. A dispute then arose whether war should be declared by command of the people, or whether a senatorial decree was enough.[53] The tribunes prevailed, by threatening to hinder the levy, and forced the consul Quinctius to refer the question of war to the people. All the centuries voted for it. In this respect also the plebs had the better, that they made good their wish that consuls should not be elected for the following year.

XXXI. Four military tribunes with consular powers were elected, Titus Quinctius Poenus, who had just been consul, Gaius Furius, Marcus Postumius, and Aulus Cornelius Cossus. Of these, Cossus had charge of the City; the three others held a levy and marching against Veii gave a demonstration how unprofitable it was in war to parcel out authority. By pursuing each his own counsels, one having this opinion, another that, they gave the enemy room to take them at a disadvantage; for their army was confused when some bade sound the charge, while others commanded the recall; and at this favorable moment the Veientes fell upon them. The camp, which was close by, received the demoralized and fleeing men, and so they suffered more disgrace than actual harm. The nation was filled with grief, for it was not used to being conquered; disgusted with the tribunes, people demanded a dictator: therein, they said, lay the hope of the state. And when they seemed likely to be thwarted in that also, by a scrupulous feeling that no one but a consul could name a dictator, the augurs were consulted and removed the impediment. Aulus Cornelius named as dictator Mamercus Aemilius and was himself appointed by Mamercus master of the horse, so true is it that when the fortune of the state required real worth, the animadversion of the censor could by no means prevent men's seeking a director of their affairs in a house undeservedly stigmatized.[54]

The Veientes, elated by their success, dispatched envoys round about to the peoples of Etruria, boasting that they had routed three Roman commanders in one fight. Nevertheless they obtained no general support from the league, though they attracted volunteers from all quarters by the prospect of booty. Only the people of Fidenae voted to renew the war; and, as though it were forbidden to commence war without a crime, as before in the blood of the ambassadors, so now they imbued their swords in that of the new settlers, and joined the men of Veii. Consultations followed between the leaders of the two nations whether they should take Veii or Fidenae for the headquarters of their campaign. Fidenae seemed the fitter; and accordingly the Veientes crossed the Tiber and transferred the war to Fidenae. At Rome there was a wild alarm. The troops were recalled from Veii, though even their spirits were much daunted in consequence of their failure, and encamped before the Colline Gate. Armed men were disposed along the walls, a cessation of the courts was proclaimed in the Forum, the shops were closed, and everything assumed more the look of a camp than of a city.

XXXII. The dictator, sending heralds this way and that through the streets, summoned the frightened citizens to an assembly, where he rebuked them for possessing hearts so easily dismayed by trivial fluctuations of fortune that on sustaining a slight reverse—and that not due to the valor of the enemy or the cowardice of the Roman army, but to a disagreement among their generals—they were seized with dread of the Veientine enemy whom they had six times defeated, and of Fidenae which they had captured almost more often than they had attacked it. Both the Romans and their enemies were the same as they had been for so many generations; they had the same courage, the same bodily vigor, the same weapons; he was himself the same dictator Mamercus Aemilius who had formerly put to flight the armies of the Veientes and the Fidenates, with the Faliscans added, before Nomentum; and, as master of the horse, Aulus Cornelius would be the same man in battle that he had shown himself in the former war, when as military tribune he had slain Lars Tolumnius, king of the Veientes, in full sight of both armies, and had borne the spoils of honor to the temple of Jupiter Feretrius. Let them remember then that theirs were the triumphs, theirs the spoils, theirs the victory; while their enemies were stained with the crime of putting envoys to death against the law of nations, with the slaughter in time of peace of settlers at Fidenae, with the broken truce, with rebelling unsuccessfully for the seventh time. Let them think of these things and arm. When once they should have pitched their camp near the camp of the enemy, he was very confident the dastardly foe would not long rejoice over the humiliation of a Roman army; but that the Roman People would perceive how much better those men had served the state who had named him for the third time dictator, than had those who, because he had torn from the censorship its tyrannical powers, had fixed a stigma upon his second dictatorship. Then, having offered vows to the gods, he marched out and encamped a mile and a half this side of Fidenae, protected on his right by mountains, on his left by the river Tiber. His lieutenant Titus Quinctius Poenus he commanded to secure the mountains and secretly to occupy the ridge which lay to the enemy's rear.

On the morrow, when the Etruscans, in high feather at what, on the previous day, had been more good luck than good fighting, sallied forth to offer battle, the dictator delayed a little, till his scouts should report that Quinctius had come out on the ridge near the citadel of Fidenae; and then forming his infantry in line of battle led them at the double against the enemy. He directed the master of the horse not to begin to fight until he got his orders: when he required the help of the cavalry, he would himself give the signal; let him then bear himself as one mindful of his battle with a king, of his glorious offering, of Romulus and Jupiter Feretrius. The armies came together with great fury. The Romans were consumed with hatred. "Traitors" was the name they gave the Fidenates, and "brigands" the men of

Veii; they called them breakers of truces, stained with the horrid murder of ambassadors, sprinkled with the gore of their own settlers, faithless allies and cowardly enemies; and fed their rage at once with deeds and with words.

XXXIII. They had shaken the enemy's resistance at the very first onset, when suddenly the gates of Fidenae were flung open and a strange kind of army, never seen before or heard of, came pouring out. Fire was the weapon of that vast multitude, and blazing torches threw a glare upon the entire throng when, as though inspired with a wild insanity, they rushed headlong on their enemy. For an instant the strangeness of this kind of battle dismayed the Romans. Then the dictator, calling up the master of the horse and his cavalry, sending for Quinctius to come down from the mountains, and urging on the fight himself, hurried to the left wing, which, as though it found itself in a conflagration rather than a line of battle, had shrunk back in terror from the flames, and in a loud voice cried out: "Will you quit your post, subdued with smoke like a swarm of bees, and yield to an unarmed foe? Will you not extinguish fire with the sword? Will you not seize these self-same brands, and each for himself—if we must fight with fire, not with javelins—attack them with their own weapons? Come, call to mind the Roman name, your fathers' valor and your own; turn this blaze upon the enemy's city and destroy Fidenae with its own flames, since your kindness was powerless to gain its friendship! The blood of your envoys and your colonists and your devastated borders exhort you to do as I say." At the dictator's command the whole array was set in motion. Here they caught up torches which had been flung away; there they wrested them violently from their bearers: both sides were armed with fire. The master of the horse on his part invented a new kind of cavalry-fighting. Commanding his men to pull off the bridles from their horses, he led the way, and setting spurs to his own, was carried by the unbridled charger into the midst of the flames. The other horses too were urged on and bore their riders at full tilt against the enemy; while the dust that rose and mingled with the smoke darkened the eyes both of the men and of their mounts. But the sight which had frightened the infantry had no terror for the horses, and the cavalry overthrew their enemies in heaps wherever they advanced. Then a new shout was heard. Both armies in astonishment looked that way; and when the dictator called out that Quinctius the lieutenant and his followers had assailed the enemy in the rear, the cheering was renewed, and he pressed home his own attack more sharply. Now that two battle-fronts and two distinct attacks hemmed in the Etruscans and forced them back from front and rear; and there was no way for them to flee, either back into their camp or into the mountains, whence a new foe had appeared to block their path; and the horses, with loose reins, had borne their riders far and wide; the Veientes for the most part ran in disorder to the Tiber, while those of the Fidenates who survived turned towards the city of Fidenae. In their panic they fled into the middle of the carnage. Some were cut down on the banks of the river; others, forced into the water, were swept away by the current; even experienced swimmers were borne down by weariness and wounds and fear; only a few out of the many swam across. The other party was carried on through the camp to the city. Thither the Romans too pushed forward in the impetuosity of the pursuit—especially Quinctius, and with him those who had just come down from the hills and were the freshest soldiers for the work, having arrived at the close of the battle.

XXXIV. After these troops, mingling with the enemy, had entered the gate, they made their way on to the wall, where they raised a signal to show their friends that the town was taken. When the dictator saw it—for by this time he had himself penetrated to the deserted camp of the enemy, he checked his soldiers, who were eager to scatter in search of booty, by encouraging the hope that they would find larger spoils in the city; and, leading them to the gate, was received within the walls and marched directly to the citadel, whither he saw that the throng of fugitives was rushing. Nor was the slaughter in the city less than it had been in the battle, until they threw away their arms, and asking nothing but their lives, surrendered to the dictator. The city and the camp were sacked. Next day the cavalrymen and centuri-ons drew lots for a single captive each, while those who had shown conspicuous bravery received two. The rest were sold at auction, and the dictator marched his victorious army, enriched with plunder, back to Rome, and triumphed. After commanding his master of the horse to lay down his office, he himself abdicated, giving up in peace on the sixteenth day the supreme authority he had received in time of war and danger. Certain annalists have recorded that there was a naval battle also with the Veientes, near Fidenae, a thing equally difficult and incredible; for even today the river is not wide enough for that, and in those times it was somewhat narrower, as we learn from the old writers; unless possibly there were a few ships assembled to dispute the passage of the river and this was exaggerated, as so often happens, by those who added to the inscription[55] the false claim of a naval victory.

XXXV. The next year there were military tribunes with consular powers, namely Aulus Sempronius Atratinus, Lucius Quinctius Cincinnatus, Lucius Furius Medullinus, Lucius Horatius Barbatus. The Veientes were granted a truce of twenty years, and the Aequi one of three, though they had asked for a longer one. There was a respite also from civil disturbances.

The following year was noteworthy neither for foreign war nor dissension at home, but gained celebrity from the games which had been vowed during the war and were splendidly carried out by the military tribunes and attended by a great concourse of neighboring peoples. The tribunes with consular authority were Appius Claudius Crassus, Spurius Nautius Rutulus, Lucius Sergius Fidenas, and Sextus Julius Iulus. The spectacle was rendered the more agreeable to the visitors by the courtesy which their hosts had united in a resolution to extend to them. After the games seditious speeches were made by the plebeian tribunes, who berated the populace because, in their besotted admiration of the men they hated, they kept themselves in perpetual servitude, and not only dared not aspire to claim participation in the consulship, but even in the matter of choosing military tribunes—an election open alike to patricians and plebeians—took no thought either for themselves or for their friends. Let them cease therefore to wonder why no one busied himself for the good of the plebs; toil was bestowed and danger risked, they said, in causes which held out hopes of emolument and honor; there was nothing men would not attempt if those who made great efforts were afforded the prospect of great rewards; but that someone plebeian tribune should rush blindly into a struggle where the risk was enormous and the reward was nothing, and in consequence of which he might be certain that the patricians, against whom he would be striving, would pursue him with relentless animosity, and that the plebs, for whom he would have fought, would not add the least tittle to his honors, was a thing to be neither expected nor demanded. Great hearts were begotten of great honors. No plebeian would despise himself when plebeians should cease to be despised. It was high time they made trial in one or two eases, to see whether there were some plebeian fit to hold high office, or whether it were almost a portent and a miracle that there should exist any brave and energetic man of plebeian origin. By exerting their utmost force they had carried the point that military tribunes with consular powers might be chosen even from the plebs. Men whose worth had been proven at home and in the field had stood for the office; during the first years they had been buffeted about, rejected, and laughed at by the patricians; finally, they had ceased to expose themselves to insult. They could see no reason, they said, why they should not even repeal a statute which authorized something that would never come; there would surely be less shame in the injustice of the law than in being passed over on account of their own unworthiness.

XXXVI. Speeches of this sort, being listened to with approval, incited certain men to stand for the military tribuneship, with the promise that they would propose in their term of office such and such measures of advantage to the plebs. Hopes were held out of dividing up the public domain and planting colonies, and of levying a tax on the occupants of the land and distributing the money as pay for the soldiers.[56] The military tribunes then watched for an opportunity when people were out of town, and recalling the senators by a secret notification, got the senate to pass a resolution, in the absence of the tribunes of the plebs, that since the Volsci were rumored to have made a plundering expedition into the country of the Hernici, the tribunes of the soldiers should go and investigate the affair, and that a consular election should be held. The tribunes set out, leaving Appius Claudius, the decemvir's son, as prefect of the City. He was an energetic young man and imbued from his very cradle with hatred of the tribunes and the plebs. The plebeian tribunes had no ground of contention either with the absent officials who had obtained the resolution of the senate, or with Appius, now that the thing was done.

XXXVII. Gaius Sempronius Atratinus and Quintus Fabius Vibulanus were elected consuls.

A foreign episode, but worth relating, is ascribed to this year, viz. that Volturnum, the Etruscan city which is now Capua, was taken by the Samnites, and named Capua from their leader Capys, or, as is more probable, from its champaign country.[57] Now they captured it after being admitted by the Etruscans—who were worn out with fighting—to a share in the city and its fields; then, on a holiday, when the old settlers were heavy with sleep and feasting, the newcomers fell upon them in the night and slew them.

In the train of these events,[58] the consuls whom I have named took up their duties, on the 13th of December. By this time not only had those who had been dispatched for this purpose reported that a Volscian invasion was imminent, but envoys from the Latins, and the Hernici as well, announced that never before had the Volscians been more energetic, whether in selecting generals or in levying an army; that everywhere men were muttering that they must either give up forever all thoughts of arms and war, and submit to the yoke, or must not lag behind those with whom they were contending for supremacy, either in courage or in endurance or in military discipline. Their tidings were true, but they caused no answerable activity among the senators; and Gaius Sempronius, to whom the command had been assigned by lot, trusting to fortune as though it were the most constant thing in the world, because he had commanded the victorious nation against the people they had defeated, conducted everything so carelessly and rashly that Roman discipline was more in evidence in the Volscian army than in the Roman. Accordingly Fortune, as on many another occasion, waited on desert. In the first battle, which Sempronius entered without caution or deliberation, his line was not strengthened with reserves nor was his cavalry skilfully posted, when the fighting began. The battle-cries were the first intimation how the affair was likely to go; for the enemy's was louder and fuller, that of the Romans dissonant and uneven and, dragging more with each repetition, betrayed the faintness of their hearts. This caused the enemy to charge the more boldly, thrusting with shields and making play with swords. On the Roman side helmets nodded, as their wearers looked this way and that for help, and irresolute soldiers made falteringly for the nearest group; at one moment the standards would be left behind by the retreat of the front-rankers, at the next they would be falling back among their proper maniples. It was not yet a definite flight, not yet a victory; the Romans sought rather to protect themselves than to fight; the Volscians advanced and bore hard against the Roman line, but saw more of their enemies killed than running away.

XXXVIII. But now the Romans were everywhere falling back, and it was in vain that Sempronius the consul upbraided or encouraged them. There was no virtue either in his authority or in his dignity; and his men would presently have shown the enemy their backs, had not a cavalry decurion[59] named Sextus Tempanius, just as the situation was becoming desperate, come with prompt courage to the rescue. In a loud voice he cried out that the horsemen who wished to save the state should leap down from their horses, and when the troopers in every squadron had bestirred themselves as if at the command of the consul, he added: "Unless this bucklered[60] cohort stops the enemy's rush it is all over with our supremacy. Follow my spear as your guidon;[61] show Romans and Volscians that when you are mounted no cavalry are your equals, nor any infantry, when you fight on foot!" When a cheer had shown their approval of this exhortation, he advanced with uplifted spear. Wherever they went they forced a passage; holding their targets up before them, they charged where they saw the distress of their friends was greatest. The fortune of the day was restored at every point where their onset carried them; nor was there any doubt that if those few men could have been present everywhere at the same time the enemy would have turned tail.

XXXIX. When the Volscian general saw that their attack could not anywhere be stopped, he ordered his troops to give ground to the men with bucklers, the enemy's new cohort, until, carried forward in their rush, they should be cut off from their friends. On this being done, the horsemen were intercepted, and were unable to break through in the same way as they had got over, since their enemies were most thickly crowded together where they had made their path. When the consul and the Roman legions could nowhere see the soldiers who a moment before had been a shield to the entire army, they pressed forward to save at any cost so many heroic men from being surrounded and borne down by the enemy. The Volscians, facing two ways, sustained on one side the onset of the consul and the legions, and on the other front pressed home their attack upon Tempanius and his troopers; who, having failed, in spite of many attempts, to force their way through to their friends, had seized a certain mound and, forming a circle, were defending themselves, not without taking vengeance on their assailants. The battle did not end till nightfall. Neither did the consul relax his efforts anywhere, but kept the enemy engaged as long as there was any light. Darkness put a stop to the indecisive struggle, and the terror in each camp was such, in consequence of men's ignorance of the outcome, that both armies, abandoning their wounded and a good part of their baggage, retreated to the nearest hills, as though defeated. Nevertheless the mound was besieged till after midnight. But when word was brought to the besiegers that their camp was abandoned, they too supposed that their side had been defeated, and every man fled where his panic led him in the darkness. Tempanius feared an ambush and kept his soldiers close till daylight. Then, descending with a few followers to reconnoitre, he discovered by questioning some wounded enemies that the camp of the Volscians was deserted, whereupon he joyfully called his men down from the hill and made his way into the Roman camp. There he found everything abandoned and forlorn and the same desolation he had met with on the ground of the enemy; and, before the Volsci could learn of their blunder and return, he carried with him such of the wounded as he was able, and not knowing what way the consul had gone, took the nearest road to the City.

XL. Thither the rumor of an unsuccessful engagement and the abandonment of the camp had already made its way, and more than all the rest the horsemen had been mourned, with public as well as private lamentations. The consul Fabius was keeping watch before the gates—for the panic had permeated even the City—when cavalry were espied a long way off, and caused no little trepidation, since men knew not who they could be. But being soon after recognized, they turned the people's fear to such rejoicing that the City was filled with the noise of congratulations on the safe and victorious return of the horse; and from the houses which a little while before had been filled with sadness and had bewailed their sons as dead, the inhabitants ran out into the street, and trembling mothers and wives, heedless of decorum in their happiness, hurried to meet the troops, and flung themselves with utter abandonment into the arms of their loved ones, being scarcely able to control themselves for joy. The plebeian tribunes, who had set a day for the trial of Marcus Postumius and Titus Quinctius, because of their responsibility for the reverse at Veii, thought a favorable opportunity was afforded by the odium recently incurred by the consul Sempronius for renewing men's displeasure with them. So, having called a meeting, they loudly declared that the state had been betrayed at Veii by its generals; and that then, because they had gone scot free, the army fighting with the Volsci had been betrayed by the consul, their heroic cavalry given over to slaughter, and the camp basely abandoned. Then Gaius Junius, one of the tribunes, commanded the cavalryman Tempanius to be called, and turning to him spoke as follows: "Sextus Tempanius, I ask you whether you think that Gaius Sempronius the consul either joined battle at a suitable moment, or strengthened his line with supports, or performed any of the duties of a good consul; and whether you yourself, when the Roman legions had been beaten, dismounted the cavalry of your own motion and restored the fortunes of the battle; then, when you and your troopers had been cut off from our line, if either the consul himself came to your rescue or sent supports; furthermore, whether you had any help anywhere next day, or you and your cohort forced a way to the camp by your own valor; whether you found any consul in the camp and any army, or a deserted camp and wounded and forsaken soldiers. In the name of your courage and your loyalty, which alone have preserved the republic in this war, you must now answer these questions; finally you must tell us where Gaius Sempronius and our legions are; whether you were abandoned, or yourself abandoned the consul and the army; in one word, whether we have been defeated or victorious."

XLI. To these questions Tempanius is said to have replied in homely terms but with a soldierly dignity, in which was neither self-praise nor self-complacent criticism of others. Touching the degree of skill in military matters possessed by Gaius Sempronius, it was not for a soldier, he said, to appraise a general: that had been the Roman People's business when it elected Sempronius consul at the comitia. It was not, therefore, to him that they must address inquiries concerning the strategy of commanders and the qualifications of consuls; even the weighing of such abilities demanded great mental and intellectual powers. But that which he had seen he was able to report; and he had seen the consul, before he had himself been cut off from the main army, fighting in the front line, encouraging his men, and moving about amidst the standards of the Romans and the enemy's missiles. He had afterwards been carried out of sight of his friends; but still, from the din and shouting, he had made out that the struggle had been prolonged till nightfall, and he did not believe that it had been possible to break through to the hillock which he himself had held, in view of the enemy's numbers. Where the army was, he did not know; he supposed that, just as he himself had protected himself and his men by taking up a strong position, so likewise the consul, in order to save his army, had occupied a place of greater security than the camp. And he did not believe that the Volsci were any better off than the Roman People; chance and darkness had at every point confused both armies. On his going on to beg that they would not detain him, exhausted by toil and wounds, it is said that he was dismissed with the highest praise, no less for his moderation than for his bravery. Meanwhile the consul had already reached the shrine of Quies[62] on the Labican road. Thither wagons and beasts of burden were dispatched from the City, and brought the soldiers back, weary from fighting and the night-march. A little later the consul entered the City, and showed no less concern to extol Tempanius with well-merited praise than to clear himself of blame. While the citizens were grieving over their defeat, and were filled with resentment against their commanders, Marcus Postumius, who had been military tribune with consular authority at Veii, was brought before them for trial and condemned to pay a fine of ten thousand pounds of bronze.[63] Titus Quinctius his colleague, having been victorious both in the Volscian country, when consul under the auspices of the dictator Postumius Tubertus, and at Fidenae, as lieutenant to the other dictator, Mamercus Aemilius, shifted all the blame for the present campaign upon his colleague who had already been condemned, and was acquitted by all the tribes. It is said that the memory of his father Cincinnatus, whom the people venerated, was a help to him, and also the fact that Quinctius Capitolinus, now well-stricken in years, supplicated and implored them not to suffer him, who had but a little time to live, to be the bearer of such sad news to Cincinnatus.

XLII. The plebs elected in their absence Sextus: Tempanius, Marcus Asellius, Tiberius Antistius, and Tiberius Spurillius to be plebeian tribunes. These were men whom the cavalry had also chosen, at the instance of Tempanius, to act as centurions over them.[64] The senate, feeling that the hatred of Sempronius made the title of consul offensive, ordered the election of military tribunes with consular powers. The successful candidates were Lucius Manlius Capitolinus, Quintus Antonius Merenda, Lucius Papirius Mugillanus. At the very beginning of the year Lucius Hortensius, tribune of the plebs, brought an action against Gaius Sempronius, consul of the year before. The tribune's four colleagues besought him in full sight of the Roman People not to persecute their general, in whom nothing could be reckoned amiss save his ill-fortune; but this Hortensius would not brook, regarding it as a test of his perseverance and persuaded that the defendant was relying not on the entreaties of the tribunes, which were thrown out merely to preserve appearances, but on their veto. And so, turning now to Sempronius, he demanded to be told where the well-known patrician spirit was, and where the courage that placed its confident reliance upon innocence; was it in the shadow of the tribunate that a former consul had found a hiding-place? And again, addressing his colleagues, he asked, "But what do you mean to do, if I persist in prosecuting the defendant? Will you rob the people of their rights and overthrow the authority of the tribunes?" When they replied that the authority of the Roman People was supreme over Sempronius and all other men, and that they neither desired nor were able to annul the people's judgment; but that if their entreaties in behalf of their commander, who stood in the relation of a parent to them, should prove ineffectual, they would put on mourning with him, then Hortensius declared, "The Roman plebs shall not see its tribunes clad in mourning. Gaius Sempronius may go free, for me, since his command has gained him this, to be so beloved by his soldiers." Nor was the loyalty of the four tribunes more pleasing to both plebs and senators than was the disposition of Hortensius to yield so readily to reasonable entreaties.

Fortune now ceased to favor the Aequi,[65] who had accepted the dubious victory of the Volsci as their own.

XLIII. The next year Numerius Fabius Vibulanus and Titus Quinctius Capitolinus, the son of Capitolinus, were consuls. Under the leadership of Fabius, to whom this command had been assigned by lot, nothing worthy of relation was accomplished. The Aequi had scarce made an irresolute show of battle when they were routed and driven disgracefully from the field, and the consul got no credit by the affair. He was accordingly denied a triumph; but because he had relieved the ignominy incurred by Sempronius' defeat, he was allowed to enter the City in an ovation.

But while the war had been concluded with less of a struggle than men had feared, in the City tranquillity gave place to unexpected and serious quarrels, which broke out between the plebs and the senators, and began over the duplication of the number of quaestors. This measure—that besides the two city quaestors two others should be elected to assist the consuls in the administration of wars—was proposed by the consuls and received the hearty approval of the senate, but the tribunes of the plebs made a fight to have half of the quaestors—hitherto patricians had been chosen—taken from the plebs. Against this provision both consuls and senators at first exerted themselves with all their might; afterwards they were ready to concede that, just as in the case of tribunes with consular powers, so likewise with the quaestors, the people should be unrestricted in their choice; but making no headway with this offer, they dropped the whole question of enlarging the number of quaestors. It was then taken up where they had left it by the tribunes; and other revolutionary schemes came to the fore in quick succession, among them one for enacting an agrarian law. When the senate, because of these disturbances, preferred that consuls be elected rather than tribunes, yet was unable to pass a resolution on account of tribunician vetoes, the government passed from the consuls to an interrex; nor was even this accomplished without a violent struggle, for the tribunes tried to prevent the patricians from holding a meeting. The greater part of the ensuing year dragged on with contests between the new tribunes and several interreges. At one time the tribunes would keep the patricians from meeting to appoint an interrex; at another time they would interpose their veto against the interrex, that the senate might not pass a resolution to hold the consular elections. Finally Lucius Papirius Mugillanus was named interrex, and upbraiding now the senators, now the tribunes of the plebs, reminded them how the state, abandoned and forsaken by men, had been protected by the providential care of Heaven, and existed by the grace of the Veientine truce and the dilatory policy of the Aequi. If an alarm should break out in that quarter, was it their pleasure that the republic should be caught without a patrician magistrate? That there should be no army, no general to enroll an army? Or did they expect to beat off a foreign foe with a civil war? But if both should come at once, the help of the gods themselves would scarce suffice to stay the destruction of the Roman commonwealth. Why would they not every man abate somewhat of his full rights and compromise harmoniously on a middle course, the Fathers consenting that military tribunes should be chosen instead of consuls, the tribunes interposing no veto to prevent four quaestors being taken promiscuously from plebeians and patricians by free election of the people?

XLIV. The election of tribunes was held first. The tribunes with consular powers who were chosen were all patricians, namely Lucius Quinctius Cincinnatus (for the third time), Lucius Furius Medullinus (for the second time), Marcus Manlius, and Aulus Sempronius Atratinus. The last-named held the election for quaestors. Among the several plebeians who sought the place were the son of a plebeian tribune, named Aulus Antistius, and the brother of another, Sextus Pompilius. Yet neither the authority nor the support of these men could prevent the people from giving the preference, because of their noble birth, to men whose fathers and grandfathers they had seen consuls. This made all the tribunes furious, but more than all the rest Pompilius and Antistius, who were incensed at the defeat of their kinsmen. What in the world, they asked, was the meaning of this? Had neither their own services nor the wrongs which the patricians had inflicted, nor even the pleasure of exercising a right—since what had before been unlawful was now permitted—availed to elect a single quaestor from the plebs, let alone a military tribune? Of no avail had been a father's entreaties for his son, a brother's for his brother, not though they had been tribunes of the plebs, and invested with an inviolable office, created for the protection of liberty. There was fraud in the matter, beyond question, and Aulus Sempronius had employed more artifice than honesty in the election. It was by his wrong-doing, they complained, that their relations had been defeated for office. And so, since they could not attack the man himself, secure as he was not only in his innocence but in the magistracy which he was filling, they turned their anger upon Gaius Sempronius, the cousin of Atratinus; and prosecuted him, with the cooperation of their colleague Marcus Canuleius, on the score of the humiliation suffered in the Volscian war. The same tribunes frequently mentioned in the senate the division of the public lands, a measure which Gaius Sempronius had always stoutly resisted, for they reckoned—and rightly—that either he would abandon the cause and his defense would become a matter of less concern to the patricians, or that persevering in his attitude he would give offense, up to the moment of his trial, to the plebeians. He chose to face the storm of unpopularity and to injure his own cause rather than be found wanting in that of the nation; and he held fast to the same opinion, that there should be no largess, for that would redound to the advantage of the three tribunes. It was not land for the plebs they were then looking for, he declared, but hatred for himself; he was as ready as another to confront that tempest with a courageous heart; nor ought the senate to set so high a value upon himself or any other citizen that their tenderness for him should bring about a general disaster. His spirit was not a whit less firm when the day of trial came. He pleaded his own cause; the senators exerted in vain every means of mollifying the plebs; and he was condemned to pay a fine of fifteen thousand *asses*.

The same year a Vestal virgin named Postumia was put on trial for unchastity. She was innocent of the charge, though open to suspicion because of her pretty clothes and the unmaidenly freedom of her wit. After she had been remanded and then acquitted, the pontifex maximus, in the name of the college, commanded her to abstain from jests, and to dress rather with regard to sanctity than coquetry. In this same year Cumae, a city which the Greeks then held, was captured by the Campanians.

The ensuing year had as military tribunes with consular powers Agrippa Menenius Lanatus, Publius Lucretius Tricipitinus, and Spurius Nautius Rutulus.

XLV. It was a year remarkable, thanks to the good fortune of the Roman People, for a great danger but not a disaster. The slaves conspired to set fire to the City at points remote from one another, and, while the people should be busy everywhere with rescuing their houses, to seize the Citadel and the Capitol with an armed force. Jupiter brought their wicked schemes to naught, and on the evidence of two of their number the guilty were arrested and punished. Each informant was rewarded from the public treasury with ten thousand pounds of bronze—which passed for wealth in those days—and with freedom.

The Aequi then began to prepare again for war; and word was brought to Rome on good authority that new enemies, the Labicani, were making common cause with the old ones. As for the Aequi, the citizens had by now grown accustomed to war with them, as to an annual occurrence; but they dispatched envoys to Labici, and having got them back with an ambiguous answer, from which it appeared that though war was not as yet being organized, yet peace would not long continue, they commissioned the Tusculans to watch that no fresh outbreak should occur at that place.

To the military tribunes with consular authority who held office the ensuing year, Lucius Sergius Fidenas, Marcus Papirius

Mugillanus, and Gaius Servilius, son of the Priscus who as dictator had captured Fidenae, there came, just as they had entered on their magistracy, ambassadors from Tusculum, who announced that the Labicani had armed and, after devastating the Tusculan countryside in company with an Aequian army, had encamped on Algidus. Thereupon war was declared against the Labicani, and the senate resolved that two of the tribunes should proceed to the front, while one attended to matters in Rome. At this a dispute immediately broke out amongst the tribunes, each of whom boasted of his superiority as a general and spurned the care of the City as a thankless and ignoble task. While the astonished senators watched this unseemly rivalry amongst the colleagues, Quintus Servilius exclaimed, "Since you have no respect for this order nor for the republic, a father's authority shall end your quarrel. My son shall preside over the City, without recourse to lots. I only hope that those who are eager to make the campaign may conduct it with more consideration and harmony than they display in seeking it."

XLVI. It was determined not to make a general levy on the entire people, but ten tribes were chosen by lot. From these the two tribunes enrolled the men of military age and led them to war. The bickerings which had commenced between them in the City grew much hotter in the camp, from the same eagerness to command; they could not agree on anything; each strove for his own opinion; each desired his own plans and his own orders to be the only valid ones; each despised the other and was in turn despised by him, until at last, reproved by their lieutenants, they arranged to exercise the supreme command on alternate days. When the report of this reached Rome, it is said that Quintus Servilius, taught by years and experience, besought the immortal gods that the strife between the tribunes might not result more disastrously to the republic than had been the case at Veii, and as though certain defeat were imminent, urged his son to enlist soldiers and make ready arms. Nor was he a false prophet. For under the leadership of Lucius Sergius, whose day it was to command, the Romans found themselves in an unfavorable position close to the enemy's camp, whither they had been drawn, when the Aequi feigned fear and retired to their rampart, by the vain hope of capturing it; and there they were suddenly attacked by the Aequi and driven pellmell down a sloping valley, where many of them, as they rather tumbled down than retreated, were overtaken and put to the sword. That day they defended their camp with difficulty, and on the next, when the enemy had almost surrounded it, they abandoned it by a disgraceful flight through the opposite gate. The generals and their lieutenants and such of the army's strength as kept to the standards made for Tusculum: the others, scattering through the fields, this way and that, hastened to Rome by divers roads and reported a much heavier defeat than had been sustained. There was the less dismay for the reason that the event had tallied with men's apprehensions, and because reserves which they could look to in the hour of danger had been made ready by the tribune of the soldiers. It was by his orders too that the lesser magistrates had quieted the confusion in the City, when the scouts whom he had hurriedly sent out reported that the generals and the army were at Tusculum, and that the enemy had not broken camp. And—what raised men's courage most—Quintus Servilius Priscus was in consequence of a senatorial decree named dictator—a man whose clear vision in public affairs the state had proved on many previous occasions, but particularly in the outcome of this war, because he alone had viewed the quarrel of the tribunes with anxiety, before their defeat. Having appointed his son, by whom, when military tribune, he had himself been pronounced dictator, to be master of the horse, as some authorities have recorded; for others write that Servilius Ahala was master of the horse that year, he set out with a fresh army for the war, sent for the troops which were at Tusculum, and fixed his camp two miles from the enemy.

XLVII. In consequence of their success, the Aequi had taken over the arrogance and carelessness which the Roman generals had shown, and the result was seen in the very first battle. When the dictator had attacked with his cavalry and had thrown the enemy's front ranks into confusion, he ordered the legions to advance rapidly, and when one of his standard-bearers hesitated, cut him down. So eager for combat were the troops, that the Aequi could not stop their rush, and when, defeated in the field, they had withdrawn to their camp in a disordered flight, it was stormed with less expenditure of time and effort than the battle itself had cost. Having captured and sacked the camp, the dictator relinquished the plunder to his soldiers; and the cavalry, which had pursued the enemy as they fled from their encampment, came back with the report that all the Labicani, after their defeat, and a great part of the Aequi, had taken refuge in Labici. Next day the army marched to Labici and, drawing a cordon about the town, stormed it with ladders and plundered it. Leading his victorious army back to Rome, the dictator resigned his office eight days after his appointment; and the senate seized the opportunity, before the tribunes of the plebs could stir up agrarian troubles by proposing a division of the Labican territory, to resolve, in a largely-attended meeting, that a colony should be planted in Labici. Fifteen hundred colonists were sent from the City, and each received two *iugera*.[66]

The year that followed the capture of Labici, having as military tribunes with consular powers Agrippa Menenius Lanatus, Gaius Servilius Structus, and Publius Lucretius Tricipitinus (all these for the second time), together with Spurius Rutilius Crassus; and the succeeding year, with Aulus Sempronius Atratinus (for his third term) and Marcus Papirius Mugillanus and Spurius Nautius Rutulus (for their second) were a period of tranquillity in foreign relations but of civil discord arising out of agrarian laws.

XLVIII. Those who stirred up the people were Spurius Maecilius, tribune of the plebs for the fourth time, and Marcus Metilius, for the third, both having been elected in their absence. On their proposing a law that the land which had been captured from enemies should be divided up among the citizens, a plebiscite which would mean the confiscation of the fortunes of a great part of the nobles—for there was scarcely any land, as might be expected in the case of a city situated on alien soil, which had not been gained by force of arms; nor was much, if any, of that which had been sold or assigned by the state held by other than plebeians, it appeared that a desperate struggle was at hand between the plebs and the patricians. The military tribunes had hit upon no plan of action either in the senate or in the private conferences which they held with the leading men, when Appius Claudius, grandson of him who had been decemvir for drawing up the laws, himself the youngest of the council of senators, announced—so the story goes—that he was bringing them from his house an old family device; for it had been his great-grandfather[67] Appius Claudius who had pointed out to the senators that the only way to break the power of the tribunes lay through the veto of their colleagues. It was not difficult for the leading men of the state to induce upstart politicians[68] to change their minds, if they would but suit their discourse meantime rather to the exigencies of the crisis than to their lofty station. The sentiments of such fellows varied with their fortunes: when they saw that their colleagues, by taking the lead in the management of affairs, had appropriated all the favor of the populace in advance and had left no room there for themselves, they would incline without reluctance to the cause of the senate, by supporting which they might gain the goodwill not only of the order as a whole, but also of the foremost senators. When they had all expressed their approval, and especially Quintus Servilius Priscus, who praised the young man as one who had not degenerated from the Claudian stock, everybody was given the task of inducing such of the tribunician college as he could to interpose their vetoes. The senate adjourned and the leading members began to canvass the tribunes. By arguments in which they mingled warnings with the promise that their action would earn the tribunes the personal gratitude of individuals, as well as that of the senate as a body, they got six men to promise their opposition. Next day when the senate, in accordance with a preconcerted plan, had taken up the question of the sedition which Maecilius and Metilius were beginning by proposing a donation of the most objectionable type, the principal senators made speeches in which each took occasion to say that he could think of nothing to suggest and saw no help for the situation anywhere save in the assistance of the tribunes; this was the power to whose protection the harassed republic, like a private citizen in distress, now fled for succor; it was a glorious thing both for the men themselves and for their office that the tribunate possessed no less strength for the resistance of its wicked colleagues than for troubling the senate and promoting discord between the orders. Loud shouts were then heard from the entire senate and appeals were addressed to the tribunes from every part of the Curia. Then, after silence had been

obtained, those who had been won over by the favor of the chief senators declared their readiness to veto the measure which their colleagues
had proposed but the senate deemed subversive of the republic. The
thanks of the senate were voted the protesters. The authors of the bill
convened an assembly, and accusing their colleagues of being traitors
to the interests of the plebs and slaves of the consulars, and in other
ways bitterly denouncing them, withdrew their measure.

XLIX. There would have been two wars in the ensuing year, in
which Publius Cornelius Cossus, Gaius Valerius Potitus, Quintus
Quinctius Cincinnatus, and Numerius Fabius Vibulanus were military tribunes with consular powers, had not the war with Veii been
delayed, thanks to the superstition of the Veientine leaders, whose
farms an overflow of the Tiber had laid waste, chiefly by ruining the
farmhouses. At the same time the Aequi were deterred by the defeat
they had suffered three years before from marching to the assistance
of the Bolani, a tribe of their own race. These people had made
incursions into the neighboring territory of Labici and attacked the
new settlers. The consequences of this outrage they had hoped to
avoid by means of the cooperation of all the Aequi; but, having been
abandoned by their friends, they lost their town and their lands, in
a war which does not even merit description, as the result of a siege
and a single skirmish. An attempt on the part of Lucius Decius, a
plebeian tribune, to carry a law providing that colonists should be
sent to Bolae too, as well as to Labici, was frustrated through the
intervention of his colleagues, who intimated that they would permit
no plebiscite to pass unless it had the warrant of the senate.

Bolae was retaken the next year, and the Aequi planted a colony
there and strengthened the town with new defenders. Rome now
had the following military tribunes with consular powers, Gnaeus
Cornelius Cossus, Lucius Valerius Potitus, Quintus Fabius Vibulanus
(for the second time), and Marcus Postumius Regillensis. To this
last was intrusted the campaign against the Aequi. He was a wrong-
headed man, yet he showed it more in the hour of victory than during
the campaign. For he was energetic in raising an army and leading
it to Bolae, where, after breaking the spirit of the Aequi in some
trifling engagements, he finally forced an entrance into the town.

He then diverted the quarrel from the enemy to his fellow-citizens; and though he had proclaimed at the time of the attack that the booty should belong to the soldiers, when he had taken the town he broke his promise. This, I am inclined to believe, was the cause of the army's resentment, rather than the fact that in a recently-plundered city inhabited by new settlers, there was less booty than the tribune had predicted. The ill-feeling was increased, when, being sent for by his colleagues on account of tribunician disturbances, he had returned to the City, by a stupid and almost insane remark he was heard to make in an assembly, where Marcus Sextius, a plebeian tribune, in introducing an agrarian measure, announced that he should propose also that colonists be dispatched to Bolae—for it was proper, he said, that the city and lands of the Bolani should belong to those who had captured them in war. "Woe to my soldiers," exclaimed Postumius, "unless they hold their peace!"—a saying which presently, on being reported to the senators, offended them no less than it had the assembly. And the tribune of the plebs, a keen and not uneloquent man, having got for one of his adversaries a man of haughty spirit and unbridled tongue, whom he could irritate and provoke to say things that would not only make himself disliked but his cause and the entire senate as well, made a point of involving Postumius in a dispute more often than any other member of the college of military tribunes. On this particular occasion, after that savage and brutal threat, he cried, "Do you hear him, Quirites, threatening his soldiers with punishment like slaves? Shall this wild beast seem to you, notwithstanding, more deserving of so great an office than those who would present you with a city and with lands, and send you out to colonies; who would provide a home for your old age; who fight for your interests against these cruel and insolent adversaries? And does it surprise you that so few espouse your cause? What are they to expect of you? Those offices which you give by preference to your opponents, rather than to the champions of the Roman People? You groaned just now when you heard his remark. What of it? If you should be asked to vote this very moment, you would elect this man who threatens you with chastisement in preference to those who wish to secure you lands and houses and fortunes."

L. When this saying of Postumius reached the troops, it stirred
up much greater indignation in the camp: did the man who had
fraudulently cut off his soldiers from their spoils also threaten them
with punishment? And while they murmured openly, the quaestor
Publius Sestius, thinking that the mutiny could be quelled with
the same violence which had occasioned it, sent a lictor to arrest a
certain brawling soldier; whereupon shouts and objurgations broke
forth, and Sestius was hit with a stone and retreated from the scuffle,
while the man who had wounded him thundered after him that the
quaestor had got what the general had threatened to give his men.
Being summoned to deal with this disturbance, Postumius aggra-
vated everything by his harsh inquisitions and savage punishments.
Finally his anger got beyond all bounds, and when the shout of
those whom he had ordered to be put to death under a hurdle[69] had
caused a crowd to gather, he ran down in a frenzy of passion from his
tribunal to those who would have interrupted the execution. There,
when the lictors and centurions assailed the mob and tried to drive
them back, on this side and on that, resentment ran so high that a
military tribune was overwhelmed with a volley of stones from his
own soldiers. This dreadful deed having been announced in Rome,
the tribunes of the soldiers wished to institute a senatorial inquiry
into the death of their colleague, but the plebeian tribunes interposed their vetoes. The dispute was closely connected with another
struggle. The senators had become apprehensive lest the plebs, what
with their fear of investigations and their indignation, should elect
military tribunes from their own class; they therefore used all their
efforts to have consuls chosen. Since the plebeian tribunes would not
allow the resolution of the senate[70] to go through, and also vetoed the
election of consuls, the state reverted to an interregnum. The victory
then rested with the senators.

LI. Quintus Fabius Vibulanus, acting as interrex, held an election, and Aulus Cornelius Cossus and Lucius Furius Medullinus were
chosen consuls. In their consulship, early in the year, a senatorial
resolution was passed that the tribunes should bring the investigation of Postumius's murder before the plebs at the earliest possible
moment, and that the plebs should appoint whomsoever they wished

to have charge of the inquiry. The plebs unanimously referred the matter to the consuls. They accomplished their task with the utmost moderation and leniency, punishing a few only, and these are generally believed to have committed suicide; yet they were unable to prevent the transaction from being bitterly resented by the plebs, who complained that the measures which had been proposed in their interests lay all this while neglected, whereas the law that was passed concerning their punishment and their lives was carried out at once, and most effectually. It would have been a very suitable occasion, now that the mutiny had been avenged, to appease their anger by offering to divide the Bolan territory. Had the senators done this, they would have lessened men's desire for the agrarian law which was meant to expel the patricians from their wrongful occupation of the public domain. As it was, a sense of injury was aroused by the very circumstance that the nobility not only persisted in retaining the public lands, which they held by force, but would not even divide among the plebeians the unoccupied ground which had recently been taken from the enemy and would soon, they thought, become, like all the rest, the booty of a few.

The same year the Volsci laid waste the borders of the Hernici, and the legions were led out to meet them by the consul Furius. Not finding the enemy there, they captured Ferentinum, to which a great number of Volsci had retired. There was less plunder there than they had expected, because the Volsci, having small hopes of defending the town, removed their possessions by night and abandoned it; next day, when it was taken, it was practically deserted. The town itself and its territory were given to the Hernici.

LII. After this year, which the moderation of the tribunes had made a quiet one, came the plebeian tribuneship of Lucius Icilius, when Quintus Fabius Ambustus and Gaius Furius Paculus were consuls. While Icilius, at the very outset of the year, was endeavoring to stir up sedition by the promulgation of agrarian laws, as if it had been the appointed task of his name and family, a pestilence broke out, which, though it was more threatening than fatal, diverted men's thoughts from the Forum and political conflicts to their homes and the care of the sick, and is thought to have been less hurtful than the sedition would have been. The state had escaped with very few deaths, considering the great number of those who had fallen ill, when the year of pestilence was succeeded, in the consulship of Marcus Papirius Atratinus and Gaius Nautius Rutulus, by a scarcity of corn, owing to the neglect of tillage usual at such times. Indeed the famine would have been more baneful than the disease, had they not supplemented the supply of corn by dispatching emissaries to all the peoples round about who dwelt on the Tuscan sea or by the Tiber, to purchase it. The Samnites who held Capua and Cumae insolently refused to permit the envoys to trade with them, but the Sicilian tyrants,[71] on the contrary, lent them generous assistance; and the largest supplies of all were brought down the Tiber, with the hearty goodwill of the Etruscans. The consuls experienced a lack of men in the afflicted City, and, being unable to find more than one senator for an embassy, were obliged to add two knights to each. With the exception of the disease and the shortage of corn, there was no internal or foreign trouble during these two years. But no sooner had these anxieties departed, than there came an outbreak of all the ills which were wont to harass the state, domestic quarrels and war abroad.

LIII. In the consulship of Marcus Aemilius and Gaius Valerius Potitus the Aequi prepared to go to war, and the Volsci, though they did not take up arms as a nation, made the campaign as volunteers serving for pay. When, on the rumor of their advance, for they had already crossed over into Latin and Hernican territory, Valerius the consul was raising troops, and Marcus Menenius, tribune of the plebs and proposer of an agrarian law, was obstructing the levy, and everybody who did not wish to go was availing himself of the tribune's protection and refusing the oath, on a sudden came the news that the citadel of Carventum had been seized by the enemy. This humiliation not only gave the patricians the means of stirring up feeling against Menenius, but supplied the rest of the tribunes, who had already been persuaded to veto the agrarian law, with a more justifiable pretext for resisting their colleague. The dispute was long drawn out. The consuls called gods and men to witness that the responsibility for whatever defeat or disgrace had already been or threatened to be visited on them by the enemy would rest with Menenius, because of his interference with the levy; Menenius, on the other hand, protested loudly that if the occupants of the public domain would surrender their illegal possession of it, he was prepared to withdraw his opposition to the muster. At this juncture nine tribunes interposed a resolution which ended the contention. They proclaimed in the name of the college that they would support the consul Gaius Valerius if, in enforcing the levy, he resorted, despite the veto of their colleague, to fines and other forms of coercion against those who refused to serve. Armed with this decree, the consul caused the few who appealed to the tribune to be haled before him; the rest were cowed into taking the oath. The army marched to the citadel of Carventum; and although the soldiers were hated by the consul and returned his hostility, yet the moment they came to the place, they manfully drove out the garrison and recovered the stronghold, which had been laid open to attack by the negligence that had permitted men to slip away from the garrison in quest of booty. There was a considerable accumulation of spoils from this constant raiding, because everything had been heaped up there for safety. All this the consul ordered the quaestors to sell at auction and place the proceeds in the public treasury, giving out word that the army should share in the plunder only when the men had not refused to serve. This increased the enmity of plebs and soldiers towards the consul. And so when he entered the City in an ovation, as the senate had decreed, the soldiers, with military freedom, shouted out rude verses now abusing the consul and now praising Menenius, while at every mention of the tribune's name the enthusiasm of the attendant populace vied with the voices of the men in cheers and applause. This circumstance caused the patricians more anxiety than the sauciness of the soldiers towards the consul, which was virtually an established custom; and as though they made no question that Menenius would be chosen for one of the military tribunes, if he were a candidate, they held a consular election and so excluded him.

LIV. The consuls elected were Gnaeus Cornelius Cossus and (for the second time) Lucius Furius Medullinus. Never before had the plebs felt so aggrieved that they were not allowed to choose military tribunes. They showed their disappointment, and likewise avenged it, at the election of quaestors, when plebeians were for the first time chosen to that office; though among the four to be elected room was made for one patrician, Caeso Fabius Ambustus. Three plebeians, Quintus Silius, Publius Aelius, and Publius Pupius, were preferred before young men of the most distinguished families. I find that those who encouraged the people to make so free with their votes were the Icilii. Three members of that family, a family most hostile to the patricians, had been made plebeian tribunes for that year, in consequence of the many great hopes they had held out to the populace, always more than eager to accept such promises. These men had declared that they would make no move in their behalf, if even in the election of quaestors—the only election which the senate had left open to both classes—the people could not find sufficient resolution to accomplish what they had so long wished to do and the laws permitted. And so the plebs felt that they had won a great victory, not estimating the significance of that quaestorship by the limits of the office itself, but feeling that the way to consulships and triumphs was thrown open to new men. The patricians, on the other hand, were as angry as though they had not merely shared their offices with the plebs but had lost them. They said that if such things were to be, it was wrong for them to rear children, who after being driven out from the places of their forefathers would behold others in possession of their honors, and would be left, without power or authority, to serve no other purpose than to offer up sacrifices, as salii and flamens,[72] for the people. The feelings of both sides were overwrought. The plebs had plucked up courage and they had three very distinguished leaders for the popular cause. The patricians, perceiving that every election where the plebs were free to choose either sort of candidate would be like that of the quaestors, strove to bring about a consular election, which was not yet open to both orders. The Icilii, on the contrary, maintained that military tribunes should be chosen; it was high time, they said, that the plebs were given their share of honors.

LV. But the consuls had no measure on foot which the tribunes could oppose and so wring from them what they wanted, when, by a wonderful piece of luck, the Volsci and Aequi were reported to have crossed the border and raided the lands of the Latins and the Hernici. As the consuls, in order to meet this invasion, were commencing to raise an army, in pursuance of a resolution of the senate, the tribunes obstructed the levy with all their might, declaring that the incident had been a fortunate one for the plebeians and themselves. There were three of them, and they were all very active and belonged to a family which might now be called noble, considering that they were plebeians. Two of them assumed the task of keeping constant watch on the consuls, each taking one of them; to the third was given the duty of haranguing the plebs, for the purpose, now of restraining, now of urging them on. The consuls could neither bring about the levy, nor the tribunes the election, they desired. Then, as fortune was inclining to the cause of the plebs, came couriers who reported that while the soldiers who were in garrison at the citadel of Carventum had dispersed to plunder, the Aequi had come, and killing the few guards, had rushed the place. Some of the soldiers had been cut down as they were hurrying back to the fortress, others as they roamed the fields. This national reverse added strength to the contention of the tribunes. It was in vain they were importuned to cease at last their opposition to the war. They yielded neither to the public need nor to men's hatred of themselves, and carried their point—that the senate should pass a decree for the election of military tribunes. It was, however, expressly provided that no one should be accepted as a candidate who had that year been tribune of the plebs, and that no tribune of the Plebs should be re-elected. It is evident that the senate wished to stigmatize the Icilii, whom they charged with seeking the consulship[73] as a reward for their seditious conduct while tribunes. The levy was then begun and preparation made for war, with the consent of all the orders. Whether both consuls marched to the citadel of Carventum, or one stayed behind to hold an election, is uncertain in view of the contradictory accounts of the authorities. Thus much is clear (for in this they do not differ), that the Romans, after a long and futile siege, retired from the citadel of Carventum and recaptured Verrugo,[74] in the Volscian country, with the same army, which spread great devastation both among the Aequi and in the territory of the Volsci, and gathered enormous spoils.

LVI. At Rome, though the plebeians were so far victorious as to have the election they preferred, yet in the outcome of the election the patricians won the day. For the military tribunes with consular authority were all three, contrary to the universal expectation, chosen from the patricians, viz., Gaius Julius Iulus, Publius Cornelius Cossus, and Gaius Servilius Ahala. The patricians are said to have employed a ruse (and the Icilii taxed them with it at the time), in that they mixed a rabble of unworthy competitors with the deserving, and the disgust which the notorious turpitude of certain of them provoked turned the people against the plebeian candidates.

Then came a rumor that the Volsci and Aequi, whether encouraged by their defense of the citadel of Carventum or angered by the loss of the garrison at Verrugo, had risen in prodigious strength; that the Antiates were the head and front of the war; that their envoys had gone about among the tribes of both races, upbraiding their cowardice in having hidden behind their walls the year before and allowed the Romans to pillage their lands and overwhelm the garrison at Verrugo. They would presently be sending out, not merely armed expeditions across their borders, but colonies too; and not only, they said, had the Romans divided up their possessions amongst themselves, but they had even taken Ferentinum from them and bestowed it on the Hernici. These words aroused indignation, and a number of young men were enlisted wherever the envoys went. So the forces of all the tribes drew together at Antium, where they encamped and waited for the enemy. When these things had been reported at Rome, amid excitement even greater than the situation warranted, the senate at once had recourse to its final counsel in emergencies, and ordered the appointment of a dictator. It is said that Julius and Cornelius resented this, and that a very bitter discussion took place. In vain the leading senators complained that the military tribunes were not amenable to senatorial control, and eventually appealed to the tribunes of the plebs and reminded them that their authority had in a similar case operated to restrain the consuls. But the tribunes of the plebs were delighted with the want of harmony amongst the senators. They could give no assistance, they said, to men who did not regard them as citizens, or even as human beings. If someday offices were thrown open to all, and they were given a share in the government, they would then see to it that no proud magistrate thwarted the decrees of the senate. Meanwhile let the patricians live with no regard for laws and magistracies, and let the tribunes act as they saw fit.

LVII. This quarrel, so inopportune at a time when a great war was in hand, had quite taken possession of men's thoughts, and for a long time Julius and Cornelius—first one and then the other—had argued that, since they were themselves quite capable of directing that campaign, it was unfair that they should be summarily deprived of the office which the people had intrusted to them; when Servilius Ahala arose and said that he had been so long silent not because of any doubt as to his opinion—for what good citizen considered his own interests apart from those of the nation? But because he had wished that his colleagues should of their own free will give in to the senators' authority, instead of suffering the power of the tribunes to be invoked against them. Even then, if the circumstances allowed of it, he would gladly, he said, have given them time to retreat from their too obstinate contention; but since war's necessity did not wait upon man's deliberations, he should place the public welfare above the favor of his colleagues; and if the senate held to its opinion, he should name a dictator that night, contenting himself, if anyone vetoed the senate's resolution, with the expression of its wishes. Having by this course gained the well-merited praise and friendly support of all, he named as dictator Publius Cornelius, by whom he was himself appointed master of the horse, thus showing such persons as considered the case of his colleagues and himself that favor and high office sometimes come more easily when men do not covet them. The war was no way noteworthy. In a single battle, and an easy one, they defeated the enemy at Antium. The victorious army laid waste the Volscian country and took by storm a fortress at Lake Fucinus, where three thousand men were taken prisoners, the rest being driven within their city-walls, leaving their fields defenseless. The dictator, after so conducting the campaign that he seemed barely to have taken advantage of his luck, returned to the City, with more good fortune than renown, and resigned his magistracy. The tribunes of the soldiers, without saying a word about electing consuls, I suppose because of their indignation at the appointment of a dictator, proclaimed an election of military tribunes. At that the patricians were more concerned than ever, as they might well be when they saw their cause betrayed by their own fellows. Accordingly, just as in the preceding year they had used the least worthy of the plebeian competitors to arouse a dislike of them all, even the deserving, so at this time, by setting up as candidates the senators of the greatest splendor and popularity, they secured all the places, in order that no plebeian might be chosen. Four men were elected, all of whom had held that office before. They were Lucius Furius Medullinus, Gaius Valerius Potitus, Numerius Fabius Vibulanus, and Gaius Servilius Ahala. This last was continued in office partly for his other good qualities, partly because of the approval he had just gained by his singular moderation.

LVIII. In that year, since the term of the truce with Veii had run out, steps were taken to demand restitution, through ambassadors and fetials. Arriving at the frontier, these men were met by an embassy of the Veientes, who asked them not to proceed to Veii until they themselves should have gone before the Roman senate. The senate, considering that the Veientes were in the throes of civil discord, agreed not to demand a settlement of them; so far were they from taking advantage of another people's difficulties. And in the Volscian country the Romans suffered a disaster, in the loss of their garrison at Verrugo. On that occasion the element of time was of such moment that, although the troops who were being besieged there by the Volsci appealed for help and might have been relieved if their friends had made haste, yet the army dispatched for that purpose only arrived in season to surprise the enemy as they were dispersed in quest of booty, just after putting the garrison to the sword. The delay was due quite as much to the tribunes as to the senate, for they got reports that the garrison was making a strenuous resistance and failed to consider that no valor can transcend the limits of human endurance. But the heroic soldiers were not unavenged, living or dead.

The following year, when Publius and Gnaeus Cornelius Cossus, Numerius Fabius Ambustus, and Lucius Valerius Potitus were consular tribunes, war broke out with Veii on account of the insolent reply of the Veientine senate, who, when envoys demanded restitution of them, bade them be answered that unless they got quickly out from their city and their borders, they would give them what Lars Tolumnius had given the others.[75] This angered the Fathers, and they decreed that the military tribunes should propose to the people a declaration of war on the Veientes at the earliest possible day. As soon as this was promulgated, the young men protested loudly that the Volscian war was not yet brought to a conclusion; two garrisons had just been destroyed, and the other outposts were being held at great risk; not a year went by without a pitched battle; and as though they had not troubles enough, a new war was being started with a neighboring and very powerful people, who were sure to raise all Etruria against them.

This smouldering discontent was fanned into a blaze by the plebeian tribunes. They persistently declared that it was the plebs with whom the senators were chiefly at war; them they deliberately plagued with campaigning and exposed to be slaughtered by the enemy; them they kept at a distance from the City, and assigned to foreign service, lest they might have thoughts, if they remained peaceably at home, of liberty and colonies, and might agitate for public lands or the free use of their votes. And laying hold of veteran soldiers, they enumerated the campaigns of each and his wounds and scars; asking where one could now find a whole place on their bodies to receive fresh wounds, or what blood they had left to shed for their country. When the tribunes by repeating these arguments in their talk and in their speeches had produced in the plebs a reluctance to undertake the war, the authors of the bill put off the time for voting on it, since it was clear that if subjected to the storm of disapproval it would fail to pass.

LIX. Meantime it was determined that the military tribunes should lead the army into the country of the Volsci; only Gnaeus Cornelius was left in Rome. The three tribunes, on its appearing that the Volsci had no camp anywhere and did not propose to risk a battle, divided their army into three and advanced in different directions to lay waste the country. Valerius marched upon Antium, Cornelius against Ecetrae, and wherever they went they plundered farms and buildings far and wide, to divide the forces of the Volsci; Fabius led his troops to Anxur, the principal object of their attack, and laid siege to it, without doing any pillaging. Anxur, the Tarracinae of our day,[76] was a city which sloped down towards the marshes. On this side Fabius threatened an assault, while four cohorts marched round under Gaius Servilius Ahala, and seizing the hill which overhangs the city, assailed the walls from this superior position, where there was no force to oppose them, with great noise and confusion. Hearing the din, the soldiers who were defending the lowest part of the town against Fabius were bewildered, and permitted him to bring up scaling-ladders; and soon the whole place was alive with enemies, who for a long time gave no quarter, slaughtering without distinction those who fled and those who resisted, the armed and the unarmed. And so the vanquished, since they could hope for no mercy if they yielded, were compelled to fight; when suddenly the command was given that none should be hurt but those who carried weapons. Thereupon, all the survivors voluntarily laid down their arms, and about twenty-five hundred of them were taken alive. Fabius made his soldiers leave the rest of the spoils until his colleagues could come up, saying that their armies had helped to capture Anxur by diverting the rest of the Volsci from the defense of that place. When they arrived, the three armies sacked the town, which long years of prosperity had filled with riches. It was this generous treatment on the part of their commanders which first reconciled the plebs to the patricians. In addition to this the senate then granted the people the most seasonable boon which has ever been bestowed on them by the chiefs of the state, when they decreed, without waiting for any suggestion by the plebs or their tribunes, that the soldiers should be paid from the public treasury, whereas till then every man had served at his own costs.

LX. Nothing, it is said, was ever welcomed by the plebs with such rejoicing. Crowds gathered at the Curia and men grasped the hands of the senators as they came out, saying that they were rightly called Fathers, and confessing that they had brought it to pass that no one, so long as he retained a particle of strength, would grudge his life's blood to so generous a country. Not only were they pleased at the advantage that their property would at least not diminish while their bodies were impressed for the service of the state, but the voluntary character of the offer, which had never been mooted by plebeian tribunes nor extorted by any words of their own, multiplied their satisfaction and increased their gratitude. The tribunes of the plebs were the only persons who did not partake in the general joy and good-feeling of both orders. They said that the measure would neither be so agreeable to the Fathers nor so favorable to the whole body of the citizens as the latter believed; it was a plan which at first sight had promised to be better than experience would prove it. For where, they asked, could the money be got together, save by imposing a tribute on the people? The senators had therefore been generous at other men's expense; and even though everyone else should submit to it, those who had already earned their discharge would not endure that others should serve on better terms than they had themselves enjoyed, and that the same men who had paid their own expenses should also contribute to the expenses of others. By these arguments they influenced a part of the plebs. Finally, when the assessment had already been proclaimed, the tribunes even announced that they would protect anybody who should refuse to contribute to a tax for paying the soldiers. The Fathers had made a good beginning and persevered in supporting it. They were themselves the first to contribute, and since there was as yet no silver coinage,[77] some of them brought uncoined bronze in waggons to the treasury, and even made a display of their contributing. After the senators had paid most faithfully, according to their rating, the chief men of the plebs, friends of the nobles, began, as had been agreed, to bring in their quota. When the crowd saw that these men were applauded by the patricians and were looked upon as good citizens by those of military age, they quickly rejected the protection of the tribunes and vied with one another who should be the first to pay. And on the law being passed declaring war on the Veientes, an army consisting in great part of volunteers marched, under command of the new military tribunes, upon that city.

LXI. Now the tribunes were Titus Quinctius Capitolinus, Quintus Quinctius Cincinnatus, Gaius Julius Iulus (for the second time), Aulus Manlius, Lucius Furius Medullinus (for the third time), and Manius Aemilius Mamercus. By them Veii was for the first time besieged. Shortly after this siege began, the Etruscans held a numerously attended council at the shrine of Voltumna, but could reach no decision as to whether the entire nation should go to war in defense of the Veientes. The siege languished during the year that followed, for some of the tribunes and a part of the army were called away to fight the Volsci.

The military tribunes with consular powers for this year were Gaius Valerius Potitus (for the third time), Manius Sergius Fidenas, Publius Cornelius Maluginensis, Gnaeus Cornelius Cossus, Gaius Fabius Ambustus, and (for the second time) Spurius Nautius Rutulus. A pitched battle was fought with the Volsci between Ferentinum and Ecetra, in which fortune favored the Romans. The tribunes then laid siege to Artena, a Volscian town. While attempting a sortie the enemy were driven back into the city and afforded the Romans an opportunity of forcing an entrance, so that the whole place, except the citadel, was captured; to this fortress, which was naturally strong, a band of armed men retired; below the citadel a large number were killed or taken prisoner. The citadel was then besieged, but could neither be taken by assault, having a sufficient garrison in proportion to its area, nor appeared likely to surrender, for the whole public store of grain had been conveyed into the fortress before the capture of the town. The Romans would have withdrawn, discouraged, had not a slave betrayed the place into their hands. This man admitted some soldiers by way of a steep approach, and they captured it and slew the sentries; whereupon the rest of the garrison was seized with a sudden panic and surrendered. After demolishing the citadel and the town of Artena, the legions were withdrawn from the Volsci and all the might of Rome was brought to bear upon Veii. The traitor was given the property of two families as a reward, besides his liberty, and was named Servius Romanus.[78] There are those who think that Artena had belonged to the Veientes, not to the Volsci. Their mistake is due to the fact that there was a city of the same name between Caere and Veii; but this place was destroyed by the Roman kings,[79] and it had been a dependency of Caere, not of Veii; the other town of the same name, whose overthrow I have just related, was in Volscian territory.

Summary of Book IV

A LAW ABOUT THE MARRIAGE OF PATRICIANS AND PLEBEIANS WAS carried by the tribunes, after a violent struggle, against the opposition of the patricians. The tribunes . . .[1] of the plebs. For some years the affairs of the Roman People at home and in the field were administered through this kind of magistracy. Likewise censors were then elected for the first time. The land taken from the Ardeates by the decision of the people was restored and colonists were sent out to it. When the Roman People was in sore straits on account of a famine, Spurius Maelius, a Roman knight, distributed corn to the people at his own expense. Having by this act gained the favor of the plebs, he aimed at royal power and was killed by Gaius Servilius Ahala, the master of the horse, at the command of the dictator Quintus[2] Cincinnatus; Lucius Minucius gave evidence against him and was presented with a gilded ox. When the envoys of the Romans had been slain by the Fidenates, because they had fallen in the service of the state, statues were erected to them on the rostra. Cornelius Cossus, the military tribune, killed Tolumnius, king of the Veientes, and returned with the second spoils of honor. Mamercus Aemilius, the dictator, limited the office of censor, which was wont to be held for five years, to the period of eighteen months; for this he was stigmatized by the senators. Fidenae was subjugated and colonists were sent thither; the Fidenates, having slain these men and revolted, were defeated by Mamercus Aemilius the dictator, and Fidenae was captured. A conspiracy of the slaves was suppressed. Postumius, the military tribune, was for his cruelty put to death by his army. Pay from the public treasury was then for the first time given the soldiers. It contains also campaigns waged against the Volsci and the Fidenates and the Faliscans.

Book v

I. Peace was now established elsewhere, but Romans and Veientes were at war, and their rage and animosity were such that the end was clearly at hand for those that should be vanquished. Each people held an election very different from that of the other. The Romans enlarged the number of their military tribunes with consular authority, and elected eight,[1] a greater number than ever before, to wit, Manius Aemilius Mamercus (for the second time), Lucius Valerius Potitus (for the third), Appius Claudius Crassus, Marcus Quinctilius Varus, Lucius Julius Iulus, Marcus Postumius, Marcus Furius Camillus, Marcus Postumius Albinus. But the Veientes, weary of annual canvassing, which was sometimes the cause of brawls, chose a king. This gave offense to the feelings of the Etruscan peoples, who loathed not more the institution of kings than the King himself. He had for sometime been hateful to the nation by reason of his wealth and arrogance, since he had violently broken up a solemn festival, which it is impious to interrupt, in his resentment of a political rebuff; and because the suffrages of the Twelve Peoples had returned another man as priest in preference to him, he had suddenly carried off the actors, most of whom were his own slaves, in the middle of the games. And so the nation which was devoted beyond all others to religious rites (and all the more because it excelled in the art of observing them) voted to refuse its help to the men of Veii, so long as they should obey a king. This vote the Veientes would not suffer to be mentioned, in their fear of the King, who had a way of treating the man by whom any such saying was reported as a leader in sedition, not as the bearer of an idle tale. Although the Romans got word that things were quiet in Etruria, still, because they heard that this question came up at all their meetings, they so constructed their works as to have a double fortification, one facing Veii, to oppose the sallies of the townsfolk, the other confronting Etruria, to shut off any assistance that might come from thence.

II. As the Roman generals hoped more from a siege than from an assault, they even began the erection of winter quarters—a new thing to the Roman soldier—and planned to carry the campaign on, straight through the winter. When news of this came to Rome, to the plebeian tribunes, who had now for a long time been unable to hit upon any pretext for agitation, they hurried before the assembly and set to work upon the passions of the commons: So this was the reason that the soldiers had been granted pay! They had not been mistaken in thinking that this gift of their opponents would be smeared with poison. The liberty of the commons had been sold; the young men, having been permanently removed and banished from the City and from the state, were no longer free, even in winter and the stormy season, to see to their homes and their affairs. What, they asked, did their hearers suppose to be the reason for making the service continuous? They would assuredly find no other motive than this: lest, through the presence in large numbers of the young men in whom lay all the vigor of the commons, something might be accomplished for the people's good. Moreover, they were far more ruthlessly abused and trodden down than were the Veientes, who, for their part, spent the winter in their houses, safeguarding their city by means of strong walls and natural defenses, whilst the Roman soldiers were enduring toil and danger, overwhelmed with snows and frosts, in tents, not even laying aside their weapons in the winter time, a season of respite from all wars both by land and by sea. Such slavery as this neither kings, nor the proud consuls who came before the establishment of the tribunician power, nor the stern authority of a dictator, nor harsh decemvirs, had laid upon them, that they should wage perennial war. Pray what would those men do if they should become consuls or dictators, who had made the semblance of consular authority so savage and truculent? But the commons were only getting their deserts. There had been no room even amongst eight military tribunes for a single plebeian. Heretofore the patricians had been wont with the utmost exertion to fill three places in a year: now they were advancing eight abreast to make good their authority, and there was never a commoner hanging on to the crowd, were it only to remind his colleagues that their soldiers were not slaves but freemen and fellow citizens; whom, at least in winter, they were bound to bring back to the shelter of their houses, and to leave them some portion of the year to look after their parents, their children, and their wives, and to use their liberty and elect magistrates.

As they shouted forth these and suchlike arguments, they found an opponent not unequal to them in Appius Claudius, whom his colleagues had left behind to repress sedition on the part of the tribunes. He was a man experienced from his youth up in contentions with the plebs, and I have related how, some years before, he had advised that the intervention of their colleagues be used to break the power of the tribunes.[2]

III. The man not only had a nimble wit but was already a practiced orator, and he delivered on this occasion a speech to the following effect: "If it has ever been a question, Quirites, whether it was for your sake or their own that the tribunes of the commons have always encouraged sedition, I am certain that the doubt has this year been resolved; and not only do I rejoice that you have at length cleared up a long misunderstanding, but I congratulate both you, and on your account the state as well, that it has happened at a time, of all others, when your affairs are prospering. Or is there anyone who doubts that no wrongs which you have suffered, if haply such there have sometimes been, have ever so offended and stirred up the plebeian tribunes as has the boon which the Fathers bestowed upon the commons, when they granted pay for military service? What else do you believe they were afraid of then, or are seeking now to shatter, but the harmony of the orders, which they regard as very apt to overthrow the tribunician authority? Indeed they are like quack-salvers seeking employment, since they desire that there should always be some disease in the body politic, that there may be something which you may call them in to cure. Pray, are you tribunes defending the commons, or attacking them? Are you adversaries of the soldiers, or their advocates? Or perhaps this is your plea: 'Whatever the Fathers do displeases us, be it in behalf of the commons or against them'; and just as masters forbid outsiders to have aught to do with their slaves, and think it right that they should abstain alike from benefiting and from harming them, so you deny the Fathers intercourse with the commons, lest we by our friendliness and liberality encourage them, or they become dutiful and obedient to us. How much more, if you had in you the slightest—I say not patriotism, but—humanity, ought you rather to have favored, and, so far as in you lay, to have encouraged the kindly spirit of the Fathers and the complaisance of the plebs? And if this harmony should last, who would not make bold to warrant that our empire would soon be the greatest among the neighboring peoples?

IV. I shall presently explain, in regard to this plan of my colleagues, who have not been willing to withdraw the army from Veii with its task unaccomplished, how not merely profitable but even necessary it was. But first I wish to speak about the actual condition of the soldiers; and I think that if I should express my meaning not in your presence only but also in the camp, the army itself would judge it reasonable. Indeed, though I were unable to think of anything to urge myself, I could be quite content with the speeches of my opponents. They were lately insisting that pay ought not to be given to the men, because it never had been given. How then can they object, if to those who have gained some new advantage be allotted new labor also, in proportion. Nowhere, as a rule, is service given without recompense, nor recompense except for service; toil and pleasure, most unlike in nature, have been linked together in a sort of natural bond. Formerly the soldier was vexed that he must serve the state at his own cost; yet he was happy to be able, for a half of the year, to till his own field and gain the means of keeping himself and his family, whether he were at home or with the army. Now he is happy that the state affords him gain, and is glad to receive his pay. Let him therefore be resigned to remaining away a little longer from his home and his property, which is now under no heavy charges. Why, if the commonwealth should call him to a reckoning, would it not justly say, "You have a year's stipend, render a year's service; do you think it right that for a campaign of six months you should receive the pay of twelve?" I dislike to dwell upon this point, Quirites; for it is thus that men who employ mercenaries ought to argue; we would deal as though with fellow citizens, and we think it only right that you deal with us as with your native country. Either we ought not to have undertaken the war, or we ought to conduct it as befits the Roman People, and end it as quickly as possible. And we shall end it, if we press our beleaguered foes, and quit them not till we have fulfilled our hopes and captured Veii. Truly, if there were no other reason, the very indignity of the thing should compel us to persist! Did all Greece once, for one woman's sake, war ten years against a city so far from home, with all those lands and seas between? And does it irk us, being less than twenty miles away and almost within sight of Rome, to maintain a siege for a single year? Doubtless our reason for fighting is a trivial one, and we have no proper and sufficient grievance to incite us to persevere! Seven times have they renewed the war; never have they kept faith in peace; our fields they have pillaged a thousand times; they forced the Fidenates to forsake us; our settlers there they put to death; it was they who instigated, in violation of the law of nations, the impious murder of our envoys; they sought to raise up all Etruria against us, and they are striving to this end today; when our ambassadors sought redress they well-nigh did them bodily injury.

V. With such enemies ought we to wage a faint-hearted and dilatory war? If so just grounds of resentment have no power to move us, pray have the following considerations none? The city is hemmed in with vast siege-works, which confine the enemy within his walls; he has not cultivated his land, and what was cultivated has been laid waste in the war; if we bring our army back, who can doubt that not only a desire for revenge, but also necessity, constraining them to plunder others since they have lost their own possessions, will cause them to invade our territory? So we are not postponing the war, if we act on your advice, but are receiving it within our own borders. And what of that matter which specially concerns the soldiers, whom the worthy plebeian tribunes formerly wished to rob of their pay, but are now desirous of protecting? How does it stand with them? The rampart and the trench, each involving prodigious toil, they have carried all that distance; forts they erected only a few at first, but since then, with the growth of the army, they have built very many; they have thrown up earthworks, not only against the city, but also facing Etruria, if any aid should come from that side; what need to speak of towers, mantlets, penthouses, and the rest of the equipment for storming towns? When they have expended all this labor, and the end of their task is at last in sight, do you vote for abandoning these things, that when summer comes they may sweat and toil again to produce them afresh? How much less effort it requires to guard what is already made, and to press on and persevere and put an end to our anxiety! For surely it is a thing soon done, if we carry it through without stopping, and do not ourselves drag out our hopes with these interruptions and delays. I talk of the loss of time and labor; what of the danger that we run by putting off the war? Do the frequent debates in Etruria about the dispatch of succors to Veii allow us to forget it? Just now they are angry and resentful, and declare that they will send none; for all they care, we may capture Veii. But who is to guarantee that if we postpone the campaign they will hereafter feel the same: since if you slacken, a greater and more numerous embassy will set out, and since what now offends the Etruscans—the setting up of a king at Veii—may be altered with the lapse of time or by agreement of the citizens, to the end that thereby they may regain the goodwill of Etruria; or with the consent of the King himself, who would not wish his sovereignty to hurt the safety of his people? See how many undesirable consequences attend that line of policy: the loss of works constructed with such effort; the imminent devastation of our fields; the Etruscans, instead of the Veientes only, aroused to war with us. It is thus, tribunes, that you would manage matters, much as though in dealing with a sick man, who if he would undergo a strict regimen might begin at once to recover, you should protract his illness and perhaps render it incurable, by indulging his immediate desire for meat and drink.

VI. If it were of no moment to this war, it was yet, I assure you, of the utmost importance for military discipline that our soldiers become accustomed not only to pluck a victory within their grasp, but if a campaign should be even more protracted, to put up with the tedium and await the outcome of their hopes, however long-deferred; and if a war be not finished in a summer, to stay for winter, nor, like birds of passage, cast about at once, on the approach of autumn, for shelter and covert. Do the eagerness, pray, and delight that men have in hunting carry them through snow and frost into the mountains and the forests; and shall not we use in the stress of war the same resolution which even sport and pleasure are wont to call out? Do we think the bodies of our soldiers so effeminate, their hearts so faint, that they cannot endure to be one winter in camp, away from home; that like sailors they must wage war with an eye on the weather, observing the seasons, incapable of withstanding heat or cold? They would certainly blush if anyone should charge them with this, and would maintain that manly endurance was in their souls and bodies, and that they could campaign as well in winter as in summer; that they had given the tribunes no commission to protect softness and idleness; and that they were mindful that their grandsires had not founded the tribunician power in the shade or under roofs.

It is due to the valor of your soldiers, it is due to the Roman name, that you should look not merely to Veii and this present war that is upon us, but should seek for the years to come a reputation that will serve you in other wars and amongst all other nations. Do you suppose there will be no great difference in men's opinion of us, whether our neighbors conclude the Roman People to be such, that if a city withstand the brunt of their first assault for a very brief time, it need thenceforward have no fears; or whether our name inspire such dread, that men believe that once a Roman army has sat down before a town, it will never budge, either from the weariness of a protracted siege or from the rigors of winter, that it knows no other end of war but victory, and relies in its campaigns not more on swiftness than on perseverance? For perseverance, needful in every kind of warfare, is especially so in besieging cities, since fortifications and natural advantages make most of them impregnable, and time itself subdues them, with hunger and thirst, and captures them, as it shall capture Veii, unless the plebeian tribunes help our enemies, and the Veientes find in Rome those succors which they are seeking to no purpose in Etruria.

Could anything happen which would so please the Veientes as that factions should spring up, first in the City of Rome, and then, as though by contagion, in the camp? But our enemies, by Heaven, are so well disciplined that no weariness of the blockade nor even of kingly rule has occasioned the smallest revolt among them; neither has the Etruscans' denial of help provoked their spirit; for whosoever prompts sedition shall forthwith die the death; nor shall any man there have license to say what is said with impunity to you. Death by cudgelling is the wage of him who forsakes the standards or quits his post; but those who advise the men to abandon their standards and desert the camp gain a hearing, not with one or two soldiers, but with whole armies, openly, in public meetings; so accustomed are you to hear with complacency whatever a tribune says, even if it tends to betray the City and to undo the state; and captivated by the charm of that authority, you suffer any wickedness whatsoever to lurk beneath it. It only remains for them to utter in camp and in the presence of the soldiers the view which they noisily publish here, and to corrupt the armies and not to suffer them to obey their leaders. For in the upshot liberty has come to mean at Rome, that a man respect neither senate nor magistrates, nor laws, nor ancestral customs, nor institutions of the fathers, nor military discipline.

VII. Appius was already holding his own with the tribunes of the plebs, even in public meetings,[3] when a sudden disaster, from a source which could least have been anticipated, befell the army before Veii, giving Appius the advantage in the argument, while it increased the mutual goodwill of the orders and their ardor for a more vigorous prosecution of the siege. For when they had pushed forward the terrace towards the town, and had all but brought the mantlets into contact with the walls, more intent upon erecting their works by day than on guarding them by night, the gate was suddenly flung open, and a vast horde, most of them armed with torches, hurled fire on the works, and in an hour's time terrace and mantlets, that had taken so long to make, were consumed in the flames; and many men perished by the sword or the fire, in vain efforts to save them. When the news of this came to Rome, it filled the City with sadness, the senate with anxiety and apprehension, lest they might now indeed be unable to check the disaffection, either in the City or the camp, and the tribunes might crow over the commonwealth as though they had overthrown it; when lo! Those who were of equestrian rating, but had not received horses from the state, having first taken counsel together, came to the senate, and being granted a hearing, volunteered to serve on their own horses. These men had no sooner received a vote of thanks from the senate, in the most honorable terms, and the report of it had spread to the Forum and the City, than the plebeians suddenly ran together to the Curia, and declared that it was now the turn of the foot-soldiers to proffer extraordinary service to the state, whether it would have them march to Veii, or anywhere else; if they should be led to Veii, they promised that they would not quit their ground until they had taken the enemy's city. Then indeed the senate could scarce control its already overflowing joy; for they did not, as with the knights, issue an order to the magistrates to thank them, nor did they call them into the Curia to receive an answer, neither did the senate keep within the House; but each for himself cried out from above,[4] to the multitude standing in the Comitium, and by speech and gesture signified the general joy. Rome was blest, they said, and invincible and eternal, by reason of this noble harmony; they praised the knights, they praised the plebeians, they extolled the very day itself, and confessed that the courtesy and goodwill of the senate had been surpassed. Fathers and commoners mingled their tears of joy, till the Fathers were recalled into the senate-house, and decreed that the military tribunes should hold an assembly and thank the infantry and the knights, and say to them that the senate would remember their loyalty to their country, and that it was voted that all who had volunteered to serve out of their due order should receive pay. The knights, too, were granted a definite money allowance. Then for the first time cavalry-men began to serve on their own horses. The volunteer army, having marched to Veii, not only replaced the works that had been lost, but added new ones. The city dispatched provisions with more than its former zeal, that nothing might be lacking to an army that had deserved so well.

VIII. The ensuing year had for consular tribunes Gaius Servilius Ahala (for the third time), Quintus Servilius, Lucius Verginius, Quintus Sulpicius, Aulus Manlius (for the second time), and Manius Sergius (for the second time). In their term of office, while everyone was intent on the war with Veii, the garrison at Anxur was neglected; soldiers were given furlough, Volscian traders were admitted without discrimination, and, the sentinels at the gates being suddenly over-powered, the town was taken. Not many soldiers perished, because they were all, except the sick, occupied, like sutlers, with trafficking in the country-side and the towns near by. Nor were things any better at Veii, which was at that time the nation's chief concern; for the Roman commanders showed more jealousy of one another than spirit in dealing with the enemy, whose forces moreover were enlarged by the unexpected accession of the Capenates and the Faliscans. These two Etruscan peoples, being nearest in situation, believed that if the Veientes were conquered it would be their turn next to face a Roman invasion. The Faliscans, besides, had incurred hostility on their own account, because they had been mixed up before in the war with Fidenae.[5] So they exchanged embassies, bound themselves by an oath, and their armies suddenly appeared before Veii. It happened that they attacked the camp at that point where the tribune Manius Sergius was in command, and great was the terror they inspired, since the Romans thought that all Etruria had risen and was come with a mighty array against them. The same belief roused up the Veientes in the town. Thus a two-fold attack was directed against the camp. The soldiers rallied into groups, facing now this way and now that, yet were unable either quite to confine the Veientes within the siege-lines, or to ward off the attack upon their own defenses and protect themselves from the enemy outside. Their only hope was if help should come from the larger camp, so that the legions might face different ways, some of them confronting the Capenates and Faliscans, and others the sortie of the townsfolk. But that camp was under the command of Verginius, who was privately hated by Sergius and returned his enmity. This man, though word was brought that many bastions had been stormed and the ramparts scaled, and that the enemy were attacking on both sides, held his troops under arms, saying that if his colleague needed help he would let him know. His pride found a match in the other's obstinacy, and Sergius, lest he should seem to have required any aid of his rival, preferred defeat at the hands of the enemy to victory gained through a fellow citizen. For a long time the Romans were slaughtered between the two attacking armies; finally they abandoned their works, and a very few escaped into the larger camp, while Sergius himself, with the chief part of his men, kept on to Rome. It was there decided, on his throwing all the blame upon his colleague, to summon Verginius from camp, and in the meanwhile put lieutenants in command of it. The affair was then debated in the senate and the colleagues heaped abuse on one another. There were but few who spoke for the commonwealth: most of them argued for one or the other disputant, according as each was swayed by private interest or favor.

IX. The leading senators held, that whether the fault or the misfortune of the commanders were the cause of this shameful disaster, they ought not to await the regular time for elections, but proceed at once to choose new military tribunes, to begin their magistracy on the first of October. While the members were voting for this proposal, the other military tribunes raised no objection; but of all people Sergius and Verginius, the very men on account of whom it was evident that the senate was disgusted with the magistrates of that year, first begged to be spared the humiliation, then vetoed the senate's decree,[6] declaring that they would not resign their authority before the thirteenth of December, the accustomed day for entering upon office. Whereupon the tribunes of the plebs, who so long as harmony prevailed and the affairs of the City prospered, had reluctantly held their tongues, suddenly broke out and threatened the tribunes of the soldiers, that unless they submitted to the senate they would send them to prison. Then Gaius Servilius Ahala, a military tribune, said: "So far as concerns you, tribunes of the commons, and your menaces, I should indeed willingly put it to the proof how you have in your threats as little legality as courage; but it is impious to oppose the authority of the senate. Accordingly do you give over seeking in our quarrels occasion for working mischief, and my colleagues shall either do as the senate decrees, or if they persist in stubborn opposition, I will forthwith name a dictator, to compel them to lay down their authority." This speech was universally approved, and the Fathers rejoiced that they needed not the trumpery threats of the tribunician power, but had found another and a greater force to coerce the magistrates; and the latter, overborne by the unanimity of feeling, held an election of military tribunes, to begin service on October the first, and before that date resigned their office.

X. The consular tribuneship of Lucius Valerius Potitus (for the fourth term), Marcus Furius Camillus (for the second[7]), Manius Aemilius Mamercus (for the third), Gnaeus Cornelius Cossus (for the second), Caeso Fabius Ambustus, and Lucius Julius Iulus,[8] was a time of great activity both at home and in the field. For they made war at many points simultaneously, before Veii, at Capena, at Falerii, and in the Volscian country—to recover Anxur from the enemy; and in Rome both the levy and the payment of the war-tax occasioned difficulties, a quarrel sprang up over the co-optation of plebeian tribunes, and the trials of the two who had lately exercised consular powers aroused no small commotion. The first concern of the military tribunes was to levy troops, and they not only enrolled the younger men, but also compelled the seniors to enlist for service in guarding the City. But the more they increased the number of the soldiers, the more money they required for pay. This they tried to collect by taxation; but those who remained at home contributed with reluctance, because they had also in defense of the City to perform the labor of soldiers and serve the commonwealth. To make this obligation, heavy in itself, seem yet more grievous, the tribunes of the plebs delivered seditious speeches, in which they alleged that the senators had established pay for the troops for this reason, that they might ruin one half of the plebs with fighting and the other half with taxation. They were now drawing out a single war into its third year, and were purposely misconducting it, that they might conduct it the longer. Again, with one levy they had enrolled armies for four wars, and had haled away even boys and old men. Now they were confounding winter with summer, to allow no rest ever to the unhappy commons, on whom finally they had even imposed a tax; that when they should drag home their bodies spent with toil, with wounds, and at last with old age, and should then find all things gone to waste in the long absence of the owners, they might pay tribute out of their diminished property, and return to the state many times, as it were with usury, the wages they had received as soldiers.

What with the levy and the tax and the weightier cares that preoccupied men's minds, they were unable on the day of election to return the full number of plebeian tribunes. An effort was then made to obtain the co-optation of patricians for the vacant places. When this failed, nevertheless, in order to invalidate the law, it was brought about that Gaius Lacerius and Marcus Acutius should be chosen tribunes, without doubt through patrician influence.[9]

XI. It so happened that in that year one of the tribunes was Gnaeus Trebonius, whose name and family seemed to make it his duty to defend the Trebonian law. This man said that what the Fathers had formerly aimed at (and had been foiled on their first attempting), the tribunes of the soldiers had finally extorted; he asseverated that the Trebonian law had been done away with, and that the tribunes of the plebs had been appointed not by the votes of the people but at the dictation of the nobles; that things had come to such a pass, that they must perforce have either patricians or the satellites of patricians for tribunes of the plebs; their sacred laws were being taken away, the tribunician power wrested from them. This was done, he declared, by the knavery of the patricians, the rascality and the treason of his colleagues.

Men were burning with resentment, not only against the patricians, but also against the tribunes of the plebs, both those who had been co-opted and those who had co-opted them, when three of the college, Publius Curatius, Marcus Metilius, and Marcus Minucius, being alarmed at their own situation,[10] fell violently upon Sergius and Verginius, the military tribunes of the previous year, and by appointing them a day for trial turned against them the anger and displeasure which the plebs had evinced towards themselves. They reminded their hearers, that those who were aggrieved by the levy, or the tax, or the protracted service and the long duration of the war, those who sorrowed for the calamity that befell at Veii, those whose houses were in mourning for the loss of sons, brothers, kinsmen or connections, that all those now had the right and the power, thanks to the speakers, of avenging the nation's grief and their own private sorrow on the two culprits; for of all their sufferings Sergius and Verginius were the cause; and this their accusers were not more forward to maintain than the defendants to confess, who, equally guilty, threw the blame on one another, Verginius taxing Sergius with his flight, while Sergius complained of Verginius's treachery. Their madness had been so incredible, that it was much more probable that they had done the thing upon agreement, with the collusion of the senators; who having before given opportunity to the Veientes to set fire to their works, in order to prolong the war, had now betrayed the army and delivered up a Roman camp to the Faliscans. They were doing everything to wear out the young men before Veii, and prevent the tribunes from bringing before the people the question of land and other advantages to the plebs, and from pushing their measures in well-attended assemblies and thwarting the conspiracy of the patricians. Judgment was already given against the accused both by the senate and by the Roman People, and also by their own college; for the senate had by its decree removed them from authority, and when they refused to abdicate their office, their colleagues had coerced them by threatening to appoint a dictator, and the Roman People had elected tribunes to assume their duties, not on the thirteenth of December, the usual date, but immediately, on October the first, believing that the state could endure no longer if the incumbents should remain in place; yet, in spite of all, these men, stigmatized and fore-judged by so many adverse verdicts, presented themselves for trial by the people, and fancied that they were quit and sufficiently mulcted because they were made private citizens two months before their time; not perceiving that they had then merely been deprived of the power to do further mischief, not punished, since their colleagues, too, were turned out of office, though they had certainly done no wrong. Let the Quirites call back the spirit they had shown when the recent calamity had occurred, when they had beheld the flight and confusion of their troops, as they stumbled, wounded and dismayed, through the City gates, accusing neither fortune nor any of the gods, but these their leaders. They were sure that there was not a man present in the assembly who had not on that day cursed and execrated the lives, the houses, and the fortunes of Lucius Verginius and Manius Sergius. It was not reasonable that their hearers, having a legal and moral right in the matter, should not use their power against those upon whom each one of them had invoked the wrath of Heaven. The gods themselves never laid hands upon the guilty; it was enough if they armed with an opportunity for vengeance those who had been wronged.

XII. Incited by these speeches, the plebs condemned the accused to pay each a fine of 10,000 pounds of bronze. It was in vain that Sergius blamed Fortune and the common chance of war, while Verginius begged that he might not be more unlucky at home than he had been in the campaign. On them the wrath of the people was poured out, and the co-optation of the tribunes and the evasion of the Trebonian law were almost forgotten.

The victorious tribunes, that the plebs might have an immediate reward for its judgment, proposed a land-law and forbade the gathering of the war-tax, notwithstanding that pay was needed for so many armies, whose campaigning, though successful, yet failed to realize the desired end in any war. Thus, at Veii, they recovered the lost camp and strengthened it with fortresses and garrisons, led by the military tribunes Manius Aemilius and Caeso Fabius; Marcus Furius in the Faliscan country, and Gnaeus Cornelius in the territory of Capena, meeting no enemies afield, drove off booty, and burning farmhouses and crops, laid waste the land, but the towns they neither assaulted nor besieged; in the Volscian country, however, after ravaging the fields, they made a futile attack on Anxur, which was seated on an eminence, and finding force to be unavailing, began to invest it with a stockade and trench, under Valerius Potitus, who had got the command against the Volsci.

While military affairs were in this posture, a quarrel that broke out at home aroused more energy than went to their making of wars; and since the tax could not be taken up, on account of the tribunes, and the generals were sent no money, while the soldiers were clamoring for their pay, the camp, too, was like to have been disrupted by the contagion of mutiny in the City. In the midst of this hostility which the plebs felt towards the patricians, though the plebeian tribunes said that the time was now come to establish liberty, and to transfer the highest office from such as Sergius and Verginius to stout and courageous commoners, yet they got no further than the election of one plebeian (by way of asserting their right), namely, Publius Licinius Calvus, to be military tribune with consular powers; the others chosen were patricians: Publius Manlius, Lucius Titinius, Publius Maelius, Lucius Furius Medullinus, Lucius Publilius Volscus. The plebeians themselves were amazed that they had gained so important a point, and not alone the man who had been chosen, one that had held no offices before but was only a senator of long standing, now well on in years. There is no unanimity of opinion why he was selected as the first and fittest to taste of the new honors. Some think it was the favor of his cousin[11] Gnaeus Cornelius, who as tribune of the soldiers the year before had granted triple pay to the cavalrymen,[12] that got him his promotion to so great an office; others, that he himself made a timely speech on the harmony of the orders, which pleased both patricians and plebeians. Overjoyed at their victory in this election, the tribunes of the plebs withdrew that opposition to the tax which was the greatest obstacle to the business of the state, and it was obediently paid in and dispatched to the army.

XIII. Anxur of the Volsci was speedily recaptured, a holiday having relaxed the vigilance of their guard. This year was remarkable for so cold and snowy a winter, that the roads were blocked and the Tiber became unnavigable. The price of corn, owing to the supply which they had brought in before, did not go up. Publius Licinius had obtained his magistracy without any disorders, rejoicing the commons more than he offended the patricians, and in the same spirit he conducted it; the people therefore became desirous of returning plebeians at the next election of consular tribunes. Marcus Veturius was the sole patrician candidate to get in; all the other military tribunes with consular authority were commoners, as the result of an all but unanimous vote of the centuries. Their names were Marcus Pomponius, Gnaeus Duillius, Volero Publilius, Gnaeus Genucius, Lucius Atilius.

The severe winter was succeeded, whether in consequence of the sudden change from such inclement weather to the opposite extreme, or for some other reason, by a summer that was noxious and baleful to all living creatures. Unable to discover what caused the incurable ravages of this distemper, or would put an end to them, the senate voted to consult the Sibylline Books. The duumvirs in charge of the sacred rites then celebrated the first lectisternium[13] ever held in Rome, and for the space of eight days sacrificed to Apollo, to Latona and Diana, to Hercules, to Mercury and to Neptune, spreading three couches for them with all the splendor then attainable. They also observed the rite in their homes. All through the City, they say, doors stood wide open, all kinds of viands were set out for general consumption, all comers were welcomed, whether known or not, and men even exchanged kind and courteous words with personal enemies; there was a truce to quarrelling and litigation; even prisoners were loosed from their chains for those days, and they scrupled thenceforth to imprison men whom the gods had thus befriended.

Meantime alarms were multiplied at Veii, where three wars were rolled into one. For, precisely as before, the Capenates and the Faliscans came suddenly to raise the siege, and the Romans fought about their works against three armies, which attacked them on both sides. What helped them most, was the recollection how Sergius and Verginius had been condemned. And so from the principal camp, where the delay had occurred on the former occasion, troops were dispatched by a short circuit and fell upon the Capenates in the rear, as they faced the rampart of the Romans. Beginning there, the battle carried terror even among the Faliscans, who were wavering, when a timely sally from the camp put them to flight. Then, as they retreated, the victors pursued them with great slaughter; and not long after a party that was raiding the territory of the Capenates happened to fall in with them and destroyed such as had survived the battle. Of the Veientes likewise, many, as they fled back to the town, were slain before the gates, when their friends, fearing lest the Romans should burst in along with them, had closed the portals, and barred out the hindmost of their own people.

XIV. Such were the events of this year. And now the time drew near for choosing military tribunes and the Fathers were almost more concerned about the election than about the war, perceiving that the highest authority had been not merely shared with the plebs, but well-nigh lost to themselves. They therefore arranged that their most distinguished members should stand, men whom they believed the electors would be ashamed to pass over, and at the same time they themselves, as if they had all been candidates, left no stone unturned, and called to their aid not only men, but the gods as well, by raising a religious scruple anent the election held two years before. In the year before the last, they said, there had been an intolerable winter, like a warning from Heaven. Last year had come not prodigies but actual realities: a pestilence had descended upon the fields and the City, clearly proceeding from the anger of the gods, whom they must propitiate in order to avert the plague, as the fateful Books had indicated; it had seemed to the gods an affront that an election held under their auspices should prostitute honors and confound family distinctions. The people were awed not only by the dignity of the candidates, but by the fear of Heaven, and to be military tribunes with consular powers chose all patricians, and chiefly the most illustrious among them, as follows: Lucius Valerius Potitus (for the fifth time), Marcus Valerius Maximus, Marcus Furius Camillus (for the second time), Lucius Furius Medullinus (for the third), Q. Servilius Fidenas (for the second), Quintus Sulpicius Camerinus (for the second). These tribunes achieved absolutely nothing noteworthy at Veii, but employed all their strength in pillaging. The two chief commanders, Potitus and Camillus, one at Falerii, the other at Capena, carried off huge spoils and left nothing untouched that iron or fire could destroy.

XV. Meanwhile many portents were reported, most of which, because they had only one witness each to vouch for them, obtained no credence and were slighted; and, besides, when the Etruscans, whose services they employed to avert evil omens, were at war with them, they had no soothsayers. One thing occasioned universal anxiety, namely that the lake in the Alban Wood, without any rains or other cause to make it less than a miracle, rose to an unwonted height. To inquire what the gods could possibly foretell by that prodigy, envoys were sent to the Delphic oracle. But a nearer interpreter of the fates presented himself, an old man of Veii, who, while the Roman and Etruscan soldiers were scoffing at one another as they stood guard at the outposts, declared in a prophetic strain that until the water should be drawn off from the Alban Lake the Romans never could take Veii. At first they made light of this as an idle taunt; then they began to talk it over; presently one of the Roman outpost inquired of the townsman nearest him (for owing to the long continuance of the war they had now got into the way of conversing together) who that man was who threw out mysterious hints regarding the Alban Lake. When he heard that, he was a soothsayer, being himself not without a touch of superstition, he alleged a desire to consult him about the averting of a domestic portent, if he could spare the time, and so enticed the seer to a conference. And when they had walked a little way apart from the friends of both, unarmed and fearing nothing, the stalwart young Roman laid hold of the feeble old man in the sight of them all, and despite an unavailing hubbub raised by the Etruscans, bore him off to his own fellows. There they had him before the general, who sent him on to Rome, to the senate. When the Fathers questioned him what it was he had meant about the Alban Lake, he answered that the gods must surely have been incensed at the people of Veii on the day when they put it into his mind to reveal the destruction destined to befall his native city; and so what he had then uttered under divine inspiration, he could not now unsay and recall; and perhaps in concealing what the immortal gods wished to be published guilt was incurred no less than by disclosing what should be hid. Thus then it was written in the books of fate, thus handed down in the lore of the Etruscans, that when the Alban water should overflow, if then the Romans should duly draw it off, they would be given the victory over the Veientes; until that should come to pass, the gods would not abandon the walls of Veii. He then went on to explain the appointed method of draining it. But the senators, making slight account of his authority, as not sufficiently trustworthy in so grave a matter, determined to wait for their deputies with the response of the Pythian oracle.[14]

XVI. But before these envoys could return from Delphi or an expiation be devised for the Alban portent, new military tribunes with consular authority came in; these were Lucius Julius Iulus,[15] Lucius Furius Medullinus (for the fourth time), Lucius Sergius Fidenas, Aulus Postumius Regillensis, Publius Cornelius Maluginensis, and Aulus Manlius.[16] In that year a new enemy arose in the Tarquinienses, who seeing the Romans beset with many wars at once, against the Volsci, who were laying siege to the garrison at Anxur, against the Aequi, who were attacking the Roman colony at Labici, and also against the men of Veii, of Falerii, and of Capena, and perceiving that affairs within the City were no less troubled, owing to contentions betwixt the patricians and the plebs, believed that in these circumstances they had an opportunity to do the Romans a hurt, and sent out light-armed detachments to raid their territory; for they thought that either the Romans would put up with the wrong, to avoid the burden of another war, or would take the field with a small and therefore inadequate army. The indignation of the Romans was greater than their concern for the damage wrought by the Tarquinienses; so they neither made strenuous efforts to prepare, nor deferred taking action to a distant date. Aulus Postumius and Lucius Iulus, without holding a regular levy—for this the plebeian tribunes hindered—but with a company consisting almost solely of volunteers whom they had induced to join by their exhortations, marched out by cross-country ways through the territory of Caere, and surprised the Tarquinienses as they were returning from their depradations laden with booty. Many men they slew, all they stripped of their baggage; and having recovered the spoils of their own fields, returned to Rome. Two days were allowed the owners to identify their property; on the third all that had not been recognized—chiefly things belonging to the enemy themselves—was sold under the spear[17] and the proceeds divided amongst the soldiers.

The other campaigns, especially the one at Veii, were indecisive. And now the Romans, despairing of human aid, were looking to destiny and the gods, when the deputies returned from Delphi, bringing the oracle's response, which corresponded with the utterance of the captive seer: "Roman, see that thou suffer not the Alban water to be confined within the lake, nor to fret its own channel to the sea; thou shalt draw it forth and water the fields withal, and spread it abroad till it be lost in rivulets; after that press boldly on against the walls of the foe, and know that over that city which thou dost beleaguer for so many years, the fates now disclosed have given thee the victory. When thou hast ended the war with conquest, bring to my temple an ample gift, and repeat and accomplish in customary wise the ancestral rites thou hast neglected."

XVII. The captive soothsayer began from that moment to be held in great repute, and the military tribunes, Cornelius and Postumius, set out to employ him about the expiation of the Alban prodigy and the due appeasement of the gods. At length it was discovered wherein the gods taxed them with neglecting ceremonies or omitting a festival: it was assuredly nothing else than that magistrates in whose election there had been a flaw had improperly proclaimed the Latin games and the sacrifice on the Alban Mount[18]; only one atonement for these errors was open to them, to make the tribunes of the soldiers resign their office, to take the auspices afresh, and to begin an interregnum. By decree of the senate these things were done. There were three successive interreges, Lucius Valerius, Quintus Servilius Fidenas, Marcus Furius Camillus. In the meantime there were continuous disturbances, and the plebeian tribunes blocked the election, until it had first been agreed that the majority of the military tribunes should be chosen out of the commons.

While this was going on, the Etruscans met in council at the Fane of Voltumna; where the Capenates and Faliscans proposed that all the nations of Etruria should unite in a common resolution and design to raise the siege of Veii. The council made answer that they had before refused the Veientes this request, on the ground that they had no right to ask help from those whom they had not cared to look to for advice in so weighty a matter. Just then, however, the plight of their country itself denied the petition. There was now in the greatest part of Etruria a strange race, new settlers, with whom they were neither securely at peace nor yet certain to have war. Nevertheless, out of regard for the blood and the name and the present perils of their kinsmen, they would grant that if any of their young men wished to serve in that war, they might do so without let or hindrance. Of such recruits it was said at Rome that a great number had come in; and so domestic differences began to subside, as generally happens, in the face of a common danger.

XVIII. It occasioned the Fathers no displeasure when the prerogative centuries[19] chose Publius Licinius Calvus tribune of the soldiers, without his seeking office; he was a man whose moderation had been proven in his former term, but was now become superannuated. It was clear that all who had been his colleagues in that same year would also be returned, one after the other, to wit: Lucius Titinius, Publius Maenius, Gnaeus Genucius, Lucius Atilius. But before they were declared to the duly assembled tribes, Licinius spoke as follows, having obtained permission of the interrex: "It is an omen of harmony, as I perceive, Quirites, a thing most needful at this juncture, that you seek for the ensuing year, when in your voting you remember our former magistracy; but whereas in my colleagues you are choosing again the same men, and all the better for experience, in me you see no longer the same Publius Licinius, of whom but the shadow and the name are left. My strength of body is decayed, my sight and hearing dulled, memory fails me, and the vigor of my mind is impaired. Here," he cried, laying hold of his son, "here is a young man, the effigy and likeness of him you formerly chose for military tribune first of all plebeians. Him have I bred up in my own principles, and in my stead I give and dedicate him to the state, and I pray you, Quirites, who without my seeking have offered me the office, that you grant it to him, who seeks it, and to the prayers I have added in his behalf." The father was granted his request, and the son, Publius Licinius, was declared military tribune with consular powers, together with those I have named above. Titinius and Genucius, tribunes of the soldiers, having marched against the Faliscans and Capenates, brought more spirit than generalship to their conduct of the war, and plunged into an ambush. Genucius, atoning for his rashness by an honorable death, fell fighting among the foremost, in front of the standards; Titinius rallied his men, who had been thrown into great confusion, on a little eminence, and made a stand, yet he would not risk an engagement on level ground. The disgrace outweighed the defeat, which had almost proved disastrous, so great was the panic which it caused, not only in Rome, where a greatly exaggerated report of the affair had been received, but also in the camp before Veii. There the soldiers could hardly be restrained from flight, for a rumor had run through the camp that the victorious Capenates and Faliscans, having slaughtered the Roman commanders and their army, were close at hand, with all the manhood of Etruria. Accounts even more alarming had been credited at Rome: that the camp at Veii was already under attack; that already a division of the enemy was marching to assail the City. There was a rush to the walls, and the women, drawn from their houses by the general consternation, betook themselves to prayer in the temples, and besought the gods to ward off destruction from the houses and shrines of the City and from the walls of Rome, and to turn that panic against Veii, if the sacred rites had been duly renewed and the portents expiated.

XIX. And now the games and the Latin Festival had been repeated, now the water had been let out from the Alban Lake upon the fields, and the doom of Veii drew on apace. Accordingly the commander destined to destroy that city and to save his country, Marcus Furius Camillus, was appointed dictator, and named Publius Cornelius Scipio as his master of the horse. The change in the command at once made a change in all things else; there was new hope and a new spirit, and even the fortune of the City seemed to be renewed. The dictator's first act was to visit military punishment upon those who had fled from Veii in the panic there, and to teach his men that the enemy was not the worst thing they had to fear. He then fixed the levy for a certain day, and in the interval hastened to Veii to encourage his soldiers; thence he returned to Rome to enroll the new army, and found no one who refused to serve. Even foreign troops, Latins and Hernicans, came with promises to help in this war, and the dictator thanked them in the senate.[20] All things being now in readiness for the campaign, Camillus vowed, in pursuance of a senatorial decree, to celebrate the great games,[21] if he should capture Veii, and to restore and dedicate anew the temple of Mater Matuta, which in time gone by had been consecrated by King Servius Tullius. Marching out from the City, where he left a greater feeling of suspense than of confidence, he first engaged the Faliscans and Capenates, in the Nepesine country. There all his measures, being executed with consummate skill and prudence, were attended, as generally happens, with good fortune. Not only did he rout the enemy in battle, but he also deprived them of their camp and got possession of enormous booty, the chief part of which was made over to the quaestor, and no great quantity given to the soldiers. He then led his army to Veii, where he increased the number of redoubts, and withdrawing the troops from the skirmishes which frequently took place, on the spur of the moment, in the space between the town wall and the stockade, by an edict forbidding any man to fight without orders, he employed them in digging. Of all the works, much the greatest and most laborious was a mine they began to drive into the enemy's citadel. That this work might not be interrupted nor the same men become exhausted by perpetually toiling under ground, he divided the workers into six parties and assigned them six-hour shifts in rotation; night and day the work went on unceasingly, till they had made a way into the citadel.

XX. The dictator saw that victory was at last within his grasp, and that a city of great wealth was on the point of being taken, with booty more than if all previous wars had been put together. Lest, therefore, he might incur either the resentment of the soldiers, in consequence of a niggardly division of the spoils, or the ill-will of the Fathers, if he were lavish in sharing them out, he wrote to the senate, that thanks to the favor of the immortal gods, his own direction, and the patient efforts of his troops, Veii would presently be in the power of the Roman People, and asked what disposition they proposed making of the plunder. The senate was divided between two opinions; the aged Publius Licinius, who was the first, they say, that his son called upon to speak,[22] advised making public proclamation that the people decreed that whoso desired a share in the spoils should proceed to the camp at Veii; the other plan was that of Appius Claudius, who declared that such largess was without example,[23] reckless, unfair, and ill-advised; if they were persuaded once for all that it was wicked that money captured from the enemy should lie in the treasury, which had been exhausted by the wars, he urged them to pay the soldiers out of it, that the plebs might have so much the less war-tax to contribute[24]; this was a boon of which all families alike would feel the benefit, nor would the hands of idle city-folk, greedy of pillage, pluck away the rewards of valiant fighting men—since it commonly turned out that in proportion as a man was prone to seek a leading share of toil and danger, he was slow in plundering. Licinius argued, on the other hand, that this money would breed endless suspicion and hate, and would furnish grounds for accusations before the plebs, and so for agitation and revolutionary laws; it was better, therefore, to win over by this gift the sympathies of the commons, to succor them, exhausted and impoverished as they were by so many years' taxation, and to let them enjoy the spoils and fruits of that war in which they had well-nigh grown old men; there would in every instance be more satisfaction and pleasure in what a man took with his own hand from the enemy and brought home, than if he received many times its value at the discretion of another; the dictator himself would fain avoid the enmity and charges arising from this business, and therefore had handed it over to the senate; the senate, likewise, in its turn, should refer the question to the plebs, and let every man keep what the fortune of war might give him. This policy seemed the safer, since it would make the senate popular. Accordingly, proclamation was made that all who liked might go to the dictator in camp, to share in the plunder of Veii.

XXI. A vast throng went out, and filled the camp. Then the dictator, after taking the auspices, came forth and commanded the troops to arm. "Under thy leadership," he cried, "Pythian Apollo, and inspired by thy will, I advance to destroy the city of Veii, and to thee I promise a tithe of its spoils. At the same time I beseech thee, Queen Juno, that dwellest now in Veii, to come with us, when we have gotten the victory, to our City—soon to be thine, too—that a temple meet for thy majesty may there receive thee." These prayers uttered, he set forward with overwhelming numbers to assault the town on every side, that the inhabitants might not perceive the danger pressing upon them from the mine. The Veientes, unconscious that they were already given up by their own soothsayers, and by foreign oracles, that some of the gods had already been invited to share in their despoiling, while others having been entreated to quit their city were beginning to look to new homes in the temples of their enemies, and that this was the last day they were themselves to live, feared nothing less than that their defenses were undermined and their citadel already filled with foemen, and, each for himself, took up arms and ran out to the ramparts; marvelling what it meant that whereas for so many days not a Roman had stirred from his post, they should now, as though they had suddenly gone mad, be rushing blindly against the walls.

At this point men introduce a tale, how, as the King of the Veientes was sacrificing, the Roman soldiers in the mine overheard the sooth-sayer declare that to him who should cut up[25] the inwards of that victim would be given the victory, and were moved to open the mine and seize the entrails, which they bore off to the dictator. But in matters of so great antiquity I should be content if things probable were to be received as true: this story, more fit to be displayed on the stage, that delights in wonders, than to be believed, it is worth while neither to affirm nor to refute.[26]

The mine, which was then filled with picked troops, suddenly discharged its armed men into the temple of Juno, on the Veientine citadel; some of them assailed the backs of their enemies, who were on the walls; others wrenched off the bars that made fast the gates; others, when the women and slaves cast down stones and tiles from roofs, fetched fire against them. The air resounded with shouts; discordant threats of the attackers and despairing shrieks of the defenders were blended with the wailing of women and children. In a moment the armed soldiers were everywhere hurled from the walls, and the gates thrown open. A part of the Romans poured through them in a body, others scaled the deserted walls; the city was overrun with enemies; the battle raged in every quarter; then, when there had already been great carnage, the fighting began to flag, and the dictator bade the heralds proclaim that those without arms should be spared. This ended the slaughter. The unarmed began to give them-selves up, and the Romans scattered, with the dictator's permission, in quest of booty. When this was brought before him, and he saw that it was considerably larger and comprised effects of greater value than he had hoped or thought, it is said that he raised his hands to heaven and prayed that if any god or man deemed his good fortune and that of the Roman People to be excessive, it might be granted him to appease that envy with the least harm to his own private interests and to the public welfare of the Roman People. As he turned, while making this prayer, tradition states that he slipped and fell, and that this omen was seen (when men came later to gather its meaning from the event) to point to the condemnation of Camillus himself, and in the second place, to the capture of Rome, a disaster which befell a few years afterwards. So that day was spent in the slaughter of enemies and the sack of a most opulent city.

XXII. On the following day the dictator sold the free-born inhabitants into slavery.[27] This was the only money that went into the state treasury, but the commons were angry about it; as for the booty they brought back themselves, they gave the credit not to their commander, who had referred to the Fathers, that they might support his niggardliness, a matter which had lain within his own discretion, nor yet to the senators, but to the house of the Licinii, whose son had brought to a vote in the senate that popular measure which his father had proposed. When the wealth that belonged to men had now been carried away out of Veii, they began to remove the possessions of the gods and the gods themselves, but more in the manner of worshippers than of pillagers. For out of all the army youths were chosen, and made to cleanse their bodies and to put on white garments, and to them the duty was assigned of conveying Queen Juno to Rome. Reverently entering her temple, they scrupled at first to approach her with their hands, because this image was one that according to Etruscan practice none but a priest of a certain family was wont to touch; when one of them, whether divinely inspired or out of youthful jocularity, asked, "Wilt thou go, Juno, to Rome?"—whereat the others all cried out that the goddess had nodded assent. It was afterwards added to the story that she had also been heard to say that she was willing. At all events we are told that she was moved from her place with contrivances of little power, as though she accompanied them voluntarily, and was lightly and easily transferred and carried safe and sound to the Aventine, the eternal home to which the prayers of the Roman dictator had called her; and there Camillus afterwards dedicated to her the temple which he himself had vowed.

Such was the fall of Veii, the wealthiest city of the Etruscan race, which gave evidence of its greatness even in its final overthrow; since after a blockade of ten continuous summers and winters, during which time it had inflicted considerably heavier losses than it had sustained, it yet was ultimately taken, when at last even destiny fought against it, by siege-works and not by force.

XXIII. When word came to Rome that Veii was taken, although the portents had been averted and the answers of the soothsayers and the Pythian oracle were known; and though they had done all that human wisdom could do to help, in choosing Marcus Furius Camillus, greatest of all generals, to lead them; nevertheless, because they had warred there so many years with varying fortune and had suffered many a reverse, their joy, as though unexpected, knew no bounds; and ere the senate could act, the temples were all thronged with Roman matrons giving thanks to the gods. The senate decreed supplications for four days, a longer period than in any former war. Moreover, as the dictator drew near, all sorts and conditions of men ran forth to meet him in such numbers as had never welcomed a general before, and the triumph far exceeded the measure of honor usual on that day. He was himself the most conspicuous object in it, as he rode into the City on a chariot drawn by white horses; an act which struck men as being not only undemocratic, but irreverent, for they were troubled at the thought that in respect to his steeds the dictator was made equal to Jupiter and the sun-god; and the triumph, chiefly for this one reason, was more brilliant than popular.[28] He then let the contract for the temple of Queen Juno on the Aventine, and dedicated one to Mater Matuta;[29] and having fulfilled these obligations to gods and men, laid down the dictatorship.

The next thing to be discussed was the gift to Apollo, to whom Camillus said that he had solemnly promised a tenth part of the spoils. The pontiffs ruled that the people must discharge this obligation, but it was not easy to devise a method for compelling them to return the booty, that out of it the due proportion might be set apart for the sacred object. They finally resorted to what seemed the least oppressive plan, namely, that whosoever wished to acquit himself and his household of obligation on the score of the vow, should appraise his own share of the spoils, and pay in a tenth part of its value to the public treasury, to the end that it might be converted into an offering of gold befitting the grandeur of the temple and the power of the god and corresponding to the majesty of the Roman People. This contribution still further alienated the affections of the commons from Camillus.[30] In the midst of these affairs came envoys from the Volsci and the Aequi seeking peace, and their suit was granted, more that the state, worn out with so long a war, might be at rest, than because the petitioners deserved it.

XXIV. The year which followed the capture of Veii had six consular tribunes, to wit, the two Publii Cornelii, Cossus and Scipio, Marcus Valerius Maximus (for the second time), Caeso Fabius Ambustus (for the third), Lucius Furius Medullinus (for the fifth), Quintus Servilius (for the third). To the Cornelii was allotted the Faliscan war, to Valerius and Servilius the war with Capena. They attempted no cities, either by assault or by siege, but wasted the countryside and despoiled the farmers of their possessions, leaving not one fruit tree in the land nor any productive plant. This devastation overcame the resistance of the Capenates; they begged for peace and it was granted. In the Faliscan country the war went on.

At Rome, meanwhile, there were disturbances of many sorts, to quiet which the senate had voted to plant a colony on the Volscian frontier, and to enroll for that destination three thousand Roman citizens, to each of whom a board of three, appointed for the purpose, had proposed to assign three iugera[31] and seven-twelfths. This donation men were disposed to spurn, regarding it as a sop intended to divert their hopes from greater things: for why should the plebs be banished to the Volscian country, when the fair city of Veii and the Veientine lands (more fertile and extensive than those of Rome) were there in plain sight? The city, too, they preferred to the City of Rome, whether for situation, or for the splendor of its public and private buildings and its places. Nay, they even mooted the plan which certainly had a great following later, when the Gauls had captured Rome, of migrating to Veii.[32] For the rest, they intended that half of the plebs and half of the senate should dwell in Veii, regarding it as possible for the Roman people to inhabit two cities with a common polity.

This proposal the patricians opposed with such vehemence as to declare that they would sooner die in the sight of the Roman People than suffer anything of the sort to come to a vote; for when there was already so much dissension in a single city, what would it be in two? Was it possible that any man should prefer a vanquished to a victorious city, and suffer Veii captured to enjoy a greater fortune than Veii free? In fine, it was conceivable that they should be left behind in their native city by their fellow Romans; but to forsake their country and their fellow-citizens no violence should ever force them; they had no mind to follow Titus Sicinius—the tribune of the plebs who had proposed the bill—to Veii, as their founder, abandoning the god Romulus, the son of a god, the Father and Author of the Roman City.

XXV. These differences gave rise to disgraceful contentions—for the Fathers had won over some of the plebeian tribunes[33] to their opinion—and the only thing that compelled the plebs to stay their hands was this, that as often as they raised a shout, in order to begin a riot, the leaders of the senate were the first to confront the mob, bidding them visit blows, wounds, and death on them. The grey hairs of these men, their distinctions, and their honors, they shrank from outraging, and shame thwarted their rage in all similar attempts.

Camillus harangued the people constantly, and in all places. It was no wonder, he said, that the citizens had gone mad, since, bound though they were to carry out their vow, they were more concerned about everything else than about the discharge of their obligation. He would say nothing of their penny contribution—a truer name for it than tithe—since in this regard each man had bound himself as an individual, and the state was freed; but there was one thing his conscience would not suffer him to pass over in silence; to wit, that the tithe should be defined as consisting of that part only of the booty which was movable; and that nothing should be said of the captured city and its territory, which were likewise included in the vow.

Unable to agree on this point, the senate referred it to the pontiffs, who decided, after consulting with Camillus, that so far as these things had belonged to the Veientes before the vow was made, and had subsequently come into the possession of the Roman People, a tithe thereof was sacred to Apollo. Thus the city and the land came into the estimate. Money was drawn from the treasury, and the tribunes of the soldiers with consular rank were directed to purchase gold with it; and there being not enough of this metal, the matrons held meetings to consider the need, and binding themselves by a common resolution to supply the tribunes with gold, brought in all their ornaments to the treasury. No act was ever more acceptable to the senate, and to honor the matrons for their generosity, it is said to have voted that they might drive in four-wheeled carriages to festivals and games, and in two-wheeled cars on holy and working days. When the gold received from each had been appraised, in order that the moneys might be repaid, it was determined to make a golden bowl and carry it to Delphi as an offering to Apollo.

No sooner had they eased their minds of the vow, than the tribunes of the commons began again their agitation, inflaming the populace against all the nobles, but especially against Camillus, whom they charged with having reduced to naught the spoils of Veii, by devoting them to the state and to religion. If any of the leaders were absent, they were fiercely denounced; being present they outfaced their angry critics and shamed them into silence. As soon as the people saw that the question would be carried over from that year, they worked for the re-election of the tribunes of the plebs who were backing the measure;[34] and the patricians exerted themselves to do the same for its opponents. So, for the most part, the same tribunes were returned to office.

XXVI. At the voting for military tribunes, the senators with much ado obtained the election of Marcus Furius Camillus.[35] The need of a commander for the wars was their pretext, but what they really wanted was a man who would combat the lavishness of the tribunes.[36] With Camillus were elected to that office, Lucius Furius Medullinus (for the sixth time), Gaius Aemilius, Lucius Valerius Publicola, Spurius Postumius, and (for the second time) Publius

Cornelius.[37] At the outset of the year the tribunes of the commons made no move, until Marcus Furius Camillus should march against the Faliscans, for to him this war had been committed. Then came delays, and men's enthusiasm waned, while Camillus, the opponent whom they chiefly feared, won fresh renown in the Faliscan country. For though at first the enemy kept within their walls, deeming this their safest course, he compelled them, by ravaging their fields and burning their farm-houses, to come out of their city. Still, they were afraid to advance very far, and pitched their camp about a mile from, the town, trusting that it was quite safe, without other reason than the difficulty of approaching it; for the ground about it was rough and broken, and the roads were either narrow or steep. But Camillus, employing a prisoner taken in that very region for his guide, broke camp in the dead of night, and showed himself at earliest dawn in a considerably superior position. The Romans, divided into three shifts, began to build a rampart, the soldiers who were not working standing by in readiness to fight. There, when the enemy sought to hinder the work, he defeated and routed them; and so great was the panic that came over the Faliscans, that they fled in disorder past their camp, which was the nearer refuge, and made for the town; and many were slain or wounded, before, in their terror, they could rush in through the gates. The camp was taken, and the booty was paid over to the quaestors. This incensed the troops, but they were overborne by the strictness of the discipline, and admired, while they detested, their general's probity. Then came a blockade of the town, and the construction of siege-works; and sometimes, when opportunity offered, the townsfolk would raid the Roman outposts and skirmishes would ensue. Time wore on, without bringing hope to either side; the besieged had corn and other supplies, which they had laid up beforehand in greater abundance than the besiegers; and it began to seem as though the struggle would be as long drawn out as at Veii, had not Fortune, at one stroke, given the Roman general an opportunity to display the magnanimity already familiar from his exploits in war, and an early victory.

XXVII. It was customary amongst the Faliscans to employ the same person as teacher and attendant of their children, and they used to intrust a number of lads at the same time to the care of one man, a practice which still obtains in Greece. The children of the chief men, as is commonly the case, were under the tuition of one who was regarded as their foremost scholar. This man had in time of peace got into the way of leading the boys out in front of the city for play and exercise, and during the war made no change in his routine, but would draw them sometimes a shorter, sometimes a longer distance from the gate, with this and that game and story, until being farther away one day than usual, he seized the opportunity to bring them amongst the enemy's outposts, and then into the Roman camp, to the headquarters of Camillus. He then followed up his villainous act with an even more villainous speech, saying that he had given Falerii into the hands of the Romans, having delivered up to them the children of those whose fathers were in power there. On hearing this Camillus answered: "Neither the people nor the captain to whom you are come, you scoundrel, with your scoundrel's gift, is like yourself. Between us and the Faliscans is no fellowship founded on men's covenants; but the fellowship which nature has implanted in both sides is there and will abide. There are rights of war as well as of peace, and we have learnt to use them justly no less than bravely. We bear no weapons against those tender years which find mercy even in the storming of a city, but against those who are armed themselves, who, without wrong or provocation at our hands, attacked the Roman camp at Veii. Those people you have done your best to conquer by an unheard-of crime. I shall conquer them, as I conquered Veii, in the Roman way, by dint of courage, toil, and arms." He then had the fellow stripped, his hands bound behind his back, and gave him up to the boys to lead back to Falerii, providing them with rods to scourge the traitor as they drove him into town. To behold this spectacle, there was at first a great gathering together of the people, and presently the magistrates called a meeting of the senate about the strange affair, and men underwent such a revulsion of feeling, that those who a short time before, in the fury of their hate and resentment would almost have preferred the doom of Veii to the peace of Capena, were now calling for peace, with the voice of an entire city. The honesty of the Romans, and the justice of their general, were praised in market place and senate-house, and, with the consent of all, envoys proceeded to Camillus in his camp, and thence, by his permission, to the Roman senate, to surrender Falerii. Being introduced into the Curia they are said to have spoken as follows: "Conscript Fathers, you and your general have won a victory over us which no one, whether God or man, could begrudge you, and we give ourselves into your hands, believing (than which nothing can be more honorable to a victor) that we shall be better off under your government than under our own laws. The outcome of this war has afforded the human race two wholesome precedents: you have set fair-dealing in war above immediate victory; and we, challenged by your fair-dealing, have freely granted you that victory. We are under your sway; send men to receive our arms and hostages, and our city, the gates of which stand open. Neither shall you be disappointed in our fidelity nor we in your rule." Camillus was thanked both by his enemies and by his fellow citizens. The Faliscans were commanded to pay the soldiers for that year, that the Roman People might be exempted from the war tax. Peace being granted, the Roman army was led home.

XXVIII. Camillus, having returned to the City distinguished by a far better kind of glory than when he had entered it in triumph drawn by white horses—for he had conquered his enemies by justice and fair-dealing—uttered no reproaches, but the senators were ill-at-ease till they should free him, without delay, from the obligation of his vow. And so, to carry the golden bowl as a gift to Apollo at Delphi, they appointed Lucius Valerius, Lucius Sergius, and Aulus Manlius, who, being dispatched in a single warship, were captured by Liparaean pirates not far from the Sicilian Straits and carried to Liparae. It was the manner of that people to divide up the booty which they had obtained by a kind of public piracy, but it chanced that year that one Timasitheus was chief magistrate, a man more resembling the Romans than his own countrymen; who, himself revering the title of the envoys and their gift, as well as the god to whom it was being sent and the cause of the oblation, imbued also the people, who are almost always like their ruler, with a due sense of religious awe; and after entertaining the ambassadors in the guest-house of the state, even sent ships to convoy them to Delphi, and thence brought them safely back to Rome. A covenant of hospitality was made with him by decree of the senate, and gifts were presented him in the name of the state.

The same year there was a war with the Aequi, of so varied fortune that it was not clear, either at the front itself or in Rome, whether the upshot had been victory or defeat. The Roman generals were two of the military tribunes, Gaius Aemilius and Spurius Postumius. At first they exercised the command conjointly; afterwards, when they had routed the enemy in battle, they arranged that Aemilius should hold Verrugo with a garrison, while Postumius should lay waste the country. As he was leading his troops in irregular formation, somewhat carelessly in consequence of his success, the Aequi fell upon them and throwing them into confusion drove them to the nearest hills, whence the panic spread even to Verrugo, to the other army. Postumius having rallied his men in a position of safety, called them together and chid them for their alarm and flight, telling them they had been discomfited by the most craven and fugitive of foes. Whereat the army cried out as one man, that they deserved his reproaches, and confessed the enormity of their misconduct, but promised that they would themselves mend it, and that their enemies' joy should be short-lived. Demanding to be led forthwith against the camp of the Aequi—which was in full sight in the plain where they had pitched it—they professed themselves willing to undergo any punishment if they should not have stormed it before nightfall. Postumius commended them and bade them sup and be ready at the fourth watch. The enemy, too, that they might cut off any retreat by night along the road to Verrugo, from the hill where the Romans lay, were afield and met them, and the battle began before daylight, but there was a moon all night. They could see to fight as well as in the daytime; but the shouts were heard in Verrugo, the soldiers believed the Roman camp was being attacked, and so great was their consternation that, despite the efforts of Aemilius to check them and despite his appeals, they fled in a scattered rout to Tusculum. From thence a rumor was carried to Rome that Postumius and the army were destroyed. But Postumius, as soon as the first rays of light had removed all fear of ambuscades in case of a wide-spread pursuit, rode down the line, reminding his men of the promises they had given him, and inspired such ardor that the Aequi could no longer withstand their charge, and were slaughtered while they fled (as happens when rage is more concerned than valor), till their army was clean destroyed; and the gloomy tidings from Tusculum which had thrown the City into a needless fright, were succeeded by a laurel-wreathed letter from Postumius, announcing the victory of the Roman People and the annihilation of the Aequian army.

XXIX. The measures introduced by the tribunes of the plebs being still undecided, the commons strove to prolong the tenure of the supporters of the bill,[38] and the patricians to re-elect the tribunes who had vetoed it; but in the election of their own magistrates the plebeians proved the stronger, a disappointment which the Fathers avenged by passing a resolution in the senate providing for the election of consuls—a magistracy odious to the plebs. There had been no consuls for fifteen years, when they elected Lucius Lucretius Flavus, and Servius Sulpicius Camerinus. In the beginning of this year, the tribunes united in a spirited attempt—for none of the college was disposed to object—to carry the bill; and the consuls, for that very reason, were quite as active in opposing them. While the whole body politic was absorbed in this one concern, Vitellia, a Roman colony, was captured by the Aequi, in whose territory it was situated. The greatest part of the settlers escaped, for the place was taken by treachery at night and their flight through the opposite quarter of the town was unopposed, and made their way to Rome in safety. To Lucius Lucretius the consul fell the command in this affair. Marching out with his army, he defeated the enemy in a battle and returned victorious to the City, where he found a far more serious struggle impending. A day of trial had been appointed for the plebeian tribunes of two years before, namely Aulus Verginius and Quintus Pomponius, to defend whom the senate, as the patricians all agreed, was in honor bound; for no man brought any charge against their lives or the conduct of their office, except their having, out of complaisance to the Fathers, opposed the tribunician law. But the influence of the senators was out-weighed by the resentment of the plebs, and a shameful precedent was set, when the innocent

men were condemned each to pay a fine of 10,000 asses. This roused
the indignation of the senate. Camillus frankly denounced the
depravity of the commons, who having turned against their own
representatives, failed to perceive that they had by their wicked
judgment of the tribunes done away with the veto, and that in doing
away with the veto they had overthrown the tribunician power. For
if they supposed that the unbridled license of that office would be
tolerated by the Fathers, they were mistaken; if tribunician violence
could not be resisted by the help of tribunes, the senators must find
some other weapon. He rebuked the consuls also, because they had,
without protesting, allowed those tribunes who had followed the
guidance of the senate to suffer for their reliance on the guarantee of
state protection. By such sentiments, publicly expressed in speeches,
he angered the people more and more from day to day.

XXX. As to the senate, he ceased not to encourage it in opposing the law: they must go down into the Forum, when the day should
arrive for voting on it, in no other spirit than that of men who realized that they had to fight for hearth and home, for the temples
of their gods, and for the soil of their birth. So far, indeed, as the
question touched his private interest, it would actually be an honor
to him, if it were not sinful to be thinking of his own renown while
his country was struggling for life, that the city he had won should be
thronged with people; that he should daily be reminded of his glory,
and have before his eyes the town which had figured in his triumph;[39]
that all men should tread in the footsteps of his fame. But he thought
it an offense against Heaven that a city deserted and forsaken by
the immortal gods should be inhabited, and that the Roman People
should dwell on conquered soil, exchanging their victorious City for
a vanquished one.

These earnest words of their leading member so stirred the senators, old men as well as young, that on the day the law was proposed
they formed in a body and came into the Forum, where they
dispersed among the tribes, and canvassing every man his own tribesmen, began with tears to beseech them, that they would not forsake
that City for which both they and their fathers had fought with the
greatest courage and good fortune. They pointed to the Capitol, to

the shrine of Vesta, and to the other temples standing all about them; they begged them not to drive the Roman People, an exile, and a wanderer from its native land and its household gods, to the city of its enemies, nor to carry things so far that it would be better that Veii had not been taken, so that Rome might not be deserted. Since the patricians used not force but entreaties, and in their entreaties made many a reference to the gods, the greater part felt the prick of conscience, and the law was rejected by one more tribe than voted in its favor.[40] And so greatly did this victory rejoice the Fathers, that next day, at the instance of the consuls, a decree was passed by the senate, that seven *iugera* of the Veientine land should be apportioned to every plebeian, and not alone to the heads of families, but so as to reckon in all the free-born members of the household, that with such a prospect before them men might be willing to rear children.

XXXI. Appeased by this largess, the plebs made no objection to an assembly for the election of consuls, and the choice fell on Lucius Valerius Potitus and Marcus Manlius, afterwards surnamed Capitolinus.[41] These consuls celebrated the Great Games, which Marcus Furius the dictator had vowed in the war with Veii. This year saw also the dedication of a temple to Queen Juno, vowed by the same dictator in the same war; and tradition relates that the ceremony was attended by throngs of enthusiastic matrons.

A campaign in no way memorable was fought with the Aequi on Mount Algidus, the enemy being routed before they had well begun to fight. Valerius was the more persistent in cutting them down as they fled, and to him was decreed a triumph; Manlius was allowed to enter the City in an ovation.[42] In this year also a new war broke out, namely with the people of Volsinii. Owing to a famine and pestilence which arose in the Roman territories on account of drought and excessive heat, it was impossible to send an army against them; and in consequence of this the Volsinienses, having added the Sappinates[43] to their forces, were puffed up with pride and made an incursion themselves into the fields of the Romans. War was then declared against both nations.

Gaius Julius, the censor, died, and Marcus Cornelius was substituted in his place, a circumstance which was afterwards thought to have offended the gods, because in this lustrum Rome was captured; nor from that day has a censor ever been appointed in the room of one who has died.[44] The consuls, too, caught the plague, and it was voted that fresh auspices should be obtained by means of an interregnum. Accordingly, when the consuls, in obedience to the senate's decree, had abdicated, Marcus Furius Camillus was appointed interrex, and named as his successor Publius Cornelius Scipio, who, in turn, named Lucius Valerius Potitus interrex; under whom they elected six military tribunes of consular rank, so that even if any of them should fall ill the state might still have magistrates.

XXXII. On the first day of July they entered office, to wit, Lucius Lucretius, Servius Sulpicius, Marcus Aemilius, Lucius Furius Medullinus (for the seventh time), Furius Agrippa, and (for the second time) Gaius Aemilius. Of these, Lucius Lucretius and Gaius Aemilius were assigned the war with Volsinii as their province, while the Sappinates fell to Agrippa Furius and Servius Sulpicius. The Volsinienses were encountered first, in a campaign of great magnitude in respect to the enemy's numbers, though the engagement with them was no very sharp affair. Their line broke at the first assault, and in the rout eight thousand soldiers were cut off by the cavalry, and laying down their arms, surrendered. When the Sappinates heard of this campaign, they refused to risk a battle, but retired within their walls and prepared to defend themselves. The Romans plundered right and left, both the lands of Sappinum and those of Volsinii, without finding any to resist their force, until the Volsinienses wearied of the war; and upon their agreeing to restore the goods of the Roman People and furnish pay for the army for that campaign, they were granted a truce of twenty years.

The same year Marcus Caedicius, a plebeian, reported to the tribunes, that in the Nova Via, where the chapel now stands above the temple of Vesta, he had heard in the silence of the night a voice more distinct than a man's, which bade him tell the magistrates that the Gauls were approaching. This portent was neglected, as often happens, because of the informant's humble station, and because that race was remote and therefore not well known And not only did they reject the warnings of Heaven, as their doom drew nearer, but they even sent away from the City the only human assistance present with them, in the person of Marcus Furius. He had been indicted by Lucius Apuleius, tribune of the plebs, on account of the spoils of Veii, just at the time of losing his youthful son. Summoning to his house his fellow tribesmen and his clients (who formed a good part of the plebs), he sounded their feelings, and having been answered that they would make up such an amount as he might be fined, but that they could not acquit him, he departed into exile, beseeching the immortal gods that if he were an innocent man to whom that wrong was done they would speedily make his thankless fellow citizens wish to have him back. He was fined in his absence in the sum of 15,000 asses.

XXXIII. After the expulsion of that citizen whose presence, if anything in this life is certain, would have made the capture of Rome impossible, disaster approached the ill-fated City with the arrival of envoys from the men of Clusium seeking help against the Gauls. The story runs that this race, allured by the delicious fruits and especially the wine—then a novel luxury—had crossed the Alps and possessed themselves of lands that had before been tilled by the Etruscans; and that wine had been imported into Gaul expressly to entice them, by Arruns of Clusium, in his anger at the seduction of his wife by Lucumo. This youth, whose guardian he had been, was so powerful that he could not have chastised him without calling in a foreign force. He it was who is said to have guided the Gauls across the Alps, and to have suggested the attack on Clusium. Now I would not deny that Arruns or some other citizen brought the Gauls to Clusium, but that those who besieged Clusium were not the first who had passed the Alps is generally agreed. Indeed it was two hundred years before the attack on Clusium and the capture of Rome, that the Gauls first crossed over into Italy; neither were the Clusini the first of the Etruscans with whom they fought; but long before that the Gallic armies had often given battle to those who dwelt between the Apennines and the Alps.

The Tuscan sway, down to the rise of the Roman domination, stretched over a wide expanse of land and sea. How great their power was on the upper and the lower seas, by which Italy is surrounded

like an island, is apparent from the names, since the Italian races
have called one of them Tuscan, the general designation of the race,
and the other Hadriatic, from Hatria, an Etruscan colony; and the
Greeks know the same seas as Tyrrhenian and Adriatic. In the lands
which slope on either side towards one of these seas, they had twice
twelve cities; first the twelve on this side the Apennines, towards the
lower sea; to which afterwards they added the same number beyond
the Apennines, sending over as many colonies as there were original
cities, and taking possession of all the transpadane region (except
the angle belonging to the Veneti who dwell about the gulf) as far
as the Alps. The Alpine tribes have also, no doubt, the same origin,
especially the Raetians; who have been rendered so savage by the very
nature of the country as to retain nothing of their ancient character
save the sound of their speech, and even that is corrupted.

XXXIV. Concerning the migration of the Gauls into Italy we
are told as follows: While Tarquinius Priscus reigned at Rome, the
Celts, who make up one of the three divisions of Gaul, were under
the domination of the Bituriges, and this tribe supplied the Celtic
nation with a king. Ambigatus was then the man, and his talents,
together with his own and the general good fortune, had brought
him great distinction; for Gaul under his sway grew so rich in corn
and so populous, that it seemed hardly possible to govern so great a
multitude. The king, who was now an old man and wished to relieve
his kingdom of a burdensome throng, announced that he meant
to send Bellovesus and Segovesus, his sister's sons, two enterprising
young men, to find such homes as the gods might assign to them by
augury; and promised them that they should head as large a number
of emigrants as they themselves desired, so that no tribe might be
able to prevent their settlement. Whereupon to Segovesus were by
lot assigned the Hercynian highlands[45]; but to Bellovesus the gods
proposed a far pleasanter road, into Italy. Taking out with him the
surplus population of his tribes, the Bituriges, Arverni, Senones,
Haedui, Ambarri, Carnutes, and Aulerci, he marched with vast
numbers of infantry and cavalry into the country of the Tricastini.[46]

There the Alps stood over against them; and I for one do not
wonder that they seemed insuperable, for as yet no road had led

across them—as far back at all events as tradition reaches—unless one chooses to believe the stories about Hercules. While they were there fenced in as it were by the lofty mountains, and were looking about to discover where they might cross, over heights that reached the sky, into another world, superstition also held them back, because it had been reported to them that some strangers seeking lands were beset by the Salui. These were the Massilians, who had come in ships from Phocaea. The Gauls, regarding this as a good omen of their own success, lent them assistance, so that they fortified, without opposition from the Salui, the spot which they had first seized after landing. They themselves crossed the Alps through the Taurine passes and the pass of the Duria; routed the Etruscans in battle not far from the river Ticinus, and learning that they were encamped in what was called the country of the Insubres, who bore the same name as an Haeduan canton, they regarded it as a place of good omen, and founded a city there which they called Mediolanium.[47]

XXXV. Presently another band, consisting of Cenomani led by Etitovius, followed in the tracks of the earlier emigrants; and having, with the approval of Bellovesus, crossed the Alps by the same pass, established themselves where the cities of Brixia and Verona are now. After these the Libui came and settled, and the Salluvii—taking up their abode hard by the ancient tribe of the Laevi Ligures, about the river Ticinus. Then, over the Poenine Pass, came the Boii and Lingones, who finding everything taken up between the Po and the Alps, crossed the Po on rafts, and drove out not only the Etruscans, but also the Umbrians from their lands; nevertheless, they kept on the further side of the Apennines. Then the Senones, the latest to come, had their holdings from the river Utens all the way to the Aesis. This was the tribe, I find, which came to Clusium and from thence to Rome, but whether alone or assisted by all the peoples of Cisalpine Gaul, is uncertain.

The men of Clusium, alarmed by this strange invasion, when they beheld the numbers and the unfamiliar figures of the men and their novel weapons, and heard that on many a field, this side the Po and beyond it, they had put to flight the levies of Etruria; though they had no rights of alliance or of friendship with the Romans, except that they had refused to defend their kinsmen the Veientes against the Roman People; did yet dispatch envoys to Rome to ask help of the senate. As for the help, they were unsuccessful; but the three sons of Marcus Fabius Ambustus were sent as ambassadors to remonstrate with the Gauls, in the name of the senate and the Roman People, against their attack on those who had done them no wrong, and were the Roman People's allies and friends. The Romans, they said, would be obliged to defend them, even going to war, if circumstances should make it necessary; but it had seemed preferable that the war itself should, if possible, be avoided, and that they should make the acquaintance of the Gauls—a new race to them—in a friendly rather than in a hostile manner.

XXXVI. It was a peaceful embassy, had it not been for the violence of the ambassadors, who were more like Gauls than Romans. To them, when they had made known their mission in the council, the Gauls replied, that although they then heard for the first time the name of Roman, they could yet believe them to be stout-hearted men, since the Clusini had sought their aid in time of danger; and inasmuch as they had chosen to defend their allies by negotiation rather than by the sword, they would not, for their own part, spurn the peace which the Romans proposed, if the men of Clusium, who possessed more land than they could till, would surrender to the Gauls, who needed land, a portion of their territory; on no other terms could they consider granting peace. They added that they desired to be answered in the presence of the Romans, and that if land were refused them, it was under the eyes of these same Romans that they meant to fight, that they might be able to tell their friends how greatly the Gauls excelled all other men in prowess. When the Romans asked what conceivable right they had to demand land of its occupants under threat of war, and what business Gauls had in Etruria, they were truculently informed, that the new comers carried their right at the point of the sword and that all things belonged to the brave. So, angry passions being kindled on both sides, they ran to their weapons and joined battle; and the envoys, impelled by the fate which was even then urging Rome to its doom, took up arms, in defiance of the law of nations. Nor could it pass unnoticed, when in the very fore-front of the Tuscan line there were fighting three of the noblest and most valiant of the Roman youth, so conspicuous was the strangers' bravery. Nay, Quintus Fabius even rode out in front of the line, and meeting the Gallic leader as he charged boldly at the very standards of the Etruscans, ran his spear through his side and killed him. As he was engaged in despoiling his man, the Gauls recognized him, and the word passed through all the army that it was the Roman envoy. Thereupon, they gave over their anger at the Clusini and sounded the retreat, uttering threats against the Romans. Some were for marching at once on Rome; but the older men brought them over to send envoys first to complain of their wrongs, and to demand the surrender of the Fabii., in satisfaction for their violation of the law of nations. When the Gallic emissaries had stated their mission according to instructions, the senate disapproved of the conduct of the Fabii and felt the demands of the barbarians to be just; but private interest could not suffer them, in the case of men of such exalted station, to decree what they approved. And so, that the blame might not rest with the senate, if a Gallic war should chance to bring disaster, they referred the demands of the Gauls to the people for consideration; and with them wealth and influence carried so much more weight, that the men whose punishment was under discussion were elected consular tribunes for the ensuing year. At this the Gauls were enraged, as they had every right to be, and returned to their people with open threats of war. The tribunes of the soldiers chosen with the three Fabii were Quintus Sulpicius Longus, Quintus Servilius (for his fourth term), and Publius Cornelius Maluginensis.

XXXVII. Now that so heavy a calamity drew towards, such is the blindness Fortune visits on men's minds when she would have her gathering might meet with no check, that state which against the Fidenates and Veientes and other neighboring tribes had on many occasions resorted to the last expedient and named a dictator—that state, I say, though now an enemy never yet seen or heard of was rousing up war from the ocean and the remotest corners of the world, had recourse to no unusual authority or help. The tribunes whose rashness had brought on the war were in supreme command; they conducted the levy with no greater care than had usually been

employed in preparing for ordinary campaigns,[48] and even dispar-
aged the rumored seriousness of the danger. The Gauls, meanwhile,
on learning that honors had actually been conferred on men who
had violated the rights of mankind and that their embassy had been
made light of, were consumed with wrath (a passion which their
race is powerless to control), and straightway catching up their standards, set their column in rapid motion. As they marched swiftly
and noisily on, the terrified cities armed in haste, and the peasants
fled; but they signified with loud cries, wherever they came, that
Rome was their goal, and their horse and foot in an extended line
covered a vast tract of ground. Yet, though rumor and the report of
the Clusini preceded them, and after that successive messages from
other peoples, the utmost consternation was wrought in Rome by
the enemy's swiftness, which was such that the army, albeit levied as
it were *en masse* and hurriedly led out, barely covered eleven miles
before confronting him, at the point where the river Allia descends in
a very deep channel from the Crustuminian mountains, and mingles,
not far south of the highway, with the waters of the Tiber.[49] The Gauls
had already overrun all the ground in front and on both sides, and—
the race being naturally given to vainglorious outbursts—their wild
songs and discordant shouts filled all the air with a hideous noise.

XXXVIII. There the tribunes of the soldiers, without having
selected a place for a camp or fortified a position to which they might
retreat, and, forgetting even the gods, to say nothing of men, without auspices or sacrificial omens, drew up their line with the wings
extended to prevent being outflanked by the numbers of the enemy;
yet could not stretch their front as wide as his, though they thinned
it till the center was weak and scarce held together. There was a
little eminence on the right which they decided to occupy with their
reserves, a measure which, though it was the beginning of their panic
and flight, was also the sole salvation of the fugitives. For Brennus,
the Gallic chieftain, seeing the Romans to be so few, was especially
apprehensive of a stratagem. He supposed that they had seized the
higher ground for this purpose, that when the Gauls had made a
frontal attack on the battle-line of the legions, the reserves might
assail them in the flank and rear. He therefore directed his assault

against the reserves, not doubting that, if he could dislodge them, it would be easy for his greatly superior numbers to obtain a victory in the plain. Thus not only luck but generalship as well were on the side of the barbarians. In the other army there was no resemblance to Romans, either amongst officers or private soldiers. Terror and dismay had got hold of their spirits, and such complete forgetfulness of everything that a much greater number fled to Veii, a hostile city, though the Tiber was across their way, than by the straight road to Rome, to their wives and children. For a little while the reserves were protected by their position. In the rest of the field, no sooner had those who were nearest heard the shouting on their flank, and those who were farthest the outcry in their rear, than—fresh and unhurt—they ran away from their strange enemies, almost before they had caught sight of them; and so far were they from risking a combat, that they did not even return their battle-cry. None were slain in fight; but they were cut down from behind as they blocked their escape by their own struggles in the disordered rout. On the bank of the Tiber, whither the whole left wing had fled, after throwing away their arms, there was great slaughter, and many who could not swim, or lacked the strength, weighed down by their corslets and other armor, sank beneath the flood. Nevertheless, the chief part got safely to Veii, whence they not only sent no succors to Rome, but dispatched not even a messenger to tell of the defeat. From the right wing, which had stood at a distance from the river and closer to the foot of the mountain, the fugitives all made for Rome, and without stopping even to shut the city gates, sought refuge in the Citadel.

XXXIX. The very Gauls themselves, stunned by the marvellous victory they had so suddenly gained, at first stood rooted to the spot with amazement, like men that knew not what had happened; then they feared an ambush; after that they fell to collecting the spoils of the slain and erecting piles of arms, as their custom is; then at last having discovered no hostile movement anywhere, they began their march, and a little before sunset reached the environs of Rome. There, when the cavalry had reconnoitred and had reported that the gates were not closed, that no out-guards were watching before the gates, that no armed men were on the walls, astonishment held them spell-bound as before; and fearful of the night and the lie of the unknown City, they went into camp between Rome and the Anio, after sending off patrols about the walls and the rest of the gates, to find out what the enemy in their desperate case could possibly be at. As for the Romans, inasmuch as more, on escaping from the battle, had fled to Veii than to Rome, and no one supposed that any were left alive except those who had found refuge in the City, they mourned for all alike, both the living and the dead, and well nigh filled the City with lamentation. But presently their personal griefs were overwhelmed in a general panic, with the announcement that the enemy was at hand; and soon they could hear the dissonant howls and songs of the barbarians, as their squadrons roamed about the walls. During all the time that intervened before the following morning their hearts were in such suspense, that each moment they anticipated an immediate attack: on the first arrival of the enemy, because they had come close to the City—for they would have stopped at the Allia, had this not been their design; again, towards sundown, because there was little daylight left, they thought that they would enter the City before nightfall; then they concluded that they had put it off till night, to strike more fear into them. Finally the approach of dawn put them beside themselves, and close upon these restless apprehensions came the evil they were dreading, when the hostile forces entered the city gates. Yet neither that night nor the following day did the citizens at all resemble those who had fled in such consternation at the Allia. For having no hopes that they could protect the City with so small a force as remained to them, they resolved that the men of military age and the able-bodied senators should retire into the Citadel and the Capitol, with their wives and children; and, having laid in arms and provisions, should from that stronghold defend the gods, the men, and the name of Rome; that the flamen and the priestesses of Vesta should remove the sacred objects pertaining to the State far from the bloodshed and the flames, nor should their cult be abandoned till none should be left to cherish it. If the Citadel and the Capitol, where dwelt the gods; if the senate, the source of public wisdom; if the young men capable of bearing arms survived the impending destruction of the City, they could easily bear to lose the crowd of old men left behind them, who were bound to die in any case. And in order that the multitude of commoners might endure it with the more composure, the old men who had triumphed and those who had been consuls declared publicly that they would perish with those others, nor burden with bodies incapable of bearing arms in defense of the country the scanty stores of the fighting men.

XL. Such were the consolations which the old men appointed to die exchanged among themselves; then, directing their encouragement to the band of youths whom they were escorting to the Capitol and the Citadel, they committed to their valor and their young strength whatever fortune might yet be in store for a City that for three hundred and sixty years had been victorious in every war. On the departure of those who carried with them all hope and help, from those who had resolved not to survive the capture and destruction of their City, though the separation was a pitiful thing to see, yet the tears of the women, as they ran distractedly up and down, and following now these, now those, demanded of husbands and sons to what fate they were consigning them, supplied the final touch of human wretchedness. Still, the greater part of them followed their sons into the Citadel, though none either forbade or encouraged it, since what would have helped the besieged to lessen the number of non-combatants would have been inhuman. Another host—consisting chiefly of plebeians—too large for so small a hill to receive, or to support with so meager a supply of corn, streamed out of the City as though forming at last one continuous line, and took their way towards Janiculum. Thence some of them scattered through the country-side, and others made for the towns near by. They had neither leader nor concerted plan; each followed the promptings of his own hopes and his own counsels, in despair of the commonwealth.

Meanwhile the flamen of Quirinus and the Vestal virgins, with no thought for their own belongings, were consulting which of the sacred things they should carry with them, and which, because they were not strong enough to carry them all, they must leave behind, and, finally, where these objects would be safe. They judged it best to place them in jars and bury them in the shrine adjoining the flamen's house, where it is now forbidden to spit; the rest of the things they carried, sharing the burden amongst them, along the road which leads by the Sublician Bridge to Janiculum. As they mounted the hill they were perceived by a plebeian named Lucius Albinius, who had a waggon in which he was conveying his wife and children, amidst the throng of those who, unfit for war, were leaving the City. Preserving even then the distinction between divine and human, and holding it sacrilege that the priestesses of his country should go afoot, bearing the sacred objects of the Roman People, while his family were seen in a vehicle, he commanded his wife and children to get down, placed the virgins and their relics in the waggon, and brought them to Caere, whither the priestesses were bound.

XLI. At Rome meantime such arrangements for defending the Citadel as the case admitted of were now fairly complete, and the old men returned to their homes to await the coming of their enemies with hearts that were steeled to die. Such of them as had held curule magistracies, that they might face death in the trappings of their ancient rank and office, as beseemed their worth, put on the stately robes which are worn by those who conduct the *tensae*[50] or celebrate a triumph, and, thus habited, seated themselves on ivory chairs[51] in the middle of their houses. Some historians record that Marcus Folius, the pontifex maximus, led in the recitation of a solemn vow, by which they devoted themselves to death, in behalf of their country and the Roman Quirites.

The Gauls found their lust for combat cooled by the night which had intervened. At no point in the battle had they been pushed to desperate exertions, nor had they now to carry the City by assault. It was therefore without rancor or excitement that they entered Rome, on the following day, by the Colline Gate (which lay wide open), and made their way to the Forum, gazing about them at the temples of the gods and at the Citadel, which alone presented some show of war. Thence, after leaving a moderate guard to prevent any attack upon their scattered forces from Citadel or Capitol, they dispersed in quest of booty through streets where there was none to meet them, some rushing in a body into whatever houses were nearest, while others sought out the most remote, as though supposing that only such would be intact and full of plunder. But being frightened out of these by their very solitude, lest the enemy should by some ruse entrap them as they wandered apart, they came trooping back to the Forum and the places near it. There they found the dwellings of the plebeians fastened up, but the halls of the nobles open; and they hesitated almost more to enter the open houses than the shut, so nearly akin to religious awe was their feeling as they beheld seated in the vestibules, beings who, besides that their ornaments and apparel were more splendid than belonged to man, seemed also, in their majesty of countenance and in the gravity of their expression, most like to gods.

While they stood reverentially before them, as if they had been images, it is related that a Gaul stroked the beard of one of them, Marcus Papirius, which he wore long, as they all did then, whereat the Roman struck him over the head with his ivory mace, and, provoking his anger, was the first to be slain; after that the rest were massacred where they sat; and when the nobles had been murdered, there was no mercy then shown to anyone; the houses were ransacked, and after being emptied were given to the flames.

XLII. But whether it was that not all the Gauls desired to destroy the City, or that their leaders had resolved to make a certain show of burning, to inspire alarm, in hopes that the besieged might be driven to capitulate by affection for their homes, but not to burn up all the houses, in order that they might hold whatever remained of the City as a pledge to work on the feelings of their enemies—however this may have been, the fire spread by no means so freely or extensively on the first day as is commonly the case in a captured town. As the Romans looked down from their fastness and saw the City full of enemies running up and down in all the streets, while first in one quarter and then in another some new calamity would be occurring, they were unable, I do not say to keep their heads, but even to be sure of their ears and eyes. Wherever the shouting of the invaders, the lamentations of the women and children, the crackling of the flames, and the crash of falling buildings drew their attention, trembling at each sound, they turned their thoughts and their gaze that way, as though Fortune had placed them there to witness the pageant of their dying country. Of all their possessions nothing was left them to defend save their persons alone; and so much more wretched was their plight than that of all others who have ever been beleaguered, that they were cut off from their native City and confined where they could see all that belonged to them in the power of their enemies. Nor was the night more tranquil, after a day of such distress; and the night was followed by a restless day, with never a moment that had not still some fresh calamity to unfold. Yet, oppressed as they were, or rather over-whelmed, by so many misfortunes, nothing could alter their resolve; though they should see everything laid low in flames and ruins, they would stoutly defend the hill they held, however small and naked, which was all that Liberty had left. And now that the same events were occurring everyday, like men grown used to grief, they had ceased to feel their own misfortunes, looking solely to their shields and the swords in their right hands as their only remaining hope.

XLIII. The Gauls likewise, having vainly for some days waged war against only the buildings of Rome, when they saw that there was nothing left amidst the smouldering ruins of the captured City but armed enemies, who for all their disasters were not a jot appalled nor likely to yield to anything but force, took a desperate resolution to attack the Citadel. At daybreak the signal was made; and the entire host, having formed up in the Forum, gave a cheer, and raising their shields above their heads and locking them, began the ascent. The defenders on the other hand did nothing rashly or in confusion. At all the approaches they had strengthened the guard-posts, and where they saw the enemy advancing they stationed their best soldiers, and suffered them to come up, persuaded that the higher they mounted up the steep the easier it would be to drive them down. They made their stand about the middle of the declivity, and there, launch-ing their attack from the higher ground, which seemed of itself to hurl them against the foe, dislodged the Gauls, with such havoc and destruction that they never attempted to attack in that manner again, with either a part or the whole of their strength. So, relin-quishing all hope of getting up by force of arms, they prepared for a blockade. Having never till that moment considered such a thing, they had destroyed all the corn in the City with their conflagrations, and what was in the fields had all been hurriedly carried off, within the last few days, to Veii. They therefore arranged to divide their army, and employ part of it to pillage the neighboring nations and part to invest the Citadel, in order that those who held the lines might be provisioned by the foragers.

When the Gauls departed from the City, Fortune's own hand guided them to Ardea, that they might make trial of Roman manhood. Camillus was languishing there in exile, more grieved by the nation's calamity than by his own; and as he sorrowfully inveighed against gods and men, and asked, with wonder and humiliation, where those heroes were who had shared with him in the capture of Veii and Falerii, and whose gallantry in other wars had ever outrun their success, of a sudden he heard that the army of the Gauls was coming, and that the Ardeates in alarm were deliberating what to do about it. With an inspiration nothing less than divine, he pushed into the midst of their conference, though before accustomed to avoid these councils—and there, (XLIV.) "Men of Ardea," he said, "my ancient friends, and of late my fellow citizens, since your goodness would have it so and my own fortune has made it necessary, let none of you suppose me to have come forward in forgetfulness of my condition; but circumstances and our common peril oblige every man at this crisis to contribute what he can to the general defense. And when shall I show gratitude for your great kindnesses to me, if I am backward now? Or when shall you have need of me, if not in war? 'Twas by this art that I stood secure in my native City: unbeaten in war, I was driven out in time of peace by the thankless citizens. But you, men of Ardea, have now an opportunity of requiting the Roman People for such great benefits as you yourselves are mindful of, nor need I cast up to you things which you remember; and your city has an opportunity to win from our common enemy great renown in war. That people now drawing near in loose array has been endowed by nature with bodily size and courage, great indeed but vacillating; which is the reason that to every conflict they bring more terror than strength. This may be seen in their defeat of the Romans. They captured the City, which lay wide open; but a handful of men in the Citadel and the Capitol are holding them at bay; already, oppressed by the tedium of the siege, they are departing and roaming aimlessly through the country-side. They greedily gorge themselves with food and wine, and when night approaches they erect no rampart, and without pickets or sentries, throw themselves down anywhere beside a stream, in the manner of wild beasts. Just now success has rendered them even more careless than they are wont to be. If you have a mind to protect your city and not to suffer all this country to become Gaul, arm yourselves in the first watch, and follow me in force, not to a battle but a massacre. If I do not deliver them up to you fast asleep, to be butchered like cattle, I am ready to submit at Ardea to the same fate that I endured at Rome."

XLV. Well-wishers and opponents were alike persuaded that there was no such warrior in those days anywhere. Breaking up the council, they supped, and waited intently for the signal. On its being given, in the silence of the early night, they presented themselves before Camillus at the gates. They had not left the city very far behind them, when they came to the camp of the Gauls, unguarded, just as he had prophesied, and open on every side, and, giving a loud cheer, rushed upon it. There was no resistance anywhere: the whole place was a shambles, where unarmed men, relaxed in sleep, were slaughtered. Those, however, who were farthest off were frightened from the places where they lay, and ignorant of the nature of the attack or its source, fled panic-stricken, and some ran unawares straight into the enemy. The most of them were carried into the territory of Antium, where they wandered about until the towns-people sallied out and cut them off.

A similar overthrow was experienced, in the region of Veii, by the Etruscans. So far were they from pitying a City that had been their neighbor for close upon four hundred years, and was now overwhelmed by an enemy never seen or heard of before, that they chose that time to make incursions into the lands of the Romans; and laden with spoils, even meditated an attack on Veii and its garrison, the last hope of the Roman name. The Roman soldiers had seen them, as they ranged through the fields and afterwards, gathering in a body, drove the booty off before them, and could descry their camp, which was pitched not far from Veii. This made them at first to compassionate themselves; then they were seized with resentment, which soon gave way to rage: were even the Etruscans, whom they had saved from the Gauls by incurring war themselves, to make sport of their calamities? They could hardly curb an impulse to assail them on the instant; but being restrained by the centurion Quintus Caedicius, whom they had chosen to be their commander, they postponed the affair till dark. The only thing wanting was a leader like Camillus; in all else the order followed was the same, and the same success was achieved. Indeed, under the guidance of captives who had survived the nocturnal massacre, they set out on the following night and came to another band of Etruscans, at the salt-works,[52] whom they surprised and defeated with even greater carnage; and so, rejoicing in their double victory, returned to Veii.

XLVI. At Rome meanwhile the siege was for the most part languishing and all was quiet on both sides, the Gauls being solely concerned with preventing the escape of any enemy through their lines, when suddenly a young Roman attracted the wondering admiration of fellow citizens and foes. There was an annual sacrifice to be made on the Quirinal Hill by the family of the Fabii. To celebrate it Gaius Fabius Dorsuo, in the Gabinian cincture,[53] with the sacred vessels in his hands, descended from the Capitol, passed out through the midst of the enemy's pickets, and regardless of any words or threats, proceeded to the Quirinal, where he duly accomplished all the rites. He then returned by the same way, with the like resolute countenance and gait, in the full assurance of the favor of the gods whose service not even the fear of death could cause him to neglect, and rejoined his friends on the Capitol, leaving the Gauls dumbfounded by his astonishing audacity, or perhaps even moved by religious awe, a sentiment to which that race is far from indifferent.

At Veii, all this while, they were gathering from day to day, not courage merely, but strength as well. Not only were Romans coming in from the country-side, men who had been wanderers since the defeat, or the capture of the City, but volunteers were also pouring in from Latium, that they might share in the spoils. It seemed therefore that the time was now ripe to return to their native City and wrest it from the hands of the enemy; but their strong body lacked a head. The place itself reminded men of Camillus, and there were many of the soldiers who had fought successfully under his leadership and auspices. Moreover, Caedicius declared that he would suffer neither god nor man to put an end to his authority, but, remembering his station, would himself demand the appointment of a general. With the consent of all they resolved to send for Camillus from Ardea, but not till the senate at Rome had been consulted; so modest were they in their conduct of everything, preserving the proper distinctions even in their well-nigh desperate case. It was necessary at enormous risk to pass the enemy's outposts. This an active youth named Pontius Cominus undertook to do, and supporting himself on a strip of cork, floated down the Tiber to the City. Once there, he passed by the shortest way from the bank up a cliff so steep that the enemy had neglected to guard it, to the Capitol, and being brought before the magistrates delivered to them the message from the army. Then, on the senate's resolving that the *curiate comitia* should recall Camillus from exile, and that, even as the people commanded he should straightway be appointed dictator, and the soldiers have the general they desired, the messenger returned by the same route and came in haste to Veii; whence envoys were despatched to Ardea for Camillus, and fetched him to Veii; or rather—as I prefer to believe that he did not quit Ardea until he had learnt that the law was passed, since he could not change his residence without the People's command, nor take the auspices in the army till he had been appointed dictator—the curiate law was passed and Camillus declared dictator, in his absence.

XLVII. While this was going on at Veii, the Citadel of Rome and the Capitol were in very great danger. For the Gauls had noticed the tracks of a man, where the messenger from Veii had got through, or perhaps had observed for themselves that the cliff near the shrine of Carmentis[54] afforded an easy ascent. So on a starlit night they first sent forward an unarmed man to try the way; then handing up their weapons when there was a steep place, and supporting themselves by their fellows or affording support in their turn, they pulled one another up, as the ground required, and reached the summit, in such silence that not only the sentries but even the dogs—creatures easily troubled by noises in the night—were not aroused. But they could not elude the vigilance of the geese, which, being sacred to Juno, had, notwithstanding the dearth of provisions, not been killed. This was the salvation of them all; for the geese with their gabbling and clapping of their wings woke Marcus Manlius, consul of three years before and a distinguished soldier, who, catching up his weapons and at the same time calling the rest to arms, strode past his bewildered comrades to a Gaul who had already got a foothold on the crest and dislodged him with a blow from the boss of his shield. As he slipped and fell, he overturned those who were next to him, and the others in alarm let go their weapons and grasping the rocks to which they had been clinging, were slain by Manlius. And by now the rest had come together and were assailing the invaders with javelins and stones, and presently the whole company lost their footing and were flung down headlong to destruction. Then after the din was hushed, the rest of the night—so far as their excitement would permit, when even a past peril made them nervous—was given up to sleep. At dawn the trumpet summoned the soldiers to assemble before the tribunes. Good conduct and bad had both to be requited. First Manlius was praised for his courage and presented with gifts, not only by the tribunes of the soldiers, but by agreement amongst the troops, who brought each half a pound of spelt and a gill of wine to his house, which stood in the Citadel. It is a little thing to tell, but the scarcity made it a great token of affection, since everyone robbed himself of his own sustenance and bestowed what he had subtracted from his physical necessities to do honor to one man. Then the watchmen of the cliff which the enemy had scaled without being discovered were called up. Quintus Sulpicius, the tribune, announced his intention to punish them all in the military fashion; but deterred by the cries of the soldiers, who united in throwing the blame upon a single sentinel, he spared the others. This man was guilty beyond a doubt, and was flung from the rock with the approval of all. From that time the guards on both sides were more alert: the Gauls, because it had been put about that messengers were passing between Veii and Rome, the Romans, from their recollection of the peril of the night.

XLVIII. But worse than all the evils of the blockade and the war was the famine with which both armies were afflicted. The Gauls suffered also from a pestilence, being encamped between hills on low ground, parched and heated by the conflagration, where the air was filled with ashes, as well as dust, whenever a breeze sprang up. These annoyances were intolerable to a race accustomed to damp and cold, and when, distressed by the suffocating heat, they began to sicken of diseases that spread as though the victims had been cattle, they were soon too slothful to bury their dead singly, and piling the bodies up in promiscuous heaps, they burned them, causing the place to be known from that circumstance as the Gallic Pyres.[55] A truce was afterwards made with the Romans, and the commanders allowed their soldiers to talk together. Since in these conversations the Gauls used frequently to taunt their enemies with their famished state, and call on them to yield to that necessity and surrender, the Romans are said, in order to do away with this opinion, to have cast bread down from the Capitol in many places, into the outposts of the enemy. Yet at last they could neither dissemble their hunger nor endure it any longer. The dictator was now holding a levy of his own at Ardea, and having ordered the master of the horse, Lucius Valerius, to bring up his army from Veii, was mustering and drilling a force with which he might cope with the Gauls on equal terms. But the army on the Capitol was worn out with picket duty and mounting guard; and though they had got the better of all human ills, yet was there one, and that was famine, which nature would not suffer to be overcome. Day after day they looked out to see if any relief from the dictator was at hand; but at last even hope, as well as food, beginning to fail them, and their bodies growing almost too weak to sustain their armor when they went out on picket duty, they declared that they must either surrender or ransom themselves, on whatever conditions they could make; for the Gauls were hinting very plainly that no great price would be required to induce them to raise the siege. Thereupon the senate met, and instructed the tribunes of the soldiers to arrange the terms. Then, at a conference between Quintus Sulpicius the tribune and the Gallic chieftain Brennus, the affair was settled, and a thousand pounds of gold was agreed on as the price of a people that was destined presently to rule the nations. The transaction was a foul disgrace in itself, but an insult was added thereto: the weights brought by the Gauls were dishonest, and on the tribune's objecting, the insolent Gaul added his sword to the weight, and a saying intolerable to Roman ears was heard, Woe to the conquered!

XLIX. But neither gods nor men would suffer the Romans to live ransomed. For, by some chance, before the infamous payment had been consummated, and when the gold had not yet, owing to the dispute, been all weighed out, the dictator appeared and commanded the gold to be cleared away and the Gauls to leave. They objected vehemently, and insisted on the compact; but Camillus denied the validity of that compact which, subsequently to his own appointment as dictator, an inferior magistrate had made without his authorization, and warned them to prepare for battle. His own men he ordered to throw their packs in a heap, make ready their weapons, and win their country back with iron instead of gold; having before their eyes the temples of the gods, their wives and their children, the soil of their native land, with the hideous marks of war upon it, and all that religion called upon them to defend, recover, or avenge. He then drew up his line, as well as the ground permitted, on the naturally uneven surface of the half-ruined City, and saw to it that his soldiers had every advantage in choice of position and in preparation which the art of war suggested. The Gauls were taken aback; they armed, and, with more rage than judgment, charged the Romans. But now fortune had turned; now the might of Heaven and human wisdom were engaged in the cause of Rome. Accordingly, at the first shock the Gauls were routed with as little effort as they had themselves put forth to conquer on the Allia. They afterwards fought a second, more regular engagement, eight miles out on the Gabinian Way, where they had rallied from their flight, and again the generalship and auspices of Camillus overcame them. Here the carnage was universal; their camp was taken; and not a man survived to tell of the disaster. The dictator, having recovered his country from her enemies, returned in triumph to the city; and between the rough jests uttered by the soldiers, was hailed in no unmeaning terms of praise as a Romulus and Father of his Country and a second Founder of the City.

His native City, which he had saved in war, he then indubitably saved a second time, now that peace was won, by preventing the migration to Veii: though the tribunes were more zealous for the plan than ever, now that the City lay in ashes, and the plebs were of themselves more inclined to favor it. This was the reason of his not resigning the dictatorship after his triumph, for the senate besought him not to desert the state in its hour of uncertainty.

L. His first act, in conformity with his scrupulous attention to religion, was to lay before the senate such matters as pertained to the immortal gods, and to obtain the passage of a decree that all shrines, in so far as they had been in the enemy's possession, should be restored, their boundaries established, and rites of purification celebrated, and that the duumvirs should search the Books[56] for the proper rites; that a covenant of hospitality should be entered into by the state with the people of Caere, because they had received the holy things of the Roman People and its priests, and thanks to their good offices worship of the immortal gods had not been interrupted; that Capitoline Games should be held, because Jupiter Optimus Maximus had protected his own abode and the Citadel of the Roman People in its time of danger; and that Marcus Furius the dictator should to that end constitute a board consisting of men who lived on the Capitol and the Citadel. A proposal was made, too, for propitiating the voice which was heard in the night to foretell disaster before the Gallic War, and was disregarded, and a temple was ordered to be built in the Nova Via to Aius Locutius.[57] The gold which had been carried away from the Gauls and that which had been collected from other temples during the alarm and carried into the shrine of Jupiter, since there was no clear recollection where it ought to be returned, was all adjudged to be sacred and ordered to be deposited under the throne of Jupiter. Even before this the scrupulousness of the citizens had been apparent in this connection, for when the gold in the public coffers was insufficient to make up to the Gauls the stipulated sum, they had accepted what the matrons got together, that they might not touch the sacred gold. For this a vote of thanks was given to the matrons, and they were granted the honor of having eulogies pronounced at their funerals, as in the case of the men. After these measures, which related to the gods and lay within the competence of the senate, had been enacted, then, and only then, heeding the importunity of the tribunes, who were urging the plebs unceasingly to quit their ruins and emigrate to a city ready to their hand at Veii, Camillus went up into the assembly, attended by the entire senate, and discoursed as follows:

LI. So painful to me, Quirites, are these controversies with the tribunes of the plebs, that my most bitter exile knew no other solace but this, all the time that I lived at Ardea, that I was far away from these contentions. And they are likewise the cause that though you had a thousand times recalled me by resolution of the senate and the people's vote, I intended never to return. Nor have I now been induced to do so by any change in my desires, but by the alteration in your fortunes. For the issue was this, that my countrymen should abide in their own home, not that I, at any or all costs, should be with my countrymen. Even now I would gladly stop and hold my peace, were not this too the quarrel of my country; whom to fail while life endures is in other men disgraceful, but in Camillus impious. For why did we seek to win her back, why rescue her, when besieged, from the hands of the enemy, if, now that she is recovered, we voluntarily abandon her? And although, while the Gauls were victorious and in possession of the entire City, the Capitol nevertheless and the Citadel were held by the gods and men of Rome, shall we now, when the Romans are victorious and the City is regained, desert even Citadel and Capitol? Shall our prosperity make Rome more desolate than our adversity has done? Indeed, if we had no religious rites established with the founding of the City and by tradition handed down, yet so manifest has at this time the divine purpose been in the affairs of Rome, that I for one should suppose it no longer possible for men to neglect the worship of the gods. For consider these past few years in order, with their successes and reverses; you will find that all things turned out well when we obeyed the gods, and ill when we spurned them. First of all, the war with Veii. How many years we fought, and with what painful exertion! And the end came not, until, admonished by Heaven, we drew the water off from the Alban Lake. What, I beseech you, of this strange disaster that lately overwhelmed our

City? Did it come before we disregarded the voice from Heaven that announced the approach of the Gauls? Before the law of nations was violated by our envoys? Before we, that ought to have punished their fault, had passed it by, with the same indifference towards the gods? Therefore were we conquered, led captive, and put to ransom; and suffered such punishments at the hands of gods and men as to be a warning to all the world. Adversity then turned our thoughts upon religion. We fled for refuge to the Capitol and its gods, to the seat of Jupiter Optimus Maximus; of our holy things, some, in the ruin of our fortunes, we concealed in the earth, others we removed to neighboring cities out of sight of our enemies; in the worship of the gods, albeit forsaken of gods and men, yet were we unceasing. Therefore have they given us our native land again, and victory, and our ancient renown in war that we had forfeited; and against our enemies, who, blinded with greed, broke treaty and troth in the weighing of the gold, have they turned dismay and rout and slaughter.

LII. As you consider these momentous effects upon the affairs of men, of serving the deity and of neglecting him, do you begin, Quirites, to perceive how, though yet scarce clear of the wreckage of our former guilt and calamity, we are headed towards a grievous sin? We have a City founded with due observance of auspice and augury; no corner of it is not permeated by ideas of religion and the gods; for our annual sacrifices, the days are no more fixed than are the places where they may be performed. Do you intend, Quirites, to abandon all these gods, both of state and of family? How squares your conduct with that of the noble young man Gaius Fabius in the recent siege, which the enemy beheld with no less astonishment and admiration than yourselves, when he descended from the Citadel through the missiles of the Gauls and offered the annual sacrifice of the Fabian clan on the Quirinal Hill? What? Would you suffer no interruption, even in war, of family rites, but desert the national worship and the gods of Rome in time of peace? Would you have the pontiffs and the flamens less careful of the ceremonies of the state religion than a private citizen has been of the anniversary of his clan? Perhaps someone may say that we shall either do these things at Veii, or thence dispatch our priests to Rome to do them; but of these courses neither can be followed without violation of the sacred usages. For, not to enumerate all the kinds of rites and all the gods, is it possible at the feast of Jupiter[58] that the couch should be spread elsewhere than in the Capitol? Why need I speak of Vesta's eternal fires, and the image[59] which is preserved as a pledge of empire in her temple? or of your sacred shields,[60] O Mars Gradivus and Quirinus our Father? All these holy things would you leave behind on unconsecrated ground—things coeval with the City, and some more ancient than its origin?

And mark what a difference between us and our forefathers! They handed down to us certain rites to be solemnized on the Alban Mount and in Lavinium. But if we scrupled to transfer sacred rites from hostile cities to ourselves in Rome, can we shift them without sin from Rome to Veii, city of our enemies? Recollect, I beg you, how often sacrifices are renewed because some point of antique ritual has been, through carelessness or accident, omitted. What was it, a while ago, after the portent of the Alban Lake, that brought relief to the commonwealth—then in the throes of war with Veii—if not a renewal of the sacred rites and auspices? But, more than that, like men mindful of their old religious fervor, we have both brought in foreign deities to Rome and established new ones. Queen Juno was lately conveyed from Veii and enshrined on the Aventine, and how notable was that day, for the zeal of the matrons and the throng! We have ordered a temple to be built for Aius Locutius because of the voice from heaven, clearly heard in the Nova Via. We have added Capitoline Games to the other annual festivals, and by authority of the senate have established a new college for this purpose. Was there any of these things we needed to have undertaken, if we meant to retire from Rome along with the Gauls; if we remained not voluntarily in the Capitol, through so many months of siege, but constrained by fear of the enemy? We talk of sacred rites and temples; pray, what about the priests? Do you never think what a sacrilege you are about? The Vestals surely have but that one dwelling-place, from which nothing ever caused them to remove but the capture of the City; the Flamen Dialis may not lie for a single night outside the City, without sin. Will you make these priests Veientine instead of Roman? Shall thy Virgins forsake thee, Vesta, and the Flamen, as he dwells abroad, bring, night after night, such guilt upon himself and the republic? What about the other matters nearly all of which[61] we transact, after taking auspices, within the pomerium? To what oblivion and neglect do we consign them? The curiate comitia which deals with the business of war, the centuriate comitia, where you elect the consuls and military tribunes—where can these be held, with due observance of the auspices, save in the customary places? Shall we transfer them to Veii? Or shall the people, for the sake of the comitia assemble with enormous inconvenience in this City, forsaken of god and man?

LIII. "But," you will say, "while it is obvious that everything will be polluted beyond all possibility of purification, yet the situation itself compels us to leave a City which fires and falling buildings have made a wilderness, and emigrate to Veii, where everything is untouched, nor vex the helpless commons with building here." But that this is rather a pretext than a true reason is, I think, apparent to you, Quirites, without my saying so; for you remember how, before the coming of the Gauls, when our roof trees, public and private, were unharmed and our City stood uninjured, that this same proposal was urged, of migrating to Veii.[62] And consider, tribunes, how wide is the difference between my view and yours. You think that even if then it ought not to have been done, yet now at any rate it ought; I on the contrary—and be not astonished at this, till you have heard what my meaning is, even if it had been right to migrate then, with the City all intact, should not think it right to abandon these ruins now. For then our victory would have been a reason for migrating to a captured city—a reason glorious to ourselves and our posterity; but now such a removal is for us a wretched and humiliating course, and a glory to the Gauls. For we shall not seem to have left our country as victors, but to have lost it as men vanquished. It will be thought that the rout on the Allia, the capture of the City, the blockade of the Capitol, have compelled us to forsake our family gods, and sentence ourselves to banishment and exile from that place which we were powerless to defend. Have Gauls then been able to cast Rome down; and must Romans appear unable to have raised her up? What remains, if they should presently come with fresh forces—for all agree that their numbers are scarce to be believed, and should wish to dwell in this City which they have captured and you have abandoned, but that you should suffer them? What if not the Gauls but your ancient foes the Volsci and Aequi should migrate to Rome? Should you like them to be Romans, and yourselves Veientes? Or should you not prefer this to be your wilderness, rather than the city of your enemies? For my part I do not see what could be more abominable. Are you ready to stomach these outrages, these infamies, because it irks you to build? If in all the City no house could be put up better or bigger than is the famous Hut of our Founder,[63] would it not be better to live in huts, as shepherds and rustics do, amongst our sacred monuments and our household gods, than to go forth as a nation into exile? Our ancestors, refugees and herdsmen, at a time when there was nothing in this region but forests and marshes, built quickly a new City; and are we loath, though Capitol and Citadel are untouched and the temples of the gods are standing, to rebuild what has been destroyed by fire? And what each would have done for himself, if his house had been burned, shall we refuse to do together after this common conflagration?

LIV. Or suppose that by crime or chance a fire should break out at Veii, and that the wind should spread the flames, as may easily happen, until they consume a great part of the city; are we to quit it, and seek out Fidenae, or Gabii, or any other town you like, and migrate thither? Have the soil of our native City and this land which we call our mother so slight a hold on us? Is our love of country confined to buildings and rafters? And in truth I will confess to you—though I like not to recall the wrong you did me—that as often, during my absence, as I thought of my native place, all these objects came into my mind: the hills and the fields and the Tiber and the region familiar to my eyes, and this sky beneath which I had been born and reared. And I wish these things may rather move you now with love, Quirites, to make you abide in your own home, than afterwards, when you have left it, torment you with vain regrets. Not without cause did gods and men select this place for establishing our City—with its healthful hills; its convenient river, by which crops may be floated down from the midland regions and foreign commodities brought up; its sea, near enough for use, yet not exposing us, by too great propinquity, to peril from foreign fleets; a situation in the heart of Italy—a spot, in short, of a nature uniquely adapted for the expansion of a city. This is proved by the very greatness of so new a place. It is now, Quirites, in its three hundred and sixty-fifth year. Amongst all these ancient nations you have for so long a time been waging wars; and all this while—to say nothing of single cities—neither the Volsci joined with the Aequi, and all their powerful towns, nor all Etruria, with its enormous strength on land and water, and its occupancy of the entire breadth of Italy from sea to sea, has been a match for you in war. Since this is so, what a plague is the reason why you that have experienced these things should experiment with others? Granting that your valor may go elsewhere, yet surely the fortune of this place could not be taken along! Here is the Capitol, where men were told, when of old they discovered there a human head, that in that place should be the head of the world and the seat of empire; here, when the Capitol was being cleared with augural rites, Juventas and Terminus, to the vast joy of your fathers, refused to be removed; here are Vesta's fires, here the shields that were sent down from heaven, here are all the gods propitious, if you remain.

LV. The speech of Camillus is said to have moved them, particularly where he touched upon religion; but the doubtful issue was resolved by a word that was let fall in the nick of time. It was while the senate, a little later, was deliberating about these matters in the Curia Hostilia; some cohorts returning from guard-duty were marching through the Forum, and as they came to the Comitium a centurion cried out, "Standard-bearer, fix your ensign; here will be our best place to remain." Hearing this sentence the senators came out from the Curia and shouted their acceptance of the omen, and the commons gathering round them signified approval. The bill was then rejected, and people began in a random fashion to rebuild the City. The state supplied tiles, and granted everybody the right to quarry stone and to hew timber where he liked, after giving security for the completion of the structures within that year. In their haste men were careless about making straight the streets, and paying no attention to their own and others' rights, built on the vacant spaces. This is the reason that the ancient sewers, which were at first conducted through the public ways, at present frequently run under private dwellings, and the appearance of the City is like one where the ground has been appropriated rather than divided.

Summary of Book V

At the siege of Veii winter quarters were constructed for the soldiers. This, being a new departure, stirred the ire of the tribunes of the plebs, who complained that the plebs were given no rest from warfare even in winter. The cavalry began then for the first time to serve on their own mounts. An inundation from the Alban Lake having occurred, a soothsayer was captured from the enemy that he might explain it. Furius Camillus the dictator captured Veii in a ten years' siege, transferred to Rome the image of Juno, and sent a tithe of the spoils to Apollo at Delphi. When the same man was besieging the Falisci as military tribune, he restored to their parents the sons of the enemy who had been betrayed, whereupon the Falisci surrendered and he obtained the victory by his justice. On the death of one of the censors, Gaius Julius, Marcus Cornelius was chosen to fill out his term, but this was never afterwards done because in that five-year period Rome was taken. Furius Camillus, having been cited for trial by Lucius Apuleius, a tribune of the plebs, went into exile. When the Gallic Senones were besieging Clusium and the envoys sent by the senate to arrange a peace between them and the Clusini fought in the army of the Clusini, the Senones were angered and marched to the attack of Rome. Defeating the Romans on the Allia they captured the City, all but the Capitol, in which the Romans of fighting age had taken refuge, and slew the elders, who, dressed in the insignia of the offices which they had held, were sitting in the vestibules of their houses. And when, climbing up on the other side of the Capitol, they had already come out on the top of it, they were betrayed by the gabbling of geese and—chiefly by the efforts of Marcus Manlius—were flung down. Later the Romans were reduced so low by hunger as to offer a thousand pounds of gold and with this price to purchase an end of the siege. Furius Camillus, having been appointed dictator in his absence, came up with his army in the midst of this very conference about the terms of peace, and six months after their coming drove out the Gauls from Rome and cut them to pieces. Men said that they ought to remove to Veii because the City had been burned and overthrown, but this counsel was rejected, at the instance of Camillus. The people were moved also by the omen of certain words that a centurion was heard to utter, when having come into the Forum he said to his company: "Halt, soldiers, we shall do well to stop here." A temple was erected to Jupiter Capitolinus, because a voice had been heard before the capture of the City, which declared that the Gauls were coming.

ENDNOTES

INTRODUCTION

[1] Liv X. ii. There were many living in his own day, Livy says, who had seen the beaks of the ships captured from Cleonymus, which were preserved as trophies in the temple of Juno.

[2] Martial, XIV. cxliii., speaks of the thickness of Patavian tunics.

[3] Strabo. III. clxix. and V. ccxiii.; *cf.* Nissen, *Italische Landeskunde,* 2, p. 220.

[4] Plin *Epist.* I. xiv. 6, says of a young protégé: "His maternal grandmother is Sarrana Procula, from the municipality of Patavium. You know the manners of the place; yet Serrana is a pattern of strictness even to the Patavians."

[5] e.g., I. iv. 5; I. viii. 5; I. xxvi. 13.

[6] It could not well have been earlier than 27, for in I. xix. 3 and IV. xx. 7 Octavian is mentioned with the title of Augustus, which the senate only conferred on him in January of that year. Nor may we put the date much later, for in mentioning the occasions on which the temple of Janus had been closed (I. xix. 3) Livy has nothing to say of the second of the two closings which took place in his own life-time,—namely that of 25 BC.

[7] Liv. IV. xx. 7.

[8] Sen. *Epist.* 100. 9.

[9] Quint, X. i. 39 (*cf.* II. v. 20).

[10] Quint, VIII. ii. 18.

[11] Sen. *Controv.* IX. i. 14.

[12] *Ibid.* IX. ii. 26.

[13] Schanz, *Geschichte der römischen Litteratur,* ii³. 1, p. 419.

[14] *C.I.L.* v. 2975 (= Dessau, *Inscriptiones Latinae Selectae,* 2919): T Livius C. f. sibi et / suis / T. Livio T. f. Frisco f., / T. Livio T. f. Longo f., / Cassiae Sex. f. Primae / uxori.

[15] Sen. *Controv.* x. *praef.* 2.

[16] It is just possible that the conversation with Augustus mentioned in IV. xx. 7 took place at sometime after the original publication of that book, and that the reference was inserted later.

[17] Suet. *Claud.* xli.

[18] Tacitus, *Ann,* IV. xxxiv., describing the trial of Cremutius Cordus for lèse-majesté on the ground that he had published annals in which he praised Brutus and styled Cassius the "last of the Romans," makes Cremutius say in his defense: "Titus Livius, preeminent for eloquence and candor, so lauded Pompey that Augustus called him a Pompeian; yet it made no difference in their friendship."

[19] Sen. *Nat. Quaest.* V. xviii. 4.

[20] Livy once refers to his work as "my annals" (*in meos annales,* XLIII. xiii. 2), and Pliny, *N.H praef.* 16, speaks of a certain volume of Livy's "histories," but these are merely generic names.

[21] The *Periocha* of Book CXLII. ends with these events, but the mention of Varus, which is found in only one MS, is generally regarded as a late addition. Its genuineness is, however, upheld by Rossbach, in his edition, *ad loc.*

[22] Plin. *l.c.*

[23] *Geschichte der römischen* Litteratur, ii^3. 1, p. 421.

[24] Books XLI.–XLV. contain many lacunae.

[25] Thus translated by Professor Duff:
> In vellum small huge Livy now is dressed;
> My bookshelves could not hold him uncompressed.

[26] See Schanz, *op. cit.* ii^3. 1, pp. 425–428. H. A. Sanders, "The Lost Epitome of Livy" (in *Roman Historical Sources and Institutions,* p. 257), makes the interesting suggestion that it may have been written by Livy's son.

[27] See e.g., the last sentence of *Per.* II., p. 438.

[28] Schanz, p. 425.

[29] Iulii Obsequentis *Ab Anno Urbis Conditae DV Prodigiorum Liber.*

[30] Schanz, *Röm. Lit.* iv^2. 1, p. 85.

[31] See his edition, p. xxxiii.

[32] In another passage (XLIII. xiii. 2) Livy tells us that when he is writing of old-world things his spirit somehow becomes old-fashioned.

[33] Plin. *Ep.* II. iii. 8.

[34] Sen, *Suas,* vi. 22.

[35] *Agric.* x. and the passage already quoted from the *Annals* (IV. xxxiv.).

[36] Quint. *Inst. Or.* X. i. 101. There are some 400 of these inserted speeches in the extant text, some consisting of only a few lines, while others run to a length of several pages. Under Domitian a certain Mettius Pompusius made a collection of speeches by kings and generals which he took from Livy (Suet. *Dom.* x. 3).

[37] Suet. *Calig.* xxxiv. (*cf.* Schanz, p. 439.)

[38] Quint. *Inst. Or.* VIII. iii. 53.

[39] *Ibid.* X. i. 32.

[40] *Ibid.* VIII. i. 3. Pollio was also severe upon Caesar, Cicero, Catullus and Sallust!

[41] Servius on Virg. *Aen.* x. 388, Schanz, IV². i. p. 20.

[42] Hertz, *Frag.* 12 (in his edition of Livy).

[43] *Inferno,* xxviii. 12.

[44] Born in Rome, 1407.

[45] *Criticisms and Elucidations of Catullus,* London, 1905², p. 232.

[46] See the Introduction to his *Roman History.* I have taken most of the material for this paragraph from Schanz, pp. 438–441.

[47] Wachsmuth, *Einleitung in das Studium der alten Geschichte,* p. 591. Wachsmuth says: "No one even now can escape the magic of his enthralling narrative, and to his countrymen, whether contemporary or of a later generation, his style must have been absolutely fascinating. We are not surprised that Latin-speaking mankind in the time of the Empire saw the ancient history of Rome almost exclusively through the eyes of Livy."

[48] Quint. *Inst. Or.* X. i. 39; Sen. *Suas.* vi. 17 and 22.

[49] H. D. Naylor, *Latin and English Idiom,* p. 6, says: "If I were asked 'What is *the* great feature of Livy's style?' I would boldly answer: 'His brilliant use of order.'"

[50] Norden, *Antike Kunstprosa* i., p. 235.

[51] *Quint. Inst. Or. X. i. 31. Historia . . . . . est . . . proxima poetis et quodam modo carmen solutum.*

[52] Taine says: *"On ne trouve pas [chez Tite Live] l'amour infatigable de la science complète et de la vérité absolue. Il n'en a que le goût; il n'en a pas la passion"* (*Essai sur Tite Live,* p. 64).

[53] Liv. VI. i. 2.

[54] Liv. XXVII. xxxvii. 13.

[55] Dion. Hal. *Antiq. Rom.* IV. xxvi. and VIII. xxvii. Dionysius and Livy worked independently of each other, though they used common sources.

[56] A. Klotz, "Zu den Quellen der 4ten und 5ten Dekade des Livius" in *Hermes,* 1. (1915), pp. 482 and 536.

[57] He composed a comprehensive chronicle of Roman events in seven books, written in Latin.

[58] This work, also in seven books, beginning with the Aeneas-legend and coming down to the year of the author's death, 149 BC, should have been of the greatest use to Livy.

[59] Polybius was born about 210 BC, in Megalopolis, where he died at the age of 82. His great philosophical history of the Romans, from the outbreak of the Second Punic War to the fall of Corinth, in 146 BC, contained forty books. Only I.–V. are extant in their entirety, but we have extracts from VI.–XVIII., and some fragments of xix.–xl.

[60] Written after the death of C. Gracchus, in 121 BC.

[61] Claudius wrote of the period from the Gallic invasion to his own times, the Sullan age. His work had not fewer than 23 books.

[62] A. Klotz, *op. cit.,* p. 533.

⁶³ Quint. *Inst. Or.* X. i. 31: Plin. *Ep.* V. viii. 9: Cic. *De Orat.* ii. 59.

⁶⁴ See Mr. Duffs excellent remarks in the finely appreciative chapter on Livy in his *Literary History of Rome.*

BOOK I

¹ Some scholars take *rem* to mean "the practice," *sc.* of expressing confidence in one's ability.

² Livy refers to the animosities inevitably aroused by writers who dealt with such thorny subjects as the civil wars, during the lifetime of many who had taken part in them.

³ The metaphor is from a decaying building.

⁴ The monument Livy means is the body of a nation's achievements (*cf. res* in § 1), the "history" of a nation, in that objective sense of the word. This he likens to a monument of stone on which men's deeds are recorded.

⁵ See the *Iliad*, v. 576.

⁶ This, in a nutshell, is the form of the legend on which Virgil based Books vii.–xii. of the *Aeneid.*

⁷ Virgil makes Jupiter grant, as a favor to Juno, that the Trojan name shall be sunk in the Latin (*Aen.* xii. 835).

⁸ *Indiges* means "of or belonging to a certain place" (Fowler, *Fest.* p. 192). Dion. Hal. i. 64, says that the Latins made a shrine to Aeneas with an inscription in which he was called πατὴ ρ χθόνιος (*Pater Indiges*). He was also called *Deus Indiges* and *Aeneas Indiges.*

⁹ The word *lupa* was sometimes used in the sense of "courtesan."

¹⁰ The derivation here given is fanciful. The word is probably akin to *palus*, "pale," and meant a "fenced place."

¹¹ A form of the legend preserved by Dion. Hal. i. 87, and Ovid, *Fasti,* iv. 843, names Celer, whom Romulus had put in charge of the rising wall, as the slayer of Remus.

¹² Evander is said to have invented the Roman alphabet.

¹³ For the story of Cacus and the origin of the Ara Maxima see also Virgil, *Aen.* viii. 182–279; Prop. iv. 9; Ovid, *Fasti,* i. 543–586.

¹⁴ The lictors carried axes in bundles of rods, in readiness to execute the king's sentence of scourging and decapitation.

¹⁵ i.e., the Capitoline.

¹⁶ As being heads of clans, *patres familiarum.*

¹⁷ The Consualia was a harvest festival, held on August 21. Consus, the true name of the god, is from *condere*, "to store up." From the association of the festival with horses came the later identification of the god with *Neptunus Equester.* See Fowler, *Fest.* pp. 206–9.

¹⁸ Plutarch, *Rom.* 15, also gives the story, and observes that the Romans used "Talasius" as the Greeks did "Hymenaeus." See also Catullus, lxi. 134 .

[19] Jupiter Feretrius (etymology unknown) was the pure Italian Jupiter, whose worship was later overshadowed by the Etruscan god of the great temple on the Capitol. See Fowler, *Fest.* p. 229.

[20] The other instances were the victories of Cossus over Tolumnius, king of Veii (iv. 20), and of Marcellus over Viridomarus, king of the Insubrian Gauls. Propertius tells the three stories in iv. 10.

[21] As a vestal, she had to draw water from the spring of the Camenae.

[22] According to Dion. Hal. ii. 38, this was the version given by L. Calpurnius Piso. Propertius wrote the best of his aetiological poems (iv. 5) about Tarpeia.

[23] *Quirites* probably comes not from Cures, nor (as Varro thought) from the Sabine word *quiris* (*curis*), "spear," but from *curia* (*cf.* next section); it would then mean "wardsmen."

[24] For another explanation of the name see vii. 6. Varro, *L. L.* v. 14 ff., assigns this version of the story to Piso, the other to Procilius, adding a third, on the authority of Cornelius and Lutatius, to the effect that the Lacus Curtius was a place which had been struck by lightning in the consulship of a Curtius.

[25] The *curia* was a political unit the members of which had certain religious rites in common.

[26] All three names are obscure, but it is not improbable that they represent a Roman, a Sabine, and an Etruscan element in the population.

[27] Literally, "the Swift."

[28] For the deification *cf.* Cic. *de Rep.* ii. 17; Dion. Hal. ii. 56; Plut. *Rom.* xxvii. Ovid also tells the story in *Fasti,* ii. 49 ff., and *Met.* xiv. 806 ff.

[29] The Romans regularly prayed with the head cloaked.

[30] It was about 530 BC when Pythagoras settled in Croton.

[31] This was evidently written before 25 BC, when the temple was again closed by Augustus. But it was not written before 27, for it was not until that year that the title of Augustus was conferred upon the emperor. We thus arrive at an approximate date for the beginning of Livy's history.

[32] The original *ancile* was a shield fabled to have fallen from heaven. To lessen the chance of its being stolen, eleven others were made exactly like it. It was of a peculiar shape, something like a violin. See Fowler, *Fest.* p. 42.

[33] There were six of these shrines or chapels in each of the four regions of the Servian city. A procession made the round of the *Argei* on March 17; and on May 15 rush puppets, also called *Argei,* and probably correspond-ing to the shrines in number, were thrown into the Tiber by the Vestal Virgins, in the presence of the priestess of Jupiter, who was dressed in mourning. The meaning of both ceremonies is obscure. See Fowler, *Fest.* pp. 54 and 111.

[34] The *fetiales* (related to *facio,* "do") were a college of priests whose duties were to represent the state in declaring war, making peace, entering

into treaties, etc. The *pater patratus* (from *patro,* "accomplish" or "bring about") was the spokesman of the deputation.

35 By taking it upon himself to punish his sister, Horatius had usurped a function of the state, and so was guilty of treason.

36 I have adopted the view of Oldfather (*T.A.P.A.* xxxix. pp. 49 ff.) that neither hanging nor crucifixion is meant, but that the culprit was fastened to the tree and scourged to death.

37 The name of the place which commemorated the spoils reflects the tradition, rejected above by Livy, that the Horatii were Albans, the Curiatii Romans.

38 These were the so-called *Collini,* or *Agonales,* and were associated with Quirinus, as the *Palatini* (chap. xx.) were with Mars Gradivus. See also v. lii. 7.

39 Each family had its *lar,* a special deity who protected the household, and its *penates,* guardians of the *penus* (the family store of provisions).

40 When Clodius was murdered, in 52 BC, the mob burnt his body in the Curia Hostilia, which caught fire and was destroyed.

41 Each squadron contained thirty men. The total number was, therefore, the same as that of the three centuries of Romulus.

42 i.e., "Guileful Wood."

43 The institution of the fetials was ascribed in chap. xxiv. to Tullus (so also Cic. *Rep.* ii. 31). Livy is here following another authority, without taking the trouble to remove the discrepancy. Other writers (Dion. ii 72; Plut. *Numa* xii.) credit Numa with the institution.

44 This was the famous Pons Sublicius, "Pile Bridge," made of wood, without metal of any sort.

45 This prison, *the* Carcer, may still be seen at the foot of the Capitoline, between the Temple of Concord and the Curia. It is thought to be as old as any structure in Rome. It was used as a place of detention and execution for condemned criminals.

46 i.e., "Necessitous."

47 The senate had doubtless shown its disapproval of the accession of Tarquinius, who now sought to render its opposition futile by doubling the membership and appointing none but his own supporters.

48 Perhaps a reference to the hundred years' truce with Romulus (xv. 5), for Livy has not mentioned any war with Veii in the interval, though one is implied in the statement (xxxiii. 9) that the Veientes surrendered the Maesian Forest, in the reign of Ancus.

49 The organization now to be described was primarily designed to increase the fighting strength of Rome. Formerly the right to bear arms had belonged solely to the patricians. Now plebeians were to be given a place in the army, which was to be reclassified according to every man's property, i.e., his ability to provide himself a more or less complete equipment for the field. See Dion. Hal. iv. 16–21; Cic. *Rep.* ii. 39.

[50] Capital, not income. The *as* was originally a rod of copper a foot long and divided into twelve inches (*unciae*). Sometime during the regal period weight was substituted for measure in appraising the *as,* and it began to be stamped with the figure of an ox, which was the source of the Latin name for money, viz. *pecunia.* From being a full pound the *as* was gradually reduced, till, in the Second Punic War, it came to weigh only one ounce. What its value may have been in the time of Servius is a highly speculative question. See the note in the edition of Book I. by H. J. Edwards (pp. 179 ff.).

[51] *Tributum* comes from *tribus* (not *vice versa,* as Livy has it), which meant originally "third part," but lost the numerical force and became simply "part," "district," like the French "*quartier,*" which Walde compares.

[52] Dion. iv. 13, and Strabo, v. 3, 7, make Servius the first to include the Esquiline in the City. Livy appears to have thought of him as merely increasing the extent of that district. Conway and Walters adopt *O*'s *Viminalemque, Viminalem,* and Gronov's *Esquiliis,* thus reconciling Livy with Dion and Strabo.

[53] *Pomerium* at first meant the boundary-line itself, then the strip of land left free within the wall, and finally was loosely used of the strip on both sides of the wall.

[54] The reference is to the stories of Atreus and Oedipus.

[55] i.e., causes affecting the *caput* (which might mean either "life" or "civic rights") of the accused.

[56] Circe bore to Ulysses a son, Telegonus, who founded Tusculum.

[57] In the account of this treaty at xxiv. 3 no Alban colonies are mentioned, nor do we know of any. Conway and Walters, therefore, keep *colonis* of the MSS, but we should rather expect *civibus* in this context.

[58] A Roman maniple was divided into halves, and each half was combined with the half of a Latin maniple, similarly divided, to form a new unit. The maniples were not, strictly speaking, doubled.

[59] As Livy gives the sum in talents, it has been suggested that he may here be following Fabius Pictor, whose history was written in Greek. The Euboic talent was worth roughly £220 or $1,060.

[60] i.e., the Capitoline. So Propertius calls the Capitoline Jupiter "Tarpeius Pater" (IV. i. 7).

[61] Literally "Dullard."

[62] A similar scene is imagined by Tibullus, I. iii. 83 ff.

[63] For the *Celeres,* see XV. 8 and note. H. J. Edwards (*ad loc.*) thinks that the office comprised both military and civil functions—the command of the cavalry (*cf.* the *Magister Equitum* in republican times) and the presidency (as deputy of the king) of comitia and senate.

[64] The "consuls" as they were called from the time of the Decemvirate, were originally designated "praetors"; Livy is anachronistic. The "centuriate comitia" was the assembly of the people by centuries, as

classified by Servius, primarily for military ends. It is more likely that Lucretius presided over the election in the capacity of interrex (to which office Dion. iv. 84 says Lucretius was appointed by Brutus) than in that of prefect.

SUMMARY OF BOOK I

[1] According to Livy (liv. 10), Gabii was not sacked, but passed peacefully into the hands of Tarquinius. See critical note.

[2] In Livy (lv. 3) Juventa is not mentioned, and Termo appears in the form Terminus.

[3] Livy (lx. 3) says 244 years.

[4] i.e., Ancus.

BOOK II

[1] This statement is too sweeping, for Livy nowhere attributes any enlargement of the City to Numa.

[2] Later any senator might be called *pater conscriptus,* and it is possible that Livy and Festus (p. 254 m) were misled in supposing that originally the *patres* were one class of senators and the *conscripti* another. See Conway's note.

[3] Livy appears to have assumed that the new senators were plebeians, but this is almost certainly wrong. The first definite notice of a plebeian senator occurs at V. xii. 11 (400 BC).

[4] Ordinarily the Roman farmer cut the stalk close to the ear, but this time it was cut near the ground, that the crop might be completely destroyed.

[5] A staff with which the slave was touched in the ceremony of manumission. The etymology suggested in the next sentence is wrong; *Vindicius,* like *vindicta,* is derived from *vindex.*

[6] Bundles of rods which symbolized the magistrate's authority to scourge, as the axes (*secures*) did his right to put to death.

[7] Dion. Hal. (v. 21) says that Valerius was consul for the *third* time, and Horatius for the second time, when the war with Porsinna came. Mommsen thought the MSS had lost these names, and proposed to insert them directly after those in the text. But in chap. xi. 8, T. Lucretius is still the colleague of Valerius.

[8] Where there was a gate called *Porta Caelimontana,* south of the *Porta Esquilina.*

[9] From the standpoint of the inhabitants of the city, looking eastward from the walls.

[10] i.e., "Left-handed."

[11] By 241 BC the number of tribes had grown to thirty-five. After this date no new tribes were added, but newly incorporated districts were assigned to one or another of the already existing tribes. Thus certain members of the Claudian Tribe lived elsewhere than in the district "across the Anio," and those who came to Rome for elections from the original seat of the tribe were called the "Old Claudian Tribe." See note in Conway's edition of this Book.

[12] Livy has nowhere told us about these hostages. In chap. xxii. 2 the same towns give the same number of hostages. Obviously he has made distinct episodes out of different versions of the same story, misled no doubt by the different dates assigned by different annalists to the affair of Pometia.

[13] Literally "under the crown," meaning a chaplet placed on the head of a captive as an indication that he was a part of the spoils.

[14] Despite the apparently conclusive victory recorded in chap. xvi. 6.

[15] But in 300 BC a *lex Valeria de provocatione* gave the people the right to appeal from the dictator.

[16] Postumius had not held the consulship, which in chap. xviii. 5 Livy stated to have been a necessary qualification for the dictatorship.

[17] Of the sons of Tarquinius, Sextus's death is mentioned in I. lx. 2 and that of Arruns in II. vi. 9. This must therefore have been Titus (I. lvi. 6).

[18] The Saturnalia proper fell on December 17, though as many as seven days came to be devoted to the popular celebration of the festival (Macrobius, I. x. 24), which was a sort of carnival. As an old Italic feast it probably originated earlier than Livy thought. See Macrobius I. viii. 1.

[19] Neither captives nor treaty were mentioned in chap. xx., and Livy seems here to be following a different authority, possibly Valerius of Antium, whom at XXXIII. x. 8 he accuses of exaggerating numbers.

[20] The word *nexus* was used (1) of one who had borrowed money by "binding" himself to work out the debt as a virtual slave of his creditor, if unable to repay the money; (2) of one so "bound" and actually serving.

[21] But it had already been razed, as we read in chap. xvii. 6—another indication that Livy is reproducing different versions of the same story (see chap. xvi. 9 and note).

[22] Mercury was the patron of trade.

[23] (1) to persuade the senate to content the people; (2) to coerce the people.

[24] That is to say, in general; from a dictator, however, there was no appeal until a later period.

[25] Apparently the Latins, perhaps after the battle of Lake Regillus (chap. xix. f.), had been denied the right to make war, save at the pleasure of the Romans.

[26] That this apparently unique distinction was actually conferred on the Valerii is confirmed by an honorary inscription (*C.I.L.* i. 284).

[27] Livy appears to have had the other tradition in mind when he wrote III. liv. 9

[28] If Menenius was a plebeian, it is improbable that he was also, as Livy rather implies, a senator. *cf.* i. 11 and note.

[29] The same apologue is found in Xenophon, *Mem.* II. iii. 18; Cicero, *Off.* III. v. 22; and St. Paul, *Cor.* I. xii. 12.

[30] In either case the number was five from the year 471 on (lviii. 1), till it was raised to ten in the year 457.

[31] A *sextans* was the sixth part of an *as,* or pound of copper.

[32] The clients were a class distinct both from the plebs and the patricians. To the latter they stood in the feudal relation of vassal to lord. They were perhaps originally citizens of conquered towns, and were recruited by manumissions and immigration.

[33] The votive games in recognition of some special service by the gods were so named.

[34] i.e., the slave who had been scourged through the circus.

[35] Livy implies that they were not the immediate successors of the consuls for 491, and in fact he seems to have omitted two sets, Q. Sulpicius Camerinus and Serg. Larcius Flavus (490), and C. Julius Iulus and P. Pinarius Rufus (489), though at III. xxxiii. 1 and V. liv. 5 he reckons in these two years. The missing names are supplied by Dion. Hal. vii. 68 and viii. 1.

[36] For another account of Coriolanus, see Dion. Hal. viii. 12 and viii. 17–56.

[37] The temple was erected in honor of both Castor and Pollux, but was commonly referred to by the name of the former alone (e.g., Cicero, *Mil.* 91). The *duumviri* were a committee of two, appointed to oversee the construction and dedication of a temple when the man who had vowed it died without accomplishing his task.

[38] For the next four years, making seven successive years in all, the Fabii were represented in the consulate.

[39] The headquarters of the consul, who was originally called praetor.

[40] The crimson *paludamentum.*

[41] A name afterwards given to the arch from the result of this expedition.

[42] This was that Fabius, according to the legend, who was to become consul ten years later! See III. x.

[43] What was the charge? Perhaps that he had failed to support the Fabii; perhaps that he had lost Janiculum by his incompetence.

[44] i.e., from his home: the Forum was lower than the residential parts of Rome.

[45] Livy mentions another instance of a conscript's objecting to serve in a rank lower than that he had previously held, in XLII. xxxiii. 3; but it does not appear that the men had any prescriptive right in the matter.

[46] It is not clear how Livy supposed that these officials had formerly been elected. Perhaps Volero merely aimed at securing by legal sanction what the state had always recognized in practice, viz. that plebeian magistrates should be chosen by none but plebeians. But this was not Livy's view, as is clear from lviii. 1.

⁴⁷ The word *templum* might be applied to any space duly marked off by augural ceremonies. Here it means the speakers' platform in the *comitium*.

⁴⁸ To *lay waste* Roman lands they must first *enter* them, and the purpose clause depends really upon this implied meaning of *vastaverant*.

⁴⁹ This was granted in recognition of unusual valor.

⁵⁰ Held in the centuriate comitia.

⁵¹ The Romans divided the night into four equal watches, beginning at sunset.

BOOK III

¹ See II. 1. 11.

² The *iustitium* also involved the closing of shops and a general suspension of business.

³ *Fusius* is in fact only an earlier form of *Furius*. By 300 BC intervocalic *s* had developed into *r*. Livy is puzzled by the same thing in chap. viii.

⁴ The *ultimum senatus consultum* conferred dictatorial powers on the consul, and amounted to declaring a state of martial law.

⁵ The *porta decumana* was normally in the west wall, in these wars usually farthest from the enemy, hence its use in this surprise attack.

⁶ The official year began at various times in different periods, until, in 153 BC, the 1st of January was adopted.

⁷ The plebeian aedileship had been created at the same time as the plebeian tribuneship, but was not mentioned by Livy at II. xxxiii. 2.

⁸ Each of the thirty wards, or *curiae* (an account of their origin is given at I. xiii. 6), had a priest called a *curio,* to preside over its religious ceremonies. These thirty *curiones* were themselves under the presidency of a *curio maximus.*

⁹ See note on chap. iv. § 1.

¹⁰ Terentilius probably aimed at restricting the power of the patricians by a codification of *all* the laws, not merely those, as Livy seems to think, which limited the authority of the consuls. The Fasti refer to the similar board actually created ten years later, as *decemviri consulari imperio legibus scribundis* ("decemvirs with consular authority for writing the laws"), and Livy has perhaps misunderstood some such phrase in the annalist he was here following.

¹¹ The ovation was a lesser triumph, granted for a comparatively easy or bloodless victory.

¹² There was required to be an interval of twenty-four days (*trinum nundinum*) between meetings of the comitia.

¹³ For the purpose of forming by centuries, in order to vote.

¹⁴ A capital charge if proven carried with it loss of *caput,* i.e., "the full legal status of a Roman citizen." (See Greenidge, *Roman Public Life,* p. 31.)

From chap. xii. § 6, it appears that a sentence of banishment rather than death was anticipated in the present instance.

[15] A populous street lying in the hollow between the Quirinal and the Viminal on the one hand, and the Esquiline on the other.

[16] The tribunes had been created to protect plebeians against the oppression of the nobles, but there were several other occasions when patricians did not disdain to avail themselves of their help. See II. lvi. 5; IX. xxvi. 16.

[17] Verginius wished to try Caeso *in absentia*, but his colleagues, by adjourning the meeting, acquiesced in the view that a defendant had the right to avoid conviction by going into voluntary exile. In similar cases the tribes subsequently passed a resolution the effect of which was to give to this voluntary exile the binding force of a legal sentence (XXV. iv. 9; XXVI. iii. 12).

[18] The *Trastevere* was not incorporated in the City till Augustus made of it his fourteenth region.

[19] The Terentilian Law. See chap. ix.

[20] Livy implies that Coriolanus and Caeso were not the only citizens who had been compelled to leave Rome during the quarrels between senate and plebs.

[21] Caeso had taken refuge with the Etruscans (chap. xiii. § 8).

[22] The word *templum* means any place marked off with augural rites. The *templum* meant here is the Comitium.

[23] Publius Valerius, son of Volesus (I. lviii. 6), afterwards called Publicola (II. viii. 1).

[24] Cf. the funeral of his father (II. xvi. 7), and of Menenius Agrippa (II. xxxiii. 11).

[25] i.e., over their law.

[26] The soldiers ordinarily carried a ration of corn.

[27] Unidentified. Dion. Hal., X. xxi., calls the town Algidum.

[28] Livy seems here to have accepted the account of the late annalists which he had suspected in chap. xxiii. 7. An extant inscription (*C.I.L.* xv. 44) commemorating the triumph of Fabius over the Aequi and Volsci and that of Cornelius over the Antiates shows that his suspicion was unfounded.

[29] Livy here assumes that Caeso is dead, and possibly thinks of him as having perished with Herdonius.

[30] Strictly speaking, a trifle less than three acres, since the *iugerum* contained only 28,800 square feet.

[31] The Roman soldier usually carried three or four stakes, to use in making a palisade.

[32] Livy thinks of Cincinnatus as removing (or perhaps only suspending) Minucius from the consulship, in virtue of his superior authority. In 509 BC (II. ii. 7 ff.) Lucius Tarquinius had been compelled to resign by his colleague Brutus and other leading men.

[33] The first recorded instance of the bestowal of citizenship in requital of service done the state.

[34] They had not been able to pass the *Lex Terentilia.*

[35] The lowest class, paying no *tributum,* had no representation.

[36] See chap. ix. § 5 and note. Apparently the codification contemplated by Terentilius was to have been in the hands of a plebeian board.

[37] The reference is especially to the law establishing the tribunate (II. xxxiii. 1). The violation of a *sacrata lex* entailed outlawry on the offender.

[38] A circumstance which Livy did not notice in chap. xxxii.

[39] This sentence and the reference to Claudius's years and honor in chap. xxxiii. § 3 seem inapplicable to a young man, and it is probable that the decemvir was, in reality, the consul of 471 BC (see II. lvi. 5), not the nephew of C. Claudius, as Livy thought (chap. xxxv. § 9), which would make him the *son* of the consul of 471.

[40] "Fasces" is here equivalent to "lictors."

[41] This sentence supports Mommsen's view that the new legislation was intended originally to *substitute* for tribunician intercession a limitation of the consular power by written law.

[42] A *nundinum* contained 8 days. The name (novem = nine) came from the Roman way of counting the Sunday, as it were, with the old week, as well as the new.

[43] *Coitio* is an understanding between two candidates whereby the stronger transfers a part of his support to the weaker, in order to defeat a third candidate.

[44] Dion. Hal. XI. xxiii. says that Poetelius, Duillius, and Oppius were plebeians, as were probably Antonius and Rabuleius as well. But Livy tells us (IV. iii. 17) that they were all patricians.

[45] May 15th.

[46] Rome enjoyed no hegemony over Sabines and Aequians at this time, though Livy evidently thinks she did.

[47] Livy did not mention Horatius in his account of the expulsion of the kings, but he is named by Dion. Hal. IV. lxxxv. Here Livy and Dion. Hal. (XI. v), are in agreement, and are perhaps following the account of Licinius Macer.

[48] See II. ii. 1.

[49] Apparently the decemvirs were technically within their rights in claiming that they held office until the tables were ratified by popular vote.

[50] He pretended concern for Valerius, but was really prompted by a wish to further the ends of Appius, by preventing an undesirable test of men's temper.

[51] Surnamed Dentatus, and known, according to Aulus Gellius (II. xi.) as the Roman Achilles. Dion. Hal. (XI. xxv. f.) tells the story at greater length and somewhat differently.

[52] Dion. Hal. (XL. iv) mentions Icilius and Numitorius as offering to be

Verginia's *vindices,* i.e., to put in a claim to interim custody of the girl, till the suit determining her status should be decided.

53 Appius argued that Verginia was either the slave of his client or under her father's control, and in neither case free, so that an action for recovering her freedom did not lie, and it was merely a question of the title between Verginius and Marcus Claudius.

54 Some take *avus* literally, as "grandfather." See chap. liv. 11, note.

55 Livy doubtless means the crime of Appius rather than the justifiable though shocking deed of Verginius (see chap. xlviii. § 7, and chap. l. § 5).

56 Viz. by the senate and decemvirs.

57 *Comitia* is here used untechnically of the extemporized election called by Verginius.

58 Asconius (ed. Clark, p. 77) commenting on Cicero's speech *Pro Cornelio de Maiestate* (which states that the plebs on this occasion "elected ten plebeian tribunes, through the instrumentality of the pontifex, because there was no magistrate") gives the name of the *pontifex maximum* as M. Papirius. This is the first time that Livy has mentioned the *pontifex maximus,* thus implying the existence of a *college* of pontiffs. See IV. xliv.

59 *Avunculus* means properly "uncle," but sometimes "great-uncle," as I have here translated it, taking it to refer to the P. Numitorius who in chap xlv. § 4 is called *puellae avus.*

60 i.e., the plebeian aediles, two in number, elected by the plebeians to assist the tribunes, as the quaestors did the consuls, and take charge of the archives of the plebs, kept in the temple of Ceres (see 13).

61 These *decemviri stlitibus iudicandis* judged cases involving liberty or citizenship.

62 The legal experts seem to have held that there was a distinction between the status of the tribunes and that of the aediles based on the belief that the former had been given *sacrosanctitas* at the time their office and that of the aediles was established, and that any violation of their persons automatically made the violator an outlaw (*sacer*); whereas it was necessary for an aedile to bring suit against the higher magistrate and convict him of the violation, before the man became *sacer.*

63 Verginius did not mean to deprive Appius of the right to speak eventually in his own defense, as we see in chap. lvii. § 6, but merely to abridge the preliminary hearing. He therefore proposed a *sponsio (cf.* chap. xxiv. § 5) to determine the guilt or innocence of Appius on one essential point.

64 The Twelve Tables.

65 And the Volsci, apparently, see chap. lx. § 1.

66 It was not the last time, however (*cf.* VII. xvii. 9). Sometimes the consul triumphed without the authorization of either senate or plebs (X. xxxvii. 8), in which case the ceremony took place on the Alban Mount; sometimes by virtue of a plebiscite confirmed by resolution of the senate (IV. xx. 1). But unless granted by the senate the triumph was paid for by the victorious consuls, instead of by the state.

⁶⁷ More accurately "fourteen," since the reference is to the five whose election Duillius recognized, together with the nine incumbents who claimed re-election.

⁶⁸ The *lex sacrata* (II. xxxiii. 1) denied patricians access to the tribunate, but apparently there was at this time a disposition to wink at their co-optation. Tarpeius and Aternius had been consuls in 454 BC.

⁶⁹ When they co-opted patricians.

⁷⁰ Alluding to the wolf that suckled Romulus and Remus.

⁷¹ On the Latin Way.

⁷² Livy is thinking chiefly of Quinctius. From § 10 it appears that Agrippa's victory came later.

SUMMARY OF BOOK III

¹ Livy III. iii. 9 gives the numbers as 104,714. Apparently there has been a mistake in copying the Periochae due to the confusion of CIIII and VIII.

BOOK IV

¹ This is Livy's first mention of Verrugo, which was situated on a steep hill in the Trerus valley.

² The right to ascertain the will of the gods by auspices was claimed as an exclusively patrician prerogative. *Cf.* chap. vi. § 1.

³ This is inaccurate. We see from chap. i. § 2 that the suggestion was that one of the consuls *might* be (not *should* be) a plebeian.

⁴ *Dies fasti* were the days on which it was lawful to pronounce judgment. *Fasti* often means, as here, the calendar kept by the pontiffs on which such days were marked. It was not until 304 BC, when Cn. Flavius posted a list of them in the Forum (IX. xlvi. 5), that the plebeians could know with certainty when they fell.

⁵ Minutes of the proceedings of the pontifical college. They probably furnished guidance regarding ceremonies.

⁶ In the plebeian secessions of 494 and 449 BC.

⁷ The first recorded instance of the tribunician veto being exercised upon a decree of the senate.

⁸ Leaders of that element in the senate which stood for a policy of conciliation, and authors of the Valerio-Horatian laws (III. li.–lv.).

⁹ The office thus instituted (very probably by a special law, *cf.* chap. xxxv. § 10) was not finally given up till 367 BC. During this period consuls were chosen twenty-two times and tribunes fifty-one times.

[10] Other Atilii were plebeians (see e.g., Liv. v. xiii. 3), hence Niebuhr conjectured that Livy was in error in stating that the three tribunes were all patricians.

[11] The lictors, with their rods and axes.

[12] The *tabernaculum* was a tent erected on the *templum,* or place marked out for the augural ceremony. Through an aperture in its roof the sky was watched for the flight of birds. Any flaw in the procedure would vitiate the subsequent election.

[13] Perhaps the *Annales Maximi.*

[14] Livy perhaps has in mind *libri consulares,* or lists of consuls.

[15] The temple of Juno Moneta was erected on the Capitoline Hill in 344 BC (VII. xxviii. 6). The Linen Rolls which Livy tells us were preserved there contained chronological lists of magistrates.

[16] i.e., the aristocratic party.

[17] The injustice probably lay in the disregard of the guardians' traditional right to dispose of the hand of their ward. The mother herself would be a ward.

[18] This looks as though the Volscian party were free lances, since a regular army would hardly have been led by an Aequian.

[19] Apparently the Volsci had not succeeded in drawing their lines completely round the city.

[20] Whereby certain land over which Ardea and Aricia were in litigation was awarded by the Roman People to themselves. See III. lxxi. and IV. i. 4.

[21] As a *senatus consultum,* to be submitted to the people for ratification.

[22] As the ancients usually did when conscious that they were about to die. *Cf.* the story of Caesar's death in Suetonius (*Iulius,* lxxxii).

[23] The *ordo equester* here means the eighteen centuries of cavalry, and must not be confused with the later *ordo equester,* consisting of all citizens below senatorial rank, whose property was assessed at 400,000 sesterces. Maelius was a plebeian *eques.*

[24] i.e., corn-dealers.

[25] This is inexact; from I. lvi. 7 we learn that it was Brutus, the father of the young men in question, who was nephew to the king, on the mother's side.

[26] See II. xli.

[27] The reference is to Appius Claudius the decemvir.

[28] The Aequimaelium was in the Vicus Iugarius, below the Capitol. Cicero derives the name from *aequus* "just," because Maelius was justly punished (*de Domo,* 101); Varro from *aequus* "level" (*L.L.* V. 157).

[29] The Lex Trebonia of 448 BC (III. lxv. 4) required the election officials to continue the voting until ten tribunes had been chosen, but said nothing about the co-optation of an eleventh.

[30] A slight anachronism, as the speaker's platform in the Forum was not called Rostra till 338 BC, when Gaius Menenius decorated it with the *rostra* (beaks) of the ships taken at Antium (VIII. xiv. 12).

[31] i.e., where the distance from bank to bank was not too great.

[32] Their city Falerii (now Civitá Castellana) was about twenty-five miles north of Rome.

[33] A Roman camp was divided by the Via Principalis, which ran from one side to the other, with a gate at each end of it, called respectively *Porta Principalis dextra,* and *P. P. sinistra.*

[34] The *triarii* were experienced troops, a body of which made a part of each legion. They were usually, as here, kept in reserve until a crisis called for their employment (*cf.* VIII. viii.).

[35] Nepos tells us (*Att.* xx. 3) that the restoration of this temple was undertaken at the suggestion of Atticus. It was therefore probably done not later than 32 BC, the year in which Atticus died.

[36] It is possible that this paragraph was inserted by Livy, without altering the context, sometime after the original publication of Books I–V. This would account for the appearance in the preceding paragraph of the version which Livy now rejects, and also for its reappearance in chap. xxxii. *Cf.* Niebuhr, *Röm. Gesch.* ii. 517.

[37] i.e., *duumviri sacrorum,* in charge of the Sibylline books, from which they derived the form of prayer used in this service.

[38] It is typical of Livy's indifference to documents that he should not have taken the trouble to consult the Linen Rolls himself. As to the fact, Diodorus Siculus, xii. 53, gives Marcus Manlius, Quintus Sulpicius, and Servius Cornelius Cossus as military tribunes for the year 320 BC, and the statement of Antias and Tubero may have arisen from the loss of the third name, and the consequent assumption that consuls were in office.

[39] This implies that the meetings of the league were made occasions for fairs. Cp. the fair at the shrine of Feronia, I. xxx. 5.

[40] The *aerarii* were the lowest class of citizens. They could neither vote nor hold office; were not eligible for service in the legion; and shared in the burdens of the state only by the payment of taxes—*aes*—assessed by the censors, instead of being determined by the citizen's sworn declaration, as was the case with members of the five classes.

[41] *Viz.* the Sibylline Books.

[42] *Auxilium* alludes to the plebeian tribunate, *imperium* to the military tribunate with consular powers.

[43] *sc.* the plebeian tribunes.

[44] The office-seeker pipe-clayed his toga; hence *candidatus,* "candidate."

[45] Whoever offended against such a law was forfeited (*sacer*) to the gods.

[46] For fear that—their claims being then disallowed—they would be treated as deserters.

[47] Not to be confounded with the annual *Ludi Magni* established by A. Postumius after his victory at Lake Regillus, 499 BC. The present reference is to votive games to be given, in the event of victory, as payment in full for the assistance of the gods.

[48] Alluding to the story told at VIII. vii. 1.

[49] A mistake. The Carthaginians had obtained a foothold in Sicily long before this time, and (according to Herodotus, vii. 166), were defeated in a great naval battle by the Sicilians on the same day that Salamis was fought (480 BC).

[50] The same who had been consul in 435? Livy usually notes the second election to a consulship with the word *iterum*. Diodorus, xii. 72, gives our consul's name as Gaius.

[51] An earlier law (*Menenia Sextia,* 452 BC) had fixed the limit of fines which magistrates might impose on their own responsibility at two sheep for poor men and thirty oxen for rich men. The present law (*Papiria Iulia*) provided for a uniform money equivalent for these fines, *viz.* twenty and three thousand asses respectively.

[52] For the procedure of the fetials see I. xxxii.

[53] If the war was a new war it must be sanctioned by vote of the people; if merely a continuation of the old war this was unnecessary.

[54] See chap. xxiv.

[55] *sc.* under the portrait of Aemilius. Livy is thinking of the partiality characteristic of such family records.

[56] The first attempt to tax the patricians enjoying the use of the public land for the purpose of paying the soldiers, who had always been required to serve gratis. See chap. lix. § 11.

[57] The name is now connected with Greek κῆπος "orchard" or "garden" not (as Livy thought) with *campus* "plain."

[58] The events described in chap. xxxvi.

[59] The *decurion* commanded a *decuria* (ten men). There were three *decuriae* in a *turma,* or squadron, and ten *turmae* in the three centuries of horse which accompanied a legion.

[60] The *parma* ("buckler" or "target") was the trooper's shield, much smaller than the *scutum* of the foot-soldier.

[61] The *vexillum,* a small red flag, was used as a cavalry ensign.

[62] i.e., Sleep or Repose.

[63] *Aes grave* ("heavy bronze") is used to distinguish the original *as libralis* (i.e., of a pound in weight) from the reduced *as* of a later time.

[64] When they had dismounted to fight as infantry; see chap. xxxviii.

[65] Livy perhaps begins at this point to follow another annalist, who had described a successful campaign of the Aequi not noticed by his authority for what has just preceded.

[66] The *iugerum* was about five-eighths of an acre.

[67] Really his great-great-grandfather (*abavus*).

[68] The term *novus homo* was usually applied to a man who was the first of his family to hold a curule office (curule aedileship, praetorship, consulship).

[69] See the account, in I. li. 9, of the execution of Herdonius. Here water is not mentioned, and the victim was probably placed on the ground and crushed beneath the stones which were heaped upon the hurdle.

[70] Providing for the investigation of the murder of Postumius.

[71] Livy probably has Dionysius I. in mind; though in reality it was several years later when he became tyrant of Syracuse.

[72] The *salii* were a very ancient college of priests whose name was derived from a weapon-dance which figured in their ritual. The *flamen* ('kindler') was the special priest of some god, thus the *Flamen Dialis* was attached to the cult of Jupiter, the *Flamen Martialis* to that of Mars, etc.

[73] Livy here employs "consulship" as a convenient, if not quite accurate, substitute for "consular tribuneship."

[74] See IV. i. 4. Livy has not mentioned the previous loss of Verrugo to the Volsci.

[75] i.e., death (see chap. xvii).

[76] Anxur was likely the Volscian name. The present form of the name is Terracina.

[77] The elder Pliny (*N. H.* xxxiii. 42) says that the Romans did not use coined silver until the defeat of King Pyrrhus (275 BC).

[78] Later it was the custom to give a slave thus manumitted by the state the name of the officiating magistrate.

[79] Livy does not mention the incident in Book I.

SUMMARY OF BOOK IV

[1] The institution of military tribunes was evidently recorded in the words that have been lost.

[2] A mistake for Quinctius.

BOOK V

[1] Livy seems to have erred through including the names of the censors, Camillus and Albinus, in his list of tribunes, of whom there were at this time but six. See chap x. § 1 and chap. xiv § 5 and notes there.

[2] See Book IV, chap. xlviii. The Appius Claudius here mentioned was a grandson of the decemvir.

[3] Livy implies that the speech which he has reported above was delivered in the Senate.

[4] i.e., from the steps that led down to the Comitium.

[5] See IV. xvii. 11.

[6] The *senatus consultum* was no more than a 'resolution' which the presiding magistrate might, if he chose, refuse to carry out.

[7] Really the first term of Camillus. The error here and in chap. i. § 2 (see note) is tacitly corrected in chap. xiv. § 5.

[8] Not the same man as mentioned in chap. i. § 2.

[9] From the beginning no patrician might become a tribune of the plebs (II. xxxiii. 1) and in 448 the Trebonian law forbade co-optation to that office (III. lxv. 4).

[10] Perhaps these three were held accountable for the illegal step which the college had taken.

[11] Or, perhaps, step-brother.

[12] In chap. vii. § 5, there is no mention of pay; Livy means that the cavalry-man received thrice the pay of the foot-soldier.

[13] From *lectus,* "couch" and *sternere,* "to spread." The images of the gods were placed on banqueting couches and served with food.

[14] A tunnel to drain the flood-waters of the Alban Lake, 1300 yards long and from seven to ten feet high, was actually cut through the solid rock, not to bring about the capture of Veii, but to save a few hundred acres of arable land on the sloping edge within the crater (Tenney Frank, *Economic History of Rome,* p. 7).

[15] For the second time (*cf.* chap. x § 1).

[16] For the third time (*cf.* chap. viii. § 1).

[17] i.e., at public auction, the spear being set up to advertise such a sale.

[18] The Latin Festival (in honor of Jupiter Latiaris, who presided over the Latin League) was held each year, and was followed by a sacrifice, on the date proclaimed by the new consuls, or consular tribunes.

[19] The *praerogatives* were the eighteen centuries of knights, which voted first; if they agreed, the other centuries were not called. See I. xliii. 11.

[20] Livy's brevity here makes the sentence a little obscure. No doubt the Latins and Hernicans first sent envoys, and these were introduced into the senate and there thanked by the dictator.

[21] i.e., votive games in recognition of some special favor of the gods.

[22] Livy is perhaps following Licinius Macer (Introd. Vol. I, p. xxix), in recording the very irregular procedure by which the tribute passed over the patrician senators to honor his plebeian father.

[23] The booty was regularly sold and the proceeds placed in the treasury.

[24] The patricians also paid the tax; but it bore harder upon the plebeians, owing to their poverty.

[25] The Latin word is a technical term which is used of carving up, in a speci-fied way, the entrails (*prosiciae*) which were to be burnt on the altar.

[26] With this sentence compare Livy's Preface, § 6.

[27] Literally, "under the chaplet," alluding to the garlands worn by captives when they were put up for sale (Aulus Gellius, VI. iv.).

[28] Livy is probably mistaken in ascribing the unpopularity of the triumph to the supposed presumption of Camillus, since it was traditional for the triumphator to suggest a likeness to Jupiter, both in his chariot and in his costume. Resentment over the disposal of the booty is more likely to have been the reason.

[29] This temple was in the cattle-market, the Forum Boarium.

[30] See chap xxii. § 1 and chap. xxiii. § 5.

[31] The *iugerum* contained 28,800 square feet, while the English acre contains 43,560.

[32] See chap. xlix.

[33] Only two, in fact, according to chap. xxix. § 6, but one was enough to veto the motion.

[34] The proposed law mentioned in chap. xxiv. § 7.

[35] For the third time. See chap. xiv. § 5.

[36] i.e., their proposal to divide up the lands of Veii.

[37] Either Scipio or Cossus (chap. xxiv. § 1), or possibly Maluginensis (chap. xiv. § 1).

[38] Providing for the division of the Roman People between Rome and Veii. See chap. xxiv. § 7.

[39] Livy is thinking of the custom which grew up later of exhibiting in the triumphal procession models or pictures of towns, rivers, and mountains, belonging to the conquered nation.

[40] There were at this time twenty-one tribes.

[41] At VI. xvii. 5 Livy implies that Manlius was given the cognomen because of his defense of the Capitol (chap. xlvii.), but at IV. xlii. 2 a L. Manlius Capitolinus had been mentioned, and the surname was probably due to the family's residing on the Capitoline.

[42] A lesser triumph, in which the victorious general entered the City on foot.

[43] Sappinum, a town otherwise unknown, is presumed to have been situated near Volsinii.

[44] Thereafter the survivor resigned and two new censors were appointed (IX. xxxiv. 21).

[45] The *Hercynei saltus* were the upland districts of South Germany (including the Black Forest, Bohemia, and the Hartz) where both Caesar and Tacitus intimate that Celts had formerly established settlements (*B.G. VI.* xxiv.; *Germ.* xxviii.).

[46] Tribes in central Gaul some of whose names survive in the modern Bourges, Auvergne, Sens, and Chartres. The Tricastini were in the Roman province (Provence).

[47] Now Milan.

[48] According to Dionysius of Halicarnassus (XII. xix) four legions were embodied, and so many allies and auxiliary troops that at the Allia the Roman army numbered 40,000 (*cf.* Plut. *Cam.* XVIII).

[49] The exact position of the battlefield is uncertain, as the town Crustumerium has disappeared and left no trace. A brook called *Fosso Maestro,* which empties into the Tiber about eleven miles from Rome, has been thought to be the ancient Allia.

[50] Cars used in the games of the Circus to carry the images of the Gods.

[51] The curule chair was inlaid with ivory. At this period the only curule magistrates were dictators, masters of the horse, consuls, and censors.

[52] Established according to tradition, by King Ancus (I. xxxiii. 9), on the right bank of the Tiber, not far from Ostia.

[53] This was a mode of girding up the toga traditional in religious ceremonies.

[54] The mother of Evander, whose name appears in I. vii. 8 in the form Carmenta.

[55] Livy tells us in XXII. xiv. 11, that the *Busta Gallica* were in the middle of the City, but the exact site cannot be determined.

[56] The Sybilline Books

[57] The god of Utterance. This "temple" is evidently the "chapel" spoken of at chap. xxxii. § 6.

[58] On the 15th of November the senate held a stately banquet at which a couch was placed for Jupiter, and Juno and Minerva occupied stools on either side of the god.

[59] The image of Pallas (Palladium), fabled to have been brought to Italy by Aeneas.

[60] See I. xx. 4, and note.

[61] Livy has in mind one important exception: the centuriate comitia met outside the pomerium, usually in the Campus Martius.

[62] Chap. xxiv. § 7.

[63] The *casa Romuli* stood on the Palatine, on the side next the Circus Maximus, and a hut which went by this name was preserved and venerated as late as Livy's own time.

SUGGESTED READING

CHAPLIN, J. D. *Livy's Exemplary History*. Oxford: Oxford University Press, 2000.

CORNELL, T. J. *The Beginnings of Rome*. London: Routledge, 1995.

CRAWFORD, M. H. *The Roman Republic*. London: Fontana, 1992.

FELDHERR, A. *Spectacle and Society in Livy's History*. Berkeley: University of California Press, 1998.

JAEGER, M. *Livy's Written Rome*. Michigan: University of Michigan Press, 1997.

KRAUS, C. S., AND A. J. WOODMAN. *Latin Historians. Greece and Rome*. Oxford: Oxford University Press, 1997.

LUCE, T. J. *Livy: The Composition of His History*. Princeton, NJ: Princeton University Press, 1977.

MILES, G. B. *Livy: Reconstructing Early Rome*. Ithaca: Cornell University Press, 1995.

OGILVIE, R. M. *A Commentary on Livy, Books 1–5*. Oxford: Oxford University Press, 1965.

SCULLARD, H. H. *A History of the Roman World, 753–146 BC*, 4th edition. London: Routledge, 1980.

WALBANK, F. W., ED. *The Cambridge Ancient History, Volume VII, Part 2*. Cambridge: Cambridge University Press, 1989.

WALSH, P. G. *Livy, His Historical Aims and Methods*. Cambridge: Cambridge University Press, 1961

Look for the following titles, available now from
The Barnes & Noble Library of Essential Reading.

Visit your Barnes & Noble bookstore,
or shop online at *www.bn.com/loer*

BEST SELLERS

American, The	Henry James	0760773653
Arrow of Gold, The	Joseph Conrad	0760773696
Autobiography of Benjamin Franklin, The	Benjamin Franklin	0760768617
Autobiography of Charles Darwin, The	Charles Darwin	0760769087
Babylonian Life and History	E. A. Wallis Budge	0760765499
Common Law, The	Oliver Wendell Holmes	0760754985
Complete Works of Saki, The	H. H. Munro	0760773734
Conquest of Gaul, The	Julius Caesar	0760768951
Cranford	Elizabeth Gaskell	0760795983
Critique of Pure Reason	Immanual Kant	0760755949
Dolorous Passion of Our Lord Jesus Christ, The	Anne Catherine Emmerich	0760771715
Early History of Rome, The	Livy	0760770239
Egyptian Book of the Dead, The	E. A. Wallis Budge	0760768382
Elements, The	Euclid	0760763127
Flatland	Edwin A. Abbott	0760755876
Guide for the Perplexed, The	Moses Maimonides	0760757577
Hadji Murád	Leo Tolstoy	076077353X
Hannibal	Theodore Ayrault Dodge	076076896X

Title	Author	ISBN
Herland and The Yellow Wallpaper	Charlotte Perkins Gilman	0760777667
How We Think	John Dewey	0760770387
Imitation of Christ, The	Thomas À Kempis	0760755914
Innocence and Wisdom of Father Brown, The	G. K. Chesterton	0760773556
Interesting Narrative of the Life of Olaudah Equiano, The	Olaudah Equiano	0760773505
Introduction to Mathematics	Alfred North Whitehead	076076588X
Leviathan, The	Thomas Hobbes	0760755930
Life and Opinions of Tristram Shandy, Gentleman, The	Laurence Sterne	0760763054
Life of Johnson	James Boswell	0760773483
Lives of the Caesars, The	Suetonius	0760757585
Lost Girl, The	D. H. Lawrence	0760773319
Love and Freindship	Jane Austen	0760768560
Man Who Was Thursday, The	G. K. Chesterton	0760763100
Martian Tales Trilogy, The	Edgar Rice Burroughs	076075585X
Meditations	Marcus Aurelius	076075229X
Montessori Method, The	Maria Montessori	0760749957
Mosby's Memoirs	John Singleton Mosby	0760773726
Nicomachean Ethics	Aristotle	0760752362
Notes on Nursing	Florence Nightingale	0760749949
On Liberty	John Stuart Mill	0760755000
On War	Carl von Clausewitz	0760755973
Personal Memoirs of U. S. Grant	Ulysses S. Grant	0760749906
Problems of Philosophy, The	Bertrand Russell	076075604X
Relativity: The Special and the General Theory	Albert Einstein	0760759219
Rough Riders, The	Theodore Roosevelt	0760755760
Satyricon, The	Petronius	076077367X
Story of an African Farm, The	Olive Schreiner	0760773521
Tractatus Logico-Philosophicus	Ludwig Wittgenstein	0760752354
Tragic Sense of Life	Miguel de Unamuno	0760777764
Tramp Abroad, A	Mark Twain	0760773629
Travels of Marco Polo, The	Marco Polo	0760765898
Trial and Death of Socrates, The	Plato	0760762007
Up From Slavery	Booker T. Washington	0760752346
Vindication of the Rights of Woman, A	Mary Wollstonecraft	0760754942

Voyage of the *Beagle,* The	Charles Darwin	0760754969
Warden, The	Anthony Trollope	0760773610
Wealth of Nations, The	Adam Smith	0760757615
Worm Ouroboros, The	E. R. Eddison	0760773645

THE BARNES & NOBLE
LIBRARY OF ESSENTIAL READING

This newly developed series has been established to provide affordable access to books of literary, academic, and historic value—works of both well-known writers and those who deserve to be rediscovered. Selected and introduced by scholars and specialists with an intimate knowledge of the works, these volumes present complete, original texts in a modern, readable typeface— welcoming a new generation of readers to influential and important books of the past. With more than 100 titles already in print and more than 100 forthcoming, the Library of Essential Reading offers an unrivaled variety of thought, scholarship, and entertainment. Best of all, these handsome and durable paperbacks are priced to be exceptionally affordable. For a full list of titles, visit *www.bn.com/loer.*